REPRESENTING
JAZZ

REPRESENTING

JAZZ

Edited by Krin Gabbard

DUKE UNIVERSITY PRESS *Durham and London 1995*

© 1995 Duke University Press
All rights reserved
Printed in the United States of America
on acid-free paper ∞
Typeset in Trump Mediaeval by Keystone
Typesetting, Inc.
Library of Congress Cataloging-in-Publication Data
and permissions appear on the last printed page of this
book.

Contents

JAZZ AND DANCE

PICTURING JAZZ

VOCALESE: REPRESENTING JAZZ WITH JAZZ

Acknowledgments

This anthology began to take shape at the December 1990 meeting of the Modern Language Association in Chicago where I chaired a session on the representation of jazz in film, literature, and photography. Two of the essays in this volume started as short presentations there. One of them was delivered by Fred Garber, a professor of comparative literature with a passion for new projects that is as rare as it is inspiring. It was Fred who urged me to assemble essays about jazz into what he thought could become the first jazz book to adopt the critical theory that has dominated literary studies for the past two decades. Before long, I had located a fascinating assortment of jazz scholars, practically none of whom regularly taught music or jazz. Their work with jazz was a passion they cultivated within, outside, or around their work in departments of English, philosophy, African American studies, history, music, American studies, comparative literature, and film studies.

Wired in to several mini-networks of jazz scholars, I eventually found so many kindred spirits that the number of potential contributors soon numbered well above twenty. I was now faced with the depressing task of paring down the contributions to ten or twelve—the canonical number for anthologies at university presses. Fortunately, I had been in touch with Bernard Gendron, whose original work on Negrophilia in French modernism convinced me that he was someone I ought to get to know. When I complained to Professor Gendron that I had too many essays for a single collection, he consoled me by suggesting that I edit two anthologies. By happy accident, my large stack of contributions fell neatly into two equal stacks of manageable proportions. In one stack I had placed the essays that dealt with film, literature, photography, and dance;

in the second were those concerned more with jazz history and aesthetics or with specific jazz artists. You are now reading the first anthology; the second one, also published by Duke University Press, has become *Jazz Among the Discourses.*

My sincere thanks go to Professors Garber and Gendron for the crucial roles they played in the genesis of these two books. I also thank the contributors to these anthologies who patiently waited, in some cases as long as five years, to see their work in print. I also thank them for constantly revising their studies to comply with each new round of readers' reports and editorial suggestions. Happily, they always made these revisions with dispatch and without complaint.

Ken Wissoker of Duke University Press will always have my respect and gratitude for his devotion to this project and for the professional manner in which he has shepherded it through to completion. The jazz scholars commissioned by the press as anonymous readers made essential suggestions for improving the anthologies and were, I am relieved to say, sympathetic to the more heretical aspects of these anthologies. Lewis Porter provided me with ancient issues of *Down Beat* and with less tangible but no less valuable items of jazz scholarship and wisdom. The Comparative Studies Program at the State University of New York at Stony Brook, especially departmental secretary Lee Peters, cheerfully provided logistical support, and Federal Express never let me down when deadlines became tight. Finally, I thank Paula B. Gabbard for providing love and sympathy for more than twenty-one years now and for agreeing with me that screech trumpeters are phallic.

Introduction: Writing the Other History

KRIN GABBARD

A t least until recently, jazz history has been based on an evolutionary model that emphasizes a handful of master improvisers and genius composers. Many of the essays in *Representing Jazz*, as well as in its companion volume, *Jazz Among the Discourses*, have radically called this model into question.[1] Relying on various poststructuralisms as well as on discourses developed by cultural historians and literary theorists, many of the contributors have broken new ground by placing the music much more securely within specific cultural moments. Many also have undertaken the metacritical work of reading jazz histories within *their* own moments.

In another welcome anthology, *Reading Jazz*, David Meltzer has searched through eight decades of assorted texts to present a fascinating array of statements about the music. In his introductory "Pre-ramble" (3), Meltzer goes so far as to argue that jazz was "invented" by whites, who have created and maintained a discourse in order to "colonize" the music. Meltzer is comparing the "jazz" of the white critic—jazz as mythology and cultural commodity—with the extensive, elusive, often ignored musics that have been played, usually by African Americans, in various locales throughout the late nineteenth and early twentieth centuries. Until 1917, virtually all of this music was unrecorded. The word "jazz" may not have been coined by whites, but dominant American culture has continued to accept it as the master term for certain kinds of musical practice in spite of the fact that many of that music's practitioners—Duke Ellington and Anthony Braxton are only two of the most prominent—have repeatedly rejected the term.

While Meltzer sees colonization as inevitable when whites write about jazz, he also argues that he has produced a "source-book of permissible (intentional, accidental, unavoidable) racism" (4). Meltzer collects a large number of overtly racist writings about jazz, but he often juxtaposes them with nostalgic reveries on the glories of black culture. A central thesis of his book is that jazz has historically been configured to serve specific purposes for whites, who have associated it on the one hand with dark-browed primitivism and on the other with ecstatic freedom. But whether the music was demonized or romanticized, the result was the same: jazz was the safely contained world of the Other where whites knew they could find experiences unavailable to them at home.

Representing Jazz can be regarded as still more exercises in colonization and permissible racism, but I would argue that many of its contributors have examined racist and colonialist discourses with uncommon rigor. In this sense, the collected essays bring a new depth to the rapidly maturing discipline of jazz studies by concentrating on jazz myth and jazz culture rather than jazz per se (assuming for the moment that jazz can in fact be isolated from myth and culture). In spite of the new turn in jazz studies that this volume and its companion represent, we may still choose to embrace much of what has been written by traditional jazz writers, even those who are most out of date methodologically. Who can dispute, for example, the crucial importance of Louis Armstrong for early jazz? (There is, however, massive disagreement about Armstrong's stature and significance after 1929 or some other date—the *terminus ad quem* of Armstrong's great period is itself a subject of considerable debate.) But there is at least one, more subtle supposition within established jazz writing that we are not likely to question—the belief that jazz history ought to be written so that it can stand in opposition to popular misconceptions. The unspoken wisdom is that without jazz history our knowledge would depend on platitudes in the daily press as well as on trite movies and television dramas, lurid novels, sensationalizing photographs, and genre paintings. But over time, don't these artifacts begin to constitute a history of their own? Are there no reasons for looking at this other history, presumably inaccurate, presumably unavoidable? If the jazz historians are giving us a truth that is otherwise unavailable, does it necessarily follow that there is no truth in what we are told by authors, filmmakers, dancers, painters, photographers, and the rest? Can't the works of creative artists render the music as vividly as those of the critics? And even if we find these works to be flawed or even grossly inaccurate, can't we examine them critically to understand how American culture has actually received the music, with its volatile mix of black and white, high and low, sacred and profane? Isn't there value in writing this other history of jazz? The essays in *Representing Jazz* can be conceptualized as systematic assessments of what we know about jazz outside the official histories. Many of these contributions express a profound discomfort with the idea that an official jazz history *can* be written or that any representation of the music can transcend its own built-in limitations.

We might also think of these essays as charting a course that is compatible with—though by no means derived from—a path laid down by critics of popular music. For several years now, rock and roll has been inspiring a theoretically sophisticated body of scholarship. Like the Hollywood cinema, rock involves a huge industry and a highly conventionalized sign system, and thus it becomes especially accessible to critics skilled in the theories of Barthes, Foucault, Althusser, Raymond Williams, and the Frankfurt School.[2] And because rock critics, unlike their jazz counterparts, have seldom laid claim to the internalist aesthetics developed for classical music, they have been more attentive to the contexts of the music. Lawrence Grossberg has suggested a useful model for writing about rock and roll, conceptualizing it as what Michel Foucault calls "an apparatus."

> The rock and roll apparatus includes not only musical texts and practices but also economic determinations, technological possibilities, images (of performers and fans), social relations, aesthetic conventions, styles of language, movement, appearance and dance, media practices, ideological commitments and media representations of the apparatus itself. The apparatus describes "cartographies of taste" which are both synchronic and diachronic and which encompass both musical and non-musical registers of everyday life. (236)

As many commentators have pointed out, jazz writers tend to ignore these extramusical aspects of jazz by conceptualizing it as a safely autonomous domain, more dependent on rhythmic innovation than on social change. In doing so, however, they have closed themselves off from the kind of work undertaken by Grossberg and the more sophisticated commentators on pop music.[3]

As a totality, the essays in this collection take a dramatic step toward reversing this trend. The first section of the book looks at the jazz apparatus as it is played out in literature and film. If, as Thelonious Monk is alleged to have said, "writing about music is like dancing about architecture," then each of the essays in this section addresses the compromises and instructive failures in the various attempts to capture the music on film or on the page. Arthur Knight's detailed and richly contextualized analysis of the 1944 short film *Jammin' the Blues* is an excellent place to begin a study of the jazz apparatus. The film was directed and coordinated by Gjon Mili and Norman Granz, Mili a photographer for *Life* magazine, Granz a soon-to-be major jazz impresario. Both men considered themselves true friends of the music and worked hard to present it in the best light. As Knight observes, however, the filmmakers could not avoid a number of traps, the most prominent being the film's ambivalence toward the one white musician in the film, guitarist Barney Kessel, who is almost entirely camouflaged in the few scenes in which he appears. Knight is especially attentive to how discourses of art and race have been discreetly mixed both in the film and in its reception.

When Eudora Welty wrote the short story "Powerhouse" after watching a performance by Fats Waller, she was much less interested in accuracy and more concerned with finding a means of allegorizing the music through literature. Leland Chambers argues first that the several successive accounts of Gypsy's death in Welty's story can be read as parallels to the fourteen improvised choruses that Powerhouse performs at the piano. Chambers then observes that language ordinarily possesses little potential to describe what actually happens in music and that Welty solves this problem by discovering a means through which the process of jazz improvisation is clarified and reified in the mythmaking by the story's main character.

Constructing a larger view of jazz as a modernist art form, Frederick Garber considers several stories and films about jazz artists, searching out the dominant tropes that repeatedly characterize these attempts to make sense out of the music and its practitioners. On his way to identifying Bertrand Tavernier's *Round Midnight* (1986) as the most satisfying exercise in rendering the complexities of jazz, Garber critiques Dorothy Baker's novel of *Young Man with a Horn* as well as Michael Curtiz's film version (1950), Julio Cortázar's "The Pursuer," Clint Eastwood's *Bird* (1988), and Spike Lee's *Mo' Better Blues* (1990).

Like many of the contributors to *Representing Jazz*, Garber engages in a dialogue with a variety of other writers, both jazz critics (Joachim Berendt, Frederic Ramsey, Charles Edward Smith, Gunther Schuller) and critical theorists (Walter Benjamin, Roland Barthes). Like Garber, I have chosen to begin my own contribution with a discussion of jazz theory, specifically the writings of Theodor Adorno, whose attacks on the music have seldom been confronted in jazz scholarship. Although Adorno associates the music with castration, I have argued that jazz in general and the jazz trumpet in particular have been crucial to establishing a masculine identity, especially for African American artists. But because it has never been attentive to the complex articulations of masculinity within jazz, Hollywood has in a sense adopted an Adornian position, consistently casting jazz trumpeters as vulnerable to castration. In *Mo' Better Blues*, Spike Lee accepts this tradition.

In his thorough study of jazz autobiography Christopher Harlos also frames his analysis in terms of recent developments in literary theory, especially those that foreground the problems of converting lived experience into prose. This demanding transition is especially crucial to jazz writers who attempt to narrate their own lives, essentially saying in words what they have previously been able to say only in music. Harlos concentrates on what is surely the most remarkable of jazz autobiographies, *Beneath the Underdog*, written by one of the most remarkable of jazz composers, Charles Mingus. Like many of the musician/writers addressed by Harlos (Louis Armstrong, Dizzy Gillespie, Miles Davis, Art Pepper, Dicky Wells, and Sidney Bechet, among others), Mingus uses the autobiographical occasion to explore possibilities for self-discovery and even self-invention. Harlos's essay is also concerned with problems that arise when musicians collaborate with other writers and when they confront other "authenticating voices" either inside or outside the covers of their autobiographical books.

In an extension of the section on film and literature, both James Naremore and Adam Knee address *Cabin in the Sky* (1943), a major film for jazz scholarship if only because it represents the sole time that Louis Armstrong and Duke Ellington appeared in the same Hollywood film (though never in the same frame). For Naremore, the film is a catalog of contradictions based in a range of popular discourses and historical forces. Naremore is especially interested in the contrasting myths about black Americans that surface variously throughout the film: at one moment they are simple, plantation-style darkies who vacillate between singing hymns and shooting craps; at the next they represent urban sophistication and many of the same exciting, utopian diversions promised by cinema (and jazz). By the end, however, because of the film's "cultural schizophrenia" as much as in spite of it, *Cabin in the Sky* turns out to be what Naremore calls "the most visually beautiful picture about black people ever produced at the classic studios." Adam Knee is less sanguine about the film's success and less charitable toward its racial confusions. Even when the film most openly celebrates black culture—specifically when the Ellington band performs at "Jim Henry's Paradise"—the filmmakers have, according to Knee, insisted on containing black self-expression with moral judgments. For Knee, the film ultimately fails by refusing to resolve its dichotomies, always marking the black term as the negative in its several Manichaean oppositions.

The two essays on jazz dance continue the volume's special attention to the American cinema and extend the inquiry into how the apparatus is represented visually. Robert P. Crease discusses the Lindy Hop, the energetic and improvisational jazz vernacular dance that was an integral part of the jazz scene in the 1930s and 1940s. The multiple and often contradictory significations of the Lindy Hop ranged from physically exciting but asexual to carnal, cannibalistic, and obscene—an especially vivid illustration of the polarities made possible by jazz myth. Crease also discusses the peculiar difficulties of representing the Lindy Hop on film. Vernacular jazz dance, like jazz music, is both an improvisational, individualistic practice on the one hand and a collaborative one on the other. Capturing these contradictions on film involves depicting dancers as individually creative at the same time that they participate in a give-and-take with other dancers. The representation of vernacular dance on film always runs the risk of sacrificing the loose, chaotic, and multiperspectival look of the dance hall floor. The Lindy Hop is also important in Karen Backstein's essay on Mura Dehn's *The Spirit Moves: A History of Black Social Dance on Film, 1900–1986*, a decades-long project to record the evolution of African American vernacular dance. Although the Lindy Hoppers provide prominent moments in Dehn's film, the film also presents early dances such as the strut and the cakewalk, more recent developments such as break dancing, and much of what came in between. Backstein is interested in how Dehn sought alternatives to the anthology method of capturing dance history on film as well as in how Dehn negotiated her way through the various racial discourses that came and went during the many years she worked on the project.

Although the essays by Hadler and Jarrett in the "Picturing Jazz" section directly address painting and photography, both authors cast much wider nets. In 1983, Mona Hadler wrote the definitive survey of the representation of jazz in Western painting. Her contribution to this anthology looks closely at how Abstract Expressionist and Surrealist painters of the New York School actually understood their appropriation of jazz into their works. Having interviewed many of these artists herself, Hadler can even tell us which specific musicians the artists name when they express their debt to jazz. It soon becomes clear that no monolithic notion of jazz existed even among a small group of painters in New York in the 1950s. One artist even claimed Paul Whiteman as an inspiration. In addition to vastly opening up the truism that avant-garde painters were influenced by jazz, Hadler's study has larger implications for the current concept of a jazz canon with its narrowing focus on a few select individuals.

Michael Jarrett's "The Tenor's Vehicle: Reading *Way Out West*" focuses primarily on a single photograph—William Claxton's portrait of Sonny Rollins as a cowboy that appeared on the cover of Rollins's 1957 LP, *Way Out West*. But Jarrett's essay is also devoted to playfully deconstructing the most well-established tropes for writing about jazz. Citing Jacques Derrida as well as Mel Brooks, Jarrett sees the Rollins portrait as an "allegory" of jazz, comparing the saxophone player to the gunslinger and the avant-garde movement of the music to a westward advance on unexplored territory. By the time he starts listing his all-time favorite album covers, Jarrett has provided an unexpected answer to the question of how it is possible to represent jazz.

In the final essay in this anthology, Barry Keith Grant recuperates vocalese from its marginal status. Citing the scene in Eastwood's *Bird* in which Chan Parker denounces King Pleasure's vocalization of Bird's "Parker's Mood," Grant asks why this rich tradition of writing and singing lyrics to well-known jazz improvisations should be so widely dismissed by connoisseurs. In developing an aesthetics for the practice, Grant credits vocalese with demonstrating that jazz improvisers are *composers* as well as soloists. Ultimately, for Grant, the practitioners of vocalese are "among the few true oral poets in the age of digital reproduction."

Writing about jazz as an apparatus calls for a knowledge of critical theory and cultural studies alongside the more familiar methods that writers have used as they try to make sense of the music. As these brief synopses suggest, the "other history" of jazz involves much more than adjectival accounts of important recordings. Unlike many of the official histories of jazz, this "other history" requires research tools that are not primarily phonographic. And as the essays in this volume vividly demonstrate, the other history involves a great deal that is new about jazz, including much that we may not have suspected that we did not know.

Notes

1 So has the work of a handful of musicologists, most prominently Scott DeVeaux and Gary Tomlinson.
2 A full account of how these various authors and schools have come together in the study of popular culture appears in the editors' introduction to Naremore and Brantlinger.
3 Also see Frith and Horne, Marcus, and the several essays in DeCurtis's "Rock & Roll Culture" issue of *South Atlantic Quarterly*.

Works Cited

DeCurtis, Anthony. "Rock & Roll Culture." Special issue of *South Atlantic Quarterly* 90.4 (1991).

DeVeaux, Scott. "Constructing the Jazz Tradition: Jazz Historiography." *Black American Literature Forum* 25.3 (1991): 525–60.

Frith, Simon, and Howard Horne. *Art Into Pop.* London and New York: Methuen, 1987.

Gabbard, Krin, ed. *Jazz Among the Discourses.* Durham, N.C.: Duke UP, 1995.

Grossberg, Lawrence. "Another Boring Day in Paradise: Rock and Roll and the Empowerment of Everyday Life." *Popular Music.* Ed. Richard Middleton and David Horn. Vol. 4. London: Cambridge UP, 1984. 225–58.

Hadler, Mona. "Jazz and the Visual Arts." *Arts Magazine* 57.10 (June 1983): 91–101.

Marcus, Greil. *Lipstick Traces: A Secret History of the Twentieth Century.* Cambridge, Mass.: Harvard UP, 1989.

Meltzer, David, ed. *Reading Jazz.* San Francisco: Mercury House, 1993.

Naremore, James, and Patrick Brantlinger, eds. *Modernity and Mass Culture.* Bloomington: Indiana UP, 1991.

Tomlinson, Gary. "Cultural Dialogics and Jazz: A White Historian Signifies." *Disciplining Music: Musicology and Its Canons.* Ed. Katherine Bergeron and Philip V. Bohlman. Chicago: U of Chicago P, 1992. 64–94.

JAZZ IN

LITERATURE

AND FILM

Jammin' the Blues,
or the Sight of Jazz, 1944

ARTHUR KNIGHT

. . . music is heard and seldom seen. . . .—Ralph Ellison (1952)

W. H. Auden says of music . . . that it "can be made anywhere, is invisible, and does not smell." But music is made by men who are insistently visible, especially, as in jazz, when the players are their music.—Nat Hentoff (1961)

Last year some twit in a British jazz rag proclaimed the music has never been a particularly visual medium. . . . What music has this motherfucker been looking at?—Greg Tate (1992)

In his "Jazz Symposium" column in the July 1944 issue of *Esquire*, Leonard Feather, critic, impresario, and sometime composer of "modernist" jazz, asked an eclectic group of jazz musicians and aficionados, "If you had a million dollars to spend on jazz, how would you use it?" Sam Donahue, "Musician Third Class, U.S. Navy; tenor saxman, trumpeter and leader of the Navy band," answered this way:

> Well, I'd like to make an educational film, debunking the average movie musical. I'd tear down the studios' haphazard method of sloughing off good music. Instead of having some chick bursting into song somewhere in the middle of a forest, accompanied by an invisible fifty piece band from out of space, I'd work the music in logically and give the musicians a break. If I could get Duke Ellington or any great colored band, I'd fix it so you could really see the band and get to know it, instead of covering it up with a lot of jitterbug dancing and stuff. . . . I'd have all the recording done simultaneously with the

shooting of the pictures, instead of having it dubbed in separately the way they do now. That would help make the music real and spontaneous. Listen, after I got that movie on the market, all the musicals after that would just *have* to be legitimate! ("Jazz Symposium" 95)

Clearly, Donahue was aware of the conventions for representing musical performance in Hollywood musicals. He was also aware that those conventions depended on and played with the audiovisual split made possible by sound film's dual recording technologies. Further, he understood that these conventions and the technologies they drew on had racial-political implications. Hearing jazz, Donahue's comments suggest, was only part of the experience of jazz; "really see[ing] the band and get[ting] to know it" was another. But, especially if the band was "colored," really seeing and getting to know it was an experience that Hollywood conventionally denied its customers. Donahue felt confident that altering these conventions and letting audiences see as well as hear the music, no matter what color, would be "educational."

In August and September 1944 the recording and photographing were done at Warner Bros. studios for *Jammin' the Blues*, a ten-minute musical short that seems nearly, if imperfectly, built on Donahue's debunking model. Produced and distributed by Warners, *Jammin' the Blues* was created by a group of people whose relationships with Hollywood were either unusual or nonexistent. It was directed by Gjon Mili, a *Life* photographer, coordinated by Norman Granz, an apprentice film editor who was also a jazz fan just starting a career as an activist entrepreneur, and featured performances by jazz musicians of varying degrees of fame: Lester Young, Red Callender, Harry Edison, Marlowe Morris, Sid Catlett, Barney Kessel, Jo Jones, John Simmons, Illinois Jacquet, and Marie Bryant. *Jammin' the Blues* was what would later be labeled a consummate "crossover" product. It combined small group "hot jazz" and "art" photography, inserted them into the mechanisms and forms of Hollywood, and distributed the results to theaters everywhere.

Most shorts came and went without much notice, but after it was released late in December 1944, *Jammin' the Blues* attracted positive reviews from *Time, Life, Esquire, Theatre Arts, Down Beat,* the *Chicago Defender,* and *Ebony.* Walter Winchell acclaimed it on his radio show, and James Agee gave it an equivocal, though finally negative, review in the *Nation.*[1] It was also nominated for an Academy Award in the one-reel short subject category. In other words, the Hollywood industry establishment, the mainstream press, and a variety of specialty presses all found *Jammin' the Blues* worthy of special note.

If he was paying attention, Sam Donahue must have been pleased; a version of his proposed education and legitimation project seemed to be working. But very quickly his satisfaction would have turned to disappointment. *Jammin' the Blues* may have crossed over, but it did not start any trends. Hollywood musicals, whether feature-length or short, did not become any more "legitimate" from the jazz fan or player's perspective after *Jammin' the Blues* than they had been before it. Instead, *Jammin' the Blues* passed into jazz lore as an anomaly: "one of the few honest motion pictures about jazz" (Balliet 6), "a landmark" (Smith 382), "probably the most famous jazz movie of all" (Meeker entry 1637), and "the greatest film to depict jazz musicians in their natural habitat" (Driggs and Lewine 268).

Why was *Jammin' the Blues* so successful as an individual film and so unsuccessful in inspiring similar films? This essay will analyze *Jammin' the Blues* within the multiple, overlapping contexts of its production and reception in the mid-forties: the jazz scene, Hollywood, and the audiovisual politics of the representation of race in the arena of American culture. *Jammin' the Blues* provides a unique, densely encoded site for exploring the connections that music—and particularly jazz—was thought to provide between hearing, seeing, and "getting to know" other Americans. It provides an opportunity to explore the relations of peripheral *and* central, repressed *and* ascendent discourses, discourses about Hollywood film, jazz, entertainment, art, race, and American culture—discourses which standard Hollywood practice worked to control and hold separate but which, as *Jammin' the Blues* shows, sometimes overlapped, sometimes competed, and often were contradictory. Finally, *Jammin' the Blues,* when considered in this context, reveals the possibilities and limits of "education" and "legitimation" through crossover products, products in which the sight of music becomes the object of industrial mechanisms and forms.

What music looks like relates crucially to how it sounds and what it can mean. Whether viewed in performance, depicted on the cover of a score or record, or suggested by program notes or the words of a radio announcer, the "look" of music influences how listeners categorize what they hear. Is it "art" or "commercial claptrap"? Is it music or noise? What is its relation to me, to us? Music's look helps define and answer such questions.

In the United States especially, a key determinant of the look of any music has long been the race—the "color"—of the musicians who play it. A legal and social construction, built on a physical trait, color suggests where a music comes from, who it "belongs" to, and who its "natural" consumers are. At the same time, and especially in the ages of mechanical and electronic reproduction, music can seem to float free of its players; through imitation, notation, recording, broadcasting, and marketing, music can separate from "colored" social bodies.[2] Music arises out of the material circumstances of the people who make it and can work profound changes in those circumstances, yet music—most oddly, recorded music, "music as a thing" (Eisenberg 11)—seems immaterial, audible but invisible. It is intimately bound to the cultures that color represents in the United States and, at the same time, easily appropriable, deracinated, dis-colored.[3]

This dynamic makes music an especially complex cultural expression and an especially charged intercultural terrain. In the United States it has resulted in what Andrew Ross has described as a "long transactional history of white responses to black culture, of black counter-responses, and of further and often traceless negotiations, tradings, raids, and compromises," not to mention "thefts," and has made music the site of intense scrutiny of and anxiety about color (67–68). Consequently, music has become a many-faceted symbol—and a debating ground—for how color is defined and represented, where it belongs in and how it affects American society and culture. Control of the visible in and around music, in all its forms, has become a critical issue.

Jazz was the first indigenous, (semi-)vernacular music in the United States to wrestle explicitly with representing, visually and aurally, its origins and its transactional quality. It generated *scenes*, groups of like-minded musicians, critics, impresarios, and fans, which developed discourses for debating competing (though often contiguous) visions of the music, for clarifying views of jazz history, and for struggling with the music's value and status: Was the music black, white, or "mixed," and what would it mean to call a music "colored"? How transactional was its history? Was it art or entertainment? Unique, live experience or mass, recorded object? These discourses welded the aesthetic to the political and the cultural to the social across the sound and sight of the music and, in the process, influenced the way jazz was seen and heard—and how color was perceived—in the United States.

When *Jammin' the Blues* was created late in 1944, jazz and its discourses were undergoing profound shifts.[4] The end of the big-band swing era was at hand, and its replacement, small-group bebop, was percolating "underground" (in Harlem, of course), soon to surface. Mediated by the phenomenon of "hot jazz," a small-group genre that was itself split between "Dixieland" traditionalists and swing-inflected "modernism," the shift from swing to bop marked a change in jazz from a mainstream popular music to an explicit art music, which was (at least initially) assertively black and (at least nascently) cultural-nationalist. In *Blues People*, Amiri Baraka tells the story this way: "Philosophically, [late-] swing sought to involve the black culture in a platonic social blandness that would erase it forever, replacing it with the socio-cultural compromise of the 'jazzed-up' popular song . . ." (181). In Baraka's account, "[t]he willfully harsh, *anti-assimilationist* sound of bebop" was the reaction to this malaise (182). It was also, as Eric Lott has noted, the music of "a moment . . . in which unpaid historical bills were falling due" (597). According to Lott, the consequent African American "[m]ilitancy and music were undergirded by the same social facts; the music attempted to resolve at the level of style what the militancy combatted in the streets" (599).

A considerable component of bebop's "politics of style" was visual and stemmed, Baraka argues, from "young Negro[es]" realizing that color was irreducible, "that merely by being a Negro in America, one *was* a nonconformist" (188; Baraka notes that young whites were also nonconformist but that they always had a choice). Still, while bebop could react against swing, it could not entirely escape (white) swing's "involvement of black culture." Swing was wildly popular, tremendously "commercial," yet some of its most successful proponents—most notably the Benny Goodman band—had worked to use their success to slowly alter the racialized, segregated look of jazz. This process influenced jazz discourse in general during the swing era and directly involved many of the people who collaborated to make *Jammin' the Blues*. Before analyzing *Jammin' the Blues* and its representation of jazz at the transition from swing to bop, it is worth detailing the development of the look of swing—especially insofar as that look was figured as both interracial and "artistic."

Writing in the summer of 1945, the blues poet and scholar Sterling A. Brown revealed how high the stakes of the look of jazz were and how complex that look could be in a racist, industrial culture:

> Of all the arts, jazz music is probably the most democratic. Mixed units of Negroes and whites have recorded for well over a decade, and most of their records are jazz classics. . . . The mixed band meets up with difficulties, especially in the South. But completely democratic are the jam sessions, both public and private, where Negro and white musicians meet as equals to improvise collectively and create the kind of music they love. Here the performer's color does not

matter; the quality of the music he makes is the basis for comradery and respect. (26)

For Brown, visible racial mixing on the bandstand best indicated the democratic quality of jazz. At the utopian moment of the jam session, the performer's color does not matter—and, at the same time, it matters entirely. Jazz is democratic because it mixes races and because that mixing makes no difference. In Brown's vision, because music is simultaneously colored and colorless, it can become a "gift" (W. E. B. Du Bois's word) given back and forth between cultures, binding them, assuring the humanity of all parties to the exchange, and ultimately leading to a truly shared culture where each contribution is acknowledged by all. Brown is not explicit, but he seems to believe such cultural democracy will lead to social democracy: The attraction of the sound of colored people leads to an acceptance of their sight—an acceptance of *them*.[5]

However, for all the utopian qualities of his vision of jazz democracy, Brown was also a pragmatist. He recognized his vision as a vision—as specifically reliant on the visible aspects of the music—and recognized the less-than-utopian circumstances that effected the dissemination of jam session democracy. On the one hand, Brown argues, despite the excellence of the sound, some people will resist the sight of mixed jazz. On the other hand, others will be distanced from this sight by the mediation of private, consumer objects—records shorn of visible information to become commodified "classics."[6] The tension between performance, which forcefully connects sight and sound but which is relatively exclusive and can lead to "difficulties," and recording, which shears sight from sound but is relatively available and safe, is a genuine one. Though Brown chose not to address them, the other major music media—radio, print, and film—complicated his categories. Radio gave "live" sound but no sight. Print could provide sight but no sound. Film could reconnect sight with sound and could be distributed as widely as the other media, but, as Sam Donahue pointed out, the reconnection of sight to sound in film was not innocent or transparent. Together, all of these media, including a wide variety of performance situations, formed the territory for the segregated look of swing, and the people dedicated to changing that look to reflect something like Brown's vision carefully exploited each medium's unique qualities.

Precisely because they did not make the "mix" visible, records were the initial step toward institutionalizing mixing in swing.[7] In 1933 the independently wealthy record producer, critic, and social activist John Hammond set up his first recording dates with Benny Goodman, then a well-respected freelance musician. According to Hammond's auto-biography, "the most effective and constructive form of social protest" he could think of was "[t]o bring recognition to the Negro's supremacy in jazz" (68). Consequently, he wanted Goodman to record with a mixed band. Hammond recalls Goodman responding: "If it gets around that I recorded with colored guys, I won't get another job in this town [i.e., New York]" (136).

Hammond acquiesced to Goodman's fears, which he felt were well-founded, but after producing enough successful records in the depression-stunted market, Hammond collected the power in the industry to arrange mixed sessions, including dates with Goodman backing Billie Holiday and Ethel Waters and playing with pianist Teddy Wilson and saxophonist Coleman Hawkins. That one of Hammond's mixed sessions was released under the imprimatur of "The Chocolate Dandies" indicates the vestigial power of the visible in sound recording. From a present-day perspective this naming may seem "ironic," but in 1933 it had multiple, non-ironic purposes (Collier 107). It invoked what Theodor Adorno derided as " 'black jazz' as a sort of brand-name" (52) and avoided the possibility of invoking anxiety about cultural miscegenation.

In mid-1934, Goodman formed the first version of the big band that would eventually make him famous; its personnel were white, but much of its music was charted by the black arrangers Fletcher Henderson, Edgar Sampson, and Jimmy Mundy. Arrangers, like the personnel for a recording, may place their indelible stamp on a piece of music, but they are invisible. A year later, at a private jam session that might have defined Sterling Brown's vision of a jazz democracy, Goodman got reacquainted with Teddy Wilson, and in July 1935 the mixed Goodman trio cut its first records.

When the Goodman band took its first big step toward stardom, selling out the Palomar Ballroom in Los Angeles for two months in the late summer of 1935, the trio still existed only as a recording unit, never seen in public. It took another year for Goodman to make it visible. The next spring Goodman and his drummer Gene Krupa (the third member of the trio) sat in with the Fletcher Henderson orchestra at a "tea dance" held at the Congress Hotel in Chicago by the Rhythm Club, a group of white, socialite jazz fans. It marked, Goodman thought, "the first time, probably, that white and colored musicians played together for a paying audience in America" (Goodman and Kolodin 210). The Rhythm Club booked the Goodman band for a similar show late in 1936, and under some pressure from the club's promoters, Goodman included the trio on the bill. There were no complaints about the mixing onstage, and the show was a success. Thereafter, the trio, later expanded to a quartet by including Lionel Hampton, was a regular fixture of Goodman's show, live and on the radio.

The trio and quartet, however, were special instances. They played separately from the band as a discrete part of the show. *Life,* in a 1937 photo essay on the Goodman band, used the caption for a photograph of Wilson to explain: "Negro pianist Teddy Wilson has many a White admirer. Because mixed bands are not the rule in New York, Wilson is not the regular pianist but steps up twice during each evening to play in a mixed quartet" ("*Life*" 121). Furthermore, Wilson had been handpicked—"discovered"—by John Hammond because, in addition to being a great pianist, he was easy for whites to accept. Wilson was from a middle-class background and, in Hammond's estimation, "had the bearing, demeanor, and attitude toward life which would enable him to survive in a white society. . . . he not only had the talent to make it in any surroundings, but the mental and emotional equipment to do so" (116). These qualities, along with his restrained, graceful, and highly polished piano style, made Wilson a perfect match for Goodman's professorial bearing and precise playing and a perfect foil for Gene Krupa's flamboyance. As the 1937 *Life* pictures show, when Hampton, an energetic vibraphone player, joined to make the quartet, the visual "mix" was racially and attitudinally balanced: two exhibitionist percussionists, one white and one black, and two introspective melodists, one white and one black, all making beautiful music together—under carefully controlled and contained circumstances that bent but did not entirely break "the rule" of common experience and expectation (figure 1).

By the end of 1937 the Goodman band, including the trio and quartet, was nationally famous. All its units had made large-selling, critically respected records, had been featured regularly on the radio, and had been widely written about. The band had been in several movies, and the quartet had been in one, *Hollywood Hotel* (Warners, 1937; see below). The quartet had toured the country, including the South, and encountered little "unpleasantness" because of its racial mix.[8] At this point, the Goodman outfit—a small industry of its own—did three things simultaneously to further alter the look of jazz. It mixed the full band for a Carnegie Hall concert program that responded explicitly to the transactional history of the music. According to Irving Kolodin, the impulse for the concert was explicitly historical: "the 'King of Jazz' in the previous decade (Paul Whiteman) had done it; why not the 'King of Swing' in the present (1930) one?" It was implicitly racial-political.

Whiteman, who was still popular in the late thirties, had risen to fame in the twenties as the major proponent of "sweet" or "symphonic" jazz. His bands never included black players, though he did use several black arrangers (Early 281). Further, his public, visual presentations consistently erased the African American contribution to jazz. His famous Aeolian Hall and Carnegie Hall concerts in 1924 began with a brief history, "The True Form of Jazz," that burlesqued early jazz by making fun of the Original Dixieland Jazz Band, a white group from the World War I period, and ended with the premiere of Gershwin's *Rhapsody in Blue* (Whiteman and McBride 100–102). His autobiography begins with the sentence, "Jazz came to America three hundred years ago in chains" (1), but beyond the first chapter it makes no mention of African Americans and contains an illustration titled "Everybody Everywhere" that shows jazz being created by tiny Whiteman figures in costumes from Spain, Great Britain, Germany, France, and India. In his 1930 film, *King of Jazz,* a section called "The Melting Pot of Jazz" also excludes African Americans.

At the Goodman concert at Carnegie Hall the regular band, the trio, and the quartet dominated the show. But at two important points in the program the band was replaced by a mixed, all-star lineup. The first instance of this came in a section called "Twenty Years of Jazz," which pastiched white (ODJB, Beiderbecke, Ted Lewis) *and* black (Louis Armstrong, Ellington) jazz and employed three key members of the Ellington orchestra. The second was a "jam session" using six members of the Count Basie band (including Basie and Lester Young) and one of the Ellington men; here, significantly, the black players outnumbered the white players onstage, shifting the established ratios of racial mixture in the Goodman band's mixed jazz.

This Carnegie Hall concert—unlike Whiteman's symphonic jazz concert—forwarded jazz's claim as an art on its own "popular" terms. The program was dance music, though no one danced. On the one hand, this just made official for a night one common reaction to the Goodman band: "Standing and listening is what most Goodman fans do for more than half a typical Madhatten Room evening," *Life* had reported in 1937 (*"Life"* 121). On the other hand, by anchoring its audience in Carnegie Hall's seats, by disallowing even the potential for the distraction of dance, the Goodman concert ensured that its audience literally saw jazz's own "artistic" terms not just as "popular" but as racially mixed.

The Carnegie Hall concert, which was successful in drawing a sellout crowd and in garnering national media attention, accelerated both mixing in jazz and jazz's claim to be an art. Around the time that Krupa left Goodman in 1938, Lionel Hampton joined the band, occasionally sitting in on drums. In 1939 Fletcher Henderson played piano for the band. From

Figure 1. (a) Benny Goodman, (b) Gene Krupa, (c) Lionel Hampton, and (d) Teddy Wilson, as pictured in "*Life* Goes to a Party," *Life*, 1 November 1937.

late 1939 through 1941, Sid Catlett, Charlie Christian, John Simmons, and Cootie Williams played for long and shorter stretches with Goodman.[9] A few other bands mixed: Artie Shaw hired Billie Holiday. Charlie Barnet employed Frankie Newton and Lena Horne over the next few years. Gene Krupa employed Roy Eldridge in the early forties and had him sing a mixed-race and mixed-gender duet with Anita O'Day on "Let Me Off Uptown" (represented in a 1942 soundie of the same title). From the other side of the color line, Fletcher Henderson hired several white players, though he claimed that in the South they had sometimes been forced to wear blackface (Feather, September 1944, 93). Still, Horne's hiring by Barnet in 1941, well before she was a national star, was unusual enough to be headline news for the *Chicago Defender*, which noted that she was the "third vocalist to [ever] be employed by a white band" ("Joins" 1)—and which also noticed when Horne did not tour the South with Barnet and when she quit because of "trouble encountered in the so many lily white spots where the band played" ("Leana" 13).[10]

In 1938, John Hammond held the first of two "Spirituals to Swing" concerts at Carnegie Hall, both sponsored by leftist political organizations. The first concert featured an all-black roster, but the second, held in 1939, concluded with a mixed Goodman sextet—a progression that at once asserted the black sources of swing and suggested that ultimately a racially mixed outcome sprang from these sources.

Also in 1938, Café Society opened downtown with an explicit commitment to racial mixing on the bandstand and, more notably, in the audience. Previous to this, there had been racially mixed audiences, but such mixing had mostly taken place in black neighborhoods and had been tinged with a one-way sense of the exotic; now the flow of color could (in a small way) reverse, moving from Harlem to downtown. Café Society held its own Carnegie Hall concert in 1941, and in 1943 Duke Ellington initiated a series of yearly concerts at Carnegie Hall, saying, in a *Time* review, "The Negro is not merely a singing and dancing wizard but a loyal American, in spite of his social position. I want to tell America how the Negro feels about it" ("Duke" 44). Swing was becoming simultaneously popular, artistic, and insistent about racial politics.[11]

At the same time, the jam session was becoming a national myth, and jazz criticism, previously the domain of slumming classical critics, industry papers, and small specialty publications, was moving into the mainstream. The mid-thirties saw the publication of the first books of jazz history and criticism—many larded with photographs documenting the mixed evolution of jazz (e.g., Ramsey and Smith)—and a wide array of general interest periodicals began to review jazz. For instance, in January 1937 *Reader's Digest* reprinted an essay from *The Delineator* called "It's Swing!" This piece typifies much mainstream, popularizing writing on swing from this period. It emphasizes racial mixing in the music at its origins in turn-of-the-century New Orleans ("Negro, white—they jammed together") and asserts the importance of the jam session for swing players, while avoiding any uncomfortable mention of mixing in the present day. The article presents the music as serious: the audience members "have come here not to dance, but to listen." It promotes Louis Armstrong (not undeservingly) to the "King of Swing," demoting Goodman to the "Swingmaster." Nonetheless, Armstrong, a perspiring exotic "in a state of profound agitation," needs to be identified for the writer by a kindly, Rochester-like waiter: "Yes, suh, boss. That boy is Louis Armstrong" (Harvey 99–102). For all its errors and offenses, essays like this one increased swing's public exposure and kept relevant terms— race, popularity, art—in wide view.

Media activity surrounding swing peaked between 1943 and 1945. In its February 1943 issue, *Esquire* selected a mixed "All-American" jazz band. All-star bands were common to specialty magazines like *Down Beat* and to African American newspapers like the *Defender*, but in a magazine that boasted a circulation of 700,000, this was new. The same year *Look* hired Leonard Feather, then a writer and editor well known in the jazz press, to do capsule record reviews. Feather concentrated on jazz, and for the next two years he carefully balanced his column between records by black and white musicians, all of whom were shown in tiny photos next to each of Feather's paragraphs. From a current perspective this may seem insignificant, but entire issues of the magazine would go by without showing any "other" American face besides those accompanying Feather's reviews.[12] Later in 1943, *Look* and *Life* each published photo essays entitled "Jam Session." Both showed black and white players, but, unlike the *Look* essay, which was a series of individual portraits from a wide array of venues, Gjon Mili's *Life* piece documented a mixed session the photographer had set up at his loft. Each of Mili's photographs showed various mixtures of whites and blacks playing and listening together (figure 2). Unlike the writer for the 1937 *Life* piece on the Goodman band, the anonymous writer of the accompanying text for "Jam Session" felt comfortable leaving this fact unremarked.

Esquire again selected an All-American band in 1944, but that year it also assembled this mixed band onstage at the Metropolitan Opera House, broadcast the show live on the radio, and recorded it on V-disc for the troops overseas. The editorial for the issue recounted "The Upward Journey of Hot Jazz, from the Junkshops to the Met," and boasted that "this will be the first time that American Jazz has invaded that innermost sanctum of musical respectability" ("Editorial" 6). The magazine also made jazz a regular part of each issue in 1944, adding columns by Feather and Paul Eduard Smith, and it published the first of its *Jazz Yearbooks.*

The next year *Esquire* topped itself by staging, and coordinating for radio broadcast, three concerts on a single night: Louis Armstrong played from New Orleans, Benny Goodman's mixed quintet played from New York, and the Ellington orchestra, augmented by various other All-American award winners, played from the Philharmonic Auditorium in Los Angeles. As a grand finale, musicians from all three places jammed with one another over the radio—the ultimate democratic, American jam session, technologically joining races, regions of the country, and masters from different genres of jazz. Of course, in this instance this feat could only be "seen" in the listeners' imaginations—imaginations prepared by slow years of gradualist assimilation to see racially mixed, "concert" jazz as the look of American music, a look as fluid and varied as the sound of jazz.

However, Leonard Feather's explanation of the 1945 All-American awards suggests that not even the imaginations of swing *fans*, let alone the mainstream "American" imagination, were yet so developed in their visions of jazz. *"Why didn't Harry James and Jimmy and Tommy Dorsey*

Figure 2. Gjon Mili's lead photo from "Jam Session," *Life*, 11 October 1943.

win anything?" Feather asked himself rhetorically. His answer gives a sense of the visual, racial politics of the dominant jazz discourse at the end of the swing era:

> I'm glad you asked that. It brings me to the point that this ballot is based on musical values, *not* on commercial success. . . .
>
> Further, our experts are free from race prejudice. In polls in which jazz fans do the voting, the majority of winners is usually white. In our ballot, the overwhelming majority is Negro; not because anybody is anti-white or pro-Negro, but because most of the great jazzmen today happen to be colored. ("All-American" 102)

Art—"musical value"—was at stake, and, according to Feather, musical values had no intrinsic color—though commercial values, which reflected for Feather the values of (white) consumers, did.

In the September 1944 issue of *Esquire*, Feather had asked a group of black jazz players a pointed question: "How have Jim Crow tactics affected your career?" Teddy Wilson's response, grounded in the mechanics of making a living, showed in detail how white prejudice continued, despite high-profile mixed bands, to control the sight of jazz across the full range of industrial forms of music:

> The whole time I was with Benny Goodman's Quartet, from 1935 to 1939, there was no significant trouble. I lost some movie work when they wanted me to do the recording for a musical sequence in *Big Broadcast of 1936* but have a white musician substitute for me when they shot the pictures. I refused to do that. The following year Benny made *Hollywood Hotel* for Warners and they did photograph the Quartet, all of us wearing the same uniform and no suggestion of segregation. But the scene was shot in such a way that they could cut it out in movie houses down South.
>
> When I got a big band together in 1939 I found out more about how Jim Crow works against musicians. They had an equal rights law in Pennsylvania, and promoters were scared to hire colored bands because it might attract Negro patrons and they'd be risking lawsuits by refusing them admittance. That means that where a white band doing a road tour out of New York could break it up into short, convenient transportation jumps, a colored band could not break the journey until it got to Pittsburgh, the first town large enough to hold a strictly colored dance.
>
> Of course, the biggest handicap is in radio. A lot of the best locations with network wires, like the Astor and the Pennsylvania [a room Wilson *had* worked with the Goodman quartet] and the New Yorker Hotel, don't hire Negro bands, and the commercial radio shows are almost entirely impossible because the sponsors are afraid their product would be boycotted by white Southerners if they hired a colored outfit. Radio and records are the life-blood of a band, so that means that a colored band has to rely mainly on records. (93)[13]

A year earlier in Los Angeles, Norman Granz, a young film editor at MGM, had begun his own efforts on the racial-political, artistic-commercial nexus of jazz. Building on a decade of work by people like Hammond, Wilson, Goodman, Henderson, and Feather and embarking in the wartime boom rather than the depression, Granz could be explicit about his motives: "I get mad easily—about racial discrimination . . . and *Jazz at the Phil* [Granz's organization] is a good way to do something about it. Jazz is ideal to use in promoting better race relations because the American Negro has contributed so much to the history of jazz. You can't begin to understand jazz without, at the same time, beginning to understand the Negro and his contributions to our culture" ("Jazz" 36). He also could be bolder about the effect jazz was supposed to have *off* the bandstand. As Feather's and Wilson's comments suggest, mainstream American audiences were resistant to both mixed bands and mixed audiences, with the limited mixing that was taking place on records and in performances seldom being reflected, and certainly not being amplified, in the makeup of audiences.

Beginning with the first jam sessions he organized and extending through two decades of JATP concerts, tours, and records, Granz applied three rules. The musicians he hired would be paid well; there would be no dancing at his events; and there could be no segregation on either the bandstand or in the audience.[14] The first of these rules responded to exploitative club owners and promoters. The second institutionalized a trend that was already familiar from other attempts to establish jazz as an art, a concert music. The third rule was most important, because it recognized the limitations of previous efforts to mix the look of jazz—efforts that had relied on an optimistic trickle-down theory of cultural-social change. Granz's third rule attempted to ensure consumption as an act of resistance to racist conventions; it tried to direct attention both to the relation of individual consumers to the producers of the music they consumed *and* to the relations between individual, and perhaps different, consumers of the same musical product.

JATP evolved as a complex, market-driven, and market-responsive answer to a racist situation, just as at the same time bebop was developing, in part, "as a profound criticism of the failure of swing's ecstatic hopes for a modern America rooted in pluralism and individualism" (Erenberg 237). Bebop, especially in its early stages, turned to local and exclusivist modes of production and upped the musical ante with an insistence on virtuosic and "authentic" black invention.[15] JATP concentrated on national (later, international), inclusive, and conjunctive elaborations of jazz, on "mass-producing" (Balliet 3) and mass-marketing a sort of "swing-bop" fusion (Kernfeld 349), especially to the young.[16] Bop was explicitly oppositional and disjunctive, frustrated by the unfair terms of "assimilation" in the United States and refusing to play the game. JATP, which would eventually include most of the great bebop players, was also oppositional, but it wanted to change the rules of assimilation, to alter what assimilation would look like, and to shift the ground for the meaning of the term.

As these developments took place, Granz assembled the cast and crew of *Jammin' the Blues*—including Lester Young, John Simmons, and Sid Catlett, black musicians who had played in high-profile mixed groups and jam sessions, Barney Kessel, a white disciple of black guitarist Charlie Christian, and Gjon Mili, photographer of mixed jam sessions. Seen in the arc of attempts to mix and aestheticize the look of jazz, *Jammin' the Blues* functions as the first national advertisement for the JATP ideology of oppositional inclusion and progressive consumerism.

Of course, *Jammin' the Blues* was not the first Hollywood film to represent jazz. Jazz musicians had been seen on screen since before the introduction of sound, and by 1944 the sight and sound of swing bands were a regular part of musicals; the Count Basie band, for example, appeared in five musicals filmed in 1943.[17] *Jammin' the Blues* was not the first film to show a mixed band: Mae West had sung with the Ellington band in *Belle of the Nineties* (1934); Martha Raye had sung with Louis Armstrong in *Artists & Models* (1937); the Goodman quartet appeared in *Hollywood Hotel* (1937); and in *To Have and Have Not*, a film that *Jammin' the Blues* was billed with, Lauren Bacall sang with a mixed band fronted by Hoagy Carmichael. And *Jammin' the Blues* was not the first film to attempt to represent jazz in an "artistic" way or as a self-conscious art: the short *Yamacraw* (1930) illustrated James P. Johnson's tone poem for orchestra, jazz band, and chorus with expressionist imagery familiar from German film, King Vidor's *Hallelujah!* (1929), and stage productions like *Porgy* (1927) and its more famous musical version, *Porgy and Bess* (1935, revived 1941);[18] in another short, *Symphony in Black* (1935), the Ellington orchestra played a nine-minute "symphony," also intercut with expressionist images, for a white, concert hall audience.

Still, in 1944, Leonard Feather summarized how most jazz fans probably felt about Hollywood's representation of the music: "In the movies—you find [jazz] all too seldom. The bands that get the biggest film breaks generally aren't jazz outfits and even when they are, their presentation is usually inadequate. As for small groups, Hollywood has virtually ignored them" ("Jazz is" 95). Feather never specified his standards of adequacy or excellence for the representation of jazz on film, but the blueprint for a "legitimate" musical he elicited from Sam Donahue, quoted at the start of this essay, can serve as a guide. An adequate representation of jazz would focus on the music and musicians, avoiding "illogical" intrusions, whether of spectacle ("jitterbug dancers") or narrative ("chicks bursting into song in the middle of a forest"), and it would record the audio and the visual tracks simultaneously, fusing "real and spontaneous" sight and sound. Feather's more general critical standards help fill out these guidelines: The jazz itself should be "real"—challenging and demanding art, based on musical, rather than commercial, values. The players should be credited for their work. And the casting should avoid racial discrimination, recognizing at the same time that "most of the great jazzmen today happen to be colored."

Neither Donahue's blueprint nor Feather's fondness for Louis Armstrong's "delightful screen personality and natural acting ability" suggest a desire to apply any sort of simple "documentary" aesthetic to representing jazz on film ("Jazz is" 95). Although it was used in seemingly countless shorts and many features, neither Donahue nor Feather discussed Hollywood's most common convention for filming swing—"canned" performance, or putting a band on a set and letting it "play" (to prerecorded sound) directly to the camera. Presumably, then, they had little use for this convention, which seldom captured the energy or the visual "showmanship" of the music.[19] In the early forties the ideal vision of jazz on film for Donahue, Feather, and jazz players and fans in general was probably the long-rumored Orson Welles bio-pic of Louis Armstrong, a quality production that would have united the consummate "artists" of Hollywood and jazz.[20]

By these standards—or hopes—no worthy tradition of jazz on film existed in 1944. None of the films just mentioned, despite their interest and importance, focused on jazz or jazz musicians. At best, the music was incidental to the narrative, used to give depth to a character, like Mae West's Ruby Carter in *Belle of the Nineties*, or a location, like Martinique in *To Have and Have Not*. At worst, regressive, racist representation recuperated a progressive visual representation of the music; for example, in *Hollywood Hotel* a blackface number precedes the appearance of the Goodman quartet. Films that did focus on the lives of "jazz" musicians, like *Birth of the Blues* (1941), indulged in what could be called the Whiteman effect, erasing the African American contributions to jazz and making the blues the province of performers like Bing Crosby and Mary Martin.[21] (The 1934 musical *Murder at the Vanities* depicts this erasure in its most extreme form when an enraged classical conductor machine-guns the elegantly uniformed Ellington orchestra after they impress "his" audience; this murder, which is ostensibly part of the show, is not the murder of the film's title.) Otherwise, Hollywood placed black musical performers in Jim Crow specialty numbers—the position of the Basie band in all of its 1943 musicals[22]—or in completely segregated films like *Yamacraw, Stormy Weather* (1944), or *Cabin in the Sky* (1943).

The concerns of African American activists and intellectuals and the standards of the liberal, largely white discursive community of jazz fans conjoined (though not always perfectly) across dissatisfaction with these Hollywood film conventions. After decades of specific, localized protests and general complaint in the black press, in 1942 the NAACP held its national conference in Los Angeles and used the occasion to pressure Hollywood to more adequately represent African Americans.[23] Two years later, the sociologist Lawrence Reddick, analyzing the movies as "one index to what the American people have come to believe about the Negro," anatomized the nineteen "principle stereotypes of the Negro in the American mind"—among them the natural-born musician, the perfect entertainer, and the uninhibited exhibitionist (368–69). Reddick felt that, in the years since *Gone With the Wind*, Hollywood had improved its depiction of blacks, but he was still deeply dissatisfied with Jim Crow films, which were by definition "false and objectionable," and with the continued reliance on "the usual roles given to Negro actors that call for types . . . [including] various jazz musicians" (380). Jackie Lopez, the writer who reviewed *To Have and Have Not* and *Jammin' the Blues* for the *Chicago Defender*, opened her piece by referring to this continuing struggle: "The stiff lipped complaining we've been tossing Hollywood way may have some bearing on the fact that the movie town is viewing the race with new eyes" (20).

Jammin' the Blues responded to and attempted to reformulate the conventions used for representing jazz and African American musicality, even as it could not escape them. It attempted to (re)envision jazz as an art and an entertainment, as specifically African American and generally (mixed) American, as private and public, exclusive and inclusive, as spontaneous and practiced, ephemeral and commodifiable. It tried to do all this in three numbers.

The opening of *Jammin' the Blues* uses several means to announce the film's difference from standard Hollywood product of the same period (figure 3). The most obvious means is the comprehensive credits, which list all the players names in big, graphically bold type. This was uncommon recognition for any musician who was not a popular, "name" star—a vocalist or bandleader, usually. ("That we should ever live to see the day!" was Charles Emge's response in *Down Beat* [6].) The credits assure the musicians' possession of their performances, disperse the authorship

of the film, and attempt to insure its authenticity, its veracity. For uninitiated viewers, the credits serve to individuate the players and suggest
that the blues were no longer an anonymous (Negro) folk music or the
domain of Bing Crosby. For viewers in the know, the credits link the film
to the discourse about jazz, investing it with a certain documentary
power by drawing on an alternative firmament of stars. Within this
alternative star system, *Jammin' the Blues* used some of the biggest
names. In the 1944 *Down Beat* poll Lester Young (tenor saxophone) and
Sid Catlett (drums) placed first in their categories; Jo Jones (drums) followed Catlett, and Barney Kessel (guitar) was seventh in his category
("Spivak" 13). Catlett won the *Esquire* All-American gold award (first
place) in 1943, 1944, and 1945, and Young won an *Esquire* silver award
(second place) in 1945.[24] In short, the credits of *Jammin' the Blues* announce the democratic, contributory nature of these blues and assert
that this music is made by specific, excellently qualified individuals.

The symbolic currency of the stars of *Jammin' the Blues* would have
run deep for jazz fans and for other musicians (figure 3). Young, Catlett,
and Jones, despite being in their early to mid-thirties, were the aware
elder statesmen of the blues as a musical discipline. Catlett had played
with virtually everyone; Young and Jones were members of the great
Count Basie band. Musically, they self-consciously bridged the gap between swing and bebop, innovating and listening to others' innovations
but stubbornly reminding younger players of the great value of what had
come before. And Young particularly, with his coded styles of speech and
fashion, was an icon, "the first black musician to be publicly recognized
not as a happy-go-lucky entertainer, *à la* Armstrong, but as an artist of
the *demi-monde* whose discontents magnified those felt in general by
his race" (Davis 16).

The brief voice-over introduction, which immediately follows the credits, reveals the tension between Hollywood conventions and resistant
impulses for representing jazz that *Jammin' the Blues* works within and
tries to work through: "This is a jam session. Quite often these great
artists gather and play—ad lib—hot music. It could be called a midnight
symphony." On the one hand, this voice is familiar from other Hollywood shorts, documentaries, and newsreels—the voice of God, the voice
of white authority, preceding and framing what the audience sees and
hears. On the other hand, this voice is different, both in what it says and
in how and when it says it. The credits have subtly displaced the voice,
diminishing its ability to fully name what the audience will experience.
Further, the combination of the image (discussed in more detail below)
and the sound (a slow, soft piano vamp, supported by bass and drums),

Figure 3. Still frames
from the opening shot
of *Jammin' the Blues.*

both image and sound continuous and uncut at this point in the film, pulls the voice into an already existing flow that has an attraction of its own.

The voice-over begins in an authoritative, definitive mode: "This is a jam session." The subtext is something like, "You've read about and seen pictures of jam sessions, now see and hear a *real* one."[25] Then it moves to a description of "great artists" who "quite often" "gather and play—ad lib—hot music." Within the context of popular discourse about jazz, this description is complex. The players the audience is about to hear and see are "great artists"—not "folk artists" or "Negro artists." The failure to specify that the players are black violated Hollywood and standard journalistic conventions of representation in 1944,[26] and the iterative "quite often" implies repetition and practice. Nonetheless, these artists also create their art spontaneously, "ad lib." In other words, their art uses one of the principal qualities of entertainment. Hollywood musicals often worked to incorporate art into entertainment, but the voice in *Jammin' the Blues* works from the opposite direction to incorporate entertainment into art.[27] The use of "hot music"—in the words of *Down Beat*, "Jazzdom's term for one of its proudest boasts: the ad lib solo playing of its crack musicians" (Levin 14)[28]—instead of the common words "jazz" and "swing" indicates the noncommercial yet exciting aspect of the music. Shifting to the conditional mode for its last sentence, the voice reiterates this combination: "It could be called a midnight symphony." *This* artistic form takes place outside the constrictive boundaries of polite convention. This sentence claims "hot music" as a "symphonic," artistic form, but it also admits a cliché—"midnight"—that is dense with both romantic and potentially racist significations. Then the voice leaves off and lets the artists "speak" for themselves.

The body of the *Jammin' the Blues* substantiates the difference that its opening sequence claims. Midway through the voice-over, the camera still lingers on the abstract image that was under the credits—two concentric white ovals slightly off-center on a saturated black field with an occasional wisp of white smoke moving past them. As the voice-over ends, the camera draws back slowly, and at the same time the circles begin to tilt, revealing that they are the key-lit brim and crown of a saxophone player's porkpie hat; the player draws his mouthpiece to his lips and joins the tune; the camera continues to draw back, showing that the player holds a burning cigarette between the index and middle fingers of his right hand, even as they work the keys of his horn. The opening abstraction has turned into a most detailed representation. (As soon as the abstraction became recognizable as a hat, jazz aficionados would have known they were seeing Lester Young, whose porkpie was as iconic in jazz as Chaplin's bowler was in film. Then they would have recognized the odd, forty-five-degree angle at which Young held his horn. Finally, the most dedicated, the same people who stood along the front of the bandstand wherever the Basie band played, may have begun to try to catch his fingerings and his fashions.) Only after the camera has reframed its subject to show his seated figure surrounded by inky darkness is there a cut to another angle.

This opening sets the photographic strategy for the film. The image moves back and forth between medium and long shots and extreme close-ups, focusing on the visible materiality of the process of making hot music: the surfaces of instruments and clothing—of ties, trousers, shoes, and hats; the small motions of hands and fingers on valves, keys, and strings; furrowed brows and distended cheeks and tiny gestures of communication. Sometimes these images are connected through disjunctive cuts, returning the image briefly to the level of abstraction or juxtaposing various individuals with one another or the group; other times tracking and reframing link a detail to a larger image of the whole scene, an individual soloist to the group.

The setting never intrudes because there is none—only apparently limitless blackness or whiteness surrounding the players. *Jammin' the Blues* rejects the architectures of both professional and "folk" musical performance—theaters, bars, levees, barns—common to Hollywood films. Instead, it creates an undifferentiated space defined by shadow and light, a space that encourages the viewer to concentrate on the music but also, perhaps even more, encourages the observer to see how musicians look as they make their music.[29] If the jam session from the Goodman band's 1938 Carnegie Hall concert or if the "technological" jam session from *Esquire*'s 1945 All-American broadcast could have found ideal locations—ones not constrained by the visible meanings of the concert hall or the invisibility of radio—those locations would probably have looked something like the space of *Jammin' the Blues*.

The sound, which had no apparent relation to the abstract image under the titles but was suddenly bound to the image when the abstraction turned into Lester Young, continues to firmly relate to the image for the remainder of the film. As was standard Hollywood practice, most of the images were shot to prerecorded, playback sound. However, Norman Granz (credited as the film's "technical director," he recorded all the music) took extraordinary care to minimize the effects of this disjuncture. Charles Emge reported in his *Down Beat* review that: "Granz had phonograph recordings made of the solos so that the boys could take them home and memorize them. . . . Drum solos are especially difficult to synchronize. Good results were obtained by Granz by recording some of the more complicated passages, such as 'rolls,' on the set during shooting and dubbing these sections into the track" (6). This practice came as near as Hollywood would probably allow to the live recording-while-shooting that Sam Donahue thought would make musical film look and sound "real and spontaneous."

Jammin' the Blues is not a narrative, so there are no story events to intrude on the presentation of the music.[30] Instead, the film's main organizing principle is addition, expressed both aurally and visually. The first, slow number ("Midnight Symphony" [MS], which begins under the credits) is followed by a medium-tempo, vocal rendering of the standard, "On the Sunny Side of the Street" [SSS], which is followed by the concluding, up-tempo instrumental ("Jammin' the Blues" [JtB]).[31] The image track matches this increase in tempo on the soundtrack with an increase in the tempo of the editing.[32] MS uses a quintet lineup (the rhythm trio plus tenor sax and trumpet); SSS uses a sextet (rhythm trio, guitar, tenor sax, and voice); and JtB uses a septet (rhythm trio, guitar, two tenor saxophones, and trumpet). So an increasing instrumental depth and complexity accompany the music's increasing tempo.

The visual track parallels this intensification in three ways. First, with one exception, the visual track accurately records these lineups, resulting in increasingly "crowded" compositions (see figure 4). (The exception is SSS, where, though the guitar is clearly audible, we see no guitarist. I will interpret this absence below.) Second, the film adds a new photographic effect with each song. SSS adds silhouette to the chiaroscuro established in MS, and JtB adds multiple exposure (see figures 5a and 10). Finally, beginning in SSS, the film adds an additional space. In MS all of the players clearly occupied the same space, but in SSS Lester Young is shown away from the other musicians. This new space, while it seems as "real" as the film's primary space, has a phantasmagoric quality in that shots from Young's position show Marie Bryant (the vocalist) sitting alone, even though the master shot shows her in the midst of the rhythm players (see figure 4b). JtB fills this same phantasmic space with a pair of jitterbug dancers (see figure 5b).

But, if *Jammin' the Blues* is not organized narratively, neither is it a typical Hollywood "canned" performance. Coincident with its additive organization, *Jammin' the Blues* posits an evolving relationship between its performers and the camera. When the film begins, the musicians are not arrayed frontally, as if playing for an implied audience, but in a sort of loose circle or U. The camera has the mobility to seek them out and peer at them from almost any angle or distance, but none of the players look directly at the camera, at the viewer; rather, they seem to serve as their own audience. In SSS, Bryant, seen in tightly framed close-up, looks obliquely past the camera—but not directly at it. The fact that she is singing increases a sense of address, but the shot, reverse-shot editing (the same editing used to show conversations in films with dialogue) variously shows her addressing the bassist and, then, Lester Young.[33] However, SSS does contain two quick insert shots, one of the pianist and one of the bassist looking directly at the camera. JtB begins with a master shot showing the band more frontally aligned (this effect is created by the three horn players standing in line) (see figure 4c), gives the aggressive, overblown, upper-register tenor saxophone of Illinois Jacquet the last and longest solo played directly to the camera (figure 6), and concludes with the drummer, Jo Jones, smiling directly at the camera and acknowledging the audience with a nod (figure 7).

As it gains aural and visual speed and density, *Jammin' the Blues* also moves from the oblique abstractness of its opening to a direct, concrete, (self-)referential close. The players move from the unsmiling introspection of Lester Young to the grinning extroversion of Jo Jones. And as the musicians play more and more intensely and more and more directly to the camera, the film creates an additional imaginative space in which it finally places a pair of jitterbug dancers, forging a possible point of entry for an audience. Through its careful organization, *Jammin' the Blues* attempts to transform its viewers from outsiders to insiders, from voyeurs and eavesdroppers to acknowledged audience members and possible participants.

For comparison, consider another Warner Bros. musical short, *Dixieland Jamboree* (1945). Here the title and production credits appear over a drawing of white-gloved hands playing a banjo and attended by thick lips and rolling eyes, all apparently held together by an invisible body. This image alludes directly to blackface minstrelsy and is repeated, in some variation, in virtually every Hollywood film dealing with minstrelsy or with black musicians (figure 8). Music ranging from "spirituals" to Tin Pan Alley accompanies a rapid montage of images of stevedores, field hands, "happy darkies," a blackface performer, and outtakes from *Jammin' the Blues*. Over this a stentorian voice intones:

> Always music has been an intimate part of a people's existence. And in America, the Negro has given to music a newer, greater significance, attaining a superb perfection, a pulsating, inescapable style. Talented with the gift of rhythm and a spontaneity of improvisation,

Figure 4. Establishing shots of the bands in (a) "Midnight Symphony"; *on facing page*: (b) "On the Sunny Side of the Street"; (c) "Jammin' the Blues."

the American Negro has fused the past with the present to create an art that is characteristic of our time, dancing, singing, and playing such music that swings the whole world to the matchless rhythm of the Five Racketeers and Eunice Wilson. . . .

Wilson and the Racketeers (a vaudeville blues singer and a novelty quintet) appear in a canned performance in front of a backdrop of watermelon slices (figure 9). The film goes on to show canned performances by the Three Whippets (a dance team), Adelaide Hall (a "sentimental" singer), the Nicholas Brothers (dancers), and Cab Calloway (commercial jazz).

In slightly different order and without the Calloway number, the body of this film was released in 1936 as *All-Colored Vaudeville Show*, but in 1945 Warners recycled it, adding Calloway and the "ethnographic" voice-over. While *Dixieland Jamboree* does not claim to be about any specific type of music, but rather claims to be about black music and blackness in general, nonetheless it shows the regressive representations of black performers and music that *Jammin' the Blues* would have been seen against. That *All-Colored Vaudeville Show* could return as *Dixieland Jamboree* speaks volumes about Hollywood's lack of sensitivity to African American concerns; what is more, Warner Bros. was considered one

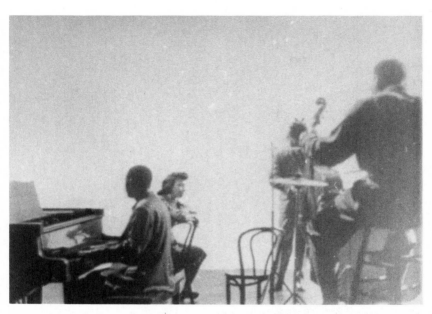

Figure 5. The "imagined" space in (a) "On the Sunny Side of the Street" (compare with figure 4b) and (b) "Jammin' the Blues" (compare with figure 4c).

of the most socially conscious studios (Reddick 379). This short vividly illustrates why critics like Lawrence Reddick were wary of Hollywood depictions of blacks as musicians and entertainers. Moreover, by using images appropriated from *Jammin' the Blues*, *Dixieland Jamboree* makes the importance of context clear. Flanked by images of men loading cotton and barefooted youngsters playing kazoos, a few brief seconds of Lester Young, accompanied by a trumpet playing a variation on "Dixie," hardly seems special. The words of the voice-over, the programmatic assemblage of the music, and the careless mixture of images work very differently—and toward different ends—from their equivalents in *Jammin' the Blues*. And the canned performances, with images often poorly matched to sound, have seemingly nothing in common with the performances in *Jammin' the Blues*.

Yet, for all of their important differences, *Dixieland Jamboree* and *Jammin' the Blues* have similarities that reveal the limits of *Jammin' the Blues'* escape from Hollywood conventions. The carefully deployed iconography, space, organization, and pattern of address of *Jammin' the Blues* would have been available for negative, ungenerous readings, espe-

cially in the context of the racist image creation that *Dixieland Jamboree* represents. The space in *Jammin' the Blues,* even as it draws together the individuality and collectivity of the musicians, suggests hermeticism, complete interiority, and a divorce from any "organic" public. The film's organization leads to exhibitionist gestures that are closer to Cab Calloway's "commercial" entertainment than concentrated, "artistic" musicianship.[34] This pattern is amplified by the shifts in the film's address and iconography. While the film initially challenges the viewer to understand and make sense of the cultural forms it represents, it ends by easing the challenge, directly addressing the audience, and presenting images of the jitterbugging couple (which Sam Donahue named as Hollywood's primary method of "covering up" black bands) and the grinning black man. This last image in particular—especially as embodied in Louis Armstrong's performance persona—was probably the most widely disseminated image of black musicianship in the world, and it had become a key image in the reformulation of the look of mid-1940s jazz, an image associated with the "tomming" that bebop formed itself against. Writing in the journal *Conjunctions* about Miles Davis, who codified on trumpet

Figure 6. Illinois Jacquet at the climax of "Jammin' the Blues."

the "cool" playing style that Lester Young originated on tenor saxophone, Quincy Troupe recalled the meaning of *not* smiling for an audience: "Besides the magisterial, deep-cool hipness of his musical language, the aspects of Miles that affected me most were his urbane veneer and his detached sure sense of himself as royalty, as untouchable in a touch everything world. . . . Miles's refusal to grin in front of white audiences like so many other black entertainers made a statement to me" (80).[35] Troupe's words could be reformulated to describe the opening of *Jammin' the Blues* but not its close.

Perhaps the aspect *Jammin' the Blues* has most in common with *Dixieland Jamboree,* and with other Hollywood representations of jazz, is the fact that it makes jazz look like an *unmixed* music—that it appears to be, though it is not, a Jim Crow film. Given the trajectory of racial mixing traced in the first half of this essay, and given the places of many of *Jammin' the Blues'* key collaborators in that trajectory, this fact marks a disappointing compromise. However, the nuances of this compromise are important for what they reveal about the recalcitrance of Hollywood conventions and about strategies for chipping away at that recalcitrance—and the presumed recalcitrance of the "American" mind these conventions represented.[36]

Jammin' the Blues does include the white guitar player Barney Kessel, but his "inclusion" is carefully managed. According to Charles Emge in *Down Beat:*

> Mr. Studio objected to the appearance of a white musician with Negroes. Of course, he didn't object personally, but it just wouldn't go with Southern audiences. Granz was asked to eliminate Barney Kessel or to get a Negro guitarist to "fake" his playing in the picture. Granz refused but had to be satisfied with photography that hides the fact that Kessel is white from all but the most discerning eyes. (6)[37]

In fact, Granz settled for both more and less in his struggle with "Mr. Studio." Before Kessel ever appears (in JtB, the film's closing tune), Kessel's presence is first—and exclusively—*audible* on the soundtrack during SSS.

"On the Sunny Side of the Street" is the central and most familiar song in *Jammin' the Blues.* In light of the knowledge of Kessel's veiled inclusion in SSS, the visuals chosen to accompany the song seem to allegorize the lyric about "crossing over" and moving from the "shade" into the sun.[38] At the start of the number a dissolve moves through "the reflection of a singer [Marie Bryant] on the ebony mirror of a piano top" (Isaacs 725) and changes the color of background from the black of MS to white (figure 10). When the camera shifts from its close-up of Bryant to an establishing shot, it centers the frame on an empty chair (figure 4b). The absent but audible Kessel arrives as a ghost, an unused chair and a pale wash of (his) color suffusing the film's only popular song.

In 1945 crossover was not yet a term used to designate music that

Figure 7. Jo Jones from the end of *Jammin' the Blues.*

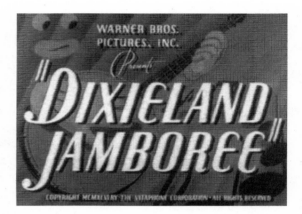

Figure 8. Title card from
Dixieland Jamboree.

was successful with both blacks and whites—or, more precisely, music
played by blacks and popular with blacks that then became popular with
whites. However, according to Henry Louis Gates and Gerald Early, the
trope of crossing over had long been rich with meaning in African American discourses. It signified death, passing for white (Gates 200), "both a
pure rebirth and a mongrelized synergism," and "the weight of one's
previous location bearing down on where you are now" (Early xiii). But
the "dead" person in *Jammin' the Blues,* the person with the invisible
body (which in Ralph Ellison's terms would be passing for black), the
person who should not consort (before institutionally imagined "southern" eyes) with the "other" race and who represented musical-social
mongrelization was white. When Hollywood erased African Americans
in mixed bands, or in its narratives of American life, it made the illusion
complete by replacing them with white stand-ins. Kessel's absent presence in SSS is more complex. It refuses Hollywood convention, even if
the convention would have played in reverse; it sounds as a small testimony to the black jazz musicians who disappeared from the sight of the
mainstream audience as jazz struggled to cross over and become a respected "American" art; and it stands as a reminder of the power of
whiteness in America.

Ultimately, Kessel does "appear" during *Jammin' the Blues'* eponymous last song, deep in the shadows at the edge of the frame, multiply
exposed, and in extreme close-up (figure 11). Kessel's fragmented and
obscured image in JtB serves as the coded but visible sign of the film's—
and jazz's—resistance to Hollywood conventions, a sign available only to
the most "discerning eyes" (eyes that would presumably have accompanied knowledgeable ears). For those able to read the code, Kessel's
veiled inclusion in the film reverses standard notions of minority/major-

Figure 9. Eunice Wilson and the Three Racketeers from *Dixieland Jamboree*.

ity and the typical "tokenism" of mixing in predominantly white bands. It recalls Leonard Feather's casual formulation—"most of the great jazzmen today happen to be colored"—but suggests that, nonetheless, jazz should not be categorized only as "Negro" or "colored," a category that the mainstream could use too easily to dismiss or exoticize the music. In the headline for a story written to accompany its review of *Jammin' the Blues*, *Ebony* magazine deciphered the code for its readers: "Jamming Jumps the Color Line" (8).

Recounting her experience of *Jammin' the Blues* at the State and Lake theater in downtown Chicago, the *Chicago Defender* reviewer Jackie Lopez was rhapsodic: "For those ten minutes you held on to the arms rests of your seat, and you were saying to yourself over and over again: 'This is art. This is art.' Just a ten minute dose of really fine jazz . . ." (20). To Lopez, the film, along with its feature-length companion, *To Have and Have Not*, indicated "Hollywood has potentialities," that it could see that black people are "like anyone else." James Agee in *The Nation* found *Jammin' the Blues* "one of the few musical shorts I have ever got even fair pleasure out of hearing, and the only one . . . which was not a killing bore to watch." But where Lopez saw art, Agee saw pretense and

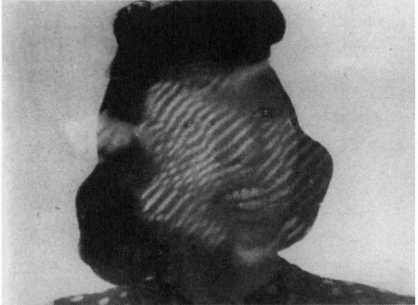

Figure 10. The transition from black to white background between "Midnight Symphony" and "On the Sunny Side of the Street."

"middlebrow highbrow" artiness (753). He was not interested in the color of the cast, which he did not mention. Agee was a minority of one among the reviewers of *Jammin' the Blues*. The other reviewers applauded the film in terms less breathless than but similar to Lopez's, and aside from the writers in *Down Beat* and *Ebony*, most, like Lopez, described what they saw (and heard) as a "Negro" film. In an unsigned capsule review for *Time*, Agee joined the majority, while pointing out that the film's "new," "artistic" qualities were new only by Hollywood standards; Agee also took this opportunity to point out that the cast was not all-Negro, and he named most of the players (50).

Agee's critical stuttering and Lopez's hopeful excitement are symptomatic of the tensions and contradictions that *Jammin' the Blues* was trying to mediate. On the one hand, "art" proves that black people are like everyone else—except, in order for the art to be made (on film, at any rate), black people could not *be* with anyone else, at least not in the United States. (*To Have and Have Not* does show mixing, which impressed Lopez, though she pointed out that the film was set in Martinique.) On the other hand, in Agee's formulation (which he had made

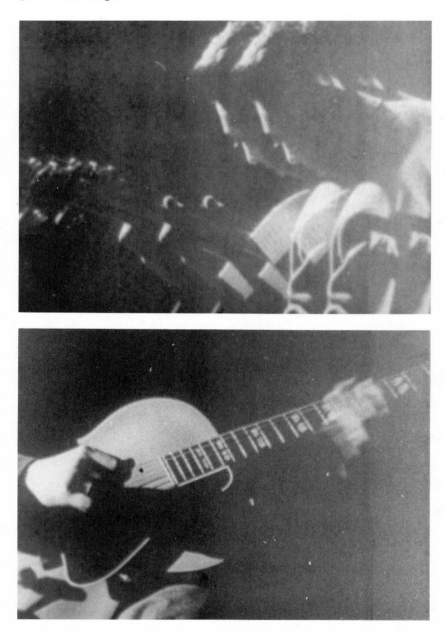

Figure 11. Barney Kessel in "Jammin' the Blues"; see also the far right of figure 4c.

explicit in his 1944 essay "Pseudo-Folk"), the striving for "art" reduces black people to everyone else, corrupting and decaying the true "folk" nature of the Negro (219–23). Finally, such positions, incorporated and enforced by Hollywood, left little room for the types of negotiation *Jammin' the Blues* was attempting.

The categories that *Jammin' the Blues* partakes of and tries to fuse mark the complexity of the film's project, the complexity of music as a social-cultural, visual and aural representation, and the contradictions of the United States as a "community" in the mid-1940s. *Jammin' the Blues* simultaneously worked to emphasize the creativity and humanity of African American musicians, to be color-blind, and to be racially mixed, but it did this work at a moment when the impulse behind such simultaneity was not yet widely acceptable. The film's careful orchestration—and compromise—of these multiple desires allowed it to be made in Hollywood and made it available and exciting to a wide audience. But the complexity of these desires ensured that—despite many hopes—refinements, expansions or even generic repetitions of *Jammin' the Blues'* model for making jazz music visible on film would not be soon in coming.

Notes

The research for this essay was supported by an ACLS/Luce Dissertation Fellowship in American Art. Thanks to the Mass Culture Workshop at the University of Chicago (especially Candace Mirza, Shari Roberts, Pam Robertson, and Hank Sartin), Miriam Hansen, Lauren Berlant, David Thompson, and Martha Howard for many careful readings of this essay.

1 [Agee,] "Jammin' the Blues"; "Speaking of Pictures"; Feather, "Jazz is Where You Find It," May 1945; Isaacs 725; Emge; Lopez; "Jam Session in Movieland"; Agee, "Films" 753.

2 For an analysis of the uses of the "audio-visual disjuncture" in recorded music, see Corbett.

3 A 1945 General Electric advertisement plays on this quality of music, especially as it is mediated through mass culture. Under a full-color image of the lady in the tutti-frutti hat, a headline shouts, "Carmen Miranda's voice in natural color—a thrill only FM radio captures!" Under a smaller, black-and-white image of Miranda, a tiny caption reads: "Conventional radio—lacks color and richness. Something is missing" (2). What is missing, of course, is not the full range of Miranda's singing voice but the spectacle of her *colorful* image, needed to lend credence to her "ethnic" voice.

4 For detailed examinations of these discursive shifts, see Erenberg and Gendron.

5 Brown's vision was not new, though it was more specific than many other descriptions of jazz as a democratic art; see, for example, Rogers. For a scathing countervision of jazz as "pseudo-democratic," see Adorno.

6   It is important to remember that, before the introduction of the LP in the late forties, records carried little of the visual information (whether in the form of illustrations and photographs or in forms suggested by liner notes and musician credits) that became common beginning in the fifties.

7   The events I discuss throughout this section are not important because they were momentous "firsts"—none of them were. Rather they are important because they were attempts to change conventions within the music industry and to make previously local, isolated practices appear "popular," normal, regular. Collier's *Benny Goodman and the Swing Era* has been invaluable for specifying the chronology of mixing in general and in the Goodman band in particular, though my interpretations of these events often differ from his.

8   This word is Goodman's (229). It refers only to direct harassment and does not include the routine humiliations of segregation, like separate and inferior accommodations for touring black musicians, that Wilson and Hampton experienced. Also see Collier 173–76.

9   None of these integrated bands were visually documented as thoroughly as the trio or quartet; as far as I know, none of them were ever filmed.

10   For more on mixing, see Monroe, "Swingin' the News" 19 Apr. and "Mixing's."

11   Probably the best-remembered musical manifestation of this trend was Billie Holiday's performing and recording of "Strange Fruit"—an account of a lynching—beginning in 1939.

12   When Feather was replaced in 1945, the *Look* reviews began to address a wider range of music, and the photos were replaced with line drawings meant to represent the music in question, rather than a specific musician. See also Feather, "Politics," for an account of how racial representation worked in the jazz press of the thirties and forties.

13   Wilson mistook which *Big Broadcast* he was excluded from—it was *1937*, not *1936*.

14   For more on Granz, JATP, and its various spin-offs, see Balliet; Feather, "The Granzwagon"; McDonough; Newton 182–85; and Horricks.

15   The initial insularity of bebop was partially economic and extramusical. Significant developments in the music occurred during the first musicians' union recording ban, of 1942–43. However, this insularity also stemmed from iconoclastic intention. Stories abound of the difficulty and strangeness of the music (many would say "noise") at Minton's Playhouse and Monroe's Uptown House in Harlem—weird rhythms and times, difficult keys, and odd ("wrong") harmonies with obscure melodies. Less consistent are accounts of the motives of the innovators' intentions. Many writers say the innovators did not want to be "ripped off" by whites; others say they did not want to be ripped off by *commercializers* (who, most likely, would have been white). The difference between these accounts is subtle, but Ralph Ellison, who adhered to the second, makes a point that suggests the difference is important: "there was no policy of racial discrimination at Minton's" (212).

16   Kernfeld sees the swing-bop hybrid as one defined by common elements of band size and instrumentation, which small swing groups (like the Goodman trio, quartet, and sextet) and bebop groups shared, and by the melding of swing's "tunefulness" with bebop's "rhythmic complexity" and speed.

17   This was the Basie band's big Hollywood year. The films were *Stage Door Canteen, The Hit Parade of 1943, Reveille With Beverlie, Crazy House,* and *Top Man.*

18   For more on the direct links between the visual styles of the stage *Porgy* and *Hallelujah!,* see Altman.

19   On the early development of this convention, see Wolfe. For insight into how some jazz players felt about "showmanship" during the mid-forties, see Miller.

20   See "Orson Welles" and Feather, "Jazz is." In fact, this bio-pic was to be a condensed history of jazz and was one proposed section of the aborted *It's All True.*

21   In his regular "Swingin' the News" column in the entertainment section of the *Chicago Defender,* Al Monroe noted this quality of *Birth of the Blues*—"The premiere in Memphis last Friday was nauseating to those who read between the lines while all those movie folk paraded and spoke"—and suggested renaming the film "The Development of the Blues" (Nov. 13).

22   An unsigned *Defender* article about the 1939 Paramount musical *St. Louis Blues* hints at how this convention looked to many African Americans: "Miss Sullivan [a jazz singer known for "swinging" folk songs like "Loch Lomond"] does not only do specialty numbers in the film. She is as important to the story as is lovely Dorothy Lamour and Lloyd Nolan. She is introduced early in the picture and remains throughout the entire entertainment" ("Maxine Sullivan" 10). While it is true that Sullivan appeared throughout the film, she played the usual maid role.

23   The most complete account of the NAACP's intervention in Hollywood is Cripps, "Slow Fade" 348–89. For an example of protest in the black press (inspired in these instances by *Gone With the Wind*), see Morris, "Hollywood" and "Should."

24   Goffin, 1943 74 and 1944 29; Feather, "All-American" 28.

25   In 1944 Columbia released a musical called *Jam Session.* David Meeker claims that the black players in the mixed Charlie Barnet band "do not appear on camera, as white actors sat in their places," entry 1629.

26   A passage from a short story by Harlem Renaissance writer Rudolph Fisher demonstrates the power of this convention by noting the power of inverting it: "And [in North Carolina] there were occasional 'colored' newspapers from New York: newspapers that mentioned Negroes without comment, but always spoke of a white person as 'So-and-so, white.' That was the point. In Harlem black was white" (58).

27   For examinations of the ideology of entertainment in the musical, see Feuer and Dyer.

28   For a less honorific account, which sees hot jazz as an "artistic" fantasy bribe for the bourgeois intelligentsia, see Adorno 51.

29   This space developed out of intersecting technical, aesthetic, and informational concerns in Gjon Mili's photographic work. Mili was a "fast motion" photographer; he used the same stroboscopic technology that creates images of bullets piercing apples. Just as in those famous photos, Mili's photos use plain backgrounds to focus on the uncanniness of "frozen" motion. In this regard, the photos in "Jam Session" (figure 3) are uncharacteristic. For a more typical example of his work, see Mili's photo essay, "The Lindy Hop."

30   The lack of narrative in *Jammin' the Blues* is not simply because of its brevity. Leonard Maltin notes that "a conflict existed in the method of making musical shorts; one school of thought believed the camera should be set up and the

performers should perform, period. The other school favored having a story line and working in the musical numbers as part of an overall plot" (211).

31   Both "Midnight Symphony" and "Jammin' the Blues" were "unpublished" pieces, which meant they were "written" in rehearsals and recorded for the soundtrack; consequently, audiences could not have been familiar with these tunes. "On the Sunny Side of the Street" was very familiar to audiences, thanks in part to the million-selling record of the song made by Tommy Dorsey late in 1944.

32   Empirically this is not strictly so: The average shot length in MS is twelve seconds (2:59/15 shots), in SSS eight (3:05/23), and in JtB ten (4:08/23). However, JtB uses seventeen setups, while SSS uses only ten, and this constant reframing and reorienting adds to the speedy feel of the final tune.

33   Discussing film music, Claudia Gorbman points out that "Songs require narrative to cede to spectacle, for it seems that lyrics and action compete for attention" (20). Since Gorbman is most interested in narrative music, which does not compete for attention, she leaves this insight unexplained, but I take it that songs compete for attention because we feel, in some way, that they address us in ways instrumental music does not.

34   During the fifties, this became the general criticism of the JATP concert style; see Feather, "The Granzwagon" 179 and Balliet 8.

35   For an account of the changing meanings of Louis Armstrong in African American communities, see Early 291–300.

36   For an analysis of Hollywood's distorted reflection of (white) American racial-cultural norms, see Cripps, "Myth."

37   Of all the other reviews of *Jammin' the Blues*, only *Ebony* and *Time* noted that the film had a mixed cast, and only *Ebony*, like *Down Beat*, complained about the fact that this mixture was obscured.

38   As sung by Marie Bryant, the lyric for the second half of the chorus of SSS, written by the white Dorothy Fields, runs:

> I used to walk in the shade
> Kept my blues on parade
> But now I'm not afraid
> 'Cause my rover, my rover's crossed over.
> If I never have a cent
> Be rich like Rockefeller, babe
> Got gold dust round my feet
> On the sunny side of the street.

Works Cited

Adorno, Theodor W. "On Jazz." Trans. Jamie Owen Daniel. *Discourse* 12 (1989–90): 45–69.

Agee, James. "Films." *Nation* 16 Dec. 1944: 753.

[——.] "Jammin' the Blues." *Time* 25 Dec. 1944: 49–50.

——. "Pseudo-Folk." *Partisan Review* 11 (1944): 219–23.

Altman, Rick. *The American Film Musical.* Bloomington: Indiana UP, 1989.

Balliet, Whitney. "Pandemonium Pays Off." *The Sound of Surprise: Forty-Six Pieces on Jazz.* New York: Da Capo, 1978. 3–10.

Brown, Sterling A. "Spirituals, Blues, and Jazz." *Jam Session: An Anthology of Jazz.* Ed. Ralph J. Gleason. New York: Putnam's, 1958. 12–26.

Collier, James Lincoln. *Benny Goodman and the Swing Era.* New York: Oxford UP, 1989.

Corbett, John. "Free, Single, and Disengaged: Listening Pleasure and the Popular Music Object." *October* 54 (1990): 79–101.

Cripps, Thomas. "The Myth of the Southern Box Office: A Factor in Racial Stereotyping in American Movies, 1920–1940." *The Black Experience: Selected Essays.* Ed. James C. Curtis and Lewis L. Gould. Austin: U of Texas P, 1970. 116–44.

———. *Slow Fade to Black: The Negro in American Film, 1900–1942.* New York: Oxford UP, 1977.

Davis, Francis. "Lester Leaps In: The Difficult Life of the First Jazz Modernist." *TLS* 12 June 1992: 16.

Driggs, Frank, and Harris Lewine. *Black Beauty, White Heat: A Pictorial History of Classic Jazz, 1920–1950.* New York: Morrow, 1982.

"Duke of Jazz." *Time* 1 Feb. 1943: 44.

Dyer, Richard. "Entertainment and Utopia." *Genre: The Musical.* Ed. Rick Altman. London: Routledge, 1981. 176–89.

Early, Gerald. *Tuxedo Junction: Essays on American Culture.* New York: Ecco, 1989.

"Editorial: The Upward Journey of Hot Jazz, from the Junkshops to the Met." *Esquire* Feb. 1944: 6.

Eisenberg, Evan. *The Recording Angel: Explorations in Phonography.* New York: McGraw-Hill, 1987.

Ellison, Ralph. "The Golden Age, Time Past." *Shadow and Act.* New York: Vintage, 1964. 199–212.

Emge, Charles. "On the Beat in Hollywood." *Down Beat* 1 Dec. 1944: 6.

Erenberg, Lewis A. "Things to Come: Swing Bands, Bebop, and the Rise of a Postwar Jazz Scene." *Recasting America: Culture and Politics in the Age of the Cold War.* Ed. Lary May. Chicago: U of Chicago P. 221–45.

Feather, Leonard. "All-American Jazz Ballot, 1945." *Esquire* Feb. 1945: 28–29, 102.

———. "The Granzwagon." *From Satchmo to Miles.* 1972. New York: De Capo, 1984. 173–85.

———. "Jazz is Where You Find It." *Esquire* July 1944: 95.

———. "Jazz is Where You Find It." *Esquire* May 1945: 95.

———. "Jazz Symposium." *Esquire* July 1944: 95.

———. "Jazz Symposium." *Esquire* Sept. 1944: 93.

———. "The Politics of Jazz." [Letter to the editor.] *New Republic* 16 Dec. 1985: 6.

Feuer, Jane. "The Self-reflective Musical and the Myth of Entertainment." *Genre: The Musical.* Ed. Rick Altman. London: Routledge, 1981. 160–74.

Fisher, Rudolph. "The City of Refuge." *The New Negro: Voices of the Harlem Renaissance.* Ed. Alain Locke. 1925. New York: Atheneum, 1992. 57–74.

Gates, Henry Louis, Jr. "The Same Difference: Reading Jean Toomer, 1923–1982." *Figures in Black: Words, Signs, and the "Racial" Self.* New York: Oxford UP, 1987. 196–224.

Gendron, Bernard. "Moldy Figs and Modernists: Jazz at War (1942–1946)." *Jazz Among the Discourses.* Ed. Krin Gabbard. Durham, NC: Duke UP, 1995. 31–56.

General Electric advertisement. *Look* 6 Feb. 1945: 2.

Goffin, Robert. "*Esquire*'s All-American Band." *Esquire* Feb. 1943: 74–75, 124.

——. "*Esquire*'s All-American Jazz Band." *Esquire* Feb. 1944: 28–29.

Goodman, Benny, and Irving Kolodin. *The Kingdom of Swing.* New York: Ungar, 1939.

Gorbman, Claudia. *Unheard Melodies: Narrative Film Music.* Bloomington: Indiana UP, 1987.

Hammond, John, with Irving Townsend. *John Hammond on Record.* New York: Summit Books, 1977.

Harvey, Holman. "It's Swing!" *Reader's Digest* Jan. 1937: 99–102.

Horricks, Raymond. "Clef/Verve: A Company Report." *Profiles in Jazz: From Sidney Bechet to John Coltrane.* New Brunswick, N.J.: Transaction, 1991. 173–81.

Isaacs, Hermine Rich. "Face the Music: Films in Review." *Theatre Arts* Dec. 1944: 723–27.

"Jam Session." *Life* 11 Oct. 1943: 117–24.

"Jam Session in Movieland." *Ebony* Nov. 1945: 6–7.

"Jam Sessions." *Look* 24 Aug. 1943: 64–66.

"Jamming Jumps the Color Line." *Ebony* Nov. 1945: 8–9.

"Jazz at the Philharmonic." *Senior Scholastic* 7 Apr. 1947: 36.

"Joins White Band." *Chicago Defender* 4 Jan. 1941: 1.

Jones, LeRoi [Amiri Baraka]. *Blues People: Negro Music in White America.* New York: Morrow, 1963.

Kernfeld, Barry. "Swing-Bop Combos." *The Blackwell Guide to Recorded Jazz.* Ed. Barry Kernfeld. Oxford: Basil Blackwell, 1991.

Kolodin, Irving. Unpaginated album notes. Benny Goodman. *Live at Carnegie Hall.* 16 Jan. 1938. Columbia 40244.

"Leana [*sic*] Horne, Song Stylist in Town." *Chicago Defender* 15 Feb. 1941: 13.

Levin, Mike. "Separating the Righteous Jazz: Critic Proposes to View Records According to Grouping in Styles." *Down Beat* 11 May 1942: 14.

"*Life* Goes to a Party: To Listen to Benny Goodman and His Swing Band." *Life* 1 Nov. 1937: 120–22, 126.

Lopez, Jackie. "Is Hollywood Yielding?" *Chicago Defender* 24 Mar. 1945: 20.

Lott, Eric. "Double V, Double-Time: Bebop's Politics of Style." *Callalo* 11 (1988): 597–605. Reprinted in Krin Gabbard, ed., *Jazz Among the Discourses.* Durham, N.C.: Duke UP, 1995. 243–55.

McDonough, John. "Norman Granz: JATP Pilot. . . ." *Down Beat* Oct. 1979: 30–32.

——. "Pablo Patriarch: The Norman Granz Story Part II." *Down Beat* Nov. 1979: 35–36, 76.

Maltin, Leonard. *The Great Movie Shorts.* New York: Crown, 1972.

"Maxine Sullivan Is Regal [Theater] Screen Star." *Chicago Defender* 8 Apr. 1939: 10.

Meeker, David. *Jazz in the Movies.* New enlarged ed. New York: Da Capo, 1981.

[Mili, Gjon.] "The Lindy Hop." *Life* 23 Aug. 1943: 95–103.

Miller, Paul Eduard. "Jazz Symposium." *Esquire* Oct. 1944: 95.

Monroe, Al. "Mixing's the Thing, Lena Horne, Richmond, Cootie and Others Say." *Chicago Defender* 16 Aug. 1941: 10.

——. "Swingin' the News." *Chicago Defender* 19 Apr. 1941: 12.

——. "Swingin' the News." *Chicago Defender* 8 Nov. 1941: 13.

Morris, Earl J. "Hollywood Ignores Black America." *Pittsburgh Courier* 28 May 1938: 20.

——. "Should the Negro Ban White Motion Pictures?" *Pittsburgh Courier* 24 Sept. 1938: 21.

Newton, Francis [Eric Hobsbawm]. *The Jazz Scene.* 1959. New York: Da Capo, 1975.

"Orson Welles to Star Satchmo." *Chicago Defender* 30 Aug. 1941: 12.

Ramsey, Frederic, Jr., and Charles Edward Smith, eds. *Jazzmen.* New York: Harcourt, Brace, 1939.

Reddick, L. D. "Educational Programs for the Improvement of Race Relations: Motion Pictures, Radio, the Press, and Libraries." *Journal of Negro Education* 13 (1944): 337–89.

Rogers, J. A. "Jazz at Home." *The New Negro: Voices of the Harlem Renaissance.* Ed. Alain Locke. 1925. New York: Atheneum, 1992. 216–24.

Ross, Andrew. "Hip and the Long Front of Color." *No Respect: Intellectuals and Popular Culture.* New York: Routledge, 1989. 65–101.

Smith, Ernie. "Film." *The New Grove Dictionary of Jazz.* Ed. Barry Kernfeld. 2 vols. London: Macmillan, 1988.

"Speaking of Pictures . . . Mili's First Movie is Skillfully Lighted Jam Session." *Life* 22 Jan. 1945: 6–8.

"Spivak Gets Crown From TD [Tommy Dorsey], Duke Wins[,] Bing Is New Voice." *Down Beat* 1 Jan. 1945: 1, 13.

Troupe, Quincy. "Up Close and Personal: Miles Davis and Me." *Conjunctions* 16 (1991): 76–93.

Whiteman, Paul, and Mary Margaret McBride. *Jazz.* New York: J. H. Sears, 1926.

Wolfe, Charles. "Vitaphone Shorts and *The Jazz Singer.*" *Wide Angle* 12.3 (1990): 58–78.

Improvising and Mythmaking
in Eudora Welty's "Powerhouse"

LELAND H. CHAMBERS

I don't know much about words, but there are just a few words that describe exactly what something is. Music has suffered from that. People read something and get an idea in their minds. The only thing you can do for music is feel it and hear it.—Ornette Coleman

When Lester came out he played very melodic. . . . He was always telling a story and Bird did the same thing. That kind of musical philosophy is what I try to do because telling a story is, I think, where it's at.—Dexter Gordon

And who could ever remember any of the things he says? They are just inspired remarks that roll out of his mouth like smoke.—"Powerhouse"

Eudora Welty's "Powerhouse," originally published[1] when "swing" was the popular buzzword for what we now understand as an evolutionary step in the history of jazz, is a twice-unique story. For one thing, she never wrote another like it—that is, no other story with even a remotely similar focus. Moreover, no other story by any author I know of has been as successful in dealing with improvisation, one of the essential ingredients of jazz.[2]

It seems to me a special act of the creative instinct that a white writer of southern background coming to maturity during the 1920s and 1930s should be able to approach a particularly salient aspect of black culture with the sensitivity and understanding shown in "Powerhouse." Welty was not even especially close to the music scene, not like Kenneth Rexroth had been as far back as the twenties (Rexroth 258), nor Hayden Carruth today (Carruth passim). Yet at one moment of her life she was capable of transposing a New York exposure to Fats Waller's music (Appel 148) to her own rural Mississippi milieu and finding a language capable of penetrating to the heart of that quality of jazz which most distinguished it from both the pop music of the day and the European-derived symphonic and chamber music tradition.

To recap, Powerhouse is the name of a renowned black piano player, famous recording artist, and bandleader, playing a dance for a sparse white crowd in a Mississippi town on a rainy night. The time is the late 1930s. In the course of the evening's entertainment the band plays dance tunes largely acceptable to a white audience; they even include a detestable waltz. In the midst of performing this tune Powerhouse begins to talk to the musicians closest to him, telling of having received a telegram with the news that his wife is dead. The telegram was signed by a certain Uranus Knockwood. During the intermission, he and those three musicians go out to a small juke joint, the World Cafe, in what the narrator calls Negrotown, where Powerhouse continues the story of Gypsy and Uranus Knockwood. He tells it in three versions, each one different in its details. The story astonishes and delights the crowd of local blacks who, having recognized Powerhouse, stand around in awe. Having worked his way through all the versions, Powerhouse composes a telegram in response to the one he claimed to have received. The musicians go back to the bandstand again and play some more.

The music Powerhouse plays and the stories he tells demonstrate fundamental similarities. The two activities derive from impulses that are very close to each other but are displayed in different modes that appear to be incompatible—the inchoate but often pleasing sounds of music and the referential sense (always relative) of language. In comparison to music, language seems clear and exact. Yet language is an inadequate means of describing what music does. In "Powerhouse," though, the mediation of jazz improvisation through mythmaking turns out to be an overwhelmingly successful strategy, because since the descriptive language of narrative cannot adequately report the sounds of music and consequently the activity of improvisation, Welty substitutes a process that is in narrative form. The result is that the nature of jazz improvising becomes exemplified and clarified in the stories Powerhouse tells about the death of his wife. The analogies between the two processes of improvising and mythmaking (at least, as they appear in "Powerhouse") are based on the fact that they employ similar basic elements. The most important of these are (1) theme-and-variation and (2) collective activity. These basic elements make it possible not only to communicate successfully the sense of the music in the language of narrative, but they permit each to become a metaphor for the other, thus enabling a reciprocal means of understanding and interpretation.

Using linguistic means (words) to convey affectively what happens in music has always led to distortions of one kind or another. Only a limited number of suitable onomatopoetic words exist, and these quickly lose their capacity for a sensitive approximation of the sounds they are intended to imitate, especially since they have to be experienced within the syntax of language rather than music. Consequently, the description of music most usually becomes impressionistic (focusing on how the listener reacts while listening or else what the player feels while playing), or it is technically precise but lifeless (at least for the purposes of fiction), or else it leans on metaphors from other areas of human experience.

This analysis is complicated by the purposes that motivate every attempt to explain any aspect of music. LP liner notes for most jazz record albums were sometimes designed as much to encourage buyer interest in a specific performance as they were to explain anything about the music in a general way, especially since the potential audience for a given jazz album already enjoys a sense of what jazz is, no matter how fragmentary or misguided their understanding. Jazz historians and critics appeal to a similar audience of jazz-oriented listeners, but again with differing purposes. André Hodeir's six-and-one-half-page analysis of Fats Waller's "Keepin' Out Of Mischief Now"—a solo performance on a recording lasting three minutes and ten seconds—seeks to illustrate the continuity of musical thought possible in improvised jazz solos (169–76), and thus it is clearly addressed to those already well-informed about jazz. Martin Williams's much less technical remarks on Coleman Hawkins's tenor saxophone solo on the 1940 recording of "The Sheik of Araby" are designed to introduce basic tenets of improvisation to beginning students of jazz (*Where's The Melody?* 38–40), while his remarks on the same solo in *The Jazz Tradition* are designed to make it fit into the context of Hawkins's development as a soloist/improviser (79), this time for an audience of more experienced students of jazz. And one could go on.

Perhaps such technically precise analyses do not fall into the abyss of impressionistic writing bemoaned by the poet Hayden Carruth, who, while conceding that "technical criticism can be moderately helpful," says:

> What I know for a fact is that the kind of impressionistic writing about jazz that has been foisted on us in superabundance during the past three or four decades is utterly useless; the kind of thing done by

Whitney Balliet, Martin Williams, and sometimes Nat Hentoff. It exploits the musicians as romantic, not to say psychoneurotic, personalities, and it exploits the reader by promising what it cannot deliver, an explanation or at least a description of the expressiveness of jazz, which every fully engaged listener longs for. (48–49)

Fiction is perhaps a more appropriate place for the impressionistic description of music, but the pitfalls broached by Carruth apply equally here, especially when the stories use the description of jazz playing to go beyond the music to other concerns. In a typical complaint of the Beat Generation, John Clellon Holmes at one point in his novel *The Horn* egregiously links the playing of two performers involved in a cutting contest to certain depressing aspects of the American experience:

> Edgar . . . blew four bars of a demented cackle, and for an instant they were almost shoulder to shoulder, horn to horn, in the terrible equality of art, pouring into each wild break (it felt) the substance of their separated lives—crazy, profound Americans, both! . . . America had laid its hand on both of them. In Edgar's furious scornful bleat sounded the moronic horn of every merciless Cadillac shrieking down the highway with a wet-mouthed, giggling boy at the wheel, turning the American prairie into a graveyard of rusting chrome junk; the idiot-snarl that filled the jails and madhouses and legislatures; some final dead-wall impact. (19)

In Langston Hughes's 1934 story "The Blues I'm Playing," the piano playing of Hughes's protagonist Oceola is said to express something absolutely universal: "In the blues she made the bass note throb like tomtoms, the trebles cry like little flutes, so deep in the earth and so high in the sky that they understood everything" (Breton 71). But throughout the story, jazz is depicted as directly interwoven with the everyday lives of Oceola's people, a situation that upper-middle-class white Americans are unable to grasp or appreciate because they are so narrowly fixed on a conception of art as an expression of the highest spirituality, as exemplified in the great composers of Europe, and therefore far above the mundane. J. F. Powers ("He Don't Plant Cotton") appears to show that the satisfaction of playing jazz as one feels it is able to compensate for the bitter sting of racial denigration, as a jazz pianist gets inside her own music while ignoring the insensitive requests of a white patron:

> And Libby was pleased, watching Baby. And then, somehow, he vanished for her into the blue drum. The sticks still danced at an oblique angle on the snare, but there were no hands to them

and Libby could not see Baby on the chair. She could only feel him somewhere in the blue glow. Abandoning herself, she lost herself in the piano. Now, still without seeing him, she could feel him with a clarity and warmth beyond vision. Miniature bell notes, mostly blue, blossomed ecstatically, perished *affetuoso*, weaving themselves down into the dark beauty of the lower keys, because it was closer to the drum, and multiplied. (Breton 87)

James Baldwin's narrator in "Sonny's Blues" is a jazz pianist's elder brother who has never really understood either the younger man's hurt or the nature of jazz, until everything becomes clear to him at the high point of the story:

Sonny's fingers filled the air with life, his life. But that life contained so many others. And Sonny went all the way back, he really began with the spare, flat statement of the opening phrase of the song. Then he began to make it his. It was very beautiful because it wasn't hurried and it was no longer a lament. I seemed to hear with what burning he had made it his, with what burning we had yet to make it ours, how we could cease lamenting. Freedom lurked around us and I understood, at last, that he could help us to be free if we would listen, that he would never be free until we did. . . . And I was yet aware that this was only a moment, that the world waited outside, as hungry as a tiger, and that trouble stretched above us, longer than the sky. (Breton 129–30)

Sonny's performance, then, is also made to convey the often stated position that the freedom of jazz improvisation is the icon of an intellectual and emotional freedom that transcends any amount of social and political repression.

In fiction about jazz, then, one often finds the music interpreted to support nonmusical ideas or experiences. This is one effect of applying the referential aspects of language to the nonreferential sounds of music. Welty's story is no exception. It belongs to the third category mentioned, that which employs a controlling metaphor to permit the linguistic interpretation of music. Perhaps the nature of improvisation—at the heart of the music itself—is a more difficult concept for fiction to get at, or at least a concept less likely to produce an affective response in the reader. In any case, Powerhouse's use of theme-and-variation as he builds his successive stories about Gypsy's death and Uranus Knockwood's menacing presence, together with the collective activity of his friends and even the onlookers at the World Cafe, show that the process of mythmaking lies so close to that of jazz improvising that it can easily and unobtrusively be substituted for it.

The occasion arises when Powerhouse and his orchestra "play the one waltz they will ever consent to play—by request, 'Pagan Love Song' " (32). They have to make a concession to their audience, for after all they are performers whose livelihood depends on pleasing the dancers. As the orchestra reluctantly begins to play, "Powerhouse's head rolls and sinks like a weight between his waving shoulders. He groans, and his fingers drag into the keys heavily. . . . It is a sad song" (32). But for these musicians, there is nothing interesting about this kind of tune without first changing it radically from ¾ time to 4/4 time, for waltz time does not, *can*not, swing (or so most dance band and jazz musicians of the time thought) nor does it offer the slightest freedom to improvise (in the view of the dance band musicians of the day). Thus, "Pagan Love Song" is for them simply a "sad song," which, by and large, the musicians simply must endure.[3]

It might be worth recalling what Fats Waller might have done when playing this tune, and this is especially relevant here because the figure of Powerhouse is clearly modeled on him (Welty has said somewhere that she wrote the story rapidly, soon after seeing Waller's orchestra playing at a dance) (Appel 148). When he got hold of a sentimental song he would find a way to burlesque it, to make fun of its lyrics, and of course to improvise on it; he might even, as Powerhouse does, have made something "light and childish" of its melody by giving it a "smooch" and "loving it with his mouth" (29). Hear him do this on pop tunes like "Two Sleepy People" or "Too Tired," for example, although neither of these was a "sad song" like "Pagan Love Song."

But Powerhouse, with his apparently limitless vitality (limitless despite his own remark that "I don't carry around nothing without limit"), soon begins to talk about his wife, remarking—in a way that immediately links his verbal meanderings to his piano-playing activity—remarking with "wandering fingers," "You know what happened to me? . . . I got a telegram my wife is dead." His fingers "walk, up straight, unwillingly, three octaves." He explains: "Telegram say—here the words: Your wife is dead," and the narrator adds, "He puts 4/4 over the ¾" (33). In this tag it is possible that Powerhouse's piano playing is all that is being spoken about here—in fact, that was the way I used to take it. More than likely, however, the narrator is referring equally to the four stark beats of the words comprising the telegram, "YOUR WIFE IS DEAD," implying in this way that Powerhouse's stories are essentially so like his piano improvising that both may be dealt with using the same vocabulary.

Moreover, to insist on the parallel, the double reference continues to the end of this scene. While "Pagan Love Song" moves slowly along, Powerhouse elaborates on his telegram: "He makes triplets and begins a new chorus. He holds three fingers up," to let the other musicians know they have only three choruses more to play (33). At one point, the piano player is shown "flinging out both powerful arms for three whole beats to flex his muscles." Welty's narrator uses music-derived vocabulary to sum up the scene; when they have concluded the discussion of the telegram, the narrator remarks, "They all laughed. End of that chorus" (34). The "chorus" here could simply refer to the melody of "Pagan Love Song," especially since Powerhouse a few lines earlier has just raised three fingers high to signify the number of choruses remaining, and only a few lines later on, Powerhouse will decide to call an intermission and bring "the chorus to an end." In those places, certainly, there is no equivocation but a clear reference to merely the playing of the "sad song" of "Pagan Love." But here at this point, after the questioning of Scoot the drummer, that "disbelieving maniac," it more than likely refers also and equally to the conclusion of Powerhouse's first attempt to deal with the story of Gypsy's death.

Thus, there is no doubt that the narrative up to this point presents the story of Gypsy and Uranus Knockwood as exactly equivalent to the improvised music expected from such musicians. And once Powerhouse has brought up the theme, he must return to it, play with it, develop it, and carry it as far as he dare before relinquishing it, just as he later does with the twelve or fourteen choruses of "Somebody Loves Me," "piling them up nobody knows how" (43). In the process, the fears hidden beneath the facade of the story in its various forms will have been exposed for everyone's laughter in such a way that Powerhouse will then be able to thrust it away from him with a gesture suited to his personality.

But before he is able to do that, and as Powerhouse tells his story, we see that the theme really has two parts: the death of Gypsy is the A part, while the entry of Uranus Knockwood is the B part. Before the first variation, then, intermission comes for the musicians on the bandstand, and Powerhouse, together with the musicians who are closest to him, Little Brother, Valentine, and Scoot, goes out the back way and down the street to Negrotown and the World Cafe. There, the musicians eventually settle themselves at a table surrounded by a crowd of local onlookers who have recognized the famous piano player, and Powerhouse spreads "his performer's hands" over the tablecloth to begin the first variation on the A part. This time we hear that it is out of her love for him that Gypsy has killed herself by leaping out a hotel window. As his companions agree that this must have been the way it was, forthwith Powerhouse rejects it and starts the second variation on A, during which A takes another turn because this time Gypsy has become terribly afraid after hearing some sinister footsteps outside in the hallway (these foreshadow B) and deliberately puts on her nightgown before going over to the window to jump out. "Brains and insides everywhere," one of the others puts in, causing the onlookers to "stir in their delight" (38). The story is highly amusing to them, and they seem to think this is a performance for their enjoyment.

In the third variation, Powerhouse raises the B theme more forcefully, for the point of view in his narrative shifts from the hotel room down to the street, where Uranus Knockwood is about to discover Gypsy's body, with "her insides and brains scattered all around." He is revolted at the mess: "Jesus! he say, Look here what I'm walking round in!" This exclamation brings "halloos of laughter" from Powerhouse's audience. This development of B culminates in a stychomathic passage to which all contribute; and as they do, the event builds into a monument to collective improvisation, where even the dominating individual voice of Powerhouse becomes lost in the texture of the whole:

> "Why, he picks her up and carries her off," he says.
> "Ya! Ha!"
> "Carries her *back* around the corner . . ."
> "Oh, Powerhouse!"
> "Uranus Knockwood!"
> "Yeahhh!"
> "He take our wives when we gone!"
> "He come in when we goes out!"
> "Uh-huh!"
> "He go out when we comes in!"
> "Yeahhh!"
> "He standing behind the door!"
> "Old Uranus Knockwood."
> "You know him."
> "Middle-sized man."
> "Wears a hat."
> "That's him."

And with this performance, "Everybody in the room moans with pleasure" (39–40).

In this third variation the B section (Knockwood) has finally crowded out the A section, since for all who are present the specter of a Uranus

Knockwood in everyone's life is a more sweeping concern. Of course, the performance Powerhouse puts on probably does not represent actual circumstances, but merely the anxieties which uncertainty and conditions that seem beyond his control bring on, and eventually he is led to admit that all of his stories, his variations on A and B, "ain't the truth. . . . Truth is something else, I ain't said what yet. It's something hasn't come to me, but I ain't saying it won't." And afterward, walking back to the dance hall with his companions in the rain, Powerhouse squeezes out the last echo of the B section in a relieved farewell to it with the telegram he composes, which not only is going to "reach" Uranus Knockwood but is going to "come out on the other side" (41–42). And this to the enormous amusement of the choir of onlookers who "are afraid they will die laughing" as they accompany the fabled musicians back to the dance hall.

As if to verify the habit of improvising collectively, Powerhouse has also led his companions into another attempt to rid themselves of the Uranus Knockwood bugaboo by offering variations on the spelling of the strange name:

> "Take a telegram!" Powerhouse shouts suddenly up into the rain over the street. "Take a answer. Now what was the name?"
> They get a little tired.
> "Uranus Knockwood."
> "You ought to know."
> "Yas? Spell it to me."
> They spell it all the ways it could be spelled. It puts them in a wonderful humor.

And earlier, as the musicians were headed outside at the start of their intermission, Powerhouse had invited them to take off on still another theme:

> "Beer? Beer? You know what beer is? What do they say is beer? What's beer? Where I been?"

But this potential improvisation goes nowhere for the moment, except to substantiate Powerhouse's continual openness to moments for improvisation.

Is Powerhouse a showman/entertainer who uses the game of inventing his characters merely to provoke his audience in the World Cafe into a tingle of pleasure, as he can do with his music, or is there a genuine fear hidden beneath this playful improvisation? It seems to me that in this story the distinction does not make a lot of difference, since for Powerhouse the process of improvisation is central no matter what he does, and as such it is a function of his mysterious and appealing vitality—and this means that as both a weaver of myths and an improviser of new melodies he will find similar ways to shape his expression: theme-and-variation and collective activity.

But the narrator at first seems most intrigued by the entertainer in Powerhouse, and his role as a jazz musician seems secondary, perhaps only one aspect of his whole performance. This is so partly because Welty has chosen to substitute the mythmaking stories just where we would more logically expect to find a description of his improvising. But more important is the fact that the narrator has much more to say about his idiosyncratic behavior on the bandstand than about his actual playing. From the outset, the narrator depicts him as a grotesque but altogether unclassifiable figure, possibly even beyond the human: "You can't tell what he is. 'Nigger man'?—he looks more Asiatic, monkey, Jewish, Babylonian, Peruvian, fanatic, devil" (29). Even his approach to piano playing supports this impression, for it is not so much the nature of his music that catches the narrator's attention as it is his antics at his instrument: "He's going up the keyboard with a few fingers in some very derogatory triplet-routine, he gets higher and higher, and then he looks over the end of the piano, as if over a cliff" (31). Or again: "Then he took hold of the piano, as if he saw it for the first time in his life, and tested it for strength, hit it down in the bass, played an octave with his elbow, lifted the top, looked inside, and leaned against it with all his might" (42). Powerhouse leads his orchestra in what seem to the narrator as unorthodox but marvelously uninhibited ways: setting the tempo of a piece with a "set of rhythmic kicks to the floor," urging the band on by shouting ("not guiding them—hailing them"), calling out new pieces by number instead of name—all done in such a way as to give the impression of being totally without "any known discipline." All this, of course, is especially remarkable from the point of view of someone who is more used to the subdued stage behavior of a chamber group or perhaps a symphonic ensemble under the baton of a conductor. "He is in motion every moment," the narrator is amazed to observe; "he's in a trance; he's a person of joy, a fanatic." Even his eyebrows, "big-arched eyebrows that never stop travelling," constantly move.

Perhaps Welty was under the influence of the powerful and in 1940 still-dominant tradition among whites of depicting blacks as caricatures of human beings, figures that look funny, act funny, and say funny things. Images that before Emancipation had emphasized the kindly, docile features of Uncle Tom but after 1863 had begun to include the features of the savage and the brute, just a step away from the *unciviliza-*

tion of the African jungle (Riggs). Leonard documents many examples of the fears expressed by white Americans in the face of the music of black musicians during the 1920s and 1930s (33–41). Welty's narrator corroborates this fear in the relentless depiction of Powerhouse's face. In the first paragraph, "He has pale grey eyes, heavy lids, maybe horny like a lizard's but big glowing eyes when they're open"; his face, with a mouth that is "vast and obscene," has "a look of hideous, powerful rapture" on it (30). It is a "secret face . . . which looks like a mask—anybody's" (30). Further into the story, his face looks like "a big hot iron stove," (39) and his mouth like a "vast oven" (40); later on, it "gets to be nothing but a volcano" (43), and in the narrator's final view, "a vast, impersonal and yet furious grimace transfigures his wet face" (43).

Still, the mystery of Powerhouse's essential nature shows through in a positive, redeeming way. Partly this is because he is an entertainer, and consequently on a level with the mind-reading horse, like Nelson Eddy or the acrobats that came to town once. More importantly, perhaps, is the fact that Powerhouse is of a "darker race" and therefore mysterious and capable of the most astonishing, portentous behavior. At times he is said to possess the "promise and serenity of a sibyl touching the book" (30); moreover, "he knows, really. He cries out, but he must know exactly" (31). The narrator is in awe of something half-glimpsed and imposing that urges us to listen to "the least word, especially what they say in another language—don't let them escape you; it's the only time for hallucination, the last time" (30).

In any case, the narrator's sense of wonder is fulsome testimony to Powerhouse's charisma, which (to all but the dedicated and experienced jazz fan, which the narrator clearly is not) is bound to overshadow the improvising, or at least to prevent the narrator from seeing it as anything but another trait corroborating the funny-ugly image of the unfathomable black performer who mesmerizes the audience with his amusing and unpredictable behavior.

But it really does not matter much whether Powerhouse is seen primarily as an entertainer or as a jazz musician, because as mythmaker his utterly individual activity is shaped from both sides of his nature: his playing to his audience at the World Cafe as well as in the dance hall, with variation on amusing variation on themes that derive from the same dark underside of the self. In both kinds of expression, improvisation is central, is a function of his captivating vitality.

However, one need not be too concerned about overemphasizing the depth of Powerhouse's anxieties arising from his situation as the traveling musician, on the road for weeks and months at a time, sleeping in one cheap hotel room after another (how much worse for black bands traveling the South), never sure how he will find things when he comes in off the road. There is always the fear of "that no-good pussy-footed crooning creeper, that creeper that follow round after me, coming up like weeds behind me, following around after me everything I do and messing around on the trail I leave. Bets my numbers, sings my songs, gets close to my agent like a Betsy-bug; when I going out he just coming in" (38–39).

How does one keep from being overwhelmed by worries such as these, worries that no one can claim? Powerhouse and his three closest companions do it by externalizing their fears, projecting them in the form of figures like Gypsy (does she even exist? it does not matter whether she does or not) and Uranus Knockwood (who is more than likely a totally symbolic invention); they create several versions of narratives about them, variations on a theme, each one more extreme than the last, and when they have done that, they have brought to the surface of conscious thought the concerns of their inner beings, each time with laughter and a sense of relief.

Freud once described the workings of the unconscious as a process wherein either "we convert inner stimuli into seemingly outer events as if better to protect ourselves," or else we repress them (Bruner 277). This externalizing has two ramifications that seem to exist as the ultimate purpose of the human activity known as mythmaking. For one thing, it establishes a basis for communion with others, and it also "makes possible the containment of terror and impulse by the decorum of art and symbolism" (Bruner 277). Both of these functions of myth are clearly present in Powerhouse's stories. And this process is what is responsible for the qualities of mythmaking that most clearly resemble those essential aspects of jazz improvising: the inventing of new melodies in place of the given music, and the close collaboration into which Powerhouse draws those surrounding him. The result is a shared product: a finished piece of music, with "12 or 14 choruses piling them up no one knows how," or perhaps an expression of the musicians' collective fears concerning their respective situations at home.

By contrast, the reader notes Powerhouse's indifference to Sugar-Stick, the local hero who represents a different sort of myth. But Sugar-Stick's "heroic" accomplishment—pulling out fourteen bodies from beneath the surface of July Creek—is simply irrelevant to the needs or the deeper concerns of Powerhouse and his friends. And so the piano player ignores the wordless Sugar-Stick and his entourage; there is nothing there for him to improvise on and make his own. Instead, he embarks on a fourth version of the story before he is stopped (40).

Eventually, Powerhouse signals his control of the situation, his successful confrontation with the unconscious, by composing a telegram that will put that "crooner creeper" in his place: "Here's the answer. I got it right here. 'What in hell you talking about? Don't make any difference: I gotcha.' Name signed: Powerhouse." The attack is over for now, but it will return, and it will have to be confronted again, possibly tomorrow night at their next job.

Just how do these activities of jazz improvising and mythmaking comment on each other? That is, what qualities characteristic of one activity can be glimpsed in, attributed to, the other because of their juxtaposition in this story?

Looking at the mythmaking in the light of the jazz improvisation, we can see it now as a spontaneous activity, an improvisation within known limits, in a playful game spirit, colored by the suggestion of excess and parody, as befits the figure of Powerhouse. Further, the process of mythmaking is seen to be totally open-ended, for even though a closure of sorts is reached for the moment with the composition of the telegram that will put Uranus Knockwood in his place, the possible variations are nearly infinite, limited only by the individual's inventiveness at any given moment. Tomorrow night's job will bring another occasion to renew the activity, perhaps in a different key, using a different tune and set of chords, and allowing a wholly different resolution to the endless welling up of the musicians' fears and anxieties. Finally, like jazz improvising, mythmaking is here a collective enterprise, in which the chief improviser/storyteller, Powerhouse, is pushed on by his fellow musicians throughout several choruses. And just as it is with jazz, to participate in the inventing of these morbid, comic stories is to plunge into an expressive medium in which the playfulness masks the serious while allowing it to take voice.

On the other hand, looking in the other direction to consider what shadows the process of mythmaking casts over the most elemental denominator of jazz—that urge toward improvisation—we realize that by behaving in much the same way as jazz improvisation, mythmaking manages to impute essential characteristics to it and clarify its sources. Most importantly, the nature of mythmaking suggests that improvising too comes from the unconscious and that it also is a mechanism for resolving fears and anxieties, perhaps even a safety valve for staving off loneliness. Further, that even though at first mythmaking's practitioners—and consequently its results—are "marvelous, frightening" to the uninitiated, the stories and thus the music they stand in for are seen to have a humanizing effect that ameliorates the earlier impression of

Powerhouse as a monstrous, grotesque being. For Powerhouse's inventions on the theme of Gypsy and Uranus Knockwood end by rubbing out some of those harsh lines of caricature and replacing them with the subtle shadings of a human person glimpsed in the partly painful and partly joyous process of airing out his anxieties and coming to grips with them.

Notes

1   In her first collection of short fiction, *A Curtain of Green and Other Stories* (1941). The story is currently available in a number of sources, including a reprint of that collection. My citations will be to the story as it appears in Marcela Breton, *Hot And Cool: Jazz Stories* 29–43.

2   The story has been the subject of several articles. Some of these recognize its focus on jazz improvising. Ruth Vande Kieft actually identifies a technique of theme-and-variation, though without developing the idea, in *Eudora Welty* (New York: Twayne, 1962), 83. Alfred Appel discusses the story in detail, calling Powerhouse a "folk hero" because he is an "improvising jazzman," and finally treating the whole story as an instance of the blues, in *A Season of Dreams* 148–64. Thomas H. Getz treats the story as a piece of music and describes Welty's language as an "act of listening to Powerhouse and . . . also her *performance* of his music—a translation of his medium into hers," but emphasizes this connection as evidence that "the characters in these stories live as though life itself were a form of improvisation." "Eudora Welty: Listening To 'Powerhouse,'" *Kentucky Review* 4/2 (Winter 1983): 40–48.

3   Given that so many song titles from the 1930s are mentioned in the story, and that two or three of them occupy crucial spots in the story's development, it is tempting to look for a connecting significance in the whole collection. I do not find any pattern of relevance among these nine tunes. It is true that "Pagan Love Song" (32) impels Powerhouse into his round of mythmaking, and thus the "pagan" qualities assumed in the song title may serve to bolster the early depiction of Powerhouse as some kind of "pagan," therefore savage, caricature of humanity. But whatever relevance the song's title may possess is not reflected in the simple waltz *tune* Powerhouse uses to take off on, which was chiefly familiar in those days in a syrupy format, even though it was occasionally revitalized in a swing treatment such as that of Glenn Miller (1939), who changed it to 4/4 time and performed it extremely fast.

Other tunes are pertinent in differing ways. For example, "Honeysuckle Rose" (32) is one of Fats Waller's most famous compositions and thus is a clue to Welty's identification of Waller as a basis for her characterization of Powerhouse. "Empty Bed Blues" (36), a famous blues by Bessie Smith, was notorious for its sexual innuendo, but in this story whatever significance it may have, aside from the fact that Powerhouse's vain request for this tune indicates the jukebox is loaded with contemporary commercial hits instead of classic versions of jazz or blues, is contained in the title alone. In the story's final paragraph, "Somebody Loves Me" (43) provides a vague reference to the fears voiced in Powerhouse's narratives about his wife Gypsy, who may or may not exist, but more importantly, a phrase from this tune's lyrics (". . . Maybe it's you!") suddenly sweeps the story's reader into the picture and thus reinforces the open ambiguity of Powerhouse's improvised myth.

If the other five songs have any relevance to Powerhouse's situation, it seems to be limited to supporting the verisimilitude of the background, I suspect. The mention of "Tuxedo Junction" does bring forth a slightly puzzling bit of dialogue in the World Cafe, where Valentine and Scoot are reading off the titles of the tunes on the nickelodeon.

"Whose 'Tuxedo Junction'?" asks Powerhouse.

"You know whose."

The laconic but suggestive response implies that the answer is obvious and that the question need never have been asked (36). However, suggestive of what? Perhaps it refers to the ironic circumstance that although this instrumental dance tune was first recorded and made popular by Erskine Hawkins's orchestra (July 1939), a rather popular black band of the late thirties, when Glenn Miller recorded it (Feb. 1940), his slicker version swamped Hawkins's. Which version would be found on a jukebox in the black section of Alligator, Mississippi? Would it make any difference to a reading of the story to remind the 1940s reader (or the 1990s reader, for that matter) that versions by white orchestras of tunes originally presented by black bands and arrangers nearly always outsold the black musicians' versions? Benny Goodman continually struck it rich with tunes from Fletcher Henderson's book. Perhaps one could make the point that this circumstance contributed to Powerhouse's anguish, but I do not see anything else in the story to support this reading. Consequently, I suspect that, beyond pinning a bit of background in place, this tune title seems to serve little purpose. The same goes for "The Goona Goo" (41), the silly title of an unmemorable jukebox tune that never became popular. Yet the song is typical of a class of novelty tune that numerous dance orchestras of the day recorded and sometimes played at dances and on radio broadcasts. And it brought forth one interesting version, a good one in fact, as recorded by Tommy Dorsey's orchestra (January 1937) and featuring a fine trumpet solo by Bunny Berigan. "San" (42) was a standard out of the 1920s, occasionally revived by swing bands of the 1930s. "Sent For You Yesterday and Here You Come Today" (37) is a blues (big-band style) as sung first by Jimmy Rushing with Count Basie's orchestra (recorded 16 Feb. 1938) and slightly later by Johnny Mercer with Benny Goodman. And even though "Marie, the Dawn Is Breaking" (31) is a sentimental ballad best-known in the version recorded by Tommy Dorsey (Jan. 1937), featuring an ironic "choral" countertext to the standard lyrics as well as a superb solo by Berigan, there seem to be no echoes of this version in Welty's story.

Works Cited

Appel, Alfred, Jr. *A Season of Dreams: The Fiction of Eudora Welty*. Baton Rouge: Louisiana State UP, 1965.

Breton, Marcela. *Hot and Cool: Jazz Stories*. New York: Penguin, 1990.

Bruner, Jerome S. "Myth and Identity." *Myth and Mythmaking*. Ed. Henry A. Murray. New York: George Braziller, 1960.

Carruth, Hayden. *Sitting In: Selected Writings on Jazz, Blues, and Related Topics*. Iowa City: U of Iowa P, 1986.

Hodier, André. *Jazz: Its Evolution and Essence.* Rev. ed. Trans. David Noakes. New York: Grove, 1979.

Holmes, John Clellon. *The Horn.* 1958. New York: Thunder's Mouth, 1988.

Leonard, Neil. *Jazz and the White Americans.* Chicago: U of Chicago P, 1962.

Rexroth, Kenneth. "Some Thoughts On Jazz: As Music, As Revolt, As Mystique." *New World Writing #14.* New York: New American Library, 1958. 252–68.

Riggs, Marlon. *Ethnic Notions.* Videotape of PBS show produced for WNET, Boston, 1988.

Williams, Martin. *The Jazz Tradition.* Rev. ed. New York: Oxford UP, 1983.

——. *Where's the Melody?: A Listener's Introduction to Jazz.* 1966. New York: Da Capo, 1983.

Fabulating Jazz

FREDERICK GARBER

It has often been argued, in what I shall call the purist position, that jazz solos have no context, no palimpsestian turn. Those solos, the purist argues, take their origin and end from the moment in which they are made and the lonely figure who makes them (Joachim Berendt speaks of "the loneliness of the creative jazz musician" [Berendt 163]). In this reading of the nature of jazz there is no sharing of the scene with a role, Olivier with Henry V. In this reading, the jazz soloist is all upfront, all self, as pure as the moment of the solo he is making. Thus, the fullest meaning of "solo" would take in not only the soloist but the time of playing, for it is as singular as he is, as immediate as he is to the circumstances of utterance.

Most jazz historians affirm that Louis Armstrong made jazz a soloist's art, that the move from King Oliver's Jazz Band of 1923 to Armstrong's Hot Fives and Sevens later in the decade was a shift from the New Orleans ensemble mode to a modified format that showcased soloists, mainly Armstrong himself. Jazz had always been an individualist's art, but the nature of the context shifted as the soloist got even more upfront and alone. One ought to emphasize "alone" because the soloists do, because "alone" is more than a near-synonym for "solo," because those two words' internal rhyme points to ironies, anxieties. Neil Leonard quotes Roy Eldridge in a comment worth requoting. Eldridge recalls how, before a solo, he would mull over what he was going to do: "but when I got out there I didn't try to make the B-flat or whatever I was thinking of, because I'd go right into a void where there was no memory—nothing but me . . . I'd just be in this blank space, and the music came out anyway" (Leonard 73). Leonard, attentive to what he sees as the religious aspects of jazz, is concerned with the "incomprehensible nature" of the moment of playing; but it is the aloneness that appears to dominate Eldridge's statement, as it does in a remark Leonard quotes from Armstrong: "When I go on the bandstand I don't know nobody's out there. I don't even know you're playing with me. Play good and it will help me. I don't know you're there. I'm just playing" (Leonard 73). (Recall Berendt's comment on "the loneliness of the creative jazz musician.")

It is in part because of such comments that we argue for the crux of jazz as upfront immediacy in the moment of the solo's making. The jazz artist may enter a solo with some sense of where he will go—the story he wants to tell, as so many have put it—or he may enter the solo with little more in mind than a familiar framework of chords, as in Eldridge's comment. Whatever the baggage he brings, he enters that moment himself and occupies it solely, free to compose in a way that a performer like Olivier could never be, doing in that moment what he will do in no other. The making of a jazz solo is in and for the moment and in the place where the moment resides, unique to that occasion, unparalleled, aleatory.[1] Even a critic like Ted Gioia, uneasy with the individualism that he feels is endemic to jazz, takes a purist position on where jazz can be found. "Jazz music," he argues, "lives and dies in the moment of performance" (Gioia 83), that is, in the act of creation. What jazz has to offer, then, is a plethora of immediacies, a sequence of present moments, Charlie Parker's successive choruses on "Ko-Ko." Gioia and many others find the essential elements of jazz in "spontaneity, creativity, variety, surprise" (Gioia 111), all of those elements products of that making which lives and dies within the contours of the moment. Whatever our uneasiness with any sort of essentialism, we seem comfortable with arguing for an essence of jazz. Whatever our uneasiness with arguments for presence, we speak of the essence of jazz in terms of a singular immediacy to the moment of origin without which jazz is not purely itself. Given the fascination of many modes of modernism with essence and its presence, jazz has to be read as a mode of modernist art, in fact a paragon of sorts. On the basis of such conditions Armstrong is as much a modernist artist as the Rilke of *Malte* and the *Dinggedicht*, the Edward Weston of the peppers and the comments in his *Daybooks*.[2]

It is those dominant readings of jazz that turn it into a model of Walter Benjamin's concept of aura. When Benjamin speaks of the auratic object's "presence in time and space, its unique existence at the place where it happens to be" ("Mech Repro" 220), he speaks in terms that describe precisely the prevailing position on the jazz solo. Even critics who find that position extreme, who are looser on the question of the birth and death of jazz in the moment of performance, continue a Benjaminian reading in still another way, in relation to authenticity. Benjamin argues that "the presence of the original is the prerequisite to the concept of authenticity" ("Mech Repro" 220), that historical continuity is possible only when the original *remains present* to act as witness to its own history. Consider, then, the argument of Joachim Berendt in *The Jazz Book* that jazz improvisation is based on the "identity of improviser, composer and interpreter" (Berendt 129), another way of putting the familiar point that in jazz the artist is simultaneously composer and performer. Berendt insists that "it would be foolish to claim that choruses that are among the greatest in jazz cease to be jazz when repeated" (128), and he cites instances such as Alphonse Picou's clarinet solo on "High Society," which has for much of this century seemed as integral a part of the piece as its melody line (not an especially good example since the solo was written down in the original sheet music). Yet Berendt scuttles his refusal to assume a purist position when he goes on to assert that what he calls the "once-improvised" (cf. Barthes and the *déja-lu*) remains authentic jazz only when played by the artist who originated it: "It cannot be separated from him, notated, and given to a second or third musician to play. . . . Jazz can be reproduced solely by the musician who produced it" (128; cf. 159). Repeated solos, Berendt claims, can be taken as jazz only when played by their sole owner/originator. That contention shows exactly what Benjamin meant by authenticity, which exists only when the original continues as testimony to itself. Despite his rejection of the argument that jazz lives only in the moment, Berendt continues a version of it by confining the solo's authenticity only to the acts of its originator in moments of his absolute presence.

Still these emphases on uniqueness to the moment are only part of the way jazz works. We have to say about jazz what Barthes and others have said about language: there is no "innocent" solo that springs only from its moment, no absolute autonomy within the moment of the solo's making. In a fundamental sense the jazz solo is a text, defining "text" not only as a tissue, a weaving (*texere*), but also as a collective of ways of acting that had been defined, in part, before the making of the solo. We have to think in terms of differing modes of speech, not only between different instruments but between the same instruments at different periods of jazz. What the clarinet does within a New Orleans ensemble is very different in expectations from what the trombone does. Consider the combination of role and sound linked to the (perhaps mythic) history of the tailgate style of trombone; consider, then its difference from anything Johnny Dodds ever did on clarinet. Add to this the trombone work of Bill Harris in the 1940s, what it shares and does not share with, say, that of Kid Ory in the 1920s. Or ponder the role of the sideman, what it means to be thought of as a sideman, what one can watch emerging in the move from Oliver's early groupings through the Hot Fives and Sevens to the development of Armstrong's big bands in the early thirties. (That move also did much to define the meaning of the term "showcase.") One can put this play of conditions in still other ways, for example, in terms of the blues as a language with rock-bottom specificities as well as an extraordinary freedom to make out of those what one wills. Alternatively, one can put it as Neil Leonard does, through terms that ground his ideas about jazz as religious expression. Placing particular emphasis on the ritual aspects of jazz, Leonard argues that the jazz soloist "did not start from scratch every time he picked up his instrument" (75).

All of these issues have enough inflections of history to put history, too, in terms of the solo's textuality, to show that history, discourse, and text are as inseparable in jazz as they are everywhere else. The speaking and role-fulfilling (or anti-role-fulfilling, as in Ornette Coleman's group solos) ground themselves in the patterns of previous fulfillments, in the histories through which those roles and their attendant expectations worked themselves out at the time of a particular solo. There are other ways to put that history, arguments that the solo is a text because it is full of traces and indexes—what it means when we say that the history of jazz is present in every improvised solo, that it appears in large part through the choices one makes at any one time. These are jazz's *déja-lu*, and they are among the reasons why we can speak of jazz's intertexts and therefore of the solo as text.

But not solely text. Jazz can never be taken as any single thing but has to be taken as several together, whatever their differences. It is surely most accurate to speak of jazz as *both* auratic and textual, each playing off the other as the soloist plays his piece. Each needs the other element to be what it radically is. Each needs a context in which to be itself, and the other's relation to it is the framework of that context. That is another way of saying that one cannot be original outside the conditions that define one's originality; but it is also a way of saying that one creates within conditions, with *and* against those conditions. The primacy of improvisation is in no sense encumbered or compromised by an awareness of the frames of discourse. Our awe before the auratic is in no sense lessened because we acknowledge that aspect of the solo that has to be called text. In fact, the simultaneous presence of the auratic and the textual comes very close to defining those tensions within modernism that make jazz a primary mode of modernist art.

That makes it possible for us to speak of the semblance of authenticity in sound recordings—something that appears, for example, in the Bix Beiderbecke and Frankie Trumbauer recording of "Singin' the Blues" that does not appear in the replayings of the Beiderbecke solo, note for note, by Rex Stewart and others. In the Bix and Tram recording we listen to the sounds of a scene at which Beiderbecke *had been* present, and what we listen to repeatedly is the reproduced sound of that past participial presence, precisely the sort of anteriority we see in photographs. Gunther Schuller makes a related point in speaking of the jazz recording and the definitive performance. Such a recording is, as Schuller puts it, "a one-time thing" (Schuller x), that is, the representation of one specific performance, definitive only if it is the only available performance. Using Armstrong's "West End Blues" as the representative case, he speaks of how we have to evaluate Armstrong's solo "on the basis of a single performance that happened to be recorded in 1928 and are left to speculate on the hundreds of other performances he played of the same tune, none exactly alike, some inferior to the recording, others perhaps even more inspired" (Schuller x). In the terms that Schuller uses, there is no definitive aura, an aura for all time, because there is no definitive performance, no once-and-for-all rendition. Peculiar to each performance is the aura thereof. Sound recordings complicate the question of the definitive in precisely the same way that they complicate the authentic. Terms like "definitive" and "authentic" have to be used in special ways in conditions of this sort, some special to sound recordings, some of those special to sound recordings of jazz. What does it mean to call a recording authentic? However good the technology, these sounds are forever Other, irrevocably past participial.[3] Still, whatever our uneasiness in calling such circumstances "authentic," they are farther down the road toward the conditions of authenticity than Stewart's reproduction of the Beiderbecke solo. If the sound recording, like the photograph, shifts into special histories as soon as it is made, its indexical properties bring us as close as we can get (we should not exaggerate how much) to the auratic moment of making and the sounds of that moment.

That makes the sound recording, and the uses to which we put it, an especially intricate instance of the syntaxes of jazz. Consider the importance of recordings in jazz's history. Several critics have suggested that jazz would not have developed as it did, perhaps would not have developed at all, were it not for the phonograph. James Lincoln Collier points out what the 1917 recording by the Original Dixieland Jazz Band did for the development of jazz: "It was the single most significant event in the history of jazz. Before this record was issued jazz was an obscure folk music played mainly by a few hundred blacks and a handful of whites in New Orleans, and rarely heard elsewhere. Within weeks after this record was issued, on March 7, 'jazz' was a national craze and the five white musicians were famous" (Collier 72). This quickly became more than a matter of the latest rage. Collier, Gioia, and others have shown the significance of jazz recordings as tools for learning fundamentals (Beiderbecke copying Nick La Rocca, Parker copying Lester Young). Recordings became the primary means of distribution for the expanding discourse of jazz. Recordings, indeed, did most to make that expansion possible, spreading the news of the expectations that had to be met and undone, those strong figures whom one needed to mimic *and* to wrestle.

It is precisely because of such issues that we seriously need to develop a more complete understanding of the syntaxes of jazz. One learns how to improvise by copying, note for note, a solo that had been improvised for the moment of the recording. One learns how to make things up by playing those solos repeatedly until their radical intricacies, their on-the-spot play of texture and intertextuality, get felt in one's musical bones. What Keats called "frozen music" is halfway literal for recorded jazz. That points to another paradox ingrained in the history and nature of jazz: one learns much of the art through a process that, necessarily, goes against the most widely accepted tenets of the art. It is a process through which one learns not only the textuality of jazz but that jazz *has* a textuality. That process teaches that there are ways of doing things and not just the doing itself; that jazz is, finally, both auratic and textual. One develops one's own auratic through mimicking someone else's, through coming to understand that the auratic is not all.

Our pondering of jazz has come, inevitably, to the question of imitation, in particular to the relations of aura and representation. What is sometimes called Bixology concerns not only the study of Beiderbecke's work and life but the uses to which we have put him; and that usage takes forms as different as the syntaxes of jazz, to which it is closely related, on which it is dependent. On 25 April 1931 the Fletcher Henderson orchestra recorded "Singin' the Blues," with the solo by Rex Stewart to which I referred. Stewart reproduces, note for note, the Beiderbecke solo on the Bix and Tram "Singin' the Blues," a recording that instantly became a model for the making of jazz. Henderson handles his business shrewdly. He begins his version with a group of saxophones playing the initial Trumbauer solo, which contemporaries found nearly as impressive as the solo by Beiderbecke. By putting this production of a single person into the hands of a group, Henderson carefully establishes the artifice of his remaking, its status as pure imitation, as the purely secondary. Through this chorus Henderson announces not only the syntax of their playing, its status as past definite, but the character of his version as an open act of homage to that which is solitary and can only be imitated. That playing by a group, because it is by a group and therefore openly acknowledges itself as secondary, argues for the stubbornness of aura, its unavailability, unreproducibility. Benjamin would have understood what Henderson did and why, especially his handling of syntax. When one gets to the Stewart solo, with its single-voiced, note-for-note rendering, that attitude continues, established for the entire piece by the initial playing of the group, established even (especially) for Stewart's singular doings. If Stewart's solo seems hesitant, diffident, Beiderbecke's tone and attack obviously missing, it draws its own tonality not only from secondhand Bix but from the carefully established structure of the arrangement in which it appears, all that the arrangement implies of jazz's temporalities. Henderson's piece reflects on itself as well as on Bix and Tram, on the nature of jazz as well as on jazz's history.[4]

That is a different situation from the sort established by Red Nichols, who by 1928 was patently playing at being Beiderbecke. The Five Pennies of that period put out a mixed bag of work, some good pieces like "Nobody's Sweetheart," some commercial arrangements like "A Pretty Girl Is Like a Melody," and a pretentious "Limehouse Blues." It still startles us to hear Nichols in "Nobody's Sweetheart." It is not merely that he does better than Stewart in mimicking Beiderbecke's ways. Nichols's work at this period is a studied imitation, carefully reproducing Beiderbecke's turns and rips, getting closer than Stewart attempted to the Beiderbecke tonality (though no imitation I know of comes close to the *centricity* of Beiderbecke's notes). But Nichols's work is more than a matter of performing homage and then going on to other things—that is, what Henderson did. Nichols's Beiderbeckian mode turns up in much of his playing of the period. It shows, for example, in his solo on "Can't You Hear Me Calling, Caroline," which carries the imitation into some of its spookier reaches. His leading of the first chorus in a Five Pennies version of "Whispering" openly sounds that mode, as does his weaker solo later in that piece. And his playing, mainly lead, in the more commercial work, has much of the sound of Beiderbecke within the Whiteman orchestra.

Nichols draws aura in jazz much closer to the sort that happens when a figure like Olivier plays Othello at the Old Vic. That is the question of stage aura that so fascinated Benjamin, what happens when the aura of the actor blends with the aura of the character he plays. Yet the relations of Nichols and Beiderbecke complicate the issue considerably. What happens with Nichols is *something* like what happens with a sound recording, the emergence of a past definite within the moment's immediacies, a confluence in which no thing is exclusively one thing but is several at once. Jazz recordings do that more dramatically than other kinds of recordings, but the case of Nichols and Beiderbecke holds a peculiar balance of aura and textuality based on a peculiar confluence of the syntaxes of jazz. There is no similar confluence in Olivier's playing of Othello because the character is always upfront and immediate when played, whatever the ancient history of previous playings. It is just that renewable immediacy that leads Benjamin to speak of the aura of a character, of what holds together all of the stage playings of Faust (see below for more on those playings). But there is no renewable immediacy in Nichols's use of Beiderbecke, no sense in which Bix breaks through to the surface of the palimpsest. Nichols's playing never loses its awareness of, never lets us forget, the already-played, that is, the intertext. His work raises the predicament of secondhand aura, a paradox/oxymoron that goes to the essence of what we have always thought about jazz.

Of course, this is homage, awe, all that we saw in Henderson; but it is much more than that because it turns the performance of homage into acts of appropriation, a different kind of practice with other implications. If Nichols's way of helping himself was no secret to most of his listeners, he turned it into more than a Henderson-like meditation on jazz's temporalities. It becomes, with Red Nichols, a way of being in jazz.[5]

Those questions of aura and authenticity and their relation to sound recordings get particularly intricate in the connections of jazz and rock. Any reading of rock and roll in terms of what happens in jazz makes clear all sorts of linkages—for example, the grounding of both in the blues. Yet such readings must also attend to the specific differences that help to define each mode. Rock musicians routinely make the act of recording only the beginning of the process of producing a tape or disk. Their use of electronics for fashioning the final text extends an art that leans heavily on electronic instruments. The "weaving" that makes it possible to speak of such projects as "texts" emerges from an elaborate system of splicing and rerecording, similar to what we expect from the editing of films. (Those are the conditions of which stage actors speak when they discuss the difficult adjustment they have to make to working in films, their requisite rethinking of the nature of performance.) Of course, it is overly bald to state, without qualification, that jazz is an art of performance and rock an art of recording; yet those *are* their radical emphases. Players of rock and roll sometimes mouth their live performances, a practice that jibes perfectly with the equally frequent habit of projecting their televised images onto a large screen so that the audience as a whole can get a better look at the act. If behind such workings there are shades of Frank Morgan cranking out the Wizard of Oz, there is rarely attempted fraud in the doings of rock and roll. (One excepts instances like the case of Milli Vanilli.) Rock and roll is brassily upfront on these issues. In effect, it changes the meaning of authenticity by changing the locus of that condition: in jazz the performance is privileged, in rock and roll the recording. The open, indeed ecstatic, embrace of the secondary is what makes rock and roll a prime postmodernist art and what clarifies the place of jazz among major modernist modes. To put it in terms of Benjamin's examples, jazz finds its analogy in all of the stage actings of *Faust*, rock and roll its counterpart in the making of film.

Benjamin uses those examples in the essay on mechanical reproduction. In a footnote on the *Faust* plays he argues that "the poorest provincial staging of *Faust* is superior to a Faust film in that, ideally, it competes with the first performance at Weimar" (*Illuminations* 243). It competes, that is, because there is an actor on the stage, present and immediate, blending his aura with the aura of the figure of Faust, while even the finest filming of *Faust* cannot pretend to claim what the provincial staging claims, a connection to the source in kind if not in time. Such issues have particular point in narrative films about jazz, which tend more often to be films about the makers of jazz than about jazz itself. All sorts of peculiar ironies surround such films, based largely on the conflict between an art form we have always thought of as radically auratic and an art whose coming-into-being did as much as any other to set aura into decline. If there is a sense in which documentaries like *Let's Get Lost* (1989) and *Thelonious Monk: Straight, No Chaser* (1989) have many characteristics of the sound recording—we are looking at Chet Baker and Thelonious Monk and simultaneously listening to soundtracks of their music—there is a sense in which a narrative film about jazz, even a film about a once-extant figure like Charlie Parker, has little of even this quasiauthenticity. To put the point another way, with a sound recording and with a documentary film we can concentrate on the music and what we see of the "real" figures, while in a *cinéma-à-clef* like *Young Man with a Horn* (1950; a compensatory dream about a redeemed semblance of Beiderbecke), or a film that seeks to present the essence of Charlie Parker as played by Forest Whitaker, we have to deal with the conditions of the classic Hollywood film with its need to tell a story through a sequence of images secondary in several senses. This means that a director who accepts the auratic nature of jazz also must acknowledge and work with inherently unstable circumstances.

Consider what Clint Eastwood did with the soundtrack of *Bird*, the best-known if not the best among more recent films about jazz. Eastwood and others make much of the soundtrack's authenticity, since it draws on recordings of Parker solos from various points in his career, including some cuts that, as the blurb on the videocasette sleeve points out, had never before been released. But what Eastwood did with the solos is unusual and revealing. Though Parker's "solos" are kept intact, the backgrounds, as the blurb says, were "electronically eliminated." (The quotation marks around "solos" are actually in the blurb.) Parker's solos, the blurb continues, "were then rerecorded with accompaniment by modern musicians attuned to Yardbird's bold improvisations. It's 'like Bird was in the studio,' says music supervisor Lennie Niehaus." Whatever their success, Eastwood's instincts are evident: by keeping Parker's solos but making their context contemporary, he seeks to overcome the past participial presence inscribed in the recordings, the presence of *what had been*. He wants to put Parker closer to the moment of the film, that is, to our own moment, the only moment of aura the Benjaminian mode makes possible. Eastwood seeks to cancel or at least to mitigate the inevitable demise of aura by creating a semblance of presence for the solos of the film's subject, a semblance based on the creation of backgrounds contemporary with the film, contemporary with us. Eastwood is responding to that reading of authenticity that ties it to the continuity of the originating presence; yet he does so through a mode of recontextualizing that undoes even the semblance of authenticity and puts the question of the index into permanent instability.

That question is unstable because film, like any photograph, is radically indexical, and the ideologies of jazz privilege conditions of immediacy where no film can go, conditions especially stringent about qualities of time and place. Jazz speaks through discourses grounded in a certain mode of being. The effects of that privileging extend into the way jazz handles situations of power. Given the informing of jazz by resident ideologies and the discourses that attend them, given the bases of ideologies in relationships of power, jazz is inevitably affected (indeed, in part effected) by the claims of a politics, a politics that takes in a far broader spectrum than most histories show. It is a politics in which jazz's own ideologies confront the ideologies of other systems of power, social, cultural, political, the closing of Storyville in 1917, Louis Armstrong's transformation into a popular entertainer, the questions of status put in Spike Lee's film *Mo' Better Blues* (1990). All of these aspects of jazz, its ideologies, discourses, politics, emerge from the conditions we read at the center of jazz, the conditions that define where the power and privilege lie. We have put at the center of jazz what finally has to be seen as a circumstance of being, a way of being in the world.

II

Much that we have learned of the genealogy of jazz buttresses our temptation to fabulate jazz. Before New Orleans there was Africa, its music relived in festivals like the one in Congo Square, a weekly event until well beyond the middle of the nineteenth century (Ramsey and Smith 5–6). Even without aural records, the Sundays in the square have come down with considerable fame, absorbed into the history they sought to preserve. Their effect was, at once, to continue and relocate. Such festivals seem to have been, as Collier puts it, "almost entirely African in nature, modified only slightly to suit conditions here" (Collier 17). That would include the instruments played, largely African in kind. In this tale of ruptures and fractures, those festivals sought a species of continuity, setting themselves as members of a community of such conclaves, developments from an original condition lost to most, perhaps all, participants. Yet the festivals involved more than membership in a community. They clearly continued the desire for communality as such, reifying for this place the congregative thrust of their African models. For the sake of communality the festivals retained bundles of traces that linked these jubilees to others lost in the murkiness of origin.

We ought not to simplify the reasons for such festivals, the desires that, on all sides, impelled them into being. As Collier points out, "the vast majority of blacks, those working on the plantations of the south, were not permitted them" (Collier 17), and those who had permission used their meetings to blow off steam that otherwise could have threatened the powers that gave permission. The place of jazz within a sociocultural framework steeped in history and economics and issues of power has to complicate any points we make about it. That is especially true of the desires that impel jazz, as true as it is for the desires that impel any discourse. Jazz holds a bundle of desires with interrelations as complex as those in any art of our century (even including film, with which jazz is sometimes linked because they began about the same time). Yet the sociocultural framework, however rich the story it tells, cannot by itself tell the fullest story. Aura may be inseparable from power, may be, itself, a vital mode of power, but it also deals with more than pure issues of power. The festivals made this place of diaspora a living museum for the aura no longer available, a place of its recollection if not its restoration. That aura had to be replaced (renewal was no longer conceivable) by the instruments of exile. Speaking of any one of these elements—power, culture, aura, longing, celebration, community, and more—is also, sometimes covertly, to speak of the others. That is another way of saying that jazz enfolds a fluent and mellifluous bundle of desires.

Other aspects of those bundles help partly to explain other aspects of jazz. The festivals drew into the history of the music that became jazz a profound sense of loss that the blues came to image in another, related way. That sense also affects our readings of the history of jazz, not only the older readings but recent attempts at correction. The best of the recent histories, such as those of Collier and Schuller, seek to dispel the fog of origin that hovers about the early history of jazz, the mistiness that intensifies, which gives a source and frame to, that early sense of loss. Yet, with all these excellent studies, the early history remains a tale of traces pockmarked with lacunae. If the festivals have behind them the history of African celebrations, then the music that succeeded the festivals has behind it a history of events in turn-of-the-century New Orleans of which we know very little, events that we can touch, when we can do so at all, only through the tracings of indexes like Bunk Johnson. (Our fascination with Johnson had as much to do with what he had seen and heard ["And did you see Shelley plain?"] as with what he could play with a new set of teeth.) There is no question that these lacunae have affected our readings of jazz, sometimes in flagrant ways. The darkness that gets to be lifted only with the century's teens, whose music we know of only through the sparsest of evidence, ties in, for example, with what we can gather of rituals that come through as strange and spooky, connected with all sorts of cultural stereotypes. Take the early fascination with Ellington, which puts this issue baldly. Schuller points out how "the welter of pseudo-jungle dance or production numbers [was] the kind of thing the 'tourist,' expecting to be transported to the depths of the African jungle, had come to look for at the Cotton Club" (341). Those whom the tourists came to hear acknowledged such fascination; a number like "Jungle Nights in Harlem" "complemented the 'primitive' murals on the walls of the Cotton Club" (Schuller 343). It is partly because of such linkages that the history of jazz has come to be read as fabulous, in fact as a kind of Romance; and that history shows how Romance can turn readily into cult, into the regular making of icons, beginning with Buddy Bolden and going at least to John Coltrane. Jazz confirms the claim that our acts of fabulation cannot seriously be separated from the rest of our social lives, a point that Jelly Roll Morton knew as well as anyone. That the history of jazz has lent itself so readily to the making of myths explains much of its fascination, much of the power it has with us.

One can see such making at work in some of the best early writing on jazz, in *Jazzmen*, for example, which remains a remarkable book not only for its insights but for itself as a piece of history. After the title page and before the table of contents appears an excerpt from a letter Bunk Johnson wrote to the editors. It dwells largely on the place of "King Bolden" and Johnson himself in the New Orleans music scene between 1895 and 1896, the King Bolden band, according to Johnson, "the first Band that played jazz" (Ramsey and Smith v). Origins and royalty, the *making* of origins by powerful royalty and attendant figures: so begins the book's tonality, and it is followed by a three-page preface, all of it in italics, that goes far toward establishing the requisite prefatory awe. The preface is about New Orleans ("A fantastic and wonderful city. A city with a hundred faces" [3]), its tonality adulation, its hero an ancient king who seems never to have gone away:

> listen hard some night, listen hard at the corner of
> Rampart and Perdido and you'll hear a whacky horn playing
> an uptown jazz rag, way out and way off, filling the tune.
> That would be King Bolden, calling his children. (4)

The sound of that horn is heard in "Louis and in Joe Oliver and in Bunk" and maybe also "between the covers of a book" (the book one is reading, obviously). In this way *Jazzmen* announces itself as hagiography, putting the King in a context, a history that absorbs him and links him to a dimness in which he partakes, which covers him too: "in New Orleans you could still hear the bamboula on Congo Square when Buddy Bolden cut his first chorus on cornet" (5). The ending of this prefatory piece acts out one of the classic gestures of Romance, the homecoming that has ended Romances from *The Odyssey* on:

> Old Willy Cornish said the crowd would be over there, with Robi-
> chaux, and Bolden's Band would start right out like the killers they
> were. You could see a glow on his very dark cheek and the soft voice
> seemed to come from back there, wherever his eyes were. He said
> that he was
>   callin' our chillun home. (6)

Here the Romance hero is, himself, the place of home. Romance not only helps us to read Buddy Bolden, but Bolden helps us to read the Romance as well.

The first pages of the chapter that follows, that begins the text proper, offer some finely evocative work on the festivals at Congo Square, "a large open field at Orleans and Rampart" (6). There the slaves performed "the tribal and sexual dances which they had brought with them from the Congo," those dances "one of the unusual sights of New Orleans to which tourists were always taken" (6). (Such tourists prefigured those who went up to Harlem to hear Ellington speak the jungle.) Here, too, the line from the dances to Bolden comes through clearly, focusing in part on prowess and its effect, in Bolden on a link between sexual and musical drives. This "barber of Franklin street" was no ordinary cornetist: "the power of his sonorous tone has never been equalled" (11). In classic mythmaking mode the chapter dwells on the prowess of the King, on some of the oldest meanings of *virtue.*[6] "Soon," we hear, " 'Kid' Bolden became 'King' Bolden" (11), the chapter spelling out an implicit coronational narrative (here, shades of King Arthur). But, as often elsewhere, the question of "virtue" gets ironic very quickly. The implicit pun turns sardonic and open as the text explores Bolden's habits, which were as immoderate "for women as for hard liquor and hot music" (15).[7] It appears that Bolden, like many a Romance hero, was equally good with all these outlets for prowess. If he could draw a crowd by sticking "his horn through a hole in the fence and the people came rushing" (13–14), he could take three women along on a parade, *"all three satisfied"* (15; italics in the original).

Jazzmen completed a process that had begun in Bolden's time, turning the barber into an icon that centered potency. By all accounts his charisma, an extraordinary version of which is requisite for any icon, was dramatic and unforgettable. (Charisma is clearly part of certain aspects of aura but is not identical with it.) Bolden's reputed roughness and vigor echoed the qualities of Congo Square, the processes of history putting those qualities within a figure who took on (as only single figures can) iconicity. The fact that Bolden died in 1931, the same year as Bix Beiderbecke (both, incidentally, B. B.), could only strengthen the qualities the icon had gained.

If there surely can be no icons without aura, there may be no fabulations without icons. All of these elements come together in our earliest readings of jazz, in contemporary views of Bolden, in writings like *Jazzmen.* They continue stubbornly, as though such practices were built into the radical nature of jazz and not just the nature of our responses to jazz. One can, indeed, argue that the nature of jazz and the nature of our most prominent readings of it are so intimately linked that they appear consubstantial, strangely echoing. Consider, in jazz and its history, that which shifts and that which remains unchanged. If jazz moved, with considerable irony, from a communal context to one that makes the individual primary and central, it has always, in every context, privileged upfront immediacy in the moment of the solo's making (whatever the textual/textural history that lies behind that making). Consider, further, what that could mean with some of the emotional bases of jazz. There is, I suspect, a deeply grounded relation between the sense of loss that pervades jazz's prehistory and continues in aspects like the blues, and the emphasis found in all modes of jazz on a passionate, celebratory, immediate moment of origin, one in which we listen and, in listening, participate. I do not speak here of anything so simplistic as compensation for loss but a compulsive insistence on what can be done *now*, one that puts equal emphasis on the doing and the now. (That too is, of course, ironic, because the moment of making jazz, as well as the jazz made, becomes history as soon as experienced.) This working to the moment, for the moment's sake, meant one thing to the New Orleans ensemble and another to the separate soloist. It meant for the soloist a particular kind of pressure that the listener turns into an extraordinary "virtue." That is how the nature of jazz affects/effects our readings not only of jazz as such but of the figures involved. That is how the place of jazz within temporality affects/effects not only the nature of jazz but how we continue to interpret that nature.[8]

These issues point to resident ironies in films about jazz, from the silliest to the most exalted. Film, through Benjamin's influence, has come to stand for the defeat of the auratic; and yet films about jazz seem inevitably to take on a classical humanist emphasis, framing narratives that focus on strong creative personalities, as centering and charismatic (charisma again not fully identical with aura) as any models we have known. That is, films on jazz continue the conditions of the histories they depict, even at their worst contributing components to those histories.

Which is another way of saying that those films are as much about the components of public discourse, the relations of such discourses to the histories behind them, as they are about their ostensible (usually titular) subjects. *Young Man with a Horn* raises these issues openly, broadly, raising especially the relations of aura to cliché, that which is by definition unique to its moment and that which is by definition a pure repeat of the past. Both aura and cliché take part in the discourse of such films, aura always part of the thematics of the film, the cliché nearly always part of the presentation of aura. That tends to make the Hollywood film about jazz an oxymoronic package. *Young Man with a Horn* puts the components precisely.[9]

The title frames ride over the sounds of Harry James at his sweetest, not far from the qualities of "Ciribiribin"; an inauspicious beginning but true to the tonalities of Dorothy Baker's mawkish book. Hoagy Carmichael, the Oscar Levant of this film, pretending surprise at the encroaching camera, begins the hagiography: "Of course Rick is practically a legend now," a remark that serves not only to define a point of view but to characterize Carmichael's comments as themselves hagiography. (With all of its clumsiness, this film, like most of its betters, sometimes manages to suggest the terms of its own making.) That legend-establishing continues into the early scenes, which play over the archetype of the little blond boy, no parents and nearly no family, who roams the dark world (those scenes a precise analogy to *Oliver Twist*, Dickens's homage to the classic fairy tale). One of the finest moments in this visually obtuse film has the young Rick, his blondness prominent, sitting in the transom of a door that leads into a jazz club. The outline of the transom frames the boy in a cuddling enclosure. He is listening to his first jazz, the enclosing image suggesting the embrace of jazz that will make up for most other dearths. When one resees the film that embrace comes through as warm *and* ominous, protective *and* divisive. One looks through the frame of the transom, beyond the figure of the blond boy, toward an interior filled with black musicians, themselves within the enclosure though not as completely as the boy. Focusing as it does on the transom, this image reads like a street sign for what is inside, a sign that we therefore read as a sign about signs as well as all it intends of frames. In a better film one would treat this as complex instructions for reading, working from the inherent aura of the blond boy in the dark streets (Dickens makes much of that built-in aura) to the semiotic implications of the frame and the act of framing. But this film slips quickly into the comforts that are always available. A gentle black father figure, that teacher whom the student will eventually surpass, takes over tutelage, the only glitch in Rick's education the simply mastered matter (simple, at least, for him) of improperly holding his lip. From that point on, Rick has a relatively easy ride. His first big job is with a commercial-cum-novelty band. The predictable responses that cannot evade the comic ("You want every number played the way it is written?") unfold not only a pandering to cliché but, more seriously in terms of the way we read jazz, what the film's working insinuates of Hollywood's sense of our expectations. By this point the film is suggesting (with no awareness that it is doing so) that the aureolic glow that openly surrounds the blond boy, that glow transmuted into the immediate makings of jazz, cannot be planted in the ambience of the adult Rick, cannot sustain itself in the context of unmitigated cliché. What we think of as the essence of jazz, what some early scenes of the film work successfully to sustain, linking the child and the music in the subtlest of encounters, finds no room to continue as the film goes to grown-up Rick and comes to nothing but banalities that are the contrary of jazz.

What *Young Man with a Horn* guesses to be our sense of jazz has within it an implicit morality, built not only into the rhetoric of the film but into the discourses out of which the sense of the film emerges. That we fear and envy figures like Rick Martin, that we sense their destructiveness not only to themselves but ultimately to us, says a great deal about our attitude to aura and its implications. Consider not only Plato's *Ion*, where much of that attitude begins, but examples like "Kubla Khan," whose poet seems so scary that we are exhorted to "weave a circle round him thrice." We fear, it seems, that this wonderful potency will go wild, that the subterranean links between creation and destruction not only shade them one into another but so weaken our understanding that we cannot tell one from the other. We argue that such fascinating figures are outside our fields of discourse, that they choose to be so (or are driven to be so, which could make it even scarier). Outsider to most of us, Rick Martin seems strange even to those who share his line of work, the black father figure, the buddy, and the blond singer, who ought to understand him better than they actually do. He is told by his surrogate father, "You're kinda locked up inside yourself." Smoke says that Rick is "a guy very few people would understand." The vocalist Jo Jordan (the usual Renaissance blond, here complicated by what her friend calls her "mother instinct"), asks him, "Why do you live in left field all the time?" This attitude, too, has sunk into cliché. It is a popular culture reading of what comes down from Plato and Coleridge, consistent with most of the strata in this oppressively shoddy film; yet it shows what we intuit about the extremes of potency, our attitude toward a creating that somehow, because so intense, cannot be as easily contained within the parameters of our discourses as the work of the other, lesser, musicians in the film. Benjamin says nothing about this aspect of aura, though it is built into the relations of aura and the sacred. We cannot have such hagiographies without at least the potential that the figure whom we exalt may do in not only himself but some of us as well. Rick, fortunately, is only indirectly responsible for the death of the surrogate father he had peremptorily sent away.

These questions get more complex when we consider not only what happens to Rick Martin but what that suggests of the film's reading of our attitudes toward jazz. *Young Man with a Horn* muddles through the reasons for Rick's downfall. After Rick marries he stops going to Galba's, the jazz club where he would play after his evening stint with the White-manesque Phil Morrison orchestra. Perhaps we are meant to gather that marriage itself has weakened his passion for after-hours jazz. Rick, it seems, is no Buddy Bolden. He is unable to fight off not only his wife's jealousy of his single-minded devotion (the film makes much of her sense that she feels "half a dozen things at the same time"), but her concomitant jealousy of the music that consumes him. The film clearly suggests that it is the weakening of his ties to jazz through the pull of the demands of marriage that sends Rick to drink and near-death in the streets.

Yet at the same time, confusingly, the ending picks up the idea, never seriously broached in the film before that point, that Rick has been striving for superhuman effects, for what the Renaissance blond says is his struggle for a note that is not on the trumpet. As Smoke puts the point, when Rick's horn lets him down he goes to pieces. Yet his only open attempt to reach such a note occurs in a recording session after his separation and turn to heavy drinking. That turning suggests that his failure stems more from increasing debility than from what the horn cannot be made to do. In fact, we never really see such a struggle before that point. It comes in near the end because of the demands of the moral stance that has been implicit in the film, the stance tied to the fears that the discourse enfolds. At the end, Smoke speaks for that discourse, and the fact that another jazzman speaks it confirms that Rick is an extreme outsider whose self-laceration threatens us all. As Smoke puts the moral: Rick "learned that you cannot say everything through the end of a trumpet, and a man doesn't destroy himself just because he can't hit some high note that he dreamed up." He learned, that is, to go for "success as a human being first, and an artist second; and what an artist!" Countering the conclusion of Baker's book, the film brings Rick back into the fold, brings him, that is, down to a size we can handle, that speaks our piece, our peace. We have had our revenge on the paragon who scares us, whom we envy. However shoddy this film, it reveals, with unintended skill, much of what is at stake in Hollywood's reading of jazz.

What happens, then, to the music that drives Rick near to destruction? The emphasis in this film and in most films about jazz lies less on the music than on its players. There are several reasons for this, none separable from the others.

Classic narrative modes, Aristotelian or well-made, have always been largely about character, its making or unmaking. Most films about jazz tend to be Aristotelian, given to diagrammable plots with turning points and climaxes, beginnings, middles, and ends, building on personalities going through palpable histories. In that sense they follow the patterns of the classic Hollywood film, which mainly does its work through straightforward narration, whatever the thrust of the discourses such films put into speech. That is one reason why most films about jazz focus on personality, on the maker of the music and not on the music itself. Whatever its own personality, whatever its own predilections toward the telling of a story, the music itself seems to the fashioners of such films not part of what can be told, of that which has always been told. We hear about the music, are told what it costs its makers; but we hear most of all about those who do the making. The aura infusing the music—that which, in the playing of jazz, cannot be separated from the aura infusing the performer—gets shifted largely to the performer.

Still, such emphases take in more than the demands of classic structures or even our ambivalent fascination with figures who self-destruct. Part of what they take in comes from our tendency to subscribe to a "great man" theory of history that is as true for the history of jazz as it is for anything else. Much of the Romance that goes from the dark interiors of the Congo to the interiors of 52nd Street takes on humanist emphases; emphases found also, without coincidence, in the classic structures of plot that Hollywood took over for its own sufficient reasons. (Frank Capra, who seems to haunt a number of films about jazz, put these "great man" readings so purely that he can stand as paragon.) Hollywood films, about jazz or anything else, come out of concatenations reaching every aspect of culture, and here they reach to our readings of jazz's development, readings that are consonant with Hollywood's predilections. But there are still other reasons for Hollywood's attraction to such readings. That those interpretations take part in—echo, support—uneasy theories of history comes partly from the attraction of the idea of stars as such. Hollywood knows how to read that attraction, has the equipment and the experience to deal with it fluently. One senses an inherent sympathy between a way of reading jazz history and some of Hollywood's ways of centering energies.

Of course (but not finally; these comments cannot be exhaustive), there is the question of representation, especially of what we sense to be unrepresentable, or representable only through the byways of analogy. One can seek, with some likelihood of luck, to get across what it feels like to play such music, going past the strained attempts in *Young Man with a Horn* or *Bird* (1988) to the convincing subtleties of *Round Midnight* (1986); yet we have seen, for sufficient reasons, few attempts to get at the music itself, and that puts the emphasis, *faute de mieux*, on the creative personality. Focusing on strong central makers, collected and coherent in the fashioning of their art if in nothing else in life, such films put their most intense stress on the Romantic-Modern tradition of centripetality that Hollywood continues with remarkable vigor. Given the difficulties involved in representing jazz, that seems like an understandable choice.

The choice has considerable interest for other reasons as well: it illuminates the rhetoric inhabiting such films, and in doing so it helps us to see precisely *where* such films work, an issue inseparable from *how* such films work. Those films involve, inevitably, metonymic structures, metonymic for reasons Jakobson did not touch. They do their primary work within metonymic fields, on the play of those elements that seem open to representation, on the play of those others that seem successfully to resist all reification. Those films discuss directly what they feel can be so discussed, coming only through indirection at that which, they suggest, can only be pointed to. Their contexts are full of symbols that are also synecdoches, that, whatever their symbolic function, work mainly as representatives of a field in which they stand as one element among others. That is as true for the central figure in, say, *Bird*, as for the cymbal that flies through that film and behaves as, at once, symbol and synecdoche. *Young Man with a Horn* makes such points as clearly as any. Whatever else he is, Rick Martin is metonymic, his aura standing for—not just absorbing—that of the music he makes. Whatever the various poverties of *Young Man with a Horn*, it offers a cardinal instance of the issues in better films.

Of the issues in *Bird*, for example, which Clint Eastwood speaks of, in an interview with Nat Hentoff, as a study in the character of "a jazz personality per se" (Hentoff 26). In remarks made two years after *Round Midnight* came out, Eastwood tells Hentoff that film and television avoid serious probings of jazz because "we think of culture in European terms—European music, European art" (27). His, he suggests, will be one of the few serious readings. Elsewhere in the interview he argues that his film comes out of an indigenous black experience, "and I feel I know it as well as any white person around" (26). If *Bird* belies those boasts at many points throughout, it has the considerable virtue (compared to films like *Young Man with a Horn*) of seeking to focus on the texture of lived experience; and if, as it turns out, the comments on black experience are too reductive or general (they occur mainly in admonitions by the Gillespie figure and the Bechet-like figure whom Parker meets in Paris), if, as it turns out, the film offers little sense of what goes into making jazz (whatever the flaccidity of *Young Man with a Horn* it does attempt to render the passion), Eastwood puts his Parker into a tangled private history, into the image of a declining figure who knows that he soon will prove his biodegradability. Eastwood builds *Bird* on a coherent, cohesive narrative of decline and fall, its focus a study of personality in the classic Hollywood mold. Yet, for most of what we are shown, this person could have been a grocer instead of the major jazzman of our time, Armstrong's only peer in the history of jazz. And he would have been a limpid grocer, at least in Eastwood's reading: Eastwood's conception of Parker as a big, soft, mushy oaf has raised extensive derision, putting Parker into terms that are consistent if not fully credible. What that figure has to do with the auratic aspects of jazz comes through almost nowhere in the narrative running the film.

Yet Eastwood knows that it has to come through somewhere. And he knows, further, that history and the auratic, whatever their antipathies, cannot finally work without acknowledgment of each other. That mutual nodding happens in the way he handles the soundtrack, which argues for the purity of both history and music in terms that seem to echo purist readings of jazz but emerge as more complex than most purist remarks. His linking of sound and time, his placement of sound *in* time, comes through in his interview with Hentoff, comes through as an understanding that purity and history not only can coexist but, in fact, have to; that sound, however pure, cannot escape immersion in history:

> [*Eastwood*]. I wanted the music to really be of that era. So often, when people do period films, they start deciding, "Well, we'll update this a little bit." And it loses its purity.
> *American Film.* So, in the movie *Bird,* you extracted Parker's solos from original recordings for the soundtrack?
> *Eastwood.* Yeah, we used Bird's own recordings. No sound-alikes. On those original recordings, his solos are always up front, and it seems like everybody else kind of disappears. So we built around those solos by bringing in as many of the original sidemen as we could and then added equivalent players of today. (Hentoff 26)

Never mind the problem of finding players equivalent to Gillespie, Davis, Powell, Mingus, Roach, or Blakey; or the correlative problem of taking a solo out of its context; or the hardly credible argument that Gillespie or Davis or Powell "quietly disappears" in Parker's presence. Eastwood's excesses put aside, one can argue that he seeks to get his soundtrack to do what he did not do in the film (an argument implying that he knew what he did not do). One also can suggest that Eastwood's work with the soundtrack creates a diametrical split, the figure that moves through the narrative showing little credible connection with the sounds emerging from the alto on the track. Eastwood tries out an exacting balancing act, admirable, tricky, difficult, prone to immediate collapse into nostalgia and bathos; and in fact the act does not work, largely because of the abyss between his Parker and the one on the track; largely, that is, because of the splitting of track and text.

Yet despite these inadequacies, we can gather Eastwood's intent, his points well taken if not full well worked out. If he puts Parker originals on the soundtrack because he knows what film does to aura, he shows in the interview that he wanted those sounds to be active both then and now, to cooperate with history by arguing for their moment *and* to undo that coercion of history that cooperates with Parker in his escalating decline. In the interview Eastwood speaks of the "purity" of the music. He opens that loaded word into the context of history, the purity of the music lying not only in its immediacy to the moment but the place of that moment in history. Again we see the linkage of purity and authenticity, their elaborate interworking, their implying and requiring of each other. This time, though, we see it in terms of history, the music pure and authentic because it happened at a particular time. Eastwood also has in mind, simultaneously, that sense of authenticity we spoke of earlier, the one that insists, for example, that a solo remains pure only if played by its only begetter. We need, at this point, to quote Benjamin again: "the presence of the original is the prerequisite to the concept of authenticity" ("Mech Repro" 220), a claim to which Eastwood obviously subscribes. If purity demands historical authenticity, the music without updating, it also demands personal authenticity: "Yeah, we used Bird's own recordings. No sound-alikes" (Hentoff 26). Eastwood complicates the question of aura in ways that transcend any minimalist purism. He argues for those conditions in which history and the auratic take cognizance of each other, each drawing on the other to make itself all that it is. History and the auratic seek to involve and surpass each other. Though they remain, necessarily, permanently at war, they show, in their working, that each comes to be what it is only because the other comes to be all that *it* is. Eastwood's narrative and soundtrack mirror each other curiously, each partly a fiction, the most mixed of bags; and if these unlikely look-alikes confront each other across a chasm of Eastwood's own making, they confirm our understanding of much that is at stake in making a film about jazz.

In sum, then, most films about jazz appear in the classic Hollywood mode, grounded in narrative frames, characterological; necessarily and in many ways such films are immersed in history; jazz privileges the solo performance in its radical momentariness, making it, by definition, antihistorical; but jazz is not solely immediate because it also owns a richly textured intertextual life, a life that, by any definition, finds itself at every point immersed in history. Much of what happens in jazz, much of its excitement, emerges out of the interplay of these contrary elements, their tensions and countering struggles, the productivity of their quarrels. Michael Curtiz ignored these elements in *Young Man with a Horn*, but so do the makers of most jazz films, whatever the claims of those makers finally to state it all. Eastwood made such claims; so did Spike Lee for *Mo' Better Blues*. Yet, unlike Curtiz or Lee, Eastwood deeply intuited the radical issues involved, issues that, I argued above, cannot be separated from sociocultural systems yet are not fully absorbed by those systems, not fully identical with them.

And that puts particular ironies into another of Eastwood's statements in the interview with Hentoff, ironies that reverberate through a number of jazz films, taking residence in places like *Mo' Better Blues*. Hentoff suggests to Eastwood that most of his films extend the work of Frank Capra, especially the theme of "the loner trying to fight the system," and Eastwood agrees. In Capra films, he says, "the different person was always the one who was right." When Hentoff puts the following: "Is it fair to say that the basic theme—with variations—in your pictures is the Capra theme: the individual against the system? *Bird* would be part of that," Eastwood again agrees: "I guess that is the basic theme" (Hentoff 28).

What surprises about these points is less the easy reading of Capra than the placement of *Bird* within the Capra tradition. Rooted in nineteenth-century Byronism, in American Adamism, and in a host of other contexts, the Capra tradition ("Capra-corn") pits the lone idealist, seemingly quite mad, against a materialist system (banks, politics) that he eventually undoes, his idealism triumphant, his outsiderness vindicated. Put in the terms we have been inspecting, he is an auratic figure (always "he," goaded on by a "she" who, when she is not Jean Arthur, might as well be), and he demonstrates his prowess by bucking and beating the system. Such figures have a potency we reverence and fear, all the qualities of the paragon (consider the background of such figures in, say, Richardson's *Clarissa*); yet the qualities of the paragon cannot be contained within the contours of the system's discourse. So the system feels and so does the potent one, even when the figures long (Clarissa, Eastwood's Bird) to take part in the system that surrounds them. If the system concludes that it cannot contain their potency, it seeks to reject and destroy them, laying out its Clarissas and Birds. Capra-corn, however, claims the triumph of the paragon, the winning-out of a potency that threatens to go wild and does so just enough to compel the system to shift. Thus does the Capra-esque, put in the terms we have been developing, offer itself to be read.

Yet for *Bird*, for several reasons, this reading cannot be sustained. Capra is, for one thing, far more ambivalent (maybe even more insidious) than Capra-corn allows. The system gives a little, but it trades that little off by absorbing the pesky paragon within the bounds of its contours, that is, the realm of its discourse. Take, for example, *Lost Horizon*, apparently atypical but in fact essential Capra. Diplomat and hero, openly unhappy, Capra's protagonist gives up one system for another, for a fiercely rigid one that promises the comforts of an enclosure as well as a perfect woman (1937 sexy, performing the nurturing role of the woman-as-teacher), absolute power, and quasi-immortality. In the world of Capra's films, systems hardly lose. If one gives way to another, system *as such* usually wins out, not only the day but the film and the discourse.

That is why films like *Young Man with a Horn* take the Capraesque into the most ironic of terms. If Rick Martin bucks the system by suggesting ferocities (vision, a quest for nonmaterial prowess) that the system ought to offer, at the end the system prevails, its morality triumphant. Its discourse dominates the terms of Smoke's final speech, where he lays out the values of humility and awareness of limitations, a species of bourgeois humanism that undoes external danger. But how does this work with *Bird*? In what sense does Eastwood's Bird buck any system? Eastwood shows him bucking the accepted musical modes, as in the scene at the end where one of the characters who mocked him in Kansas City has turned to the tawdriest rhythm and blues; but this is so skimpily put, with so little discussion of what Parker offered on his own, that the terms of Bird's bucking never come through clearly. He does not buck the social system, openly or otherwise, except in the scenes in the South, too easily comic. In fact, he seems to have little social sense at all, though he shows at one point a longing for domesticity, for well-kept lawns, an impossible (for him) Westchester; and the way that longing is put in the film makes Eastwood more like Curtiz than one would expect him to be. One bucks any system on the basis of alternative values, but the only values this version of Bird supports, bop and domesticity, get little credible due. Eastwood's Bird has nothing to do with the Dirty Harries and their like. He is no quasi-Capra hero but a self-destructive personality, too hooked to die for anything but that which has hooked him, too far gone to be accepted by any fold, too inarticulate to spell out the values for which he stands. Calling him Capraesque, as Eastwood and Hentoff do, brings out the confusion in Eastwood's conception, his version of the ambivalence, the ambiguity, the unsettledness of vision, that dogs most films about jazz.

Yet Eastwood intuits much that we feel about jazz, what appears in other jazz films, what appeared in Michael Curtiz's, what was to appear in Spike Lee's.[10] One senses in many of these films a deep uneasiness about jazz, about the potency of the music as well as the creative personality. Most likely it stems from a fear of the passion that drives the jazzmaker, a fear that gets transferred to his music and his life, as though the life required drugs and drunkenness, as though the music as such were somehow responsible. That brings us back to a point that has, in fact, never left, dogging our discourse throughout: the jazzman as metonym, as one more center for aura in a system that seems to demand them. That our reading of this system is radically metonymical comes through, in various ways, in most films about jazz.

Eastwood's ambivalence appears in his seeking for so many reasons (Capra, European films, what he claims to know better than most) for making the film at all. *Bird* fascinates not only because of Eastwood's love and knowledge of jazz but for its uncertainty about itself—an uncertainty revealing an active, deep-grained awareness of much that is at stake in making a film about jazz.

That pervasive uneasiness about jazz and its makers takes a revealing, bitter form in another reading of Parker, Julio Cortázar's story "The Pursuer" (1985), a histoire à clef whose hero is plainly Bird. The unfolding of the tale reveals the complexities of the narrator's attitude toward Johnny Carter, on whom he has written a well-received book. It also reveals the depths of Carter's understanding of what he is pursuing, what he suggests he never can find (though in fact he seems to have hit on it, remarkably, once). Bruno, the narrator, fears and envies Carter, whom he describes as a natural force (a familiar, easy cop-out of the sort we often take before that which we cannot handle or comprehend). "Maybe," he says, "I am a little afraid of Johnny" (Cortázar 196). That fear takes various forms, not only fear before Johnny's energy but fear of his understanding as well. Despite Bruno's early suggestion that Johnny cannot know what he is doing ("I never pay too much attention to the things Johnny says" [194]), he actually pays lots of attention, knowing that his reading of Johnny as inarticulate cannot hold up to inspection. He speaks, but only to himself, of Johnny's "way of seeing what I didn't see and, at bottom, didn't want to see" (199). That undoing of self-deception continues in his confessing that "I envy them, I envy Johnny, that Johnny on the other side, even though nobody knows exactly what that is, the other side" (203). The narrator/critic understands a good deal, not only about himself but what drives Johnny to the pursuit. In a passage (207–9) that brilliantly puts the terms of the quest into incessant open-endedness he describes Johnny's preference for "desire rather than pleasure"

(208). Johnny himself portrays his pursuit later in the text, chastising the narrator/critic for what did not go into the book ("what you forgot to put in is me" [238]), speaking of one great moment, a moment without internal time, outside any time, a moment of pure immediacy in which he seemed to find, for once and fleetingly, what he continues to pursue.[11]

Under no obligations to the conditions of the Hollywood film or the call of the mawkishness in Dorothy Baker's book, Cortázar puts his points skillfully, cogently. He puts not only the pursuit but a set of conditions within which it can occur, putting a more credible image of Parker than the one Eastwood made, a more plausible passion of pursuit than the one Curtiz showed. Cortázar's Bird knows what those other figures do not, the seductions of system, of everything in life (the Chan figure, God, jazz itself) that seeks to calm the pursuit, to tame it, make it acceptable. His last words were "make me a mask," that with and within which he could appear to conform, seem all that the narrator wrote about, a mask that would leave him free to continue the pursuit. What Curtiz and Eastwood had made a game of winners and losers; what Curtiz had shown of the system cannily, nervously, absorbing the figure it fears and reveres; what comes through in Eastwood as Hollywoodish confusion about how and where systems work; all this appears, understood and transfigured, in Cortázar's reading of Bird. It shows in the jazzman's willingness to *seem* so long as desire stays unmitigated, stays blind but fully aware, open to all but the closure that Bruno wants for the jazzman and therefore for himself. One finds in Cortázar's reading all that Eastwood claimed but never really accomplished. Persuasive and fully tenable, "The Pursuer" probes the meaning of the auratic in jazz, its place in and out of history, the geographies in which it works, its complicities with powers that create their own credibility, our ambivalence not only toward those powers but their involvement with us.

Cortázar's open-endedness clashes with several conditions of the classic Hollywood film, especially its appetite for closure, and when Bruno speaks for himself he speaks in terms analogous to those that shape such films. Indeed, his complex motivation suggests several impulses that call for such terms. Bruno's qualms about incompletion come not only from his compulsion to prove his book correct but from elemental qualms about open-endedness as such. Each of those discomforts blends with his discomfort around Johnny Carter; and there can be no way of telling the discomforts apart because they sustain each other, in time become each other. Bruno finally captures Johnny for the discourses of the system when, at the end and Johnny dead, he refuses to incorporate into a new version of his book what he has recently learned from Johnny about the conditions of the pursuit. "The Pursuer" ends, thus, much like *Young Man with a Horn*, the hero caught and framed, but it contains a meta-discourse that repeats and explores the discourse powering vehicles like Curtiz's film. That elemental gap between discourse and metadiscourse locates, enfolds, the ironies emergent in Cortázar's tale. His reading of jazz is also a reading of our readings of jazz, the link between Curtiz and Bruno revealing relations of passion and discourse that take in and connect both audience and performer.

Bertrand Tavernier's film *Round Midnight* suggests similar relations, making it another reading of readings, producer of metadiscourse. Given his penchant in this film for understatement so restrained that it can ironize itself (this too makes metadiscourse), several early scenes in the film suggest difficult problems of reading, the problems asking simply how ironic those scenes might be. Recall, in Curtiz's film, the Oliver Twist-like boy framed in the transom, listening to jazz being made in a club, too young as well as too poor to enter and partake. Tavernier seems to echo that scene from Curtiz when he twice has Francis, not too young but clearly too poor, squat on the street outside a grate leading into the Blue Note, listening to the music of Dale Turner whom he has long idolized. If such echoing were the case, one could argue credibly for Tavernier's recall of the past in order precisely to undercut it, calling it into his film so as to make the past itself one of the subjects of the film. Tavernier plays with sentiment but never lets it take over, partly because—one could argue on the basis of this scene—he simultaneously plays with the history of films like the one he is making. Were this scene an echo, it would take in, at once, confession *and* provocation, setting multiple tonalities that Tavernier, one could argue, sets as a challenge to himself.

Given not only the visual links but Tavernier's passion for jazz as well as his steeping in the history of modern film, such a reading seems plausible. Yet we are given reason to hesitate before this uncanny echo. In an interview with Jean-Pierre Coursodon that dwells on *Round Midnight*, Tavernier speaks of his early research on the film and especially his meeting with Francis Paudras, whose relationship with Bud Powell similar to the one that the film's Francis had with Dale Turner. (This cinéma à clef opens doors to several lives, Powell, Lester Young, and Dexter Gordon himself; these at least.) Tavernier says of Francis: "he told me how, when he didn't have the money to get into the club, he would crouch on the sidewalk and listen to the music through an air vent" (Coursodon 20). Tavernier's scenes at the grate surely recall those events: the relations of Paudras and Powell are among the determining grounds of *Round Midnight,* as a title comment makes clear. But that does not entitle us to drop off the suggestion of an echo from Curtiz as an *additional,* different component, a different dimension of history. That the scenes also may echo the one in Curtiz's film (it is difficult to imagine that Tavernier did not see it) suggests that there may be signals, early in *Round Midnight,* about Tavernier's ironies and their handling of meta-discourse, the film commenting at once on lives and histories, the lives of the clef figures, the history of films about jazz.

The claim for multiple echoes, once made, seems irresistible. Still, the argument for a single source, the contention that the links are merely coincidence, is not as flat as it might appear, indeed quite the opposite. Given the unlikely chance that Tavernier missed Curtiz's film, that the scenes in the two films are independent of each other, each scene still suggests the same geography, a separate, closed-off world of makers and aficionados with elaborate roles for each. Francis, like the quasi-Oliver, gets invited inside the club by the awesome central figure, thereby gaining entry into a special world of music. Yet, as the film works out, Francis continues to live at a distance from the figure he idolizes despite their eventual sharing of an apartment. Still somehow outside the grate, he never enters the magic circle that we have woven around the makers, that the makers have, simultaneously, woven around themselves. Unlike Oliver in the transom, he is not framed by what absorbs him but stands apart from the grate whatever his passion for what it emits. Part of this has to do with the stance we heard about from Eldridge and Armstrong, the inviolable aloneness of the maker in the moments of making. Another part of it has to do with Coleridgean fear and reverence that keep us silently cooperating with the figure whom we watch as he helps us make the circle that keeps him visible and apart. Tavernier knows enough about the conditions of Dale's stance to know the conditions of Francis's, how they imply each other, implicate each other. That he knows how to handle his knowing—that, indeed, he knows of his knowing—goes far toward making this film the masterly artifact it is.

Round Midnight depends on no flying cymbals to get its points across, but on modalities of making that are nuanced, lyrical, ironic. Such making has nothing to do with what Tavernier, in the interview, calls three-act narratives (one way of putting the shape of the classic Hollywood film), but on scenes and echoes that call back and forth to each other, confirming each other while often undercutting each other. Sometimes, given what seems a Tavernierian hall of mirrors, they undercut the undercutting.

Take, for example, another exploration of what so fascinates Tavernier, the question of the stances around and in the magic circle. In one of the series of brief scenes that make up most of the film (each designed to get ripples going rather than further a firm narrative) Francis stares with gentle intensity at the clearly exhausted Dale and asks: "Are you tired?" Dale replies—slowly and with that eloquent spacing of pauses that makes Gordon's voice sound eerily like his saxophone—"I'm tired . . . of everything except the music." The film as a whole handles that point so candidly that Tavernier sometimes seems to worry about it being too plain. Probably thinking of such bluntness as not sufficiently lean, nuanced, and hesitant, Tavernier has Dale repeat the comment later in the film. Asked by a psychiatrist about his condition he says: "I'm tired of everything . . . except music," and goes on to tell the shrink, lost in awe at who is before him, about his dreams (always of music), the blood he sometimes finds on his mouthpiece, his occasional, chancy sex; precisely those subjects the psychiatrist wants to explore. Later, in a cab, Francis admits he was watching them. Dale, surprised, responds "How was I?" as though it were all just another performance; and so it might be taken except that it echoes word for word what he had said to Francis before, when his burnout was showing plainly. By speaking of his meeting with the psychiatrist as one more performance, Dale appears to undercut what he had said in the interview, cautioning Francis not to take it all too seriously, thereby protecting himself. Yet the echo of the earlier words, said frankly to Francis in an unprotected moment, no hint of irony, undercuts the undercutting, making it not so certain. The echo problematizes, ironizes, cautions us about his comments and yet, at the same time, urges us to take him at his word. Here and everywhere, Dale stays just out of reach, seemingly capturable but never completely so, a master expositor of the shifting tonalities that order Tavernier's film— tonalities that seem, at once, to cross over the magic circle and yet to end by proving that it is always inviolably there. Tavernier's reading of the experience of making jazz affects, effects, his reading of how his film should go.

That reading affects the film in its making of silences and spaces, part of that making probably fed from Gordon's vocal and musical phrasing. Gordon handles verbal cadences in a way remarkably analogous to his understated sax work, his pared-down lines and pregnant pauses, his penchant for constraint in a mode of making jazz noted for its dazzling runs, its packing of spaces with pyrotechnics that are as much of fingers as chords. Though Gordon's playing in the film lacks much of the flair and drive of his earlier work, when he was among the supreme bebop tenor players, its suggestions of a mode of being, its echoes in his work, in his speech, in his manner of self-handling, show a coherence of being-in-the-world that does much to make his performance as extraordinary as it is. Tavernier's handling of his film continues his work in *Un Dimanche à la Campagne* [*A Sunday in the Country*] (1984), which has much, thematic and modal, in common with *Round Midnight*. That handling coalesces with what Gordon brought to the film, his work confirming, extending, the modalities Tavernier brought.

Consider Tavernier's treatment of silence and empty spaces, their analogies brought out with nuanced but regular insistence throughout *Round Midnight*. One looks at but not through doors that are partly open, looks at them down the empty corridors of sleazy Paris hotels, the sounds of hidden instruments warming up behind those doors. Sometimes one hears in those scenes the sounds of a club session going on at another location, sometimes the sounds of Dale telling what it was like to have been himself. Sometimes one sees down narrow streets that echo the corridors in their emptiness, the sounds from hidden sources interspersed among the sights. In this film about the making of sounds there are silences and empty spaces that speak in subdued eloquence. They work in the speech of Gordon and the direction of Tavernier, working with and enhancing the sounds of music and musicmakers, working in a way that John Cage would understand, speaking of lives as well as the music made in those lives. Music is made in such silences, and the lives decline within them, as Dale's is doing in the film, perhaps as his prowess is doing. "I keep wondering whether I still have something to give": this amid his agreements with the remarks of those around him that he and several others have taught all the rest, that he is still the best. Being and playing fuse in the figure of Dale/Dexter, being and filming fuse in the modalities of *Round Midnight*. Remarkable for its economies, the film speaks, through those economies, an understanding of jazz that is nuanced, profound, convincing.

That understanding speaks in Tavernier's handling of the soundtrack, which ought to be a bugaboo in any film on jazz. Unlike other films of its kind, *Round Midnight* immerses itself in the music of which it speaks, presenting extensive selections and sometimes entire pieces—multiple choruses of "Body and Soul," for example, played while the camera shifts from figure to figure, solo to solo. The film explores the music as much as it explores Dale, and it shows how those explorings contain, create each other. It lays out what jazz musicians mean when they speak of telling a story, the narrative within the solo complementing, counterpointing, the narrative driving the film. The mode of this film's story comes closer in kind and quality to the mode of jazz solo-making than to the mode of the standard three-acter, the classic Hollywood film. That is one of the ways in which Tavernier undoes what would bind down Eastwood. That is one of his motives for presenting extensive solos and entire pieces, their storymaking helping to shape the mode of the film that contains them.

The fusion Tavernier seeks in working soundtrack and tale together appears in another part of the bugaboo, that relation of aura and history which dogs every system of recorded jazz. Tavernier's notes to the compact disc of the soundtrack lay out some of the issues:

> On my first meeting with Herbie [Hancock], we immediately agreed on certain principles. We wouldn't try to duplicate exactly the music of the fifties. "Otherwise," declared Herbie, "we might just as well use the Blue Note records." We wanted to avoid a rigid or scholarly approach to the musical style. . . . Filming the music live was a real challenge for the musicians. We never really knew where we were going and there could be enormous differences between two takes.

He explores the issues further in the interview with Coursodon:

> In the musical sequences, the camera work *had* to adapt to the music constantly because the music was improvised, and all of it was recorded directly while filming—which no one thought we could manage to do. We never knew in advance what the musicians were going to do, how many choruses they were going to take. A number that went on for four minutes in one take might go on for seven in the next. I was lucky to get a wonderful camera operator who is a musician himself and who patterned his camera moves after the harmonic structure of the compositions, so that he could smoothly track along a musician playing a solo and move past him just as he completed it. (23)

In one sense Tavernier wanted the purest authenticity: "I never seriously considered using anybody but an actual musician. It had to be someone who not only could play the part, but also had the appropriate musical style for the period" (Coursodon 20). The sounds, however, would have to be the ones recorded on film while music and film were being made; that is, no Blue Note records, no sounds of earlier solos. The sounds would be authentic in a Benjaminian sense because they were the sounds of someone who, by virtue of his continuing presence, confirms the purity of authenticity; and they would be authentic in still another sense because the music was made in front of a contemporary camera and what that camera recorded was the moment of the music's making (the making that, as Tavernier points out several times, was never the same before or after). Tavernier seeks to overcome what was to damage *Bird*, the fracturing in the relationship between sight and sound. He gets as close as one can to the moment of making, hearing *and* seeing it. Tavernier knew the issues as well as any maker of such films, knew what he could do to make those issues work.

But he also, finally, knew what he could never do, knew that the filming of a jazz solo is always as much about films, their requisite otherness, their built-in historicity, as about the solo itself. Taking a hint from the life of Francis Paudras, who had made home movies of Powell and other musicians, Tavernier has his Francis take movies of Dale and others playing. Those films make the viewers smile, but the films are always in black and white, their shadings strikingly grayed among the subdued, nuanced colors of the rest of *Round Midnight.* Thus does Tavernier describe the art he uses to describe another art. His own art is always distanced and other, always black and white in contrast to the saturated hues of the immediate making of jazz. In commenting on his own art, he comments on another, comments on the making of jazz, its relation to history and the moment, to the tonalities that surround the making, to our readings of that making as radically auratic. Complete in its acknowledgment of requisite incompletion, *Round Midnight* shows the story as fully as it can be shown.

Notes

1 David Antin's talk-poems are close in mode to jazz solos. They too perform in aleatory modes, taking off from the mood of the moment. They too are grounded in questions about aura and its relation to improvisation. Comparable points can be made about the Canadian group the Four Horsemen, whose improvised combination of language and music works out of analogous conditions.

2 Benjamin would obviously reject the suggestion that Rilke and Weston are modernists, given the meaning he attributes to modernism in the essay on mechanical reproduction. Not only does he equate modernism with the postauratic, but he begins the essay with an attack on "outmoded concepts, such as creativity and genius, eternal value and mystery" ("Mech Repro" 218), concepts which, of course, underlie Rilke and Weston. Yet the central creative presence, the passionate quest for aura, the uniqueness of the work as well as the moments of making and experiencing, however they appear as anathema to Benjamin, are as characteristic of modernism as anything else about it. The presence of those issues in figures like Rilke and Weston—or, say, Yeats and Steichen—establishes that point unmistakably. Benjamin focuses on a question that had been felt and worked over for at least a hundred years. His essay demonstrates how modernism is most accurately seen as radically ambivalent on these issues, an ambivalence that can

be shown within his own work as a whole. It also suggests that Benjamin's ideas were most fully realized in postmodernism.

3　Much the same questions can be asked of any photograph: what is the authentic photograph, given that there is no original photograph but only an original negative? If authenticity, in Benjamin's terms, has to do with the presence of the original, what does it mean when someone other than the maker of the negative makes an image from the negative? Further, the photograph, like the recording, "presents" that which is irrevocably Other, that which indeed becomes Other as soon as it can be represented. This leads, inevitably, to the question broached below about the relationship between jazz and representation, an issue that needs far more study and that will, like others broached, emphasize how jazz exemplifies modernist preoccupations.

4　On 3 March 1929, Paul Whiteman played a version of "Singin' the Blues" in which a four-saxophone chorus reproduced Trumbauer's original solo, no doubt with Trumbauer himself as part of that group (Sudhalter and Evans 377). (In Berendt's reading of authenticity that would make Trumbauer's playing authentic, but not the playing of the others.) Earlier, on 10 January 1929, Whiteman had recorded a version with a small group under the name of "Bee Palmer with the Frank Trumbauer Orchestra" (Sudhalter and Evans 462). It has "Trumbauer and two other reeds [playing] a scored version of his 1927 Okeh solo." In this rendering, Beiderbecke had a thirty-two-bar solo. The full orchestra played the final chorus, "spotlighting four trombones," with Beiderbecke "coming up over the ensemble to ride out the last eight bars." That recording was never issued, and the masters appear to have vanished. Though the Whiteman version may have influenced Henderson's rendering, it seems unlikely, given what we know of Whiteman's arrangers, that his version had any of the subtleties of Henderson's arrangement.

5　It helps a great deal to compare Nichols's appropriations with the postmodern versions of Sherrie Levine. Levine argues against the primacy of the central, self-constituting creator, with all the attendant issues of uniqueness and "ownership." Nichols, on the other hand, confirms just those qualities, his unshakable awe affirming the centrality of Beiderbecke's aura. Jazz's emphasis on the auratic is as intense and pervasive as the equivalent emphasis in figures as different as Rilke and Yeats.

6　As the OED puts it, virtue is "the power or operative influence inherent in a supernatural or divine being." Though that meaning is said to be archaic and obsolete, the cult of Bolden (and Armstrong and Beiderbecke and Parker and Coltrane) shows that its context is as present as ever. What Bolden has that the others do not is a fogginess of origin that is part of his grandeur. (Recall the shepherd in *The Prelude* who seems enlarged to gigantic size by the fog that surrounds him.) Secularized (though never completely so; it always enfolds a sacral residue) "virtue" comes to enclose "manly excellence, manliness, courage, valour." If one thinks of those capacities specifically in terms of "prowess," one brings back up what has never really left, the relation of our reading of jazz to our reading of Romance, a mode that never loses its ancient ties to myth. For more on cult and related issues, see the valuable study on jazz and myth by Neil Leonard.

7　I do not say that the pun is put forth by Ramsey and Smith, but that it is available in our reading of their text.

8　There is an implicit argument in jazz that what we know best (in fact, all we can really know) is found in immediacy. Suggestions of such an epistemology appear routinely throughout modernism, as early as proto-modernists like Henry Adams and as late as most late modernist performance art.

9   For another reading of the film as "Classic Hollywood," see Gabbard.

10 The ending of Lee's disappointing and muddled *Mo' Better Blues* comes right out of Capra, without a hint of irony. It is one of the purest examples available of the absorption of the auratic figure and his music into prevailing cultural values.

11 Cortázar's tale suggests still other Romance elements in the workings of jazz, particularly the quest. It is a version of the quest that ties profoundly into the acts of other auratic figures for whom the quest is all. Such figures inhabit the second part of Rilke's *Notebooks of Malte Laurids Brigge*, the saints and women lovers, the Prodigal Son, and, in hope if not in accomplishment, Malte himself. Cortázar touches, in this tale, at some of the deeper reaches of modernism, some of its profounder probings of myth and desire. Jazz, his tale suggests, does the same sort of probing.

Works Cited

Benjamin, Walter. "A Short History of Photography." *Classic Essays on Photography.* Ed. Alan Trachtenberg. Trans. P. Patton. New Haven, Conn.: Leete's Island Books, 1980. 199–216.

——. "The Work of Art in the Age of Mechanical Reproduction." *Illuminations.* Ed. Hannah Arendt. Trans. Harry Zohn. New York: Schocken, 1969. 217–51.

Berendt, Joachim. *The Jazz Book: From New Orleans to Rock and Free Jazz.* Trans. Dan Morgenstern and Helmut and Barbara Bredigkeit. New York: Lawrence Hill, 1975.

Collier, James Lincoln. *The Making of Jazz.* New York: Dell, 1978.

Cortázar, Julio. "The Pursuer." *Blow-Up and Other Stories.* Trans. Paul Blackburn. New York: Pantheon, 1985. 182–247.

Coursodon, Jean-Pierre. "Round Midnight: An Interview with Bertrand Tavernier." *Cinéaste* 15.2 (1986): 20–23.

Gabbard, Krin. "Wrong Man with a Horn." *University of Hartford Studies in Literature* 21 (1989): 13–24.

Gioia, Ted. *The Imperfect Art: Reflections on Jazz and Modern Culture.* New York: Oxford UP, 1988.

Hentoff, Nat. "Flight of Fancy." *American Film* 13 (Sept. 1988): 24–31.

Leonard, Neil. *Jazz: Myth and Religion.* New York: Oxford UP, 1987.

Ramsey, Frederic, Jr., and Charles Edward Smith, eds. *Jazzmen.* 1939. New York: Harcourt Brace Jovanovich, 1967.

Schuller, Gunther. *Early Jazz: Its Roots and Musical Development.* New York: Oxford UP, 1968.

Sudhalter, Richard M., and Philip R. Evans. *Bix: Man and Legend.* New York: Schirmer, 1974.

Signifyin(g) the Phallus: Mo' Better Blues
and Representations of the Jazz Trumpet

KRIN GABBARD

Virgil Thomson had compared the performances of famed jazz trumpeter, Louis Armstrong, to those of the great castrati *of the eighteenth century.—Theodor Adorno, "Perennial Fashion—Jazz"*

Adorno's appropriation of Virgil Thomson's comment on Armstrong is typical of Adorno's notorious and possibly uninformed attacks on jazz.[1] Although he argues both in "Perennial Fashion—Jazz" and in his earlier essay "On Jazz" that the music brings about the castration of the *listener,* Adorno supports this thesis by suggesting that one of the music's most prominent *producers* was in some way emasculated. Earlier in "Perennial Fashion—Jazz," Adorno had associated the jazz performer with "the eccentric clown" and "the early film comics" (129). If Adorno had Armstrong in mind in these remarks, he was probably aware that, like many African American performers, the trumpeter was frequently asked to play the epicene clown when he appeared in American movies. But Adorno ignores the patterns of racism in the culture industry that demanded the demasculization of black jazz performers. Other than castration, he admits no alternative—positive or negative—to an undefined masculinity just as he makes no attempt to distinguish the diverse forms of masculine expression among different races and social classes. Adorno also appears unaware of the many ways in which a performer like Armstrong found his way around Hollywood's constraints. Perhaps the most extreme example of the movie industry's attempts to emasculate Armstrong is the scene in *Going Places* (1938) in which he is made to sing a love song to a horse. But here as in so much of his self-presentation, Armstrong may have been subverting the racist program of the film by overplaying and Signifyin(g) on his presenters. "Signifying" has long been an African American term for the art of talking about, criticizing, ridiculing, and/or putting one over on the listener. Henry Louis Gates, Jr., has made this practice—which he writes as "Signifyin(g)" in order to distinguish it from the Standard English sense of the word—a central concept in his work on African American literature.[2]

An even more arresting instance of Armstrong's ability to overcome demeaning material is his performance in the short subject *Rhapsody in Black and Blue* (1932). Playing at the invitation of the "King of Jazz-mania" on a highly stylized set, Armstrong appears dressed in a leopard skin, up to his knees in soap bubbles. After mugging his way through a chorus of "Shine," Armstrong raises his trumpet, adopts an erect stance, and becomes a different figure, completely in charge of his horn and his sexual persona. When the film cuts to a medium shot of the docilely grinning Tubby Hall at the drums, the contrast is striking.[3]

Although most Americans now recall Armstrong as a smiling clown, he regularly used his trumpet to express phallic masculinity along with a great deal of the sexual innuendo that was already an essential element of jazz performance (see figure 1). When Hollywood's racial codes allowed, Armstrong was even given license to represent his sexuality in more conventional ways as, for example, when he performed erotically charged duets with the black actress Dorothy Dandridge in *Pillow to Post* (1945) and with Billie Holiday in *New Orleans* (1947). Adorno's association of Armstrong with castration has not been defended, even by Adorno's most tenacious advocates. While Miriam Hansen has brilliantly constructed a positive aesthetics of cinema out of Adorno's largely negative writings on film, no one is likely to tease a corresponding jazz aesthetic out of essays such as "Perennial Fashion—Jazz."[4]

Louis Armstrong was only the first of many African American jazz artists to attract international attention by establishing phallic authority with that most piercing of instruments, the trumpet. Dizzy Gillespie, a celebrated musical descendant of Armstrong who frequently spoke of the "virility" of black jazz, may have been Signifyin(g) on the phallic nature of his instrument when he bent the bell upward as if to simulate an erection (see figure 2). In the forty years since Gillespie bent his bell, however, a new generation of trumpet players has emerged who, while not abandoning the libidinal recesses of jazz, have moved away from the more explicitly virile possibilities of the instrument. Although these

Figure 1. Louis Armstrong in his prime.

younger musicians have in no way embraced castration, they seem much less interested in phallic display. Their stylistic orientations might be called "post-phallic."[5]

As writer and director of *Mo' Better Blues* (1990), Spike Lee has confronted this tradition, if only because he hired Terence Blanchard to dub in the trumpet solos for his protagonist, Bleek Gilliam (Denzel Washington). The choice is significant because Blanchard plays in a style with distinct post-phallic qualities. But as has long been the case, the codes of sexual signification developed through the history of jazz have been profoundly repressed within the traditions of classical cinema. *Mo' Better Blues*, Spike Lee's most personal film prior to *Crooklyn* (1994), falls back on a well-established pattern in Hollywood films that calls into question the masculinity of jazz trumpet players, even white ones. Adorno's thesis that jazz leads to some type of symbolic castration is validated by *Mo' Better Blues* as well as by several American films that preceded it, including *Young Man with a Horn* (1950), *The Five Pennies* (1959), and *New York, New York* (1977). Probably without intending to do so, Lee has brought Terence Blanchard's sound into his film, even though Blanchard's post-phallic trumpet undermines the film's reaffirmation of the

Figure 2. Dizzy Gillespie, his horn turned ever skyward.

traditional sexual roles that Hollywood has promoted throughout the century.

A term such as post-phallic may be even more problematic than words such as phallic, masculine, and castration, especially now that increasingly large numbers of critics have addressed the inevitable slippage of such terms. Among the many useful articles addressing "male trouble" in the journal *Camera Obscura*, I find Thomas DiPiero's "The Patriarch Is Not (Just) a Man" to be especially helpful in formulating a discourse of the phallus among jazz artists. DiPiero argues that possessing a phallus (in the sense of social and cultural empowerment) and being male are not necessarily the same thing:[6] phallic entitlement is just as dependent on "one's racial and class identity, along with one's sexual orientation, national identity, and a host of other qualities" (103). For DiPiero, masculinity is by no means monolithic and ought to be understood "as an unstable nexus of social and political phenomena, rather than as a mystified, consistent source of power and control" (118). Given the long history of violence and disempowerment endured by African Americans, there is no question that black masculinity constitutes an even more unstable nexus. With its complex history of Signifyin(g) and encoding, jazz offers abundant examples of how black artists have refused to abide by prescribed and proscribed notions of phallic masculinity. A striking but not exceptional example is Cecil Taylor, a gay jazz pianist who has for several decades played an unrelentingly aggressive, experimental music.

As Eric Lott has convincingly demonstrated in his work on blackface minstrelsy in the nineteenth century, white America's view of black masculinity has always been riddled with contradictions. As was often the case with Louis Armstrong, the black male was a figure of hyper-masculinity at the same time that he was considered pathetically un-manly (Lott; Frederickson). This must have been especially true for Armstrong in the 1920s and 1930s when the jazz trumpet was most flamboyantly representative of sexuality among African American musi-cians. As with many aspects of black culture, jazz provided its practi-tioners with wide latitude for expressing masculinity while avoiding the less mediated assertions of phallic power that were regularly punished by white culture. If it is true that no one ever possesses the phallus of the father—the first phallus that anyone desires—then all of us, male and female alike, are castrated.[7] The trumpet can then be conceptualized as a compensatory, even hysterical mechanism to ward off castration. By extension, as DiPiero has argued (118), *any* display of masculinity is essentially hysterical. The inescapably hysterical underpinnings of the jazz trumpet must be acknowledged even for a figure such as Armstrong, who deftly negotiated racial and sexual taboos by carefully coding his phallic display. One of my purposes here is to distinguish the joyous and subversive if compensatory phallicism of musicians such as Armstrong from the castration (as in loss of subjecthood) that Adorno in a blanket way attributes to jazz but *not* to "autonomous" art.

On the most obvious level, the phallicism of the jazz trumpet resides in pitch, speed of execution, and emotional intensity, all of which Arm-strong greatly expanded in the 1920s.[8] The many artists who followed Armstrong have found numerous ways of dealing with this dimension of the trumpet. By contrast, we may not choose to characterize the Euro-centric virtuoso who can play high and fast as necessarily phallic; what a symphony player might call bad technique—an extremely wide vibrato or a "smeared" note, for example—can become a forceful, even virtuosic device in the hands of a jazz trumpeter. Stage deportment and the musi-cian's clothing can also become part of a phallic style. Consider the pel-vic thrusts that Dizzy Gillespie performed during the 1940s and 1950s[9] or the "Prince of Darkness" mode in which Miles Davis clothed himself during his final two decades.

If African American artists have understood how to manipulate musi-cal codes of masculine sexuality,[10] they have also been aware on some level of the artificiality of phallic display. Although most jazzmen would probably not agree with DiPiero's thesis that masculinity "can only ever be hysterical" (118), they have been capable of Signifyin(g) on received notions of the masculine. One of the most common ways in which trumpeters have played on the phallic nature of their instrument is by adopting the role of self-effacing *eiron* where the strutting *alazon* is expected. Gillespie, for example, would fend off other trumpet players— especially young, ambitious ones—by underplaying; when preceded in a sequence of solos by a flashy young trumpeter, Gillespie would "cut" his opponent with short, piquant, often humorous phrases. Cat Anderson, who for many years played extraordinarily high notes in trumpet solos with the Duke Ellington orchestra (Ellington would tell audiences that Anderson's final stratospheric note was "a high C above Hyannis Port"), is Signifyin(g) on his own reputation as well as on his audience's expectations in a 1976 recording with a band led by Bill Berry. Anderson is about to solo on "Boy Meets Horn," a tune that Ellington and Rex Stewart wrote in the late 1930s to feature Stewart's playful, half-valve cornet style. Berry announces that Cat Anderson will perform "Boy Meets Horn" and then adds, "although in this case it's more like Superman." In his solo, however, Anderson stays almost exclusively within the middle register, frequently offering a precise imitation of Stewart's original reading of the tune.

A useful contrast to the Signifyin(g) black artist is the white jazz trumpeter Maynard Ferguson, who simply plays as high as possible in order to establish his power unself-consciously and without irony. This is not to say that whites or women cannot signify or play a role in the history of the jazz trumpet. On the one hand, many have internalized and transformed styles associated with African American males: the black female trumpeter Valaida Snow, who flourished in the 1930s and 1940s, recorded in a distinctly Armstrongian style, as did the white Harry James, who grew up playing in traveling circus bands directed by his father. In the 1920s white trumpeters like Bix Beiderbecke and Red Nichols, whose middle-class, midwestern backgrounds provided few of the conditions that prompted black artists to develop phallic styles, created distinct paradigms of their own.

Today a number of talented female trumpeters are regularly disrupting any attempt to mark the instrument as exclusively male. I would specifically cite the case of Rebecca Coupe Franks, a white woman who is fully in control of the phallic elements of the tradition at the same time that she is capable of substantial lyricism. Although not at all unserious,

Franks appears to enjoy herself as she addresses the history of the jazz trumpet, often quoting from canonical recordings and clearly Signifyin(g) on her predecessors as well as on her audience's gender expectations.[11]

Still, the dominant figures in the history of the jazz trumpet have been African Americans, especially those who used the trumpet to express masculinity at historical moments when other, comparable expressions were dangerous. What separates a "trumpet jock" like Maynard Ferguson from a figure such as Louis Armstrong is Armstrong's ability to do more than simply overwhelm the competition with pitch, volume, and speed. Like many African American entertainers of his generation, Armstrong made Signifyin(g) a regular feature of his performance persona, engaging in a great deal of ribaldry and self-deprecation. Part of Armstrong's success was surely related to his ability to play the sexual *and* the asexual jester in different registers and at different moments in a performance.[12] Although Armstrong did not give the impression that he was a sexual threat to all the women in his audience, he often kept a teasing edge on his ribaldry. Along with the poetry and pathos, there was a libidinal energy in Armstrong's solos that could create a kind of foreplay leading up to climaxes. Accordingly, members of his band are said to have referred to their accompanying figures on Armstrong's 1931 recording of "Star Dust" as "the fucking rhythm" (Radano).

Most of the important trumpeters who came of age in the 1930s and 1940s—Roy Eldridge, Buck Clayton, Frankie Newton, Hot Lips Page, Charlie Shavers, Dizzy Gillespie—were the aesthetic progeny of Armstrong, all of them adopting styles with phallic elements. In fact, almost all of Armstrong's disciples relished the opportunity to establish their authority, regularly taking on challengers in "cutting contests."[13] In the years after World War II, when jazz was about to establish itself permanently as an art music, Fats Navarro, Clifford Brown, and Miles Davis were each at one time or another in a position to become the most prominent inheritor of the Armstrong/Gillespie legacy. Navarro died the death of a drug addict in 1950 at the age of twenty-six, and in 1956 Clifford Brown was killed on the Pennsylvania Turnpike at age twenty-five. The field was effectively left open for Miles Davis, already well established since the mid-1940s and undoubtedly the most influential trumpeter since Armstrong. At the son of a dentist in East St. Louis, Illinois, Davis may also have been the first important black trumpeter from a comfortable, middle-class background. Many phallic elements persisted in Davis's playing, including spikes into the upper register, fast runs throughout the range of the instrument, and an often exaggerated feel for climaxes. He was also conspicuous in refusing to develop an ingratiating performance persona, often turning his back on audiences, ignoring their applause, and leaving the stage when other musicians were soloing.[14] Always attentive to sartorial elegance, Davis adopted a highly ornate style of dress at roughly the same time in the late 1960s that he electrified his band and embraced forms of music closer to the popular mainstream.[15] Although one of the platitudes of jazz history posits a decline in Miles Davis's playing after the late 1960s, many qualities that surrounded his playing enhanced the phallicism of his image. The heavily amplified volume of his final bands is only the most obvious example of this change.

In spite of Davis's desire to create an almost exaggerated masculine identity, as early as the 1940s he was using his trumpet to reveal emotional depth and introspection, even vulnerability. When Davis made a "mistake"—when his tone faltered or he seemed to miss a note—the cause was soulfulness and sensitivity rather than some shortcoming of technical prowess.[16] (Davis's ability to aestheticize the "clam," or missed note, should be considered alongside the Hollywood trope discussed below in which failure to hit the right note symbolizes a trumpet player's sexual impotence.) Without attempting to explain the complex development of Miles Davis's style over forty-five years,[17] I would point out that what came to be known as the "cool" aspects of his playing have influenced a great many players in a great many ways. Since the 1950s, many of the most critically acclaimed black trumpeters have been ironists (Clark Terry, Don Cherry, Lester Bowie, Olu Dara) and introverts (Art Farmer, Clarence Shaw, Booker Little, Ted Curson) rather than dominators and extroverts.[18] Art Farmer may be the best example of an artist working in a post-phallic style derived from emotional codes developed by Davis. While Davis was a man of slight stature who nevertheless posed provocatively in boxing gear for a notorious album cover,[19] Art Farmer is tall and large-boned. His lyricism, soft tone, hesitant delivery, and lack of stage mannerisms all represent a retreat from phallic bravado.[20] Farmer's style might be called post-phallic rather than nonphallic because, on the one hand, it in no way suggests that Farmer has accepted castration, lost his subjecthood, or refused the sexuality of the idiom; on the other hand, there is no obvious hysterical edge to Farmer's self-presentation that spills over into showy displays of technique or extramusical affectation.

In the last few years a post-phallic style has become the norm among a group of young musicians who have taken the fantastically successful Wynton Marsalis as their model.[21] Marsalis, Wallace Roney, Marlon Jordan, and Terence Blanchard all play in a frequently understated manner that conventionalizes—a more severe critic might say commodifies—Miles Davis's modal improvisations from the mid-1960s. Like many jazz musicians of recent decades, the younger musicians have transformed the withdrawn but elegant performance image of Davis's middle period into an affectless stage presence and a highly conservative dress code. Without renouncing the romance and sexuality that have always been fundamental to jazz, and without completely abandoning speed and high pitch, these trumpeters have substituted finesse and control for theatrics and ostentation.

The emergence of a post-Davis, post-phallic style in the 1980s is surely overdetermined. Recalling DiPiero's statement that maleness is manifested differently within different races and social classes (and at different historical moments), we might associate the rise of the post-phallic trumpet style with a group of African Americans who are more affluent, better-educated, and/or more class-conscious, and who thus feel less impelled to demonstrate their masculinity with the provocative gestures of ostensibly working-class musics such as rap and hip-hop. By avoiding the flamboyant displays of more popular and more visible forms, jazz artists have maintained the obligatory "otherness" of their music. At the same time, a large population of fans has nourished the music of Wynton Marsalis, Marcus Roberts, and their peers: it is an upscale music that bears marks of both the contemporary and the classical but favors smooth elegance over the rough-edged forms of more experimental and/or progressive jazz.[22] Revealingly, the New Old Jazz in the early 1990s began to grace television advertisements as a signifier of affluence and sophistication. For example, a Marsalis clone can be heard playing trumpet on the soundtrack of a commercial for the Infiniti, a luxury car. We might also consider the possibility that musicians like Marsalis and Blanchard are Signifyin(g) on old and/or lower-class notions of masculinity by backing away from phallic posturing.

At any rate, Marsalis is disproportionately more popular than someone like Jon Faddis, an exceptionally phallic trumpeter who *might* have been a better choice to dub in Bleek Gilliam's solos in *Mo' Better Blues*. In stature and carriage Faddis even resembles Denzel Washington, in stark contrast to the diminutive Blanchard. A protégé of Dizzy Gillespie, Faddis regularly appeared on the same venues with his master and evoked gestures of approval from Gillespie whenever the younger man negotiated particularly impressive improvisations.[23] Blanchard, on the other hand, could trace his parentage almost entirely to Miles Davis. Unlike Gillespie, Davis was a highly problematic father figure, who regarded with suspicion a generation of young players who took up a style that he had abandoned twenty-five years earlier.[24] If Harold Bloom's theories of the dynamics of influence among post-Enlightenment poets are applicable to jazz history, both Faddis and Blanchard might be considered weak poets, anxious about their influences. Playing with confidence and expansiveness as he rifles through the legacy of the strong poet Gillespie, Faddis's style might be understood in terms of Bloom's trope *apophrades:* the work of the precursor is completely absorbed by the ephebe, who identifies with the strong poet to the point of replacing him or re-creating him as if he never existed. By contrast, Blanchard's work suggests the ratio of *askesis* as he turns inward with a pared-down, resigned version of Davis's more sweeping vision. Blanchard sometimes appears unusually self-effacing in his recordings and appearances, especially in the years before Spike Lee began shooting *Mo' Better Blues.* In fact, according to Lee's companion volume for the film, Blanchard was not performing in public during the filming because he was in the process of developing a more effective embouchure (158). But Blanchard must not be written off because he has not reached Faddis's level of technical flash. In addition to complementing and perhaps enhancing our understanding of Signifyin(g) in jazz, Bloom's work offers the advantage of placing the two trumpeters within a system that is free of value judgments. In terms of how masculine codes are articulated in music, however, Blanchard may in fact be more interesting for pursuing the complicated legacy of Miles Davis. On *Black Pearl* (1988), the last recording he made before changing his embouchure, Blanchard provides one of the most convincing demonstrations of how the trumpet can be made to speak a compelling, romantic language devoid of phallic bravado.

Spike Lee probably did not come up with the original idea to hire Terence Blanchard as the trumpet voice of Bleek Gilliam in *Mo' Better Blues.* Blanchard more likely was recommended to Lee by saxophonist Branford Marsalis (Wynton's brother), who acted in Lee's 1988 film *School Daze,* contributed much of the music for *Mo' Better Blues,* and recorded the saxophone solos that are dubbed in for Shadow Henderson (Wesley Snipes). On one hand, Blanchard's restrained playing is appropriate to the obsessive artistic personality that Lee gave to Bleek Gilliam. On the other, Blanchard's decidedly post-phallic style is not what we might expect from a character who declares, "It's a dick thing," when asked to justify his need for two regular sex partners (figure 3). Bleek Gilliam is presented first as a musician too obsessed with his art to develop real feelings for either of his two women; at the end of the film, after he gives up the jazz life, he is "saved" by one and becomes a bourgeois patriarch. While it can be argued that the first role leads to

Figure 3. Joie Lee,
Denzel Washington, and
Cynda Williams in *Mo'*
Better Blues (1990).

nagging, castrating behavior by both women, and that the second involves the emasculating act of begging for salvation from one woman,
little in Bleek's character is consistent with the self-consciousness and
sexual complexity of Blanchard's playing.

In his interviews and in the companion volume to *Mo' Better Blues*
(39–40), Spike Lee has singled out *Round Midnight* (1986) and *Bird* (1988)
as films that do not accurately portray the lives of jazz artists. But these
are not the only films about jazz musicians, including jazz trumpet
players as in *Mo' Better Blues*. In fact, the phallic symbolism of the jazz
trumpet has not been lost on Hollywood filmmakers. For example, when
Robert Wagner in *All the Fine Young Cannibals* (1960) reencounters his
lover after a long absence, he thrusts the bell of his trumpet into the air
and executes a long glissando into a high note. Although Goldie Hawn
refuses Kurt Russell's advances for five months in *Swing Shift* (1984), she
takes him home to her bed the first night she hears him play the trumpet.
Christine Lahti, *Swing Shift*'s other heroine, also succumbs to Russell's
allure after her first experience of his music. In *I Dood It* (1943), an early
film directed by Vincente Minnelli, Lena Horne appears in a production
number that invokes the biblical story of Jericho. When a black jazz

trumpeter joins Horne on stage in the Jericho segment, the walls (hymen) come tumbling down after the musician reaches his highest note. The trumpeter then collapses as well, his body drained of tumescence after the musical climax.

In other films, however, the trumpet's obvious phallicism is connected with impotence or vulnerability to castration in much the same way as in *Mo' Better Blues*. A more general comparison here would cite a long history of narratives in which excessive masculinity is constantly undermined by performance anxiety as well as by the fear that sex with a woman will limit a man's strength in a variety of "manly" pursuits such as sporting events. In *Raging Bull* (1980), for example, Martin Scorsese (for whom Spike Lee has expressed admiration) drew attention to Jake LaMotta's conviction that sexual intercourse would hinder his success as a boxer. When this trope is translated into the plots of jazz films, the trumpet brings substantial fragility to an otherwise highly masculine male: in *Birth of the Blues* (1941), when Bing Crosby comes to blows with Brian Donlevy, Crosby is urged not to hit cornetist Donlevy in the lip. More revealingly, there is a common scene in which the trumpet player's inability to hit the right notes is a metaphor for his sexual or masculine inadequacy. There are examples of this situation in at least two films that preceded *Mo' Better Blues: Young Man with a Horn* and *The Five Pennies*.

As some reviewers of *Mo' Better Blues* observed, Rick Martin (Kirk Douglas), the eponymous hero of *Young Man with a Horn* (figure 4), bears a certain resemblance to Bleek Gilliam in that both trumpeters are obsessive artists torn between two women. In part because he has married the emasculating Amy North (Lauren Bacall) instead of the nurturing Jo Jordan (Doris Day), Rick cannot command the upper register at a recording session with singer Jordan. Stricken with panic, he begins a long decline that culminates when he collapses in the street, his castration made explicit as a car runs over his trumpet (Gabbard, "Wrong Man"). At this point, instead of dying—as in Dorothy Baker's novel on which the film is based—Rick is apparently nursed back to health by Jo Jordan, at whose recording session he is playing confidently as the film ends. As Rick once again ascends to the higher registers of his instrument, the film's narrator tells us that Rick learned "to be a success as a human being first and an artist second." In other words, Rick regains the phallus through normative monogamous sexuality rather than through art, not at all unlike Bleek Gilliam in Spike Lee's film.

In *The Five Pennies*, a film biography of Red Nichols, Nichols dubbed in the trumpet solos for Danny Kaye (figure 5). In the middle of the film,

Figure 4. Kirk Douglas and Doris Day in *Young Man with a Horn* (1950).

after the protagonist blames himself and the excesses of his career for his daughter's crippling attack of polio, he destroys his horn and takes a job as a common laborer. Years later, Nichols is provoked into playing when several teenagers, who have come to celebrate his daughter's birthday, express ignorance of his earlier achievements. One young man says, "My father told me all about you. . . . He said you were smart to get out of the business before the parade passed you by." Outraged at this slight and intent on proving that he is still musically potent, Nichols is conveniently handed a cornet by his wife, who sees an opportunity to bring him back to the music after many years. Although he plays a highly embellished version of "Indiana" for a few bars, Nichols stops in frustration when he fluffs a high note. All of his daughter's friends then leave the house in embarrassment, one of them explaining, "I have homework to do." Nichols's eventual comeback performance is marked not by renewed success as a musician but by the realization that the love of his family is what really matters. At the climactic moment in the final scene, Nichols is invited to dance by his daughter who has suddenly regained the near complete use of her legs. Again, love and family sustain the musician where jazz cannot.

I should also point out that Jackie Gleason's Ralph Kramden, one of the

Figure 5. Danny Kaye and Barbara Bel Geddes in *The Five Pennies* (1959).

most castrated males in the history of television, continually fails to hit the high notes on his old trumpet in an episode of the *Honeymooners*. Similarly, in the 1960s and 1970s comedian Jackie Vernon presented himself as a resigned loser, often bringing a battered cornet into his stand-up routine. Appropriately, Vernon's range was limited to the lower registers. There is, finally, the character of Ish Kabibble (Merwyn Bogue), a tall, solemn comedian with bangs who was regularly featured with Kay Kyser's popular dance band in the 1930s and 1940s. Kabibble has posed holding a damaged horn with the bell bent upward, slightly reminiscent of the trademark trumpet of Dizzy Gillespie. Here, however, the resemblance ends: rather than phallic power, the broken horn of Ish Kabibble jokingly symbolizes his lack of conventional manliness.[25] I would argue that the hypermasculine image of premodern black trumpeters is a structuring absence in the personae of all three white comedians.

Spike Lee resurrects the trope of the impotent trumpeter at the climax of *Mo' Better Blues* when Bleek Gilliam walks into the Dizzy Club where his old group is performing, now led by his musical and sexual rival Shadow Henderson. Bleek has just undergone a long recovery from a severe injury to his lip, and as is often the case in a narrative when the hero has been out of circulation for a while, important issues are about to be resolved. Earlier scenes in *Mo' Better Blues* suggested that these issues would involve the debate between Bleek and Shadow over what kind of music the band ought to be playing. In an initial scene, Bleek had accused Shadow of "ego-grandstanding" during a solo, as if the saxophonist were compromising his art to please the unsophisticated listeners in the house. Later, at a party, Shadow had called Bleek "a grandiose motherfucker" for playing his own personal brand of jazz and then complaining because audiences ignored the music. None of these issues, however, are directly addressed at the film's conclusion.

When Bleek walks into Dizzy's, the group is playing behind a vocal by Clarke Bentancourt (Cynda Williams), formerly one of Bleek's two lovers, now a bedmate of Shadow. Bleek had earlier declared Clarke to be unprepared to sing jazz, and in fact her singing recalls Joni Mitchell rather than canonical female jazz vocalists such as Billie Holiday, Sarah Vaughan, Betty Carter, or Abbey Lincoln, who appears in *Mo' Better Blues* in the nonsinging role of Bleek's mother. The audience in the club, however, appears to be enjoying her singing while Lee's camera glamorizes her with star close-ups. When Bleek joins his old group on the bandstand, the film might have shown the two horn players squaring off in a cutting contest, or Bleek might have rallied his old sidemen to play a more complex or more soulful form of jazz after the bland, bleached performance by Clarke. When he takes his solo chorus, however, Bleek finds himself unable to maintain command over his trumpet and suffers the same humiliation as the protagonists in *Young Man with a Horn* and *The Five Pennies*. In all three films (as well as in *I Dood It*), the analogies with sexual performance are reinforced by placing the narratives' key women in close proximity to the infirm trumpeters.

In disgrace, Bleek walks out of the club and hands his trumpet to Giant, his incompetent manager played by Spike Lee. In a striking scene that exhibits what Michael Wood has called the "perfectly overblown" qualities of Classical Hollywood, Giant walks after Bleek in a heavy rainstorm. As the camera raises to shoot down from a great height and as the diegetic music from the club becomes empathically extradiegetic, the Chaplinesque Giant holds up the trumpet and shouts, "I won't sell it, Bleek, I won't sell it." Bleek then appears at the apartment of his other girlfriend, Indigo (Joie Lee). After he asks her to save his life, a montage shows them married and raising a son while the John Coltrane quartet's recording of the "Acknowledgement" section of *A Love Supreme* plays on the soundtrack.

The presence of Coltrane's music is one of the film's several problematic appropriations of jazz. Recorded in 1964 to celebrate his discovery of

God, saxophonist Coltrane presented *A Love Supreme* as a single suite, a unique addition to his discography at that moment. Lee says that his film was originally titled *A Love Supreme* but that Coltrane's widow refused him permission unless he excised absolutely all foul language from the film, a compromise Lee was unwilling to make (Holley 54). Coltrane purists might object that the film relegates the saxophonist's expression of his religious conversion to the background of a largely secular account of marriage and family and that Coltrane's music accompanies the hero's renunciation of jazz, even though it is in the language of this tradition that Coltrane chose to communicate his most profound convictions. There is also a certain incoherence in the film's suggestion that Shadow has succeeded as a musician (and as the lover of Clarke) by embracing a compromised form of jazz scorned by Bleek; in fact, the Marsalis/Blanchard style of jazz trumpet has proven to be quite successful with real-life audiences, and the film shows Bleek to be a crowd-pleasing entertainer with a substantial following.

According to the published script for *Mo' Better Blues*, Bleek becomes a music teacher sometime after the incident at the Dizzy Club (283), but we are not told what kinds of music or what approaches he teaches, and the film itself provides no information at all about Bleek's new career in its last scenes. What we do know is that Bleek, like the hero of *Young Man with a Horn*, has chosen the less sexual of his two women, given up his obsessive artistic aspirations, and become a better person. Bleek Gilliam is still another of Hollywood's jazz artists who runs the risk of castration—on several levels—so long as he remains devoted to his music. Early on, he makes a great fuss when Clarke bites his lip in their love play and actually draws blood. This hint of castration is a foreshadowing of the climactic scene in which Bleek's mouth *and* trumpet are brutally maimed when he tries to save his manager from two toughs hired to punish Giant for falling behind in his gambling debts. In spite of his public statements that *Mo' Better Blues* would correct the myth of the doomed jazz artist presented in *Bird* and *Round Midnight*, Spike Lee has made another film about a self-destructive jazz musician. The hero is not a drug addict or an alcoholic, but he can only be saved by abandoning jazz. Once he renounces the music, the film suggests, his masculinity is restored as he ascends to the role of strong father.

The final scene of *Mo' Better Blues*, designed to parallel closely the opening moments of the film, reveals much about Lee's attitudes toward jazz and masculinity. Both scenes are shot in the same Brooklyn brownstone, and the same actor plays both the young Bleek and Miles, the son of Bleek and Indigo. When young Bleek is urged by his peers to join them

in a game of baseball in the opening scene, the boy's mother forbids it,
insisting that he stay in and practice the trumpet. Bleek's father is unable
to prevent the mother from denying the boy his time with his friends.
The film then cuts from a shot of young Bleek practicing to the mature
Bleek performing in a club. From the outset, *Mo' Better Blues* has linked
the life of the jazz artist to matriarchy and the denial of normally sanctioned masculine behavior. The final scene precisely duplicates dialogue
and camera setups of the opening scene, but it ultimately shows the
young trumpeter being allowed to put down his horn and play with
his friends. Unlike his father, Bleek successfully intervenes when the
mother insists that the boy continue his practice session. Although
the son is named Miles, and although Bleek is seen teaching him to play
the trumpet, the ending suggests that the boy will not be forced into
the jazz life with its attendant hazards.

The idealization of baseball in *Mo' Better Blues* has been noted by
Viveca Gretton, who has published a perceptive article on the 1980s
renaissance of baseball films. As in *Bull Durham* (1988), *The Slugger's
Wife* (1985), *Long Gone* (1987), *Eight Men Out* (1988), *Stealing Home*
(1988), *Major League* (1989), *The Natural* (1984), and especially *Field of
Dreams* (1989), *Mo' Better Blues* uses baseball as a vehicle for the rees-
tablishment of patriarchy.[26] Hollywood has found in baseball—especially
the baseball of a premodern era—a domain in which an old-fashioned
paradigm of phallic masculinity can be presented as natural and uncom-
plicated. *Field of Dreams* in particular identifies this beleaguered form of
masculinity as not merely benign but actually as the key to reforging ties
with the problematic fathers whose values were rejected in the 1960s. As
Gretton points out, however, the guilty nostalgia of the new baseball
films represses a number of ugly subtexts. For our purposes, the most
glaring is the racism of premodern major league baseball that excluded
African Americans until 1947.

In *Mo' Better Blues*, Lee largely ignores the racist aspects of baseball
history that correspond closely to the exploitation of black jazz artists
portrayed in the film. Houston A. Baker, Jr., has applied a Fanonian
reading to Spike Lee's *Do the Right Thing* (1989) in which Sal, the owner
of the pizzeria, can be understood as a typical white colonizer: "These are
my people. They grew up on my pizza. I love these people, especially the
attractive young females." Similarly, in *Mo' Better Blues*, the Flatbush
brothers have colonized black jazzmen while presenting themselves as
honest businessmen doing their job. In a gesture of friendship, they offer
their cousin to Bleek as a new manager at the same time that they refuse
to give him a larger portion of the receipts from his performances. The

jazzman is condemned to the degraded life of an alienated laborer, his subjecthood at risk. But the film forgets the exploitation of black athletes that has long been central to the institution of baseball. Significantly, the protagonists in Lee's films wear jerseys associated with Jackie Robinson and Willie Mays; as in *Field of Dreams*, earlier baseball suggests a maleness that is unapologetic and unambiguous rather than contested. It is to a ball game, not to music, that Bleek sends his own son at the end of the film, just as Bleek had earlier bonded with his own father as they played pitch and catch.

There are a number of possible reasons why Lee would make a film that portrays sports and patriarchal family life as healthy alternatives to jazz. On one level, *Mo' Better Blues* marks the inevitable movement of an independent filmmaker toward familiar models of sexuality and cultural behavior as his budgets and audiences expand: the concluding montage, with its earnest portraits of masculinity and femininity based in childrearing marriage, would have been unthinkable in Lee's earlier films. With *Mo' Better Blues*, Lee also may have been extending the role of spokesperson bestowed on him by the media after his extremely effective commercials for Jesse Jackson's presidential campaign appeared on television in 1988 and even more so after *Do the Right Thing* became linked to contemporary events in New York City during the summer of 1989. Lee has accepted this advocate's role by appearing frequently on news and talk shows and consenting to regular interviews. He may still be the only black filmmaker to make this transition: it is difficult to imagine Mario van Peebles, Charles Burnett, or Prince (the auteur of two films in his own right) discussing race relations with Ted Koppel on *Nightline*. Certainly because of this public image, Lee was widely criticized for making films that were not sufficiently "realistic" by people with widely different takes on reality. This kind of criticism may have impelled Lee to end *Mo' Better Blues* with the portrait of a black family led by a strong father.[27] In *Do the Right Thing*, by contrast, Lee himself had played a father who neglected his son and the boy's mother. A similar trajectory toward "positive images" characterizes the progress of Lee's character Mars Blackmon, the streetwise trickster figure who first appeared in Lee's *She's Gotta Have It* (1986). After playing Mars in his witty television commercials for Nike shoes with basketball star Michael Jordan, Lee eventually made a public service message in which Mars and Jordan urge young people to stay in school.

In addition, Lee appears to harbor an ambivalence toward jazz that may be related to feelings about his father's career as a jazz artist. In the companion volume to *Mo' Better Blues*, the filmmaker has said that his father, Bill Lee, an established jazz bassist, refused to play the electric bass during the 1960s and was thus unable to find regular employment (163). Consequently, Spike Lee's mother went to work as a school-teacher, the same profession practiced by Indigo, the character played by Spike's sister (Joie Lee) who "saves" Bleek Gilliam. Spike Lee has also written that his mother was "the heavy" in the house while his father was a passive figure (43), the same constellation we see in young Bleek Gilliam's family. As Sharon Willis has written, "Giant happens to have Spike's face, but the film seems to want to say that the real 'Spike Lee' figure is Bleek" (250). Although the son has hired his father to provide jazz scores for all of his films prior to *Jungle Fever* (1991), the younger Lee apparently remains conflicted about the music and about his father's unwillingness to compromise by playing something other than jazz.[28] Accordingly, one can choose to portray Bill Lee as a principled artist refusing to sell out or as a stubborn man clinging to an anachronism in spite of his family's needs. Spike Lee's account of his family must be regarded as one more text to be interpreted rather than as the real-life situation that explains the film. In this context, *Mo' Better Blues* can be understood as Spike Lee's attempt to rewrite his own story: jazz may have a place in this revised version, but not if it interferes with family harmony. Significantly, Bleek Gilliam's sympathetic if passive father is a former professional baseball player rather than a jazz artist. Furthermore, there is no real jazz community in *Mo' Better Blues* outside of Bleek and his sidemen, and Bleek never interacts with a "strong poet" and/or trumpet mentor. Thus Bleek can give up jazz without disturbing some larger tradition that is inseparable from his performance career.

If Spike Lee is more comfortable with codes of masculinity connected with baseball than with jazz, he has also gravitated toward the highly representable codes of masculinity established for rap music. The most memorable performance scene in *Mo' Better Blues* takes place when Bleek turns around his baseball cap and sings "Pop Top 40 R 'n' B Urban Contemporary Easy Listening Funk Love" while adopting the body language of a rapper rather than a jazz artist, a strong contrast to the post-phallic stance he adopts while playing the trumpet elsewhere in the film. It is extremely difficult to imagine Wynton Marsalis or Terence Blanchard crossing class boundaries to abandon their affectless stage poses for more than a moment. The film ends, revealingly, with the rap group Gangstarr singing "Jazz Thing" while the credits role. Lee's own view of jazz is probably summarized in Gangstarr's lyrics that position jazz as the revered but obsolete forerunner of more contemporary—and more provocative—forms of African American expression. Baseball is supremely representable; its codes have been thoroughly conventionalized in several decades of films and in the heroic close-ups we know so well from watching the game on television. Similarly, rap has quickly developed a highly conventionalized mode of performed masculinity that has become a regular feature of music videos, some of which have been directed by Lee himself.

Lee's affinity for rap and sports must be understood in the context of the choices he faces as a filmmaker. Unlike baseball and rap, jazz operates with a set of codes that are extremely difficult to represent, especially those forms that work against familiar models of masculinity; the Hollywood convention that "missed" notes can only symbolize a trumpeter's impotence provides a strong case in point. David James has identified the qualities that prevent the representation of a cultural development when it cannot be commodified in several intertextual, complementary depictions. James cites Madonna, Ronald Reagan, and the Olympics as easily represented phenomena that can be recognized in television, magazines, posters, and any number of other media and discourses. By contrast, "any social program that is not reducible to the priorities of this totalized machine is effectively unrepresentable" (79). James lists "the British miners' strike, AIDS, systemic judicial racism in the United States," and the U.S. defeat in Vietnam (79) as phenomena that cannot be assimilated within the mythologies of contemporary culture industries. Certainly all avant-garde forms of art belong in this list, with the post-phallic codes of jazz a legitimate if less conspicuous example.

Spike Lee was acting within prescribed cultural/cinematic practice when he equated the jazz life with self-destructiveness (the attack on Bleek's mouth is the most gripping moment in the film) and then indicated his hero's redeemed masculinity through the perennially effective spectacles of a wedding and the birth of a child. Speculating about the life that Bleek accepts after his embouchure has been damaged by the two toughs, Lee has written, "Out of the devastation that comes from not being able to play professionally, Bleek finds himself. And he finds that he can love and be loved. I really don't think Bleek could have been a happily married family man if it weren't for the accident" (68). An alternative ending to *Mo' Better Blues* in which Bleek can love and be loved *and* play jazz would have required a radical if not impossible revision of mainstream American cinema.

Several films provide relevant comparisons to this theme that the jazz life is incompatible with sustained romantic love. *Young Man with a Horn*, in which the protagonist becomes "a human being first and an artist second," is the clearest example. Although not unsympathetic to the music, *Paris Blues* (1961) ends with its protagonist—an American jazz artist (Paul Newman) living in Paris—confirming his commitment to jazz by sending his lover (Joanne Woodward) back home to the States. In *Swing Shift*, Kurt Russell leaves behind both of his lovers to go on the road with a group of black jazz musicians. Martin Scorsese, who may be Spike Lee's strong poet, contributed to this tradition in *New York, New York* (1977) by attributing the central couple's breakup at least in part to the uncompromising desire of Robert DeNiro to play modern jazz rather than the more commercial forms that emerged after the big-band era.

As I suggested, the post-phallic trumpet of Terence Blanchard is and is not a logical choice for the sounds that appear to emanate from the horn of Bleek Gilliam in *Mo' Better Blues*. On the one hand, the confidence and swagger of a Jon Faddis would have been inconsistent with the protagonist's decision to give up his craft after one humiliation. (In fact, as John Gennari has observed, no experienced jazz artist would have ventured into a club in the first place if he had any doubt about the condition of his embouchure [517]). On the other hand, the complex re-thinkings of phallic masculinity implicit in Blanchard's music are inconsistent with the conclusion of the film: its idealization of sports and normative gender roles represses the vulnerability, sensuality, and introspection of Blanchard's trumpet solos. Lee celebrates the same modes of masculinity on which Blanchard may in fact be Signifyin(g).

Adorno's thesis that the audience for jazz is told, "give up your masculinity, let yourself be castrated," is especially relevant to the issues raised by the history of the jazz trumpet in general and by *Mo' Better Blues* in particular. In "Perennial Fashion—Jazz," Adorno creates a scenario that recalls the opening and closing scenes of Lee's film:

> A child who prefers to listen to serious music or practice the piano rather than watch a baseball game or television will have to suffer as a "sissy" in his class or in the other groups to which he belongs and which embody far more authority than parents or teacher. The expressive impulse is exposed to the same threat of castration that is symbolized and mechanically and ritually subdued in jazz. (131)

Like Adorno's theorized child, the young Bleek is condemned by his peers for accepting a practice session with his trumpet rather than a game of baseball. But Lee and Adorno submit their similar scenarios to sharply different interpretations. For Lee, the child can resist castration by moving toward baseball; for Adorno, sports and jazz are virtually identical in their regressive character.[29] The two interpretations intersect only in the association of castration with the child's move toward jazz.

Although he was critical of Freud's bourgeois privileging of normative genital sexuality (Huyssen 27), Adorno reveals a familiar bias, associating good, autonomous art with manliness and consumer art with femininity.[30] Most importantly, Adorno has confused jazz with the truly industrialized music of popular culture.[31] Even when he was writing his essays on the music, there were a great many jazz artists whose work could pass muster according to his definition of autonomous art. In the late 1950s and 1960s, musicians such as Cecil Taylor, Ornette Coleman, John Coltrane, and Charles Mingus were producing musics that fit many of the categories of "protest," "inaudibility," and "nonsubsumability" that Adorno in his *Philosophy of Modern Music* created to license the music of Arnold Schoenberg. Even earlier, jazz musicians had developed expressive modes that strongly undermined Adorno's dichotomy of masculine autonomous art and castrated jazz. Ironically, Hollywood—which Adorno held in contempt—has been as reluctant as Adorno to look past the uncritical association of jazz with castration.

Notes

I thank Steven Elworth, Louise O. Vasvari, Ronald M. Radano, Maureen Turim, Lewis Porter, Frederick Garber, Kevin Whitehead, Christopher Harlos, Peter Lehman, Ilsa J. Bick, Rob Walser, John L. Fell, Ingrid Monson, and Eric Smoodin for their comments on early drafts of this essay.

1 According to Ulrich Schönherr, Adorno wrote his jazz criticism "in almost complete ignorance of the subject" (87).

2 For the application of Gates's Signifyin(g) aesthetic to jazz, see Tomlinson; Gabbard, "The Quoter and His Culture."

3 The relevant portion of *Rhapsody in Black and Blue* appears in the documentary *Satchmo* (1989) that also includes footage of Armstrong singing "Jeepers Creepers" to a horse in *Going Places*. As one reader of this essay observed, Harpo Marx provides another revealing comparison to Armstrong: both are liminal figures who change drastically when they turn to their respective musical instruments. Unlike Armstrong, however, Harpo Marx changes from a skirt-chasing satyr into serious musician with no sexual persona. Appropriately, in some of the Marx Brothers' post-Paramount films of 1933 and after, Harpo plays the harp surrounded by children.

4 But see Gendron for a practical application of Adorno's work to popular musics along with a critique of its limitations.

5 I thank Steven Elworth for coining the term "post-phallic."

6 The penis as physical organ is distinguished from the more symbolic phallus in several discourses. For the extraordinarily influential work of Jacques Lacan on

the phallus as the signifier par excellence, see Silverman, *The Subject of Semiotics*. Daniel Rancour-Laferriere draws on sociobiology and semiotics as well as psychoanalysis to make a more interdisciplinary but complementary argument in "Some Semiotic Aspects of the Human Penis."

7   See Silverman, "Masochism and Male Subjectivity." DiPiero makes the important distinction between castration as "bodily mutilation restricted to males" and the "psychic alienation all subjects undergo upon access to the symbolic order," pointing out that a great deal of psychoanalytic writing has conflated the two (113).

8   Of course, the combination of blowing and fingering associated with tubular instruments has been sexualized at least since the Renaissance. See, for example, the entries for "pipe," "bugle" and "horn" in Partridge's *Shakespeare's Bawdy*.

9   For a revealing record of Gillespie's performance persona, see the videocassette *Jivin' in Be-Bop*.

10   For a sophisticated analysis of gender codings in Western music, see McClary.

11   Future recordings by Franks promise to reveal even more of her Signifyin(g) abilities.

12   Armstrong's career is treated extensively and unromantically by Collier. Giddins's *Satchmo* is an idealized but thoughtful view of Armstrong's role in American culture and in some ways a response to Collier. For an enlightening account of how Armstrong was able subversively to "orchestrate" his own story in spite of the censors and editors of his three autobiographical texts, see Kenney.

13   This kind of competition is captured in the 1958 battle between Buck Clayton and Charlie Shavers through a series of chase choruses on "This Can't Be Love," anthologized on the videocassette *Trumpet Kings*.

14   Davis clearly associated an ingratiating stage persona with Uncle Tomism. In his autobiography, he places a photograph of Louis Armstrong on the same page among pictures of Beulah, Buckwheat, and Rochester. The caption reads, "Some of the images of black people that I would fight against throughout my career. I loved Satchmo, but I couldn't stand all that grinning he did."

15   Davis poses with his wardrobe in a photograph included in *Miles: The Autobiography*, plate 88.

16   Hear Davis's famous fluff on "My Funny Valentine." By not editing this portion of the performance, the producers at Columbia Records were promoting the image of Davis as the profound but fragile genius. I would also cite this recording as an excellent example of how Davis alternated strongly phallic elements of his playing with moments of post-phallic vulnerability. For a brilliant and extensive analysis of Davis's "My Funny Valentine," see Walser.

17   For a concise account, see Giddins, "Miles's Wiles."

18   Of course, Ray Nance, Sonny Berman, and Rex Stewart all played in "ironic" styles in the 1930s and 1940s. This is also not to suggest that aggressive trumpeters, black and white, ceased to exist after the 1950s. Lee Morgan, a virtuoso player who was strongly influenced by Gillespie and Clifford Brown, died in 1972. Freddie Hubbard, another technically proficient, sometimes flamboyant horn player, is still active, as are young phallic trumpeters such as Jon Faddis, Brian Lynch, Philip Harper, and Roy Hargrove.

19   The picture is on the cover of Miles Davis, *Tune Up*. Released in 1977, this album collects Davis's Prestige recordings from 1953 and 1954.

20 A video record of a 1982 Farmer performance is included in the "Jazz at the Smithsonian" series.

21 When he appeared on the cover of *Time* (22 Oct. 1990), Marsalis was declared by the magazine to be a "full-fledged superstar." The cover article placed his gross income in the seven-figure range (71). Marsalis's ability to reach a large audience of serious and casual jazz fans surely owes a great deal to the considerable cachet he has gained by regular performances of both jazz *and* classical music. I should also point out that Marsalis moved away from the Miles Davis legacy around 1990 and began exploring other modes, such as the growling, blues-based style of Cootie Williams.

22 It could even be argued that the tenor saxophone replaced the trumpet as the most phallic jazz instrument sometime in the 1950s. While Miles Davis was turning inward, John Coltrane was aggressively opening up new modes of expression on the tenor. Today, the most phallic and most adventurous hornmen may be tenor saxophonists Sonny Rollins, David Murray, and until his untimely death, George Adams. For Rollins, see *Saxophone Colossus*; for Murray, see *David Murray Quartet Live at the Village Vanguard*; Adams appears in *Charles Mingus's Epitaph*.

23 The relationship between Gillespie and Faddis was clearly evident at the Wolf Trap performance. For an example of Faddis's self-assured Signifyin(g) on the music of earlier trumpet masters, hear his album *Legacy*.

24 In 1988, when Davis was asked to talk about *Miles Smiles*, his 1966 LP that epitomizes the style imitated by players such as Marsalis, Blanchard, and Wallace Roney, Davis responded, "I can't remember it" (Ephland 18). Davis had an especially confrontational relationship with Wynton Marsalis. After criticizing one another in the press for several months, Marsalis walked on stage one night in 1986 in hopes of playing with Davis when both musicians were in Vancouver at a jazz festival. Miles wrote in his autobiography that he told Marsalis, "Man, get the fuck off the stage" and then stopped his band until Marsalis left. See *Miles: The Autobiography*, 374. Marsalis has responded to these remarks in Helland, 16. To my knowledge, Davis never appeared on the same stage with Terence Blanchard, but at the Montreux Jazz and Blues Festival of July 1991—just two months before he died—Davis participated in a highly unusual revival of his early work with Gil Evans and traded solos with Wallace Roney.

25 Performing with a conventionally shaped trumpet, Ish Kabibble appears with Kay Kyser in the nine films that featured Kyser's band from 1939 until 1944. For the comedian's own story, see Bogue and Reilly.

26 In *A League of Their Own* (1992), even female teams function according to the well-established paradigm of Hollywood's baseball films; at its conclusion, the film powerfully reinscribes mainstream sex and gender roles after superficially interrogating them throughout.

27 When asked by Henry Louis Gates, Jr., why he put a "fairy-tale ending" on *Mo' Better Blues*, Spike Lee responded, "I don't know why it's unrealistic for a couple, a black couple, to be happily married and have a child at the end of a movie. We suppose to end up broke and OD-ing in some little funky hotel in the lower east side?" (197).

28 Lee may also have been working through ambivalence about his father's life in *Jungle Fever*, which addresses the romance between a black man and a white

woman. Bill Lee married a white woman after the death of Spike's mother, and Spike has candidly told interviewers that he does not get along well with his stepmother. See Richolson's interview. In the overtly autobiographical *Crooklyn* (1994), the director offers a more detailed portrait of his father as a failed artist whose solo concert is attended only by a small group of friends and family. Most significantly, the child in the film who represents the young Spike deeply resents being forced to attend his father's concert on a night when he would have preferred to be watching the Knicks compete for the NBA championship.

29 Adorno makes this connection explicitly in "On the Fetish-Character in Music and the Regression of Listening": "These smart chaps can be found everywhere and are able to do everything themselves: the advanced student who in every gathering is ready to play jazz with machinelike precision for dancing and entertainment; the gas station attendant who hums his syncopation ingenuously while filling up the tank; the listening expert who can identify every band and immerse himself in the history of jazz as if it were Holy Writ. He is nearest to the sportsman: if not to the football player himself, then to the swaggering fellow who dominates the stands" (291).

30 Modleski is sensitive to the positive association of men with production and the negative associations of women with consumption in "Femininity as Mas(s)querade: A Feminist Approach to Mass Culture."

31 "Likewise, when Adorno remarks that 'the extent to which jazz has anything at all to do with genuine black music is highly questionable,' he is referring to the popular, commercially produced hits that were accessible to any European civil servant on the radio, and not to what now would be recognized as authentically *black* jazz, a jazz of which few white Europeans in the 1930s would have been aware" (Daniel 41).

Works Cited

Adorno, Theodor. "On Jazz." Trans. Jamie Owen Daniel. *Discourse* 12.1 (Fall–Winter 1989–90): 45–69.

——. "On the Fetish-Character in Music and the Regression of Listening." *The Essential Frankfurt School Reader.* Ed. Andrew Arato and Eike Gebhardt. New York: Urizen, 1978.

——. "Perennial Fashion—Jazz." *Prisms.* Trans. Samuel and Shierry Weber. Cambridge, Mass.: MIT P, 1981.

——. *Philosophy of Modern Music.* Trans. Anne G. Mitchell and Wesley V. Blomster. New York: Seabury, 1973.

Baker, Houston A., Jr. "Spike Lee and Popular Culture." Paper delivered at the Humanities Institute, State University of New York at Stony Brook. Apr. 1991.

Bloom, Harold. *The Anxiety of Influence.* New York: Oxford UP, 1973.

Bogue, Merwyn, with Gladys Bogue Reilly. *Ish Kabibble: The Autobiography of Merwyn Bogue.* Baton Rouge: Louisiana State UP, 1989.

Collier, James Lincoln. *Louis Armstrong: An American Genius.* New York: Oxford UP, 1983.

Daniel, Jamie Owen. "Introduction to Adorno's 'On Jazz.'" *Discourse* 12.1 (Fall–Winter 1989–90): 39–44.

Davis, Miles, with Quincy Troupe. *Miles: The Autobiography.* New York: Simon, 1989.

DiPiero, Thomas. "The Patriarch Is Not (Just) a Man." *Camera Obscura* 25–26 (Jan.–May 1991): 101–24.

Ephland, John. "Miles: The Interview." *Down Beat* Dec. 1988: 18.

Fredrickson, George M. "The Negro As Beast." *The Black Image in the White Mind.* New York: Harper, 1971. 256–82.

Gabbard, Krin. "The Quoter and His Culture." *Jazz in Mind: Essays on the History and Meanings of Jazz.* Ed. Reginald T. Buckner and Steven Weiland. Detroit: Wayne State UP, 1991. 92–111.

——. "Wrong Man with a Horn." *University of Hartford Studies in Literature* 21.3 (1989): 13–24.

Gates, Henry Louis, Jr. "Final Cut: Spike Lee and Henry Louis Gates, Jr., Rap on Race, Politics, and Black Cinema." *Transaction* 52 (1991): 176–204.

——. *The Signifying Monkey: A Theory of Afro-American Literary Criticism.* New York: Oxford UP, 1988.

Gendron, Bernard. "Theodor Adorno Meets the Cadillacs." *Studies in Entertainment: Critical Approaches to Mass Culture.* Ed. Tania Modleski. Bloomington: Indiana UP, 1986. 18–38.

Gennari, John. "Jazz Criticism: Its Development and Ideologies." *Black American Literature Forum* 25.3 (1991): 449–523.

Giddins, Gary. "Miles's Wiles." *Rhythm-a-ning: Jazz Tradition and Innovation in the '80s.* New York: Oxford UP, 1985. 78–85.

——. *Satchmo.* New York: Doubleday, 1988.

Gretton, Viveca. "You Could Look It Up: Notes Towards a Reading of Baseball, History, and Ideology in the Dominant Cinema." *CineAction* 21–22 (Summer–Fall 1990): 70–75.

Hansen, Miriam. "Introduction to Adorno, 'Transparencies on Film' (1966)." *New German Critique* 24–25 (Fall–Winter 1981–82): 186–98.

Helland, Dave. "Wynton: Prophet in Standard Time." *Down Beat* Sept. 1990: 16.

Holley, Eugene, Jr. "The Black Director and the Sinner Jazzman." *Pulse!* Sept. 1990: 54.

Huyssen, Andreas. *After the Great Divide: Modernism, Mass Culture, Postmodernism.* Bloomington: Indiana UP, 1986.

James, David. "Rock and Roll in Representations of the Invasion of Vietnam." *Representations* 29 (Winter 1990): 78–98.

Kenney, William Howland. " 'Going to Meet the Man': Louis Armstrong's Autobiographies." *Journal of the Society for the Study of the Multi-Ethnic Literature of the United States* 15.2 (Summer 1988): 27–46.

Lee, Spike, with Lisa Jones. *Mo' Better Blues: The Companion Volume to the Universal Pictures Film.* New York: Simon, 1990.

Lott, Eric. *Love and Theft: Blackface Minstrelsy and the American Working Class.* New York: Oxford UP, 1993.

McClary, Susan. *Feminine Endings: Music, Gender, and Sexuality.* Minneapolis: U of Minnesota P, 1991.

Modleski, Tania. "Femininity as Mas(s)querade: A Feminist Approach to Mass Culture." *High Theory/Low Culture.* Ed. Colin MacCabe. New York: St. Martin's, 1986. 37–52.

Partridge, Eric. *Shakespeare's Bawdy: A Literary and Psychological Essay and a Comprehensive Glossary.* Rev. ed. London: Routledge and Kegan Paul, 1968.

Radano, Ronald M. Personal communication. 6 Jan. 1992.

Rancour-Laferriere, Daniel. "Some Semiotic Aspects of the Human Penis." *Versus* 24 (1979): 37–82.

Richolson, Janice Mosier. "He's Gotta Have It: An Interview With Spike Lee." *Cinéaste* Dec. 1991: 12–15.

Schönherr, Ulrich. "Adorno and Jazz: Reflections on a Failed Encounter." *Telos* 87 (Spring 1991): 85–96.

Silverman, Kaja. "Masochism and Male Subjectivity." *Camera Obscura* 17 (May 1988): 31–67.

———. *The Subject of Semiotics.* New York: Oxford UP, 1983.

Tomlinson, Gary. "Cultural Dialogics and Jazz: A White Historian Signifies." *Disciplining Music: Musicology and Its Canons.* Ed. Katherine Bergeron and Philip V. Bohlman. Chicago: U of Chicago P, 1992. 64–94.

Walser, Robert. "Out of Notes: Signification, Interpretation, and the Problem of Miles Davis." *Jazz Among the Discourses.* Ed. Krin Gabbard. Durham, N.C.: Duke UP, 1995. 165–88.

Willis, Sharon. Comments after Jim Merod's "A World Without Whole Notes: The Intellectual Subtext of Spike Lee's *Blues.*" *Boundary* 2 18.2 (Summer 1991): 250.

Discography

Berry, Bill. "Boy Meets Horn." Rec. July 1976. *Hello Rev.* Concord CJ-27.

Davis." *Jazz Among the Discourses.* Ed. Krin Gabbard. Durham, N.C.: Duke UP, 1995. 165–88.

———. *Tune Up.* Prestige P-24077.

Faddis, Jon. *Legacy.* Rec. Aug. 1985. Concord CJ-291.

Franks, Rebecca Coupe. *Suit of Armor.* Rec. 2 Feb. 1991. Justice Records 0901-2.

Harrison, Donald, and Terence Blanchard. *Black Pearl.* Rec. 1988. CBS 44216.

Snow, Valaida. *Hot Snow.* Foremothers, Vol. 2. Rosetta Records 1305.

Videography

Charles Mingus's Epitaph. Rec. 1989 at New York's Lincoln Center by British Television Channel 4 and broadcast on the Bravo cable network in 1990.

David Murray Quartet Live at the Village Vanguard (1986). Directed by Bruce Buschel. Video Artists International 60094.

Art Farmer: Jazz at the Smithsonian (1982). Kultur 1272.

Dizzy Gillespie's 70th Birthday, Live at Wolf Trap. Rec. 6 June 1987. Directed by Phillip Byrd and broadcast on PBS in 1988.

Jivin' in Be-Bop (1947). Directed by Leonard Anderson. Jazz Classics JVCV-115.

Satchmo (1989). Directed by Gary Giddins. CMV Enterprises 49024.

Saxophone Colossus (1986). Directed by Robert Mugge.

Jazz Autobiography: Theory, Practice, Politics

CHRISTOPHER HARLOS

I remember one day being in a music history class and a white woman was the teacher. She was up in front of the class saying that the reason black people played the blues was because they were poor and had to pick cotton. So they were sad and that's where the blues came from, their sadness. My hand went up in a flash and I stood up and said, "I'm from East St. Louis and my father is rich, he's a dentist, and I play the blues. My father didn't never pick no cotton and I didn't wake up this morning sad and start playing the blues. There's more to it than that." Well, the bitch turned green and didn't say nothing after that. Man, she was teaching that shit from out of a book written by someone who didn't know what the fuck he was talking about. That's the kind of shit that was happening at Juilliard and after a while I got tired of it. —Miles: The Autobiography

In the five decades since Miles Davis's brief encounter with institutionalized music history at Juilliard, the gradual acceptance of jazz studies on the American campus is indicative of a more general call for research in areas of popular culture previously considered beyond the purview of traditional scholarship. Lewis Porter spoke of jazz studies "coming of age in the academic world" as late as 1988, and even more recently there is evidence of a genuine historiographical self-awareness, Scott DeVeaux's compelling critique of the jazz textbook macro-narrative, and Gary Tomlinson's related essay on the "dialogics" of jazz discourse being two such signs. Both essays draw attention to a symptomatic and recurrent breakdown in the way jazz history has been commonly conceptualized: as a linear and altogether coherent progression, straightforward and logical in its development, and built on a well-established canon—rather than as a complex of musical forms and cultures in a perpetual state of collision, revolution, and redefinition. In contrast to Miles's succinct comment on the establishment version of black music history, such theorizing only serves as evidence that jazz historiography is just now catching up—some fifty years later—with the intuitive observation of an exasperated undergraduate that there is, simply, "more to it than that."

But the claim that jazz history is really much more complicated than the textbook version designed for the undergraduate curriculum should be neither surprising nor controversial. At issue is the means through which the experience of jazz musicians has been traditionally transformed into written prose—and in the wake of these recent historiographical stirrings are questions concerning the position from which any such *master narrative* might be constructed: its genealogy; the tacit goals it seeks to advance; and, perhaps most importantly, what voices, elements, or incidents that narrative might seek to suppress. Subject over the years to the pressures of economic interdependence in a highly volatile and ultimately shrinking market, the alliance between writers and jazz musicians has been fragile, producing a body of writing specifically tooled for a readership of supporting patrons. So it is no accident that such a dynamic tended to avoid specific reference to friction or even open animosity between the musicians and those wielding the substantial power of the press—much less toward promoters, club owners, or record companies. Obviously, for publishers to reveal contempt among musicians for the establishment would be to undermine the establishment's authority, and since the majority of jazz writing has sprung, until about 1991, from a few dozen industry-dependent critic/journalists, the accepted *mode of production* remained fairly stable by keeping acrimony in check.

Now, however, in two distinct but related movements, it is possible to observe a significant transformation in jazz writing's business-as-usual. The one movement, within which musicologists like Tomlinson, DeVeaux, and Porter could be cast, is discovered in the expansion of jazz titles among scholarly presses and academic journals—attributable to the growing acknowledgment that jazz has affected twentieth-century world culture in numerous ways not yet completely understood. The other movement in this transformation is manifested in the fact that since the early 1980s jazz literature has been inundated with autobiographies—especially as an entire generation of survivors rapidly dwindles. During the ten-year period from 1983 until 1993, dozens of book-length, first-person, nonfiction narratives published under the name of a jazz musician were added to an already sizable list of autobiographical works representing a wide spectrum of players from every generation and style: stories from leaders, headliners, and sidemen; stories about Chicago in the twenties, the road in the thirties, about the East Coast in the forties, the West Coast in the fifties, about expatriates in Europe; stories about long careers, short careers; about survival; about creating art—all of which also represent a wide range of approaches to the act of self-inscription.

One particular autobiography that points some new directions for jazz scholarship is Milt Hinton's *Bass Line* (written with David Berger). As one of the most recorded and respected musicians in jazz history, Hinton offers a carefully detailed, first-hand account of a remarkable career; one balanced between traveling with Cab Calloway's big band in the 1940s, and the greatly different demands of the New York studio scene in the fifties and sixties. But *Bass Line*'s documentary value, beyond the interest and elegance of its narrative, is that Hinton includes more than two hundred photographs from his own collection—pictures of almost every major jazz figure in rehearsal and performance settings—taken over the course of forty years; and so vast is Hinton's reserve of photographs that he subsequently published a companion piece, *Over Time.* Hinton's one-of-a-kind legacy to jazz history provides a profoundly rich perspective on the life of one sensitive musician-historian; when juxtaposed with other books from the 1983–93 period, it is further evidence that despite the slight critical attention received so far, such a substantial body of primary material can have tremendous ramifications—both for jazz studies and for scholarly work on autobiography. So the fact that the growing academic interest in jazz would appear simultaneously with the plethora of autobiography, particularly as we approach the fin de siècle, seems more than merely coincidental—for not only are there new primary materials to be examined and considered, but surely, the synthesis of the jazz sensibility with "the culture of autobiography" has produced texts whose literary and cultural interest parallels, or even surpasses, the biographical information made newly available in such works.[1]

II

An early whispering of what the personal stories of jazz musicians—taken en bloc—might have to offer appears in Gary Giddins's brief introduction to pianist Hampton Hawes's *Raise Up Off Me*, a book from a cluster of late seventies' autobiographies, including Dizzy Gillespie's *To BE, or Not . . . to BOP*, and Art Pepper's *Straight Life*. In his attempt to locate *Raise Up Off Me*, one of the first autobiographies by a postwar bebopper, Giddins quickly looks at a number of books by earlier musicians (Jelly Roll Morton, Sidney Bechet, Mezz Mezzrow and others), suggesting that the "small, little-known genre of autobiographical works not only provides insight into the music and its makers, but also sheds light on race relations, Bohemian attitudes toward sex and drugs, alienation, and the predicament of the black artist in America." Giddins perceptively foresees an expanded role for jazz autobiography within a broader reading of American music and popular culture, but his suggestion ultimately begs the question as to how one might go about extracting or interpreting any "light" emanating from the works under consideration. Even to christen a given collection of texts a genre is to tacitly accept a number of literary conventions (in both writing and reading) that privilege features that may or may not be useful to a wholesale reading of jazz autobiographies. As a result, running parallel to the sociopolitical topics suggested by Giddins, there is the related question of how jazz musicians use, challenge, or transform the institution of autobiography itself.[2]

With these questions in mind, the present essay proposes to examine the emerging body of jazz autobiography in terms that explicitly track the dynamic at work in a jazz player's transition from a musical to a literary subject. One motivation behind the jazz player's move to autobiography, for example, is signaled in the opening of *Treat It Gentle,* where Sidney Bechet states flatly, "You know there's people, they got the wrong idea of Jazz," and then a few pages later asserts that it was only "a name white people have given to the music." Likewise, in *Music Is My Mistress,* Duke Ellington makes a point of the fact that he was disinclined to use the term "jazz" as a way of classifying his own musical endeavors. For Bechet and Ellington at least, one attraction to autobiography was the opportunity to deconstruct the label *jazz* (both denotatively and connotatively) as the binary other against which so-called "serious" or "legitimate" music was defined and subsequently marginalized (a project Ellington, for one, continued throughout his life). Implied in the terminological uneasiness expressed by Ellington and Bechet, however, is a deeper and more complicated set of conditions that informs the relationship between the jazz musician and jazz history; and for jazz musicians, the turn to autobiography is regarded as a genuine opportunity to seize narrative authority. So, to follow Giddins's suggestion, looking for possible insights to be gleaned from a collective reading of jazz autobiography quickly leads to the discovery that for many jazz musicians one source of the "alienation" and "predicament" to which Giddins refers is often previously written prose; that is, dissatisfaction with jazz writing is a theme that immediately surfaces in a number of autobiographical works.

In one of the handful of published essays to treat jazz autobiography as such, Kathy Ogren has already called attention to an annoyance with jazz writing expressed by two early musicians, pianist Willie "The Lion" Smith and guitarist Danny Barker, in their personal narratives. Barker says of his motivation to turn to autobiography: "Many books came on the scene together with many falsehoods, lies, and cooked up stories. I read much of this crap and then I was told I should write some truth and explanations of many jazz subjects that were not clearly explained" (120–21). Smith, a native New Yorker, complains bitterly about the early "jazz books, most of them written by non-playing so-called critics," that tended to discount musicians who came from anywhere but the Delta region. Though Ogren frames these passages in a somewhat different argument about storytelling and narrative performance from the one proposed here, it is hard to dismiss the contempt for jazz writing— particularly by nonmusicians—such works convey.

To take another example, in Charles Mingus's *Beneath the Underdog,* the critique is cast in slightly different terms when he lampoons a coterie of widely published jazz critics through an imagined New York jam session featuring *them* as performers: Leonard Feather on piano, Bill Coss and Gene Lees singing, Barry Ulanov on drums, Marshall Stearns on bass, Whitney Balliett as composer, John S. Wilson conducting, and Martin Williams, who can "play everything," the narrator quips, adding, "I can tell by the way he writes" (294). The dubious authority of the nonmusician writer is also depicted in an apocryphal story recounted in Art Hodes's *Hot Man* about an unnamed American jazz critic who, having recently published a book, is introduced to "Ivan," a Soviet jazz critic visiting New York. Hodes writes: "After a bit the 'Russian' says to the American critic, 'what instrument do you play?' The critic replies, 'Nothing.' The 'Russian' looks him over carefully. 'You write on jazz and you don't play an instrument? In Russia we shoot you'" (108).

But the felt distrust for writers on the part of jazz musicians can take on a much more serious and acrimonious tone. In a more direct way, *To BE, or Not . . . to BOP* shows how Dizzy Gillespie came to regard the reaction of the American press to the bebop movement of the forties. At the core of the text, in possibly its finest chapter, "Beboppers . . . the Cult," is a considered response to the popular image of the jazz musician—as a goateed, bereted, drug-using, nonpatriot—much of which was directed toward Gillespie himself. With specific reference to an article appearing in the March 25, 1946, issue of *Time,* warning of bebop's "degenerative influence on youth," he writes, "Once it got inside the marketplace, our style was subverted by the press and the music industry." "I should've sued," he continues a few lines later, "even though the chances in winning in court were slim. It was all bullshit." And for an even more explicit and sustained articulation of the contempt for jazz writing, we need only return to *Miles: The Autobiography*:

> After bebop became the rage, white music critics tried to act like they discovered it—and us—down on 52nd Street. That kind of dishonest shit makes me sick to my stomach. And when you speak out on it or don't go along with this racist bullshit, then you become a radical, a black troublemaker. (55)
>
> I wasn't going to [grin] just so that some non-playing, racist, white motherfucker could write some nice things about me. . . . So a lot of critics didn't like me back then—still don't today—because they saw me as an arrogant little nigger. Maybe I was, I don't know, *but I do know that I wasn't going to have to write about what I played and if they couldn't or wouldn't do that, then fuck them* [emphasis added]. Anyway, Max [Roach] and [Thelonious] Monk felt like that, and J. J. [Johnson] and Bud Powell, too. So that's what brought us close together, this attitude about ourselves and our music. (83)
>
> A lot of white critics kept talking about all these white jazz musicians, imitators of us, like they was some great motherfuckers and everything. Talking about Stan Getz, Dave Brubeck, Kai Winding, Lee Konitz, Lennie Tristano, and Gerry Mulligan like they was gods or something. *And some of them white guys were junkies like we were, but wasn't nobody writing about that like they was writing about us* [emphasis added]. They didn't start paying attention to white guys being junkies until Stan Getz got busted trying to break into a drugstore to cop some drugs. That shit made the headlines until people forgot and went back to just talking about black musicians being junkies. (156)
>
> [Some] musicians had become victims of the critics, most of whom are lazy and don't want to work too hard to understand contemporary musical expression and language. That's too much like work for them, so they just put it down every time. *Dumb, insensitive critics have destroyed a lot of great music and musicians who weren't as strong as I was in having the ability to say, "Fuck y'all"* [emphasis added]. (352)

Though anyone accustomed to Miles's scorching whisper would expect some level of invective to surface in *The Autobiography*, his attack against writers, when read on the heels of the others mentioned above, raises an important question about the extent to which such views are prevalent within a more general range of jazz autobiography. If there is an overarching sentiment that a good deal written about the music does not necessarily correspond with the sensibility or even lived experience of the musicians themselves, then it seems reasonable to conclude that within the burgeoning collection of autobiography there exists a significant alternative to "mainstream" jazz history. So the expansion of jazz autobiography has, among other things, brought the discursive (i.e., nonmusical) voice of the jazz musician in direct contact and dialogue with history, and by consequence, the ethos of the musician-as-historian has risen exponentially. Moreover, to approach the body of jazz autobiography as a *reaction against* previous writing on jazz, to see *that* as one of its primary motivations will obviously lead to a different reading from one that would take the musician-writer relationship as being unproblematic. But lest this initial sketch seem inordinately polarized—particularly as it draws extensively upon the reported experience of one notoriously truculent trumpeter—we can hastily note many counterexamples that indicate a more positive relationship to jazz writing within musician-authored texts—some even in *Miles: The Autobiography.*

III

It should also be recognized that the historical issues raised by the jazz musician-turned-writer sketched above represent only one aspect of the complex literary subject at work/play in jazz autobiography. Having expressed themselves for so many years in more subtle ways, jazz musicians typically have more in mind than merely setting the historical record straight when they turn to writing, and specifically to autobiography.[3] In Miles's case, the account of his Juilliard experience, the "resisting arrest" incident at the front door of Birdland, or the story about his trip to the Reagan White House are just single points in what amounts to a critique of various American institutions—through the eyes of a unique "self" presented in the form of a written autobiographical text. Hence, any critical assessment of what a given jazz autobiographer is up to means considering the various components of a *writing subject* who also happens to be a jazz musician. Take, for example, the epilogue to *Music Is My Mistress,* where in an essay titled "The Mirrored Self," Duke Ellington with characteristic eloquence struggles with his newly invented literary self:

Ah, this is *us*, the us we know, and as we savor the wonderful selves-of-perfection we suddenly realize that just below our mirror, there is another reflection that is not quite so clear, not quite what we expected. This translucent surface has a tendency toward the vague: the lines are not firm and the colors not quite the same, but it is us, or should we say *me*, or rather one of our other selves? We examine this uncertain portrait and just as we feel inclined to accept it we realize that, down below this, there is still another mirror reflecting another of ourselves and more. For this third mirror is transparent, and we plainly see what is going on before and behind it, and we refuse to credit that here is still another of our selves. But there we are with four reflections, all reflections of us who look at them. We accept the first three, even with the vague and misty overtones, but the fourth, on the other side of the transparent mirror, leaves us baffled and on the verge of defeat. (451)

Apart from his explicit rumination on the problematic nature of self-inscription, Ellington also demonstrates a keenly individual understanding of autobiographical form. *Music Is My Mistress* is organized into eight separate "acts," each composed of several smaller pieces: bits of travel narrative, expository prose, poetry, photographs, and numerous character sketches (what Ellington refers to as *Dramatis Felidae* [the cast of cats]) connected, more or less, by an overall chronology. In the epilogue, immediately following the passage cited above, Ellington even proposes a mock interview where he responds with wry indignation to numerous likely-to-be-asked questions—"*Q*. When did you get on your 'blue' kick? Are there colors you dislike? *A*. My mother always saw to that my Sunday clothes were blue. When she died I was wearing a brown suit." After the last question he adds, "(The only reason an interviewer sometimes asks the interviewee stupid questions is because he thinks the interviewee is stupid)." This final twist is obviously Ellington's polite way of expanding the borders of his literary subjectivity, but this bitterly ironic self—one that speaks in a tone clearly distinguishable from the preceding text—is carefully confined to the epilogue and is thus offered more as a final reward to the diligent reader rather than as an overt political statement permeating or informing the work as a whole.

To explore the literary potential for jazz autobiography in more detail, however, I want to look a bit more closely at *Beneath the Underdog: His World as Composed by Mingus*, a text that has taken on the status of a classic in jazz literature. Cleverly framed by visits to a fictionalized psychiatrist, the Mingus autobiography, like the Ellington work, demonstrates a sophisticated take on autobiographical form. In the book's first paragraph, for example, the subject discloses his sense of decenteredness, that he is actually three-in-one: "The man who watches and waits, the man who attacks because he is afraid, and the man who wants to trust love but retreats each time he finds himself betrayed." When his therapist asks, "Which is the image you want the world to see?" Mingus replies poignantly, "What do I care what the world sees, I'm only trying to find out how I should feel about myself."

As the opening scene for an autobiography, such a deliberate and self-conscious construction immediately adds a new set of variables to the textual equation, for it signals an approach to the form saturated in literary invention. And as if that were not enough, the text itself is prefaced by a seemingly superfluous disclaimer that *"some of the names in this work have been changed and some of the characters and incidents are fictitious."* So readers of *Beneath the Underdog* must negotiate a text that provokes questions about narrative invention and *literary agency*—within the context of an autobiography, questions also likely to arouse the traditional aversion toward the conflation of what is typically considered fiction and nonfiction.

In her portion of *Mingus/Mingus*, Janet Coleman recalls how both she and Al Young were approached to edit the text: "It was a jumble, a torrent, it was like James Joyce, jazzy Joyce, and it was terrific. It had puns and wordplay, and a schizophrenic narrator." Mingus corresponded with Coleman thus: "concerned as of your opinion as far as: Does it sound clear? Does the writer sound convincing? Has he been dead and alive?" (5) Not surprisingly, *Beneath the Underdog*, which then bore the alternative titles, *Half Yaller Nigger* or *Half Yaller Schitt-Colored Nigger*, went through the hands of several potential editors and publishers before it found its way into print. First under option at McGraw-Hill, then briefly considered by Random House, Mingus traveled from publisher to publisher with a number of stipulations, most notably that he wanted the book to be published in a white leather binding with gold lettering so that it might be mistaken for the Bible. Finally published by Alfred A. Knopf in 1971, *Beneath the Underdog* had "before it reached its last editor, Nel King," Coleman recalls, been "whitened up beyond repair" (8).

Coleman's choice of words is significant because in tandem with the literary invention signaled in *Beneath the Underdog*, the presence of a black subjectivity is also communicated through a separate introductory note where Mingus expresses gratitude to editor Nel King, who he describes as *"probably the only white person who could have done it."* Moreover, during the opening scene in the psychiatrist's office, just after his comment about not knowing how to feel about himself, he continues, "I can't change the fact that they're all against me—that they don't want me to be a success." When prodded by the therapist to specify whom he means, Mingus responds: "Agents and businessmen with big offices who tell me, a black man, that I'm abnormal for thinking we should have our share of the crop we produce. Musicians are as Jim-Crowed as any black motherfucker on the street and the . . . the . . . well, *they* want to keep it that way" (4). Mingus's explicitly charged reference to racial difference on the second page of the book is remarkable, for it immediately stakes out a markedly "raced" subjectivity in which the narrative unfolds.

Jazz musicians typically bring up race as an issue early on in their autobiographies, but few (certainly none before 1971) are more candid about their contempt for white America than Mingus in *Beneath the Underdog* where it is a theme kept before the reader on practically every page.[4] The loose framing device of the psychotherapy session of the first chapter soon gives way to a more straightforward biochronology, which takes as its point of departure a 1924 incident in which the two-year-old Mingus had to be rushed to the hospital after incurring a head gash on a piece of "Goodwill-store old fashioned second-hand-me-down white folks" furniture. For the narrator at least, the specific significance of the accident, however, is that it was then that "I found myself standing outside him for the first time since he was born," observing his panicked family: "they had so much faith in this guy named God, Baby wouldn't respond. I decided to go back inside and take over until he could get himself together. No one seemed to notice as I climbed up onto the white table where Baby was laid out and materialized myself into the big hole over his left eye" (9).

Indeed, this acute sense of self-awareness is sustained throughout the text with the "I" retained only for the speaker's narrative present, (except in a few letters to critic Nat Hentoff) and all other self-reference confined to the third person (he, baby, my boy, Charles, my man, etc.). The narrative is thus orchestrated and conducted by one master self who slips in and out of the various multiple selves—intermittently engaged in a series of digressions: confrontations, dreams, letters, phone calls, poems, seductions, and fantasies.[5] In terms of its correspondence with salient incidents in Mingus's life, the story of *Beneath the Underdog* as it now stands (there are, reportedly, another few hundred of pages of unpublished manuscript) ends roughly in 1959, just after Mingus's self-referral to Bellevue Hospital, an episode that begins with Mingus wandering the city after several sleepless weeks, haunted by the voices and faces of his past, and mulling over the Kenneth Patchen poem "It's dark out, Jack" (which he and Patchen had recently performed), when he finds himself before the gates of Bellevue. Sensing imminent breakdown, he requests admittance, only to have the guard repeatedly try to persuade him to go home and try to get some rest on his own: "You don't want to come in *here*. If I was to let you in first thing you'd say when I close that door behind you is *Lemme out, I ain't crazy!*" Finally, the guard relents, calling two orderlies who "had me in a straight jacket before I knew it and I'm telling the guard, 'Maybe you were right, I don't feel so bad after all.' . . . So here I am on my first day in Bellevue and nobody knows where I am and before lunch I'm told Negroes are paranoiac and threatened with a lobotomy!" (331–33).

The R. P. McMurphy-like experience of a mental health facility inspires Mingus to compose: first a poem, "Nice of You to Have Come to My Funeral," then his list of grievances, "Hellview of Bellevue," and, finally, his famous anthem to psychiatry, "All the Things You Could Be By Now If Sigmund Freud's Wife Was Your Mother." In fact, apart from its many screens and fictions, what further distinguishes *Beneath the Underdog* from more conventionally plotted autobiographies is that in constructing the life story within the context of psychotherapy—an attempt to find out how he is "*supposed* to feel about himself"—Mingus provides a running commentary on the function of artifice within the act of self-inscription. *Beneath the Underdog* noticeably forgoes many of the self-serving strategies one typically encounters in autobiography as a way of offering a subject pursuing something distinctly separate from revising the historical record or "having his or her turn" at authorial control. So readers familiar with jazz history might be surprised to discover that there is no mention, for example, of his performance with Parker, Gillespie, Powell, and Roach at the famous Massey Hall concert in May 1953—for the past three decades regarded as one of bebop's crowning moments—nor of his contribution to jazz history by having recorded the event with his own equipment.

Three significant musical experiences that do appear, however, explicitly foreground race: the first, the switch from classical cello to bass because it was perceived as a more *Negro* instrument, "*You're black. You'll never make it in classical music no matter how good you are*" (69), and two particularly painful encounters with racism much later on (WCBS-TV's interdiction of his appearing on television with Red Norvo, and the famous onstage fire ax altercation with Juan Tizol [321–27]). All told, however, there is little detail regarding Mingus's musical career in *Beneath the Underdog*, which is not to say that the text carries less documentary value than other, more conventional autobiographical statements.[6] So while *Beneath the Underdog* does offer some portrait of Mingus the musician, much of the book's focus is on his coming to terms with social power—particularly that power associated with race, ethnicity, and sexuality. In some instances, of course, such as the initial switch from cello to bass, there is a discernible connection to be made between the racial dynamic of a specific incident and its effect on Mingus's musical career. For other incidents, however, such as those (far more numerous) involving sexuality, the immediate musical effect is less evident. In the initial scene, for example, the psychiatrist eventually brings the discussion "back to the subject"—Mingus's ambivalence regarding the power and guilt of pimping: "That's almost impossible to explain—how you feel when you're a kid and the king pimps come back to the neighborhood. They pose and twirl their new watchchains and sport their new Cadillacs and Rollses and expensive tailored clothes. It was like the closest thing to one of our kind becoming president of the U.S.A. When a young up-and-coming man reaches out to prove himself a boss pimp, its making it. That's what it meant where I come from— proving you're a man" (6).

Although Mingus is calling traditional notions of masculinity into question, these are the same notions he has nonetheless internalized. It is worth noting that at the core of the initiation narrative is the relationship with the father who, by midtext (roughly through seventeen years), has become the source of brutal beatings, castration threats, and the revelation that the younger Mingus's grandmother was white—a first cousin to Abraham Lincoln. Moreover, Mingus's father is repeatedly depicted as a vigilant guardian of the light-to-dark "pecking order" within Watts— while at the same time the boy Mingus (the "mongrel," "the underdog") encounters hostilities stemming from his liminal status—"not light enough to join the almost white elite, not dark enough to belong to the beautiful elegant blacks . . . the black hate for Whitey was turned on him, a schitt-colored halfass yella phoney." Consequently, overshadowing the initial search for the musical self is the search for the racial/ethnic self:[7]

> Whenever he looked in the mirror and asked "What am I?" he thought he could see a number of strains—Indian, African, Mexican, Asian and a certain amount of white his father boasted of. He wanted to be one or the other but he was a little of everything, wholly nothing, of no race, country, flag, or friend. . . . All he wanted was to be accepted somewhere and he still wasn't, so fuck it! . . .

He became something else. He fell in love with himself. . . .
I understood what he was trying to do. I've met a few other people on that colorless island. (65–66)

It is in his adolescent romances, however, that Mingus begins to work through or, perhaps more accurately, act out his racial/sexual anxieties: Lee-Marie, Manuela, and one seaside liaison which he describes as "the first time Charles felt completely accepted by a black negro" (92). From there, after a brief marriage to "Barbara Jane Parks" (Canilla Jean Gross), the story of his self-discovery moves through a seemingly interminable chain of relationships, tilting finally toward his pimp fantasy. So the second half of the book subsequently becomes something of a modernist literary experiment, traversing a variety of sexual frontiers: an orgy with twenty-three prostitutes; the entanglements of a biracial whore/pimp triangle with his "sweet-and-hot marshmallow-and-chocolate" confla-tion, *Donnalee*; a bestial love contest; a touch of sadomasochism; a free-for-all jazz party; the cynicism of pimping—all of it singularly energized by the transgression of a founding taboo: miscegenation.

In the midst of all of this racially charged sex-play are the recurring dreams or, perhaps more accurately, *apparitions*, of Fats Navarro, the gifted trumpeter who died in 1950 at the age of twenty six as the result of tuberculosis and heroin addiction. For Mingus, Navarro's demise is a metaphor for jazz itself, and the first of the Navarro dialogues stands as one of the most bitter commentaries on working conditions for black musicians in all of jazz nonfiction: "Jazz is big business to the white man and you can't make a move without him. We just work-ants. He owns the magazines, agencies, record companies, and all the joints that sell jazz to the public" (188). Significantly, in the same dream dialogue, Mingus casts himself as a naif, shocked by these stark revelations; when he responds by suggesting that blacks try to seize the means of production, his guide replies "You breaking into Whitey's private vault when you start telling Negroes to wake up and move in where they belong and it ain't safe, Mingus. When the day comes the black man says I want mine, then hide your family and get yourself some guns. 'Cause there ain't no better business for Whitey to be in than Jim Crow business" (190). Func-tioning, more or less, as Mingus's alter ego, Navarro's overwhelming sense of hopelessness, particularly about the vicious relationship be-tween white control of the jazz industry and the grip of heroin over musicians like himself is ultimately mitigated by Mingus's closing vi-sion of redemption, which takes on the character of a Platonic dialogue on race, religion, and cosmology.

IV

In terms of a broader reading of jazz autobiography, *Beneath the Underdog*'s unique play with the conventions of narrative nonfiction is actually more atypical than representative in form and structure; as autobiographers, jazz musicians tend to be much more conservative than Mingus in conforming to established practices of self-representation. It is, however, precisely this uniqueness that makes *Beneath the Underdog* a useful backdrop against which other jazz autobiographies can be contextualized and contrasted. In this regard, I would first call attention to the disclaimer that opens *Beneath the Underdog* as a classic example of how a given text will explicitly reveal its own assumptions about the nature of autobiography and consequently prescribe the way in which the credibility of its already marginal subject is intended to be interpreted. In the introductory pages of Art Pepper's *Straight Life*, for example, along with an epigraph from Ezra Pound, there is an explanation from Pepper's wife Laurie—the amanuensis who transcribed and edited the manuscript—that, although "a true story," there was a need, in some instances, for pseudonyms and slight alterations of narrative detail to protect certain reputations. Laurie Pepper then continues, "Attitudes, intentions, and feelings attributed by Art Pepper to anyone besides himself should be understood by the reader to be Art's impressions, not fact." Readers for whom the pleasure of autobiography is located *precisely* in the discovery of those impressions would likely find such a statement unnecessary; but apparently the editor of *Straight Life* addresses other potential readers perceived as being so ill-equipped at sorting through autobiographical material that they need to be reminded that the narrative is filtered through an overarching point of view.

Moreover, within each chapter of *Straight Life* one or more witnesses are included (some twenty-two in all) as a means of corroborating the testimony of the key witness, Pepper himself. But the introduction of third-person material in the form of corroborating witnesses tends to raise as many doubts about the subject's credibility as it alleviates—particularly when no substantial disagreement occurs in fact or circumstances.[8] The witnesses, described as "the cast of characters," are introduced, each with his or her own brief bio-blurb, immediately following the editorial warning cited above; but since the narrative would suffer no substantial loss if the witnesses were not present, the reader is left to wonder about their textual function. One significant upshot concerning the textual presence of other voices in the ostensibly autobiographical narrative is the underlying desire to "authenticate" the subject's perceptions and point of view. A similar multiwitness format is employed to an even greater extent in Dizzy Gillespie's *To BE, or Not . . . to BOP*, an autobiography that includes close to one hundred other voices, such that the majority of the text—presented as *"memoirs"*—comes from speakers other than the ostensible subject himself. The text opens with the following note: "We began this book five years ago with the aim of creating the best—the most complete, authentic, and authoritative autobiography of a jazz musician ever published. Humbled now by the many difficulties inherent in such a task, we must first thank God for our being able to complete this still imperfect and much tempered version of our original ambitious goal" (xvii).

What would it mean for an autobiography to be more or less "complete, authentic, and authoritative?" Although there is no specific reference to other jazz autobiographies, one can assume that Gillespie and Fraser perceived that certain previously published texts, perhaps even *Beneath the Underdog*, lacked those qualities that they sought to achieve in their own work and thus could be taken to be somehow incomplete, inauthentic, and less than authoritative. Furthermore, the question can be raised as to whether completeness, authenticity, and authoritativeness are more desirable in an autobiography than say, candor, confession, or coherence. Compared with the resulting collage of testimony in *To BE or Not . . . to BOP*, the narrative intervention of fewer witnesses in *Straight Life* is noticeably stronger in bringing forth narrative continuity. But, as is also true of *Straight Life*, the witnesses have a countering effect on Gillespie's overall credibility to the extent that their presence seems intended only to corroborate or substantiate the primary subject's perceptions and recollection of events. Rather than fulfill their purpose and simply validate the subject's story, the result is a text in which the subject's ethos is essentially undermined—a textual flag which cautions the reader that the "I" is insufficient or unreliable. Beyond the unspecified difficulties in writing an autobiography, that Gillespie and Fraser were content to simply see the project through to a less-than-satisfactory conclusion suggests, in this particular case, that the oscillation between autobiographical and biographical forms proved too unwieldy to manage. Regardless of any given text's explicit caution about the subject's desire or need to fictionalize, as in *Beneath the Underdog*, or to augment the autobiographical statement with the testimony of others, as in *Straight Life* and *To BE, or Not . . . to BOP*, we notice that jazz autobiographies tend to mediate their subjects in complicated ways.

One important mode of textual mediation—demonstrated in Gillespie and Fraser's use of "we" throughout the cited passage above—is collaboration, a popular but sometimes sticky method of getting a jazz artist's story into book form.[9] Since 1975, when theorist Phillipe Lejeune outlined what he then termed the "autobiographical contract"—under which a given text's author, narrator, and protagonist are taken by the reader to be identical—some scholars, most notably Albert Stone (1982), have tried to accommodate the collaborative autobiography, a contingency untreated in Lejeune's typology. Significantly, though, Stone's approach suppresses the theoretical impulse to regard collaboration as a "literary *problem*" but suggests instead that it be taken (somewhat cryptically) as a "cultural *solution*" that has produced several literary masterpieces, among them *All God's Dangers: The Life of Nat Shaw* (Rosengarten) and perhaps most notably *The Autobiography of Malcolm X.* Central to Stone's theory of collaboration is a focus on the way in which the autobiographical contract is modified in the paratextual material—titles, subtitles, prefaces, forewords, afterwords, and notes— where the terms of collaboration are generally made explicit, announcing the "grounds by which the reader measures his/her own experience of the text."

There is a substantial range in collaborative practice among autobiographers, though at times its extent is intentionally presented ambiguously—leaving readers to their own devices in figuring out how a certain text asks to be read. For example, in the case of Billie Holiday's *Lady Sings the Blues* (written with William Dufty), on the *front* cover of the Avon paperback edition it is described as a "searing, turbulent autobiography," yet it becomes a "classic American biography" on the *back* cover. Ambivalence about authorship in the Holiday/Dufty case is understandable since Holiday had little to do with the book's development; within the text itself there is no discussion of the relationship between Dufty and Holiday or in the writing process, and it has been suggested by Robert O'Meally and others that she never even read it. Dufty, a writer for the *New York Post* had access to Holiday mostly through his wife, Maely, a longtime friend of Holiday's, and, for a period, the singer's personal manager. Much of the material of the book was collected from previously published interviews from the left-liberal newspaper *PM* that Dufty pieced together into a single narrative; O'Meally's research amply demonstrates that the text contains several gross errors in historical fact as well as misguided attributions to its subject. In his biography, *Billie's Blues*, John Chilton reports that Holiday, who disliked being incorrectly labeled a blues singer, was unhappy about the title, which she originally intended to be *Bitter Crop*, a line from one of her most famous songs, "Strange Fruit"—a composition, fittingly enough, often mistakenly attributed to her.

Given the dismal collaborative circumstances of *Lady Sings the Blues* and the fact that Holiday was not even able to title her own autobiography, it is curious that Henry Louis Gates includes her on his list of authors he regrettably was unable to include in *Bearing Witness*. But the question of collaboration does not end there because, as one might expect in such a collection, Gates includes a chapter from *The Autobiography of Malcolm X*, but surprisingly makes no mention of Alex Haley in his general introduction nor in the blurb that prefaces the selection, and the fact that Gates only mentions Haley's name in the reprint acknowledgments at the end of the text is itself striking. Also on Gates's list of missing authors is the name of Theodore Rosengarten, a white historical novelist who collaborated with Alabama tenant farmer Ned Cobb (pseudonymously Nate Shaw) to produce *All God's Dangers*. That it is Rosengarten, and not Cobb/Shaw, who is named as a missing author in an anthology composed of "autobiographical statements written by black men and women between 1904 and 1990"—only further testifies to the theoretical confusion that autobiographical collaboration is liable to generate.

But to readers of jazz autobiography not especially concerned with literary theory, an explicit description of the collaborative process can also fit quite neatly into the narrative as a whole and thus enhance, rather than cloud, the meaning-making process readers typically undergo. Consider, for example, Count Basie's autobiography, *Good Morning Blues*, where he recalls being struck by the impulse to produce an autobiography while dozing on a train during a tour of England:

> What got me started was the clotheslines. I don't remember what I had been dreaming about or anything like that, but as soon as the scenery changed from the countryside to the suburbs and I saw all of those pieces of laundry flapping in the breeze on all of those sagging lines across all of the back porches, my mind flipped from England all the way to New Jersey and how the clothesline in our backyard used to look every Monday morning when I was growing up, and then what I was also thinking about was my mother.
>
> For years people have been trying to do a book about myself or to let someone else do one about me, and up to that afternoon I had always put them off. But by the time I stepped off the train I had

actually made up my mind and not long afterward I actually started
putting a few memories on tape and also jotting down little notes
about a few things. . . .

So after about a dozen years of making those little tapes and notes
and then forgetting what the hell I did with some of them, I finally
decided to bring in a co-writer and see if I could work things out with
him the same way I've spent all of these years working up materials
for the band with my staff arrangers, ever since I first got the idea
and started co-writing arrangements with Eddie Durham for Bennie
Moten in Kansas. (xi)

An exemplar of collaboration in jazz autobiography, *Good Morning
Blues* is quickly distinguished among other works in the genre by the literary stature of Albert Murray, the cowriter Basie "decided to bring in" to
help on the project. Highly respected as a scholar and writer of both fiction and nonfiction, including *The Omni-Americans* and *Stomping the
Blues* (winner of the ASCAP Deems Taylor award in 1976), Murray represents an exclusive class of literary heavyweights who accept such invita-
tions only with great reluctance and trepidation. But, we notice, it is Murray's name listed beneath the title on the book's spine, and it is *his* fine
career that is sketched in the final note, "About the Author." Yet, compared to Alex Haley's informative epilogue that serves as the final chapter
for *The Autobiography of Malcolm X* (providing valuable insight into
Haley's relationship with the autobiographical subject), Murray's three-
page afterword draws little attention to his own effort in the book's creation, only hinting at his editorial role or literary vision. We do learn that
it was he who suggested that the narrative begin with the turning point in
Basie's early career—his first live encounter with the Blue Devils—and
that from there the "sequence of chapters could be a matter of orchestration like the choruses in a Kansas City arrangement, which would also
work like a movie scenario." Such a description, one that links writing an
autobiography to the narrative logic of both music and film, is revealing
because Basie, not surprisingly, uses a music metaphor to describe the
writing process and his working relationship with Murray: "As my main
man in the research department, my co-writer also likes to *think of
himself as Count Basie's literary Count Basie* [emphasis added]; in other
words, he comps [accompanies] for me pretty much as I have always done
for my soloists and also my sections and also for my band as a whole. And
of course, we have also done a bit of four handed piano-playing, just like
Bennie Moten himself and I used to do, sometimes with two separate
pianos and sometimes on the same keyboard" (xii).

The lesson to be learned from *Good Morning Blues* is that like jazz itself, where the completely solo performance is atypical, jazz autobiography also easily lends itself to being produced on a collective basis. By initially casting himself in terms of the featured soloist, behind whom Murray's literary voicings serve to punctuate and accent, Basie's vision of the book's collaborative creation seems distinct from any notion of a purely individual effort typically associated with autobiography. Moreover, in the passage's second sentence Basie makes a subtle distinction between those occasions of accompanied soloing and four-handed playing when, presumably, he and Murray would work over specific passages together. Among the obvious differences in terms of textual production, one of the many distinctions to be made between the Holiday and Basie autobiographies is that Dufty was relying solely on previously printed material, whereas Murray had access to tape-recorded interviews from which portions of the manuscript were produced. The practice of using tape recordings, by far more common in jazz autobiography, is ultimately an adaptation of a method typically employed in more formal oral history projects, but the notion of "shared authority" still raises some question about that perilous voyage from the tape recorder onto the page.[10]

For a final glimpse of the kind of issues at stake in collaborative autobiography here, I would point to Richard Sudhalter's review-essay of various jazz autobiographies in which he cites a passage about recording methods in the 1940s from *Hamp: An Autobiography* (with James Haskins) and complains that the "tone, cadence, choice of words, simply don't *sound* like Lionel Hampton." The implication is that Hampton's description of the specific recording process would probably have been more colloquial than what appears in the book; moreover, Sudhalter scolds Hampton/Haskins for historical muddling of the technology available at the time, casting further doubt on the team's narrative authority. An informed reader of jazz autobiography, Sudhalter (himself a biographer of Bix Beiderbecke) makes a good case for the readerly expectations one might bring to jazz autobiography in terms of the story presented by the ostensible subject: he expects historical accuracy, believable dialogue, and narrative coherence. Beyond that, though, Sudhalter also wants a collaborator who is both supportive and critical, who "allows" the subject free expression, but who is also ready to "cross-examine" when details get too sketchy. In short, Sudhalter evaluates jazz autobiographical texts by the degree to which they demonstrate a rather delicate balance of historical, personal, and political detail, and curiously, in his parting comment, he appropriately shakes his finger at future "ghost-writers" reminding them to properly "understand and discharge their responsibilities," for, "without them, understanding of this unique and remarkably hardy way of making music will be infinitely the poorer" (216).

Sudhalter's lack of confidence in unassisted musician-authors demonstrates how the issue of "responsibility" in instances of collaborative autobiography can often get touchy, particularly when the question raised turns on a particular historical fact. In the afterword to *Miles: The Autobiography*, for example, Quincy Troupe relates the events that led up to when "Miles chose me to write his book," and then the "authors" go on to thank the scores of jazz personae including three earlier Davis biographers. Significantly, Stanley Crouch, Scott DeVeaux, and others have already commented extensively on the similarities between specific passages from the autobiography and other works, particularly *Milestones*, Jack Chambers's two-volume biography of Davis. So as in the case of the Holiday autobiography, it is indeed a curious condition of intertextuality when a book, ostensibly published as an autobiography, written with a professional writer, draws word-for-word accounts from earlier interviews conducted in a different context. "Troupe denies using any of it," Crouch claims, "then says, 'the man can quote himself,' then blames the publisher for 'messing up' by omitting a discography and a bibliography, and by not checking facts." Troupe's reported unwillingness to accept responsibility for the manuscript is telling, for it raises questions about who is responsible when an autobiographical text becomes controversial.

V

Though understandable, Sudhalter's admonition for would-be collaborators or editors to police their charges risks a number of textual fissures and refractions; and not surprisingly, the sticky question of how responsibility is ultimately divided between the autobiographical subject and collaborator (or editor) gets more complicated when racial difference is factored into the equation. Just about everyone now acknowledges, for example, that Louis Armstrong was not, as claimed in his sundry autobiographical statements, born on July 4, 1900—a date which, if nothing else, cleverly expresses an admirable optimism about the history of American music in this century. Of course, the idea of challenging any subject on a point as basic as a birth date smacks of the worst kind of patronization, while at the same time, just beyond the pursuit of basic historical precision stands the unsettling awareness that once having cast doubt on such a charming but founding *misrepresentation*, the balance of what has been previously accepted as accurate information in jazz autobiography can be equally called into question.

In addition to the debates on any specific biographical detail it has generated, what makes the Armstrong case even more interesting is that there were multiple "authorized" texts of his autobiography circulating simultaneously throughout his life.[11] William Kenney has argued that the demands of a white publishing establishment and readership exerted no small influence on each version and that, as a result, the image of Armstrong to emerge from the texts is highly stylized, and ultimately much different from the persona to emerge from his original manuscripts. Armstrong, for instance, preferred to punctuate long passages with ellipses rather than periods; he inventively used capitalization, inverted commas, and contractions; and his various other vernacular spellings, syntax, and grammar brought forth a highly readable (though what was taken to be an unpublishable) manuscript.[12]

Beyond issues of stylistic corruption, however, *Swing that Music* is otherwise interesting in formal terms because the Armstrong narrative is framed by a number of other voices: an introduction by Rudy Vallee; a postscript by Horace Gerlach (the text's "musical" editor) that provides a glossary of Armstrong's neologisms; and photographs of several white contemporaries from the music business that frame the narrative proper. The book is thus a discursive interplay among Vallee, Gerlach, and what amounts to two diluted Armstrong voices—what Kenney distinguishes as the "didactic" and the "vernacular" Armstrong. For Kenney, whose general focus is on Armstrong's autobiographical negotiation of the biracial jazz world, the most interesting of the four voices that appear in *Swing that Music* is the vernacular Armstrong; for despite Gerlach's clumsy intrusions, the vernacular Armstrong comes closest to an "authentic" autobiographical voice. Kenney's compelling reading of *Swing that Music* in terms of the slave narrative, that it is a "conversation between whites that frames the black star's narrative, recreating the structural characteristics of the nineteenth century former slave narratives that were similarly surrounded by the comments of white abolitionists" (48), is tagged, in part, by a brief reference to Robert Stepto's *From Behind the Veil*, the following passage from which supplies a bit more of the argument:

> In Afro-American letters, [for example], while there are notable exceptions, the battle for authorial control has been more of a race ritual than a case of patricide. Author has been pitted against author, primarily to reenact the eighteenth and nineteenth century strug-

gles between author and guarantor. The competition has rarely been between artist and artist for control of an image, line, or trope; rather, it has been between artist and authenticator (editor, publisher, guarantor, patron) for control of a fiction—usually the idea of history or of the artist's personal history—that exists outside the artist's text and functions primarily as an antagonistic force with regard to that text's imaginative properties. (45)

Kenney's implicit linking of *Swing that Music* with Stepto's formulation of an "authenticated" African American autobiography is certainly on target, but the bifurcation of Armstrong's voice into the didactic and a vernacular brings an added ambiguity that is not present in "authenticated" texts whose subject is more or less univocal. Although I will return to Kenney's schema and look more closely at the other voice—the didactic Armstrong voice against which the vernacular Armstrong struggles—I want first to consider two other brief examples that illustrate, in a somewhat less complicated way, the ramifications for a "framed" autobiographical text.

The first comes from *Pops Foster: The Autobiography of a New Orleans Jazzman* (as told to Tom Stoddard). With a foreword by Stoddard, an introduction by Bertram Turetzsky, and interchapters by Ross Russell, *Pops Foster* exhibits a formal construction similar to what Kenney identified in the Armstrong autobiography and to that described by Stepto. In the foreword, for example, Stoddard offers a description of the writing process and explains his intervention regarding various contradictions in Foster's story—that on occasion he felt that he "understood Pops and knew the story well enough to decide which was the most accurate version." Because the book appeared some three years after Foster's death, Stoddard, anticipating critical reaction, also assumes sole responsibility for the text: "I expect to be deluged with correspondence regarding inaccuracy and errors. I realize that many things in this book conflict with 'known' jazz history. But Pops was a historical source and was as entitled to say his piece as the cat who wrote that history. Frankly, after spending all that time with Pops, I would be inclined to accept his version of the story. There probably will be a number of points that I may have misunderstood or where Pops was just plain wrong. Anyone who thinks this may certainly write. I do not promise to answer all the letters" (x).

In contrast with this ambiguous editorial signal, however, the introduction takes a different approach to authentication. Turetzsky begins by comparing Foster to Domenico Dragonetti, the eighteenth-century

"Paganini of the contrabasso," friend to both Haydn and Beethoven. What makes Turetzsky's introduction so interesting is that he feels compelled to couch all of his accolades in terms of classical music, with a lengthy explanation of Foster's technique (complete with a diagram) and its similarity to the style from the "German school," and he even goes so far as to include side-by-side photographs of himself and Foster with the captions: "Pops Foster in a typical playing position" and, under his own photograph, "Bertram Turetzsky in a classical playing position." Also, Turetzsky cites testimony from numerous figures, most from the white jazz establishment, including Gunther Schuller and Bud Freeman, who, in praising Foster's gracious humility, adds parenthetically, "obviously he had not read Harriet Beecher Stowe."

The interchapters are equally troubling because Ross Russell feels compelled to continually remind the reader of "how great" Foster really was, or, even worse, to explain what Foster has just said or is about to say. Take, for example, Russell's explication of the obvious in his attempt to "clarify" Foster's rather detailed account of working conditions: "The essential point is that musicians, like other professional workers, depended on jobs for a livelihood," or, as if readers of autobiography did not know what to expect, "Continuing with his story, Pops describes the everyday events that were accompanied by live music in New Orleans." Russell also does not hesitate to offer his judgments on Foster's perceptions: "The opening paragraphs of the next chapter furnish the jazz historian with valuable information." Although obviously intended to strengthen the subject's narrative, for Russell to distinguish a few paragraphs as "valuable" not only implies that the rest of the text is of less historical "value," but reinforces his position as the authority who knows the difference.

The second example, trombonist Dicky Wells's autobiography, *The Night People*, is also brought into perspective by a number of mediating voices: (1) a brief foreword by Count Basie; (2) a preface by editor Stanley Dance; (3) a general introduction by Martin Williams; (4) an analytical essay by André Hodier originally written in 1956 as part of *Jazz: Its Evolution and Essence*; (5) a Wells discography by Chris Sheridan; and (6) an interesting glossary of jazzspeak much like one included at the end of *Swing that Music*, compiled by Dance for the most uninitiated of readers (e.g., *Whitey, n.* A white person.). Exhibiting a curious compulsion to undermine Wells's own narrative through relentless paraphrase of the obvious, Dance opens his preface to the autobiography with the not-so-startling claim that: "In telling his story here, Dicky Wells has a great deal to say about the world in which he has lived and worked as a jazz musician." Furthermore, in *The Night People* it is Dance who speaks the interchapter commentary (e.g., "this chapter is a kind of summing-up in which Dicky Wells expresses great admiration for Tommy Dorsey"), not unlike that provided by Russell in *Pops Foster.*

The Night People appeared in 1971 (Crescendo) and then in two later editions: Da Capo (1984) and the Smithsonian Institution Press (1991), the last of these including the Hodier essay, the discography, and the (retrospective) introduction by Martin Williams who, in attempting to locate the Wells work within the body of jazz autobiography, flatly claims that "stylistically the book virtually stands alone in jazz litera-ture." Literally the most "institutional" of the textual voices authen-ticating the 1991 edition of *The Night People,* Williams brings to his task an implied aesthetic for jazz nonfiction that is worth teasing out; for in many respects it crystallizes the issues taken up in the present essay. Williams's argument for the stylistic excellence of *The Night People* is grounded in the following sentence: "Wisely, Dicky Wells and Stanley Dance decided to use—unapologetically—the eminently expressive col-loquial language of Wells and his associates, with only enough change as might be needed for clarity." In raising the issue of "the expressive colloquial language," Williams touches on a key issue for the corpus as a whole: the way in which publishers represent the talk of the jazz subcul-ture. We have already noted the textual appendage of a glossary—made necessary, for the most part, by a chapter titled "Bus Talk," in which Wells interrupts the narrative and provides a few pages of representative slang. Interestingly, the diction and tone of the other chapters—written, more or less in standard prose—are markedly different from the road dialogue represented in "Bus Talk." In his interchapter commentary, Dance communicates his awareness of the abrupt shift in language and style, which he describes as "obviously concentrated"; Wells himself saw the chapter as merely "samples" of jazz lingo, and a departure from the narrative up to that point. Indeed, in the following chapter, Wells imme-diately resumes the standard prose of the previous chapters, and so it seems safe to assume that it was at the editor's prompting that "Bus Talk" was in the book at all.

The very presence of "Bus Talk," the chapter to which Basie, Williams, and Dance all direct the reader's specific attention, raises further ques-tions about the language in which the jazz subject is cast. That Williams finds it remarkable that neither Wells nor Dance feels compelled to *apologize* for the language in *The Night People* is at first puzzling, be-cause even the most prudish reader would likely find any linguistic transgressions minimal; Wells even employs the modest "b— s—"

method of presenting expletives to the reader. Yet Williams's comment is also revealing in terms of the textual mediation that his introduction—as the official spokesperson for the Smithsonian Institution—brings to the work. For in the next paragraph he goes on to make some vague distinctions concerning the "informality of language" in jazz autobiography more generally, noting the "genial terseness" of *Good Morning Blues*, the "informal warmth" of *Bass Line*, as opposed to a marked preoccupation with drug addiction (presumably captured in a more troubling prose style) in *Straight Life* and *Raise Up Off Me*. Simply put, what Williams finds so appealing about *The Night People* is that unlike these other books, Wells "gets down without ever getting dirty."

Not surprisingly, two titles conspicuously absent from Williams's brief rumination on colloquial style in jazz autobiography are *Beneath the Underdog* and *Miles: The Autobiography*, and one can only imagine how he reacted to Mingus's confessional psychonarrative, Miles's penchant for the expletive "motherfucker" (used in both its positive and negative contexts more than three hundred times in the book), or Miles's graphic account of an embarrassing cab ride shortly after his arrival in New York with Charlie Parker and a prostitute—a scene one reviewer termed "unprintable." Consequently, the institutional interventions in the case of *The Night People* illustrate the contradictory position of finding literary curiosity in the jazz musician's long-standing reappropriation and transgression of standard (American) English, while at the same time attempting to severely mitigate the strategic impact of that same reappropriation.

Williams's final point—from his position of institutional authority—concerning the ultimate value of *The Night People*, is further noteworthy, for in its thoughtless condescension it shifts the ostensible focus from style in jazz autobiography to something quite different: "Surely there is no more authentic record of how it felt to be a sideman in a great orchestra than this, or of how it felt to tour the segregated American South in the 1930s and 1940s, carrying the music to people who needed its message to give meaning to their lives" (x). Although in a chapter titled "The Hazardous Road," Wells does recount, with genuine immediacy, his own experience with violent racism and some of the ways the touring band tried to cope with the fear of sudden and unwarranted attack, nowhere in the text does Wells even come close to suggesting that "people" in the segregated South were living meaningless lives until the advent of big band music in the thirties. Indeed, Wells would likely find such a claim not only absurd but repugnant, particularly when offered in the form an "official" sanction to his own life story. Dicky Wells, who died of cancer on November 12, 1985, never saw the introduction to the 1991 edition of *The Night People*.

With these two examples in mind, then, I want to return to *Swing that Music*, the first Armstrong autobiography. What distinguishes the orchestration of voices in *Swing that Music* from the Foster or Wells autobiographies is that the Foster and Wells books provide a much clearer delineation between the authenticators and the single-voiced subject, whereas the Armstrong presents a single narrator who is in effect "double-voiced."[13] Each with his own domain, the vernacular Armstrong is presented as the authority on biographical or historical matters related to New Orleans, Chicago, and Armstrong's personal odyssey, while the didactic narrator has a broad understanding of the entire music industry. For example, the didactic Armstrong makes fine distinctions between the "old jazz," "tin pan alley," "trashy popular music," and "the fine swing music" being advocated throughout the book. The didactic Armstrong is on the cutting edge of the new swing *culture:* he knows the journals and books on jazz, the names of those behind jazz societies throughout the United States and Europe, the best places to go for jam sessions, and how jazz can be located within a much broader context of an expanding international popular culture.

More importantly, though, it is through the didactic narrator that the book's nonautobiographical component—anticipated in Vallee's introduction—becomes clear. Vallee's textual function (Kenney calls him the "emcee") is to "introduce" (to the point of defense) Armstrong on musical grounds to the skeptical reader; to argue, from a position of authority, that despite the fact that Armstrong's singing, for example, "often seem[s] to be the result of a disorganized chaotic mind struggling to express itself," that it really is—on thoughtful consideration—a product of genius and that he, Vallee, was one of the first to recognize it. Beyond the telling presumption that Armstrong would need Vallee's endorsement to establish his autobiographical credibility, there is, in addition to what Kenney describes as the "sparring" between the didactic and vernacular Armstrongs, an ongoing rhetorical struggle between Armstrong and Gerlach as well.

Among the points in the argument from the didactic Armstrong worth considering: First, that the great New Orleans jazzmen had no formal training in music, and it was precisely that noninstitutional quality that allowed them to create the new musical form. Second, in merging what had previously been regarded as two distinct spheres of artistic creation, composition *and* performance, these same musicians eschewed any reliance on musical notation, which, if applied in any systematic way,

would ultimately represent the death of the new music. (There is, however, a collection of transcribed solos at the end of the text whose presence would contradict this view.) Third, that "if those early swing musicians had gone to music schools . . . swing music would have never been
born at all." Fourth, that "real masters" (composers, authors, artists) can
be divided into two types; the one who "learns everything about his art
and what was done before him so he can go beyond it," and the other, who
"doesn't know *anything* about it—who is just plain ignorant, but has a
great deal of feeling he has to express in some way, and has to find that
way out for himself." Because, the argument goes, most swing musicians
are in the latter category, listeners of jazz's early manifestations were
struck at once by the players' strong vitality as well as by the music's
crudeness. But in the face of this celebration of natural musicianship, the
argument takes a significant turn:

> It is very true that the swing music we have today is far more refined
> and subtle and developed as an art because the swing men who
> learned how to read and understand classical music have brought
> classical influences to it. I think that may be said to be the real
> difference between the original New Orleans "jazz" and the swing
> music of today. And in taking in the classical influence, real jazz has
> gained, and not lost—it is growing into a finer and broader and richer
> music, a music that is truly American, that will surely take its place
> in time, alongside the great and permanent musics of other coun-
> tries. Until swing music came, America had no music it could really
> call its own. If you will look at the European music journals, you will
> see what their critics think of our swing music. You will see that
> they already think of it as a new and permanent music. Some of
> them even write that the swing principle of free improvisation of the
> player will affect all of music—and at last make the player, the
> instrumentalist, as important as the composer, because he too, in
> swing, becomes a composer—a player-composer. I don't know about
> that, but it is funny that swing music got its first serious recognition,
> not at home, but in Europe. During my own three years playing in
> England and on the Continent, the very finest music critics would
> come back to my dressing room, or call on me at my hotel to discuss
> the "significance" of our music and what they thought it meant.
> That never happened to me before in America, although since I have
> been brought home this last time I noticed that our own critics and
> journals are beginning to have the same kind of serious interest. I
> don't believe that I, myself, ever realized swing music was really

important until I went to Europe and saw what they thought of it. I had just been playing it and growing with it since I was a kid. (74–76)

For those who challenge the autobiographical authenticity of *Swing that Music*, passages such as this one raise questions about the amount of influence Gerlach ultimately exerted over the final draft, particularly regarding the various claims made concerning the relationship between burgeoning jazz and conventional music: (1) that jazz has only been improved by its infusion with elements (presumed absent) of the European tradition; (2) that European music critics immediately recognized its aesthetic as opposed to its entertainment value; (3) that Armstrong never seriously reflected on such issues until visiting Europe. Although it is entirely reasonable to assume that Armstrong was informed on what European jazz critics such as Gerlach or Belgian jazz enthusiast Robert Goffin were writing about jazz in the early 1930s, and (even more likely) that he was well aware of the difference in the level of interest among jazz writers there as opposed to American critics, the claim that he "never realized swing music was important" until visiting Europe is rather hard to accept as coming directly from Armstrong himself. Moreover, his use of the words "important" and "significant" raises the question of *important* or *significant to whom*, and in what context, the answer to which here seems to be the self-consciously hip non-American cognoscenti (like Gerlach) who have some stake in "raising" jazz to a level of "serious" music.

VI

The preceding pages have taken up a few of the salient critical issues— what I consider essential "pressure points"—for any assessment of jazz autobiography. To briefly summarize, the attempt here has been to (1) expose an explicit historical awareness among jazz musicians manifested in the transformation from written object to writing subject; (2) provide a reading of Charles Mingus's *Beneath the Underdog* as an exploration of possibilities for literary invention and self-discovery in jazz autobiography; (3) examine the exigencies and constraints of collaboration within the autobiographical form; (4) interrogate the formal clash between the autobiographical subject and other ostensibly authenticating textual voices. What this particular cluster of issues seems to indicate is that along with the pertinent historical information to be derived from any specific jazz autobiography or, for that matter, from the corpus as a whole, much of the textual interest ultimately circulates around the contradiction or tensions produced in the written representation of a subjectivity fundamentally grounded in what Elizabeth Tonkin calls "oracy." So judgments regarding style, such as those advanced in Martin Williams's introduction to *The Night People,* immediately bring into sharp contrast the "supplementary" or "dialogic" relationship between speech and writing, particularly when a predominantly oral discourse is cast in terms of well-established written tradition. Given that writing is the most typical domain of self-inscription, a subject's commitment to or detachment from characteristic vernacular prose thus becomes a source of considerable tension as that is the material base from which auto-biographers must fashion their text.

To conclude my remarks, I would like to touch this very broad issue by referring once again to *From Behind the Veil,* where Stepto introduces, in a somewhat different context, an intriguing notion that he calls the "discourse of distrust"—the multidirectional tension (restricted in Stepto's argument to African American letters) that links literacy with freedom, that superimposes a narrative of textual creation (manifested in a published text itself) onto the larger narrative journey to autonomy. African American literature is largely predicated on a deep faith in literacy, Stepto asserts, but also present is a counterbalancing distrust on the part of the reader toward the wholly self-conscious author who, as "writer," has already stepped beyond the prescribed bounds of a minimal writing skill needed to "tell" a story. Significantly, Stepto focuses on the distrust engendered by the tension between "storytelling" and "story-writing"; or, as he puts it, on the act of written simulation that is "fully 'about' the communicative prospects of Afro-Americans writing for American readers, black and white, given the race rituals which color listening and/or reading." Stepto continues: "The risks that the written storyteller undertakes are twofold; one is that the reader will become a hearer but not manage an authenticating response; the other is that the reader *will remain a reader* and not only belittle or reject storytelling's particular 'keen disturbance' but also issue confrontational responses which sustain altogether different definitions of literature, of literacy, and of appropriate reader response" (202).

So in adapting Stepto's argument to my own purposes here, I would claim that it is precisely the complexity of the relationship between reader and autobiographical subject—the "keen disturbances" of jazz autobiography—that renders it a rich methodological field. On the writer's side, a statement like that in Rex Stewart's prologue to *Boy Meets Horn* reveals a genuine awareness of what is at stake in the project of *textualizing* a jazz life. There, Stewart is clearly caught in a double bind;

unwilling to call himself a writer, he nonetheless writes and explicitly distances himself from cultural coding brought forth in a vernacular style. Stewart addresses the "gentle reader": "I have nothing to lose. I am not on a way out kick nor am I an alcoholic. And although I do not consider myself a writer, I feel I can spell out these pertinent thoughts for the record. One truth I have discovered: it is easier to blow a horn than to write about when, why, and how. Which is why I disavow usage of the word. And while I am being humble (for the moment) I might as well beg your indulgence for the unavoidable lapses into the vernacular of my trade. No doubt, most laymen are aware that musicos have a private language of their own" (x).

On the opposite side of the equation, for the reader of *Miles: The Autobiography* or *Straight Life,* there is the unmistakable and constant reminder of the text's *orality* and the fact that the institutional underpinnings of print culture itself are often in direct tension with the lived jazz aesthetic such texts seek to capture on the page. Apart from harkening back to a Victorian sensibility regarding published material and polite company, the standards implied in Martin Williams's praise of *The Night People*—that it "gets down without ever getting dirty"—suggest something along the lines of a discursive etiquette, which, in the context of personal narrative, leads to more highly charged issues of political correctness. One important byproduct of a candidly conversational text such as *Straight Life,* then, is its textual inversion or shift into an *anti-autobiographical* mode in which the guiding trope is an open confession of less than exemplary life; and Williams's impatience with *Straight Life,* because it is "as concerned with struggles against drug addiction" as it is with the life of a musician, reflects a common "just the (musical) facts" bias in jazz nonfiction. As a result, the presence of substantial off-the-bandstand autobiographical material (in Art Pepper's case, a litany of hustles, break-ins, drug deals, arrests, and prison time à la William Burroughs), though revealing much about subjects, can in the end offer readers a bit more than they bargained for when turning to a given work of jazz autobiography.[14]

Along with the addiction narrative, for example, one recurrent and particularly disturbing aspect of the jazz autobiography is the candid expression of a naked and often violent sexism. In many of the works under consideration the physical abuse of women becomes a motif, not only through the various and degrading names for women but also in the form of a cold-blooded revelation: Mingus's pimp story, Pepper's vivid account of his having raped a young woman in England, or Miles's rendering of the time his then-wife Cicely Tyson was forced to call the police after he hit her in the face. As a feature of autobiography, one expects self-disclosure—even of a distasteful nature—but at the same time an unabashed, unrepentant attitude about violent abuse of women can be tough on reader sensibility. The Davis/Tyson incident was so disturbing to writer Pearl Cleage that after having read *Miles: The Autobiography* she created a performance piece in 1990, "Mad at Miles," from which the following passage is excerpted (the italicized section is a refrain, repeated numerous times throughout the piece):

> I kept thinking about Cicely Tyson hiding in the basement of her house while the police were upstairs laughing with Miles. I wondered what she was thinking about, crouched down there in the darkness. I wonder if thinking about his genius made her less frightened and humiliated.
>
> I wonder if his genius made it possible for her to forgive him for *self-confessed crimes against women such that we should break his albums, burn his tapes, scratch up his CD's until he acknowledges and apologizes and rethinks his position on the Woman Question.* (19)

With Cleage's reaction to *Miles: The Autobiography*, we thus return to our initial problem of generic circumscription in considering jazz autobiography and the position from which it is best surveyed, having discovered along the way that some of the handy and traditional distinctions (i.e., fiction/nonfiction, biography/autobiography, written/oral) when superimposed on contemporary critical issues of race, class, and gender leave an array of alternatives to ponder. .

Notes

1 For a useful overview of some current issues in self-representation, see Folkenflik.
2 Anthropologist Elizabeth Tonkin takes up the politics of *genrification* within the specific context of textualized oral autobiography in chapter 3 of her provocative study, *Narrating Our Pasts.*
3 In his introduction to a recent anthology of African American autobiography, *Bearing Witness*, editor Henry Louis Gates, Jr., locates autobiography at the core of African American letters. Gates writes: "The will to power for black Americans was the will to write; and the predominant mode that this writing would assume was the shaping of a black self in words" (4). Interestingly, Gates points out that African American autobiography distinguishes itself by typically *inaugurating* (rather than summarizing) a literary life: in these cases, the autobiographical subject seeks not only self-inscription but self-invention—through writing. Gates's argument for the primacy of autobiography, powerfully supported by

numerous texts, naturally presupposes that among the various forms of self-expression available to human subjects, writing is the most obvious; as the "will to power," it is the primary way African Americans have defined themselves. But one cannot help but notice that the subjects assembled in *Bearing Witness* are those already *predisposed* to use language (whether as novelist, poet, playwright, journalist, or political activist) as their chosen mode, distinct from what might be called nonwriterly subjects, be they visual artists, athletes, or jazz musicians. Obviously, one reason for the privileging of autobiographies by those possessing natural skill with language as opposed to music is that such works demonstrate a literary sensibility that we have come to expect from "good writing."

4   Jazz autobiographies vary widely in terms of the extent to which race is explicitly developed as an issue. Pony Poindexter's *Pony Express,* for example, follows *Beneath the Underdog* in sustaining its critique of race relations throughout the text. Milt Hinton's *Bass Line* and Garvin Bushell's *Jazz from the Beginning* recall a strikingly similar boyhood trauma of witnessing a lynching. In the opening pages of *Boy Meets Horn,* Rex Stewart remembers his grandmother's calling his attention to "race and class distinctions" when she chased a white man from their front yard. Sidney Bechet's *Treat It Gentle* begins with a lengthy description of the rape of a young black woman. Buck Clayton tells of the impressive childhood experience when W. E. B. Du Bois was a guest in the home of his parents. In the opening of *Satchmo: My Life in New Orleans,* Louis Armstrong remembers being scolded for taking a seat in the front of a streetcar when he could not read the sign that said, FOR COLORED PASSENGERS ONLY, and he then recalls later experiences when black passengers outnumbered whites and happily sat where they pleased. Sammy Price begins *What Do They Want?* with an account of his learning the various uses and contexts of the word "Nigger." Also, most of these works sooner or later take up the issue of interracial tension and the hierarchy fostered by one's ability or inability to "pass" in the white community. Jelly Roll Morton's *Mr. Jelly Roll* suggests that the relationship between New Orleans' lower-class blacks and middle-class French-speaking mulattos was the founding element in the creation of jazz itself.

5   In his discussion of third-person narration in autobiography, "The Self as Other," Robert Folkenflik traces Augustinian self-loathing as the primary impetus in the confessional or conversion autobiography. Because the narrative of personal failure or tragedy is, as Folkenflik argues, fairly atypical in autobiographical writing, the successful reinvention of the self is posited as the ultimate victory. In such cases, the narrative is predicated upon the juxtaposition of the "authentic self" with one or more "false selves."

6   Consider, for example, Mingus's timeless description of his depression-era Watts high school: "The new school was all black except for a few Mexicans and Noba Oke, a Japanese boy whose family owned the most pleasant and fairly priced grocery store in the district. Noba's brother Mosa as a straight-A student at Jordan High. His younger sister Miko had been crippled by polio. They were a nice family and tolerated Negro drop-outs—called delinquents in those days—who hung out in front of their store smoking and shooting craps all afternoon and in the evening went over to Steve's Billiard Parlor on Watts's main street to shoot pool. These tough kids wore jackets and windbreakers painted with skulls and dragons and the names of their clubs—Panthers, Blue Devils, Crusaders" (45–46).

7 See Fischer. In an attempt to grapple critically with the notion of ethnicity, Fischer constructs an elaborate model drawing from representative autobiographies of variously assimilated American subcultures: American Indian, Chinese-American, Armenian-American, Mexican-American, and African American, with *Beneath the Underdog* as one example of the last category.

8 In *Straight Life*, Benny Carter's testimony is but one example of how a "qualified" statement by a supporting witness can ultimately cast doubt on the subject's credibility: "I was greatly impressed by Art's talent, his sound, his concept of playing lead, and his creative ideas. He was a handsome, clean-cut, and most mannerly boy with an affable disposition. I wasn't aware at all of Art drinking heavily or using drugs. I liked him and have only positive memories of him at that time" (49–50).

9 Among the number of well-known collaborative works already mentioned, there are a few more titles, each with its own way of describing the coauthor function: Bob Wilber's (1986) *Music Was Not Enough*, Steve Jordan's (1991) *Rhythm Man*, Barney Bigard's (1986) *With Louis and the Duke*, Andy Kirk's (1989) *Twenty Years on Wheels*, Art Hodes's (1992) *Hot Man*.

10 See, for example, Prögler.

11 In a tidy textual note that serves as preface to *Satchmo*, his own biography of Armstrong, Giddins, who refers to his subject as "the most expansive musician-writer jazz has ever known," briefly summarizes Armstrong's writing career, one that includes dozens of magazine articles, numerous letters, sketches, a group of notebooks, as well as various autobiographical manuscripts. Among these is *Swing that Music* (1936), undoubtedly one of the first texts published under the name of a jazz musician, which underwent such extensive revision at the hands of its editor that it is now regarded as corrupt—particularly when compared to the later and more well-known book, *Satchmo: My Life in New Orleans* (1954). Though also edited (albeit more sensitively), *Satchmo: My Life in New Orleans*, widely considered to have been written by Armstrong himself, covers the same formative years before his move to Chicago in 1922 and is reportedly only part of a longer manuscript—first suppressed, now lost—that candidly details Armstrong's maturity, including sundry dealings with gangsters, drugs, and the law.

12 In this regard, Kenney also mentions a review of the book by *New Yorker* jazz writer Whitney Balliett who complained that the original manuscript was "hoked-up" by the publisher and that Armstrong's written style "makes e.e. cummings seem like ladyfingers on a spree"; if left untouched, Balliett claimed, Armstrong's personality "would have come closer to the surface."

13 In his famous essay "Discourse in the Novel," Mikhail Bakhtin describes a similar condition that he calls "dialogized heteroglossia" in which an author will appropriate the language of a character. "Such speech constitutes a special type of *double-voiced discourse*. It serves two speakers at the same time and expresses simultaneously two different intentions: the direct intentions of the character who is speaking, and the refracted intention of the author. In such discourse there are two voices, two meanings and two expressions. And all the while these two voices are dialogically interrelated, they—as it were—know about each other (just as two exchanges in a dialogue know of each other and are structured in this mutual knowledge of each other); it is as if they actually hold a conversation with each other" (324).

14   In a review of *Straight Life*, Peter Schwendener explicitly addresses this issue. "It is an ugly book in many ways, full of the stale, sour, sickly smell of clinical degeneracy, or the kind of violence that never goes anywhere but just sits rotting on the page. . . . one can't help but wonder in reading it if Pepper enjoyed the violence he writes about while it was actually going on, and the sense one gets that he did makes one's pleasure in the book feel a bit warped, as if it were not really pleasure but something more like voyeurism or one of Pepper's other self described sins one were engaging in while reading. . . There's a lot to like about Pepper—his honesty and friendliness and way with words—yet there's also the sense of someone who got more positive energy from violent depression than most people get from feeling great about themselves" (247–48).

Works Cited

Armstrong, Louis. *Satchmo: My Life in New Orleans.* New York: Da Capo, 1986.

Bakhtin, Mikhail. *The Dialogic Imagination.* Austin: U of Texas P, 1981.

Barker, Danny. *A Life in Jazz.* Ed. Alyn Shapiro. New York: Oxford UP, 1986.

Bechet, Sidney. *Treat It Gentle.* New York: Da Capo, 1975.

Bigard, Barney. *With Louis and the Duke: The Autobiography of a Jazz Clarinetist.* Ed. Barry Martyn. New York: Oxford UP, 1986.

Bushell, Garvin, as told to Mark Tucker. *Jazz from the Beginning.* Ann Arbor: U of Michigan P, 1988.

Chambers, Jack. *Milestones I.* Toronto: U of Toronto P, 1983.

——. *Milestones II.* Toronto: U of Toronto P, 1985.

Cleage, Pearl. "Mad At Miles: A Black Woman's Guide to Truth." *Deals with the Devil.* New York: Ballantine, 1993.

Coleman, Bill. *Trumpet Story.* Boston: Northeastern UP, 1989.

Coleman, Janet, and Al Young. *Mingus/Mingus: Two Memoirs.* Berkeley, Calif.: Creative Arts, 1989.

Crouch, Stanley. "Play the Right Thing." *New Republic* 12 Feb. 1990: 30–36.

Davis, Miles, with Quincy Troupe. *Miles: The Autobiography.* New York: Simon, 1989.

DeVeaux, Scott. "Constructing the Jazz Tradition: Jazz Historiography." *Black American Literature Forum* 25.3 (1991): 525–60.

Ellington, Duke. *Music Is My Mistress.* New York: Da Capo, 1976.

Fischer, Michael M. J. "Ethnicity and the Post-Modern Arts of Memory." *Writing Culture: The Poetics and Politics of Ethnography.* Ed. James Clifford and George Marcus. Berkeley: U of California P, 1986. 194–233.

Folkenflik, Robert ed. *The Culture of Autobiography.* Stanford, Calif.: Stanford UP, 1993.

Foster, Pops, as told to Tom Stoddard. *Pops Foster: The Autobiography of a New Orleans Jazzman.* Berkeley: U of California P, 1971.

Gates, Henry Louis, Jr., ed. "Introduction." *Bearing Witness.* New York: Pantheon, 1991.

Giddins, Gary. "Introduction." *Raise Up Off Me,* by Hampton Hawes and Don Asher. New York: Da Capo, 1979.

——. *Satchmo.* New York: Doubleday, 1988.

Gillespie, Dizzy, with Al Fraser. *To BE, or Not . . . to BOP*. Garden City, N.Y.: Doubleday, 1979.

Hampton, Lionel, with James Haskins. *Hamp: An Autobiography*. New York: Warner, 1989.

Hawes, Hampton, and Don Asher. *Raise Up Off Me*. New York: Da Capo, 1979.

Hinton, Milt, and David Berger. *Bass Line: The Stories and Photographs of Milt Hinton*. Philadelphia: Temple UP, 1988.

———, with David Berger and Holly Maxon. *Overtime*. San Francisco: Pomegranate Art Books, 1991.

Hodes, Art, and Chadwick Hansen. *Hot Man*. Urbana: U of Illinois P, 1992.

Holiday, Billie, with William Dufty. *Lady Sings the Blues*. New York: Avon, 1956.

Jordan, Steve, with Tom Scanlan. *Rhythm Man*. Ann Arbor: U of Michigan P, 1991.

Kenney, William H., III. "Negotiating the Color Line: Louis Armstrong's Autobiographies." *Jazz in Mind*. Ed. Reginald T. Buckner and Steven Weiland. Detroit: Wayne State UP, 1991. 38–59.

Kirk, Andy, as told to Amy Lee. *Twenty Years on Wheels*. Ann Arbor: U of Michigan P, 1989.

Lejeune, Philippe. "The Autobiographical Contract." *French Literary Theory Today*. Ed. Tzvetan Todorov. Cambridge: Cambridge UP, 1982. 192–222.

Lomax, Alan, and Jelly Roll Morton. *Mister Jelly Roll: The Fortunes of Jelly Roll Morton, New Orleans Creole and "Inventor of Jazz."* Berkeley: U of California P, 1973.

Malcolm X, with Alex Haley. *The Autobiography of Malcolm X*. 1964. New York: Ballantine, 1992.

Mezzrow, Mezz, and Bernard Wolfe. *Really the Blues*. New York: Random, 1946.

Mingus, Charles. *Beneath the Underdog: His World According to Mingus*. Ed. Nel King. New York: Vintage, 1991.

Murray, Albert. *Good Morning Blues: The Autobiography of Count Basie*. New York: Random, 1985.

Ogren, Kathy. " 'Jazz Isn't Just Me': Jazz Autobiographies as Performance Personas." *Jazz in Mind*. Ed. Reginald T. Buckner and Steven Weiland. Detroit: Wayne State UP, 1991. 112–27.

O'Meally, Robert. *Lady Day: The Many Faces of Billie Holiday*. New York: Arcade, 1991.

Pepper, Art, and Laurie Pepper. *Straight Life*. New York: Schirmer, 1979.

Poindexter, Pony. *Pony Express*. Frankfurt: J.A.S. Publikationen, 1985.

Porter, Lewis. "Some Problems in Jazz Research." *Black Music Research* 8.2 (1988): 195–206.

Porter, Roy, with David Keller. *There and Back: The Roy Porter Story*. Baton Rouge: Louisiana State UP, 1991.

Price, Sammy. *What Do They Want?* Ed. Caroline Richmond. Urbana: U of Illinois P, 1990.

Prögler, J. A. "Choices in Editing Oral History: The Distillation of Dr. Hiller." *Oral History Review* 19 (1991): 1–17.

Rosengarten, Theodore. *All God's Dangers: The Life of Nate Shaw*. New York: Avon, 1974.

Schwendener, Peter. "The Sad White Jazz Man." *Tri-Quarterly* 74 (1989): 247–54.

Smith, Willie, with George Hoefer. *Music on My Mind*. New York: Da Capo, 1978.

Stepto, Robert. *From Behind the Veil.* Urbana: U of Illinois P, 1991.

Stewart, Rex. *Boy Meets Horn.* Ed. Claire Gordon. Ann Arbor: U of Michigan P, 1991.

Stone, Albert E. "Two Recreate One: The Act of Collaboration in Recent Black Auto-biography." *REAL* 1.1 (1982): 227–66.

Sudhalter, Richard. "What's Your Story, Mornin' Glory?: Reflections on Some Jazz Autobiography." *Annual Review of Jazz Studies* 5 (1991): 210–16.

Tomlinson, Gary. "Cultural Dialogics and Jazz: A White Historian Signifies." *Black Music Research Journal* 11.2 (1991): 229–63.

Tonkin, Elizabeth. *Narrating Our Pasts: The Social Construction of Oral History.* Cambridge: Cambridge UP, 1992.

Wells, Dicky, as told to Stanley Dance. *The Night People.* Washington, D.C.: Smithsonian Institution Press, 1991.

Wilber, Bob, assisted by Derek Webster. *Music Was Not Enough.* New York: Oxford UP, 1987.

EXCURSUS:

CABIN

IN THE

SKY

Uptown Folk: Blackness and Entertainment in Cabin in the Sky

JAMES NAREMORE

Between 1927 and 1954 the major Hollywood studios produced only six feature films that took place in an all-black milieu: *Hallelujah!* (MGM, 1929), *Hearts in Dixie* (Fox, 1929), *The Green Pastures* (Warner Bros., 1936), *Cabin in the Sky* (MGM, 1943), *Stormy Weather* (Twentieth Century-Fox, 1943), and *Carmen Jones* (Twentieth Century-Fox, 1954).[1] The period in question was the heyday of classic cinema, bounded at one end by the introduction of sound and at the other by a shift toward a decentered, "package unit" mode of production;[2] more importantly, 1954 was the year when the U.S. Supreme Court ordered public schools desegregated, paving the way for a civil rights movement that would have a lasting effect on all the media. Until then, any studio film purporting to deal exclusively with black experience was truly exceptional and controversial. These six films are therefore among the most unusual products of American show business. No proper history of the movies should ignore them, and they deserve far more critical analysis than they have received.[3]

Viewed from a late twentieth-century perspective, one of the most interesting of the "all Negro" productions was MGM's *Cabin in the Sky*, starring Ethel Waters, Eddie Anderson, Lena Horne, and many well-known black performers. This film warrants special attention—not only because of its considerable entertainment value, but because it appeared at a crucial juncture in the series, when African Americans were increasing their demands for better treatment from the movie industry, when black musical performers were receiving a degree of celebrity they had not enjoyed before, and when the federal government was engaged in a semiofficial drive to encourage more pictures with black casts. Although

Cabin was manufactured in Hollywood's most politically, artistically, and sexually conservative studio, it was designed to appeal to a variety of audiences, binding them together in the name of wartime solidarity; in certain ways it can be described as a liberal or historically transitional work, and it tells us important things about the complex, sometimes troubled relations between ethnicity and modernity.

Of course, in general terms, *Cabin* was no different from the other five studio-produced films about blacks. They were all products of a segregated society; they were all written, produced, and directed by whites; and they were all musicals or melodramatic narratives that made extensive use of song and dance, thus reinforcing the white culture's perception of African Americans as a fun-loving, "rhythmic" people. As a group, the six films also depended on a vivid binary opposition between city and country that structured both classic Hollywood and many aspects of the culture at large.[4] The social tensions and ideological contradictions expressed by this opposition were always crucial to any art or entertainment that involved blackness; notice, for example, how the country-city polarity functioned in early uses of "jazz," a term that had been appropriated by white songwriters from Tin Pan Alley and turned into an ambiguous, highly flexible signifier. Was jazz a primitive music, a people's music, or an entertainment music? All three possibilities were suggested by critics, and the term seemed to oscillate between diametrically opposed meanings. On the one hand, jazz was associated with flappers, skyscrapers, and the entire panoply of twentieth-century modernity; on the other hand, because it originated with African Americans who migrated to the northern cities, it connoted agrarian or precapitalist social relations, and it could be linked to a pastoral myth. Thus Jerome Kern and Oscar Hammerstein's *Show Boat* (1927) and George and Ira Gershwin's *Porgy and Bess* (1935)—two celebrated "modern" stage musicals—were grounded in folkloric treatments of blacks. Even Warners' *The Jazz Singer* (1927) evoked both the city and the country. Throughout most of the film, jazz represents a force of modernization that disrupts a conservative Jewish household; but when the protagonist enters show business, he reasserts old-fashioned values by donning blackface and singing "Mammy."

The same contrasts can be observed everywhere in *Cabin in the Sky*, which uses black-influenced popular music to tell a story about a rural community threatened by a world of gamblers and nightclubs. But as I hope to show, *Cabin* creates a different effect from earlier pictures of its type. Whatever its artistic merits (and these are far from negligible), its treatment of the country/city theme is ironic or insincere, signaling an important change in mainstream cinema's negotiation of racial issues.

Even though the film is never free of reactionary sentiments, it is in some ways an entirely modern work, generating what Richard Dyer has described as a "utopian" feeling of energy, abundance, intensity, transparency, and community—a vision of "something we want deeply that our day-to-day lives don't provide" (177).[5] Dyer qualifies his observation when he lists *Cabin* among a group of musicals that are "bought off by the nostalgia or primitivism which provides them with a point of departure" (188); nevertheless, I would argue that *Cabin*'s nostalgia is on one level superficial, and that its primitivism is transformed (for white audiences at least) into a paradoxical sophistication. Ultimately, the film participates in a kind of capitalist progress, contributing to the breakdown of a pastoral, the death of a bogus authenticity, and the growing urbanization of black images in Hollywood. In fact, there is an important sense in which *Cabin* was "saved" or "made progressive" by the very forces of mass-cultural aestheticism and commodification that leftist critics usually condemn.

To fully appreciate such ironies, we should first examine *Cabin*'s historical context, bearing in mind Mikhail Bakhtin's observation that all art operates in a "dialogically agitated and tension-filled environment" (276). For obvious reasons, the environment surrounding this particular film was especially agitated, and it requires careful scrutiny. I shall therefore propose that *Cabin* was situated uneasily among at least four conflicting discourses about blackness and entertainment in the United States during World War II.[6] These discourses were composed of a variety of texts, including speeches, newspaper items, critical and theoretical writings, and artistic representations; for the most part they were generated outside Hollywood, and they tended to cut across the usual political divisions between right and left, affecting both the production and the reception of the film. By examining each in turn, we can begin to recover *Cabin*'s historical specificity, showing how several artists at MGM responded to the racial dialogue of their day. In the process, we can begin to make informed judgments about the film's cultural politics.

I

Cabin was shaped first of all by a vestigial tradition of "folkloric" narratives having to do with poor blacks in rural southern communities. I hasten to emphasize that nothing in the film was generated by an indigenous, agrarian culture, and that folklore itself is a suspiciously modern phenomenon, born of late eighteenth-century attempts to distinguish between the learned and the popular. We should remember, however, that the discourse on the folk can have different uses. For the most part, the childlike mammies and pappies who once populated our songs, stories, and movies were figments of a reactionary white imagination—embodiments of what Peter Burke describes as everything "natural, simple, instinctive, irrational, and rooted in the local soil" (216). But another kind of folklore has been important to the historical consciousness of African Americans, and during the 1930s folkloric images of black people were frequently used by the federal government's Works Progress Administration (WPA) and the Popular Front on behalf of a progressive social agenda. The entire artistic culture of the depression was in fact somewhat "folksy" in tone, ranging from public murals to Leadbelly recordings, from the American Communist party's folk-song movement to John Steinbeck's *The Grapes of Wrath*, and from off-Broadway theatrical productions like *Mule Bone* to Pulitzer Prize hits like *The Green Pastures*.

Cabin in the Sky has an ancestry in this mostly liberal, 1930s-style folkloricism. The film was based on a 1940 Broadway musical by Lynn Root, concerning an impoverished Georgia laborer named "little Joe" who is wounded by gunfire during a dice game. Joe's devout wife, Petunia, prays for his recovery, and black emissaries of God and the Devil are sent to earth to do battle for his soul. Joe is given a short reprieve so that he can mend his ways, but the Devil complicates matters—first by allowing Joe to win the Irish sweepstakes, and then by sending a temptress to lure him away from home. In the end, Petunia's faith wins out, and she and Joe ascend into heaven. Root's quasiallegorical plot was rendered in the form of a colorful, mainstream spectacular, but many of the black performers, including such figures as Rex Ingram and Katherine Dunham, were associated in the public mind with a kind of folkloric art; indeed, the show's lyricist, John Latouche, had worked with the WPA and had written a famous depression-era cantata entitled "Ballad for Americans." Not surprisingly, when MGM purchased the property, it conceived the forthcoming film as a substitute for *Porgy and Bess* (which was unavailable for purchase), and it hired Marc Connelly, the author of *The Green Pastures*, to work on the screenplay (Minnelli 121; Harvey 41).

By the time *Cabin* went into production, however, African Americans had enlisted to fight in a war against fascism, and a second discourse about race was emerging, foreshadowing the civil rights movement of the next decade. Immediately before the war, Walter White, the executive secretary of the NAACP, had met with a group of Hollywood executives and stars—including Walter Wanger, David O. Selznick, Daryl

Zanuck, and James Cagney—to discuss "the limitation of the Negro to comic or menial roles" (quoted in *The Papers of the NAACP*, December 1940). Then in 1942 the NAACP held its national convention in Los Angeles, where White called for an end to racial stereotyping and greater participation by black workers in Hollywood craft unions. Later that same year, at the invitation of Wendell Willkie, who was at the time special counsel to the NAACP and chairman of the board of Twentieth Century-Fox, White made a similar speech to the East Coast Committee on Public Relations of the Motion Picture Producers Association, which promised him it would "effect as rapid a change as possible in the treatment of Negroes in moving pictures" (*The Papers of the NAACP*, April 1942).

Not coincidentally, *Casablanca* and *In This Our Life* were released by Warner Bros. in 1942, and several of the subsequent wartime pictures, including *Sahara* (1943) and *Bataan* (1943), showed urban blacks pitted against Nazi or Japanese antagonists. Equally important, the Office of War Information financed a handful of documentaries about black participation in combat, among them Carleton Moss and Stuart Heisler's *The Negro Soldier.* During the same period, black musical performers, some of them bearing flamboyantly aristocratic names, were featured in movies about contemporary show business: Count Basie, Duke Ellington, and Nat "King" Cole worked at Republic Pictures in 1942–43, as did Louis Armstrong and Dorothy Dandridge; and in 1944, Fox produced *Stormy Weather,* starring Lena Horne and a virtual pantheon of jazz entertainers. Meanwhile, as Thomas Cripps has pointed out, the sentimental depictions of plantation life in Julien Duvivier's *Tales of Manhattan* (1942) and Walt Disney's *Song of the South* (1946) were denounced by black organizations—this despite the fact that both films "might have been lauded for efforts in social progress" only a few years earlier (44).

When *Cabin in the Sky* and *Stormy Weather* went into production, the *New York Times* reported that both pictures had been given the explicit encouragement of the Roosevelt administration:

> Two major studios, Metro-Goldwyn Mayer and Twentieth Century-Fox, in producing pictures with all-Negro casts, are following the desires of Washington in making such films at this time. Decisions to produce the pictures, it is stated, followed official expression that the Administration felt that its program for increased employment of Negro citizens in certain heretofore restricted fields of industry would be helped by a general distribution of important pictures in which Negroes played a major part. (quoted in Bogle 136–37)

But even though Hollywood and Washington, D.C., seemed to be collaborating in an effort to employ minorities, many black leaders were dismayed by the idea of MGM's musical about rural colored folk. *Cabin* had never been the sort of picture to appeal to most white southerners, but it also threatened to offend its more liberal audience in the predominantly urban centers where Lowe's, Inc., owned theaters. One sign of the trouble the film might encounter was a letter from Hall Johnson, the conductor of a black choral group hired to perform in *Cabin,* to associate producer Albert Lewis. Johnson (who had also worked on the 1935 adaptation of *The Green Pastures*) warned that "Negroes have never forgiven the slanderous misrepresentations of [Connelly's play], and when after five successful years on the stage it was finally made into a picture, they did not hesitate to express their opinion" (quoted in Fordin 74).

Almost concurrently, an influential group of white intellectuals was voicing a sharply different complaint, growing out of what might be termed the discourse of critical modernism. Some participants in this third discursive activity believed in an indigenous folk culture that could be captured on film, but they argued that black folk and jazz music in particular had been commodified, controlled, and transformed by the media and the WPA; as a result, important local differences were being erased, and America was moving ineluctably toward a one-dimensional society. The locus classicus of such reasoning was James Agee's "Pseudo-Folk," published in *The Partisan Review* in 1944, less than a year after *Cabin in the Sky* was released. Agee was especially disturbed by the "decadence" of swing music, and he worried that the latest fashion in pop tunes would have a bad influence "among Negroes, . . . our richest contemporary source of folk art, and our best people en bloc" (407). To his ear, swing was a corruption of true jazz, which had been produced "where the deep country and the town have first fertilized each other" (405). As examples of the fake, mass-cultural populism that was destroying jazz and overtaking America like a "galloping cancer" (404), he cited the declining quality of Louis Armstrong's most recent work; the sleek, big-band arrangements of Duke Ellington; the "pseudo-savage, pseudo-'cultured' dancing" (408) of Katherine Dunham and her troupe; and Paul Robeson's performances of John Latouche's "inconceivably snobbish, esthetically execrable 'Ballad for Americans'" (406–8). Although he never mentioned *Cabin in the Sky,* he could hardly have come closer to describing it. Both Armstrong and Ellington were featured in the movie, and, as we have seen, both Dunham and Latouche had contributed to the original Broadway show.

Interestingly, Max Horkheimer and Theodor W. Adorno's *Dialectic of*

Enlightenment was roughly contemporary with Agee's essay. (The book was published in 1947, but it was written during the war, largely in California, and it carries a 1944 copyright.) In making this connection I am not suggesting an influence or equivalence. Unlike Agee, Horkheimer and Adorno came from a European Marxist tradition; they were never preoccupied by the folk (understandably so, since in Germany *völkish* theory had long been appropriated by the fascists), and for the most part they regarded jazz as a pernicious outgrowth of the culture industry.[7] Nevertheless, like many intellectuals of the left, right, and center, they believed that industrialized capitalism and big government of the interwar years was standardizing and reifying social relations, and they shared Agee's distaste for tendentious, fake, or "inauthentic" art. In 1941, Adorno had described the "utopian" element in American life as a "desperate attempt to escape the abstract sameness of things by a kind of self-made and futile *promesse du bonheur*" (quoted in Calinescu 228). For his part, Agee remained a humanist and a lover of movies; he was, however, an equally fierce critic of "sameness." In fact, when he claimed that a valuable "folk tradition" was being "thoroughly bourgeoizified" by the media (404), he was responding to the same rationalization and commodification that had given rise to the Frankfurt school's pessimistic, somewhat Weberian analysis of "late capitalism."[8]

Arthur Freed, the producer of *Cabin*, was oblivious to such critiques; as a leading executive in America's most prosperous movie studio, however, he was sensitive to charges of racism. In an attempt to avoid controversy, he gave interviews to the black press in which he addressed "the Negro problem," committing himself to a "dignified presentation of a peace-loving and loyal people," and promising to "spare nothing" on the production (quoted in Fordin 73). The last of these pronouncements was disingenuous, since *Cabin* was the lowest-budgeted musical in the history of the Freed unit; photographed in a sepia-tinted black and white, it borrowed its most spectacular visual effect—a tornado that destroys a nightclub—from *The Wizard of Oz* (1939). Even so, the studio made a considerable investment in the picture: it hired Elmer Rice and Joseph Schrank to assist Connelly with the adaptation (Schrank wrote the first draft and received the sole credit); it commissioned Harold Arlen and E. Y. Harburg to supplement the original John Latouche/Vernon Duke score; and it selected the popular radio personality Eddie Anderson to replace Dooley Wilson.

MGM's production resources, the cast of star performers, and Freed's efforts at public relations all helped the film to earn a modest profit. According to Donald Bogle, *Cabin* was received enthusiastically by black audiences in the South, and was widely shown at U.S. army camps, where Lena Horne was a special favorite (132). But tensions were evident during the shooting, and arguments over *Cabin*'s racial subject matter persisted throughout its distribution.⁹ On its release, certain reviewers were highly critical of the results. Although *Cabin* received good notices from the *New York Times* and the *New York Daily News* (the last of which had a substantial black readership), David Lardner of the *New Yorker* scoffed at MGM for trying to produce a "lovable ol' folk fantasy" (29 May 1943), and the anonymous reviewer for *Time*—none other than James Agee—charged that the studio had treated its fine cast as "picturesque, Sambo-style entertainers" (12 April 1943). *PM* magazine remarked that the film was an example of "how *not* to fulfill a pledge such as Hollywood made to Wendell Willkie last year, to treat the Negro as a first-class citizen in films" (1 June 1943). At least one review in the African American press was even more scathing. Writing in New York's *Amsterdam News* two weeks after *Cabin* had opened its successful run at the Criterion theater on Broadway, Ramona Lewis described the film as "an insult masking behind the label of folklore. . . . It pictures Negroes, heads tied up, with crap shooting inclinations and prayer meeting propensities at a time when [they] are daily proving their heroic mettle in battle and defense plant. . . . Since box office returns convince Hollywood more than anything else that it is in the right, it's too bad the actors didn't have the courage to refuse to make the film in the first place" (12 June 1943).

In different ways, each of these negative reactions was appropriate. There can be little doubt that *Cabin* was a Hollywoodish depiction of black folklore, saturated with inferential forms of racism; nor can there be any doubt that it represented a carefully managed style of mass entertainment, designed to serve the interests of a white corporation. Nevertheless, the film has a paradoxical effect, as if it wanted to dissolve binary oppositions between the town and the country, thereby unsettling the strategy of containment that usually operated in Hollywood's folkloric narratives. Placed alongside earlier pictures in the same vein, such as director King Vidor's sincere but no less racist *Hallelujah!* or the Warner Bros. adaptation of *The Green Pastures*, it seems distinctly urban· in spirit, keyed to the talents of Ethel Waters, Duke Ellington, and Lena Horne. In true Hollywood fashion the performers are treated as celebrities, so that they take on a glamorous aura and sometimes appear in cameo roles as "themselves." And because these performers have a spacious, handsomely mounted vehicle (staged on the visibly artificial, "utopian" sets that were a hallmark of the Freed unit during the forties), they are able to behave like something other than minstrel-show caricatures.[10]

This is not to excuse MGM's racism. The studio was responding in certain ways to potential criticism from its black audience, but it was also attempting to preserve the imagery of cheerful, plantation-style darkies. My point is simply that the film's folkloric project was vitiated—partly by the black critique of Hollywood, partly by the Roosevelt administration's desire to integrate certain aspects of the wartime economy, and chiefly by the growing commodification and modernization of American life. In this last regard I would also argue that *Cabin's* strong feeling of urbanity and sophistication derives in great measure from a fourth discourse about blackness, different from the ones I have described thus far: a chic, upscale "Africanism," redolent of café society, Broadway theater, and the European avant-garde.

I use the term "Africanism" in a limited and stipulated manner, to suggest a cosmopolitan artistic sensibility that pointed away from the American provinces—usually toward Harlem, Paris, French colonial Africa, and the Caribbean. This sensibility was prompted indirectly by developments within black culture itself, especially by the black internationalism described in a founding document of the Harlem Renaissance, Alain Locke's "The New Negro" (1925).[11] It also has something in common with "Negritude," a word first used in print by poet Aimé Césaire in 1939. But the particular attitude I am trying to identify was chiefly a white mythology, with distant origins in the artistic and intellectual revolutions that had swept Europe during the early twentieth century. Its progenitors would include Conrad's *Heart of Darkness* (1902), Picasso's *Les Demoiselles d'Avignon* (1907), Fry's exhibition of the postimpressionist painters (1910), Freud's *Totem and Taboo* (1913), and the Dadaist experiments with "Negro poems" or *Negergedichte* (1916).[12]

Throughout the 1920s and 1930s, as European high modernism became institutionalized, African motifs found their way into "classy" forms of decoration and entertainment, operating in almost dialectical relation with narratives about the pastoral southland. (Meanwhile, in Germany, the Nazis branded both modernist art and the newer types of black entertainment as "degenerate.") This chic, highly commodified style—raised to delirious excess by Josef von Sternberg in the "Hot Voodoo" number of *Blonde Venus* (1932)—offered a "savage" urbanity in place of a "childlike" pastoralism. It was already present to some degree in the original Broadway production of *Cabin in the Sky,* where the two primitivisms seemed to combine. It could also be heard everywhere in the work of songwriters employed by the Freed unit; for instance, Cole Porter had written a series of Africanist numbers for Broadway shows like *Jubilee* (1935) and *Panama Hattie* (1940), both of which were purchased by MGM. One of the leading exponents of the style, however, was a young director Freed hired for the film: Vincente Minnelli, who had never before been placed in charge of a feature picture.

Minnelli had begun his career in the early 1920s, at the very birth of "modern times," by taking a job as a window decorator in the Marshall Field department store in Chicago; and throughout his later tenure in Hollywood, he consistently drew on post-1870s Paris—the cradle of artistic and commercial modernity—as a source of inspiration. (See *An American in Paris* [1951], *Lust for Life* [1956], and *Gigi* [1958].) A devoted student of European painting and a great admirer of the surrealists, he was valuable to MGM precisely because, in Geoffrey Nowell-Smith's well-chosen phrase, he furthered the studio's policy of bringing "refinement to the popular" (75). He was undoubtedly offered the chance to supervise *Cabin* because during the mid-1930s he had become famous as a director-designer of sophisticated Broadway revues featuring black performers. Ethel Waters had starred in two of his most successful New York shows, including *At Home Abroad* (1934), where she was cast as the "Empress Jones," a potentate of the Belgian Congo who travels to Harlem and brings the latest styles back to her subjects. ("Cartier rings they're wearin' in their noses now," she sang.) Minnelli had also created settings for Duke Ellington's big band at Radio City, and he was responsible for the extravagant and erotic costumes Josephine Baker wore in *The Ziegfeld Follies* of 1936. Robert Benchley of the *New Yorker* snidely accused him of having a "Negroid" sense of color (quoted in Minnelli 58), but in his authorial signature and personal style he continued to exploit what Stephen Harvey has called "the totems of Africa *moderne*" (34). In 1937, *Esquire* magazine praised his own dress as "a perfect marriage of Harlem and the Left Bank" (quoted in Harvey 30).

In figure 1, an example of one of Minnelli's designs for the unproduced 1939 Broadway musical *Serena Blandish* (intended as a vehicle for Lena Horne and Ethel Waters) shows his tendency to blend surrealist motifs with an au courant Africanism. It should be emphasized that this style is no less racist than high modernism itself, and no more progressive than much of the commercial folklore of the 1930s. Like the folkloric artists, Minnelli relied on a kind of primitivism, explicitly associating blackness with sexuality, instinctiveness, and the Freudian unconscious. At the same time, however, he promoted an uptown face of jazz, tied to contemporary fashion and big-time entertainment. In this context, blackness

Figure 1. Vincente Minnelli's design for *Serena Blandish,* 1939. Photograph by permission of Lee (Mrs. Vincente) Minnelli.

began to signify both wildness and sophistication. The African imagery was as "stereotypical" as any other cultural code, but it seemed attractive and denatured by parody or playful quotation; moreover, because it was regarded by audiences as vanguard, it tended to problematize the distinction between the savage and the cultivated.

However one might describe the political effect of such designs, the important point about Minnelli's work is that he was far more attuned to contemporary New York than to the Old South, and in a picture like *Cabin* his aestheticism tended to undermine the conservative implications of the original material. This is not to suggest that he was either an auteur or an artistic subversive. On the contrary, his elegance and "exoticism" were perfectly in keeping with the institutional needs of MGM in 1943—as we can see from the studio's promotion of the picture, which tried to deemphasize the story's rural atmosphere. Consider the lobby card (figure 2) from the original release showing Lena Horne, Eddie Anderson, and Ethel Waters gathered around a picket fence. The artwork and promotional copy are appropriate to a big-city nightclub, promising "entertainment galore" and "gorgeous girls," while depicting two richly costumed figures strutting off to a dance. Although the film is less brazenly "citified" than this ad, MGM's publicity department was being reasonably faithful to the values Freed and Minnelli put on the screen.

Figure 2. MGM's promotion for *Cabin in the Sky*. © 1943, Turner Entertainment Co. All rights reserved.

II

The historical forces and discursive categories I have been describing—the vestigial folklore of the 1930s, the NAACP's mounting criticism of Hollywood, the increasing collaboration between mass entertainment and government, and the posh Africanism of high-toned Broadway musicals—have left their mark on the film, producing a kind of ideological schizophrenia. At the beginning of the credit sequence, for example, a title card announces "The Broadway Musical Play *Cabin in the Sky*," as if MGM wanted to legitimize the project by pointing to refined origins. When the credits end, however, a "crawl" moves across the screen, informing us that "Throughout the ages, powerful thoughts have been handed down through the medium of the legend, the folktale, and the fantasy. . . . This story of faith and devotion springs from that source and seeks to capture those values." Here the film seems to be claiming a different lineage, even though the word "fantasy" mingles ambiguously with appeals to patriotism, folklore, and religion, opening the possibility for a more playful reading.

To be sure, *Cabin* continues to exhibit half-hearted concern with the religious beliefs of a "simple" couple who live outside the corrupting reach of modernity, together with a pervasive nostalgia for a lost home life. As Rick Altman has pointed out, the Hollywood "folk musical" is defined by these two qualities, especially by its preoccupation with "family groupings and the home" (273). Such films often involve both a desire for adventure and a recurrent homesickness, and they tend to be resolved by a *nostos* after a period of wandering. In *Cabin*, for example, Joe is torn between the artificial "Club Paradise" and the genuine paradise of a community church; between a sexy, brown-skinned mistress and a somewhat mammyfied wife; between a fast life of wine and easy money and a domestic life of lemonade and productive labor. He strays from home to find excitement and pleasure, but then he yearns for what he has left behind, and his return (or more precisely, his recovery after a fevered, guilty dream) is essential to the happy ending.

As we have seen, *Cabin* is based on a paradigmatic tension between city and country, and it gives that tension a conservative resolution, making the town lead to Hell and the country lead to Heaven. Its racist implications become especially apparent when we realize how often the two opposed realms are depicted respectively in shades of blackness and whiteness. The nightclub is situated in a noirish street, whereas the cabin is often flooded with light; Joe wears black tie and tails when he spends the Devil's money, and a white robe when he ascends a stairway to paradise; the Devil's henchmen (costumed as big-city elevator operators) are dressed completely in black, in contrast with the soldiers of the Lord, who wear uniforms of glowing white.

But the town is nonetheless an attractive place, and the real story is elsewhere—largely in the photography, the art decoration, the costuming, the performances, and the musical numbers. In fact, to achieve a satisfying conclusion, *Cabin* finds ways to pull its two worlds into a kind of synthesis.[13] Thus the domestic woman moves briefly into the nightclub, wearing a shiny dress, performing a spectacular and amusing dance, and beating the siren at her own game. More importantly, the cabin becomes a performing space, where tap dancing and lively pop tunes bring sexuality and entertainment under the benign influence of spirituality and married love. One of the best numbers in the picture, Ethel Waters's superb rendition of "Takin' a Chance on Love," is staged in the family kitchen, and it uses the metaphor of gambling (Joe's major vice) to speak about monogamous romance.

Here as elsewhere, *Cabin* simply borrows a few stock images from a folkloric code, putting them in the service of a new form of musical theater. In the opening credits it makes a patriotic appeal to folklore, but then it uses jazz and jitterbug to perform the function of hymns and work songs in earlier movies of the type. As a "folk musical," it therefore differs sharply from *Hallelujah!*, where, according to Rick Altman, "the tempered rhythms of the spiritual, sung in unison by the gathered community," are set off against "the syncopated rhythms of jazz and the chaotic sexual drive which they invoke" (292). Unlike King Vidor, Freed and Minnelli have utterly secular imaginations, and their film contains no Manichaean musical oppositions. In fact, the only religious song heard in *Cabin* is a snippet of "Old Ship of Zion," which is immediately preceded by "Little Black Sheep," an ersatz hymn written by Yip Harburg.

Cabin might be properly described as suburban rather than folkloric, because it blends MGM's middle-class values with the Freed unit's relatively elite, Broadway ethos. To see just how much it tilts toward the city, however, one needs to step far outside the studio system, viewing it alongside Spencer Williams's *Blood of Jesus* (1941), an independent film directed by a black man and aimed at an audience of southern black churchgoers. Williams's film, which has none of the production values of MGM, was designed, in Thomas Cripps's words, "to mourn the passing of the great days when Afro-Americans were embraced by a familial certitude that would later be shattered by the great black diaspora from Southern farm to Yankee city" (92). Williams portrayed the Devil in the style of *aesthetique du cool,* and he made urban jitterbug seem a lurid music, appropriate to a world of crime and prostitution. In *Cabin,* Freed and Minnelli were able to use the same fundamentalist semantics, and yet their tone was completely different. For example, in one of the most exhilarating sequences of the picture, a high-stepping couple, dressed in the latest fashion and moving to the beat of Duke Ellington's performance of "Things Ain't What They Used to Be," enter the swinging doors of the Club Paradise; the camera dollies backward as the couple glides onto the dance floor, and then, as a crowd of neatly dressed men in zoot suits and women in bobby socks gathers around, it cranes high above the room, drifting across the scene to close in on the bandstand (figure 3). A publicity still shows the performers in the sequence and suggests the ambience of the room. Clearly, this is no smoky den of iniquity. It seems more like a showcase for a famous orchestra, and the lovely collaboration among Ellington's music, Busby Berkeley's choreography, and Minnelli's camera crane amounts to a kind of celebration.[14]

It follows that if the nightclub is treated as relatively innocent fun, religion is depicted in perfunctory or comic ways. Unlike Williams's *Blood of Jesus, Cabin* imagines the afterlife whimsically, in a style

Figure 3. *Cabin in the Sky:* Duke Ellington and dancers at Jim Henry's Paradise. ©
1943, Turner Entertainment Co.

similar to Lubitsch's *Heaven Can Wait* (also released in 1943). It never
mentions Jesus, it never shows a crucifix, and it barely alludes to scrip-
ture; instead, it offers a nonsectarian god who behaves rather like a
cosmic cost accountant, and it proffers a few simple edicts against gambling and adultery. The Devil's henchmen do their work from the "Hotel
Hades," which resembles the office of an MGM producer during a story
conference; and the entrance to Heaven—a vast, cloud-covered stairway
flanked by black cherubim—seems to have been derived from a Ziegfeld
production number.

   By the same token, the quotidian, earthbound scenes in *Cabin* resemble a pure dreamworld. Most Hollywood movies about the folk at least
claim to represent a specific place, but here the characters inhabit a poor
but utopian black universe, structured by the absence of white people
and decorated with an odd mixture of artifacts. Indeed, one of the major differences between the Broadway show and the film is that in the
film the battle between God and the Devil turns out to be something
Joe *dreams.* This change gave the picture a happy ending, and at the
same time enabled Minnelli to invest the mise-en-scène with an Afro-
Caribbean look that foreshadows his subsequent work on *Yolanda and
the Thief* (1945) and *The Pirate* (1948). In his autobiography he claims
that he struggled with MGM's art department in order to keep the cabin

from seeming "dirty" or "slovenly" (121), but his dreamy settings also tended to aestheticize poverty, motivating some condescending jokes. At one point, for example, Joe uses earnings from a local feed mill to buy Petunia a washing machine; because there is no electricity in the cabin, he places the gleaming white appliance on his porch as a symbol of prosperity. In this context, the washer becomes a surrealistic image—a bizarre *objet trouvé*, both satirizing and validating the society of consumption.

Not only the settings, but also the manners and accents in the film are heterogeneous and fantastic. Hall Johnson had written to the producers advising them to use "an honest-to-goodness Negro dialect" (quoted in Fordin 75), but the script was rendered in a series of excruciatingly condescending white versions of demotic, southern black English. Here is the way Joseph Schrank and Marc Connelly imagined Petunia praying for Joe's recovery:

> If yuh lets him die de debbil gonna git him fo' sho'. An' he aint wicked, Lawd—he jus' weak, dat's all. He ain't got no powah to resis' de debbil lest Ah watches him. (21)

And here is Joe when he discovers a pair of dice in his bedroom drawer:

> Right now I'm wrestlin' wid de devil. When I was lookin' for de necktie in de bureau drawer, I also found two clamity cubes. I aint throwed 'em away yet. If I been redeemed, why don't I pitch 'em right in de stove? (9)

Fortunately, little of this language survives in the performances—an effect that becomes especially evident in the case of a minor player, Butterfly McQueen, who never uses the spacy singsong that audiences (even audiences of films produced by blacks) had come to expect of her.[15] Petunia's prayer has been completely revised for the completed film, and Eddie Anderson delivers the speech about "clamity cubes" in the same gravelly, urban accent he used on the radio, so that it hardly sounds like the same language. At one point, Ethel Waters sings a few lines of "Happiness Is a Thing Called Joe" in a fake dialect ("He gotta smile dat make de lilac wanna grow"), but everywhere else, she sings in crisply enunciated standard English, using the slightly elocutionary vocal technique of her best-known recordings.

Where the design of the film is concerned, Minnelli seems to have taken pleasure in making a southern locale look like the big city. In one of the most revealing comments in his autobiography, he remarks that the set he liked best was "a southern ghetto, with a warm, golden look, created from a permanent version of a New York street" (122). He also tried to glamorize the featured players: whenever Ethel Waters is seen in a bandanna, she wears fashionable earrings reminiscent of the Cartier jewelry she had sung about in *At Home Abroad*; and when Lena Horne dresses up as a temptress, she exchanges her pillbox hat for a magnolia, pinning the visibly artificial blossom to her hair like Billie Holiday.[16]

Much the same thing could be said about the dressing of the sets. Minnelli painted his own "Africanist" murals on the walls of the Paradise nightclub, and he turned the cabin into a spacious interior, accented with reproductions of Victorian art. He gave Joe and Petunia an elaborate, wrought-iron bedstead, and in each of their rooms he placed white wicker chairs designed in a rococo filigree. (The same chairs show up again in 1944, helping to furnish Judy Garland's bedroom in *Meet Me in St. Louis*; in 1950 they reappear in MGM's *Two Weeks with Love*, a Jane Powell/Debbie Reynolds musical set in a fashionable Catskills resort.) To grasp the full implications of this style, we need only glance at the stills reproduced here. The first comes from Williams's *Blood of Jesus*, where a black household has been decorated with a single picture—a dime-store image of Jesus exhibiting his bleeding heart, visible at the upper left of the frame (figure 4). The second is from *Cabin*, and helps to indicate the comparative opulence of MGM. Notice especially the framed picture at the upper right of the frame, showing a white cherub kissing a sleeping boy (figure 5).

Largely because of this elaborate, exquisite decoration, *Cabin* seems remote from anything we commonly associate with folkloric movies. A deliberate exercise in *faux-naïveté*, it has more in common with what Rick Altman has called "fairy tale musicals," in the sense that it elicits identification "with fantasy, with the far away, with the imaginary" (153). Generally speaking, of course, all the classic Hollywood musicals were fairy tales; but *Cabin*'s oneiric quality has an odd relationship to its ostensible subject, making its folkloric setting seem a mere pretext. The deeper purpose of the film becomes evident when we consider two rhyming camera movements, one near the beginning of the story and one near the end. In the first, Joe stands looking at a lottery ticket he has fastened to his bedroom mirror; as he leans forward in a trance, the camera moves up and over his shoulder, advancing toward the tilted surface of the glass as if to plunge him and us into an imaginary world. In the second, Petunia looks into a mirror that has survived the devastation of the Club Paradise; she notices something reflected there, and the camera moves downward to share her viewpoint, revealing a studio-manufactured stairway leading off through the clouds. These shots contrast Joe's dream of riches

Figure 4. Set decoration for Spencer Williams's *Blood of Jesus* (1940). Photograph courtesy the Black Film Center Archive, Indiana University.

with Petunia's dream of Heaven, but they also serve as metaphors for two aspects of the Hollywood cinema. Like the movies, they appeal both to our desire for luxury and to our desire for a magical, nonmaterial existence. They invite the audience to form a subjective bond with a poor black couple, but in the process they make Joe and Petunia seem like ideal consumers of entertainment—a pair of restless American dreamers caught up in a world of music, light, and dance.

Like virtually all the Freed unit musicals, *Cabin in the Sky* involves a good deal of what Jane Feuer has termed "conservative self-reflexivity"; it banishes every social contradiction, first by appealing to its own status as entertainment, and then by presenting "a vision of human liberation which is profoundly aesthetic" (Feuer 84). Notice also that the aesthetic sensibility is always expensive, dependent on signifiers of material abundance and rarefied taste. Thus when Waters, Anderson, and Horne play the roles of folkloric characters, they do not look poor; and because they are treated as stars, they induce a feeling of playful masquerade. In a strange way this transformation of blackness into a commodity-on-display has a salutary effect, even if the display has dubious purposes. We

Figure 5. Lena Horne and Rex Ingram in *Cabin in the Sky*. © 1943, Turner Entertainment Co. All rights reserved.

might say, echoing Richard Dyer's formulation, that the film gives us the feeling of "what utopia would feel like rather than how it would be organized" (177).

Clearly, the makers of *Cabin* were taking care to keep too much social reality from intruding on the attractive surroundings. Their strategy may seem offensive when so much of the actual experience of African Americans has been suppressed or driven into a political unconscious, but *Cabin* has a complex ideological potential. From the point of view of many social critics of the time, its Hollywood surrealism and freewheeling, commodified treatment of folklore were irredeemably decadent and false; and yet its design runs against the grain of a repressive and no more "true" set of conventions. After all, there is no such thing as an "authentic" folk movie, and *Cabin* may have been better off for its evident artificiality. Freed and Minnelli were hardly social activists, but by imbuing their film with a dreamy atmosphere and an urban Africanism, they and the performers turned it into what is arguably the most visually beautiful picture about black people ever produced at the classic studios. We might say that during the early 1940s, and within the context of a white entertainment industry, their aestheticism amounted to a modestly positive gesture.

Perhaps a better way of making the same point would be to repeat the familiar Marxist axiom that capitalism represents a progressive stage in history. Unfortunately, such progress always involves injustices and ironies. As I have observed, *Cabin* and every other studio film about blacks simply reinforced the hypocritical, separate-but-equal policies of a segregated society. This injustice was compounded because whites were in charge of every behind-the-scenes aspect of the production, and because much of the debate over the film's merits was framed and conditioned by a white cultural establishment. It is ironic that *Cabin* can nonetheless be described as a step forward in the democratization of show business, and that a film containing so much nostalgia and synthetic folklore should have provided a showcase for some of the wittiest and most talented entertainers of the period. But the greatest irony of all is that the black performers, who were at last becoming full-fledged stars, were merely gaining membership in a conservative enterprise—a system devoted to praising the American way, and to promoting the values of glamour, charm, and illusion.

Notes

The author would like to acknowledge several people who contributed useful suggestions for this essay: Manthia Diawara, Gloria Gibson-Hudson, Phyllis Klotman, John Hess, John Fell, Robert Stare, Susan White, and Cary Wolfe.

1   This list excludes Paramount's *Tales of Manhattan* (1942), an anthology film with one episode involving black characters, and Disney's *Song of the South* (1946), which was largely animated.

2   The package-unit system began in 1955, but the end of the classic studios was in sight by 1954. See Bordwell, Staiger, and Thompson 330–38.

3   All six films are discussed in Cripps and Bogle. The only film to have received extensive critical treatment elsewhere is *Hallelujah!*; see, for example, Durgnat and Simmon 96–113. *Cabin in the Sky* is discussed in Harvey 40–44; see also Altman, who analyzes *Hallelujah!* and makes brief remarks on a few of the other black-cast musicals. Outside the context of director and genre studies or books on African American film, the black-cast pictures are treated as if they had only technical importance. In their monumental study of the Hollywood system, Bordwell, Staiger, and Thompson make a passing reference to *Hallelujah!*, noting its camera movements; they mention *The Green Pastures* during a discussion of the focal length of camera lenses; and they provide an image from *Carmen Jones* to illustrate CinemaScope. Two standard histories, Cook and Mast, mention only *Hallelujah!*, praising its use of sound.

4   For an extensive discussion of this theme in English literature, see Williams. For an analysis of how the country/city opposition structures classic Hollywood, see Wood 59–61.

5   A similar argument can be seen in Feuer 67–85. Both Dyer and Feuer have something in common with Walter Benjamin, who believed that mass culture's potentially utopian, collective energy was pushed in conservative directions by capitalism. See Buck-Morss 525–86. More recently, Dyer has seemed more aware of the complex discursive networks in which films operate. See, for example, his discussion of Paul Robeson's star image in *Heavenly Bodies* (1988).

6   I use the term "discourse" heuristically, to describe several conflicting voices surrounding the production of a single film. I do not claim that my survey of these voices is comprehensive, only that it is sufficiently broad to illustrate social conflicts in the period. It should also be noted that no discursive category is monologic. Each of the categories I have attempted to isolate could be divided into others, and these could be divided again, in a process of infinite regression. For additional discussion of how films can become the sites of conflicting discourse, see Stam, Marchetti, and Shohat. Where the response of actual historical spectators is concerned, I have much less to say. For an important analysis of spectatorship and race, see Diawara.

7   Adorno was a particularly hostile critic of show business. In "On the Fetish Character in Music and the Regression of Listening" (1938), he charges that "music for entertainment" serves only to assure that people are "confirmed in their neurotic stupidity" (286). See also his postwar essay, "Perennial Fashion— Jazz." Here Adorno describes jazz as a "slave" music, in which it is difficult "to isolate the authentic Negro elements" (122). Needless to say, James Agee's attitude toward commercial jazz and American blacks was different. He was also a contributor to *The Quiet One* (1949), a sensitive independent film about a lonely black boy, which Bogle compares favorably with Rossellini's *Paisà* [*Paisan*] (1946) (141–42).

8   On the relation between the Frankfurt School and Max Weber, see Adorno 190– 91, 207–19. Jameson believes that the term "late capitalism" originated with Horkheimer and Adorno, whose conception of American society was "Weberian," involving two essential features: "1) a tendential web of bureaucratic control . . . and 2) the interpenetration of government and big business" (xvii). In what I describe as the "discourse of critical modernism," there is a strong tendency to regard the mass media as opiates or instruments of social control. Compare T. S. Eliot's conservative response to the rise of movies during the 1920s: "with the encroachment of the cheap and rapid-breeding cinema, the lower classes will drop into the same state of protoplasm as the bourgeoisie" (225).

9   Until a studio executive ordered the MGM commissary integrated, most of the players ate lunch in L. B. Mayer's private dining room. See Mordden 163.

10 Bogle describes the forties as the "apex" of the "Negro Entertainment Syndrome," in which the nightclub was a recurrent setting for black performers (118–19). During the period, Ethel Waters became a major star on American radio, and Duke Ellington presented a series of forty-seven weekly, hour-long broadcasts sponsored by the U.S. Treasury Department.

11 In his influential essay, Locke claimed that American blacks of the twentieth century were involved in a "deliberate flight not only from the country to the city, but from medieval America to modern" (515): "The pulse of the Negro world has begun to beat in Harlem. A Negro newspaper carrying news material in English, French, and Spanish, gathered from all quarters of America, the West Indies and

Africa has maintained itself in Harlem for over five years. . . . Under American auspices and backing, three pan-African congresses have been held abroad for the discussion of common interests, colonial questions and the future co-operative development of Africa. . . . As with the Jew, persecution is making the Negro international" (522). For an extensive discussion of the historical importance of the "New Negro," see Gates.

12   An essay of this length cannot fully document the European fascination with Africa during the modernist period. See Torgovnick (75–140), who discusses the nexus of modernist aesthetics, colonial stereotypes, and obsessions about race and gender. For a discussion of a similar phenomenon in European avant-garde culture between the wars, see Stallabrass.

13   For a discussion of this strategy in other Hollywood genres, see Ray.

14   Notice, too, *Cabin*'s portrayal of a gambler named Domino Johnson (aka John Bubbles Sublett, the original Sportin' Life in *Porgy and Bess*), whose privileged moment is a performance of Ford Dabney and Cecil Mack's "Shine." This song (also performed by Dooley Wilson in *Casablanca* [1942] and later recorded by Bing Crosby and Frankie Laine) is one of the more uncomfortably racist moments in the film, chiefly because of its references to "curly" hair, "pearly" teeth, and fancy clothes; from the point of view of the black actor, however, it functions self-reflexively, and it is the only occasion when a character is allowed to acknowledge racial difference. Moreover, while Johnson is supposed to be a villain, we are never invited to think of him as truly dangerous. Sublett's dancing makes him seem charming, and Minnelli's camera movements suggest a rapport with the figure of the black dandy.

15   The black performers were working against the script, but I suspect MGM wanted to "dignify" the production. In any case, the effect of dialect humor or "local color" depends on context. Consider the following speech, from Langston Hughes's *Simply Heavenly* (1963): "Why, its getting so colored folks can't do nothing no more without some other Negro calling you a stereotype. Stereotype, hah! If you like a little gin, you're a stereotype. . . . If you wear a red dress, you're a stereotype. . . . Lord have mercy, honey, do-don't like no blackeyed peas and rice! Then you're a down-home Negro for true—which I is—and proud of it! I didn't come here to Harlem to get away from my people. I come here because there's more of 'em. I loves my race. I loves my people. Stereotype!" (125–26).

16   It should be noted that the most imposing and handsome males in *Cabin* are Kenneth Spencer and Rex Ingram, who play supernatural characters. In the earthly scenes, Lena Horne is an obviously sexualized female, playing a role similar to Nina Mae McKinney's in *Hallelujah! Cabin* is almost the only one of Horne's films in which she functions as an agent of the narrative and in which she moves provocatively around the set; even so, one of her singing numbers was cut because Minnelli staged it in a bubble bath.

Works Cited

Adorno, Theodor W. "On the Fetish-Character in Music and the Regression of Listening." *The Essential Frankfurt School Reader*. Ed. Andrew Arato and Eike Gebhardt. New York: Continuum, 1987. 270–99.

——. "Perennial Fashion—Jazz." *Prisms.* Trans. Samuel and Shierry Weber. Cambridge, Mass.: MIT P, 1990. 119–31.

Altman, Rick. *The Hollywood Film Musical.* Bloomington: Indiana UP, 1987.

Agee, James. "Pseudo Folk." *Agee on Film, Vol. 1.* New York: McDowell, Obolensky, 1958. 404–10.

—— (anon.). "Cinema." *Time* (12 Apr. 1943): 112.

Bakhtin, Mikhail. *The Dialogic Imagination.* Trans. Caryl Emerson and Michael Holquist. Austin: U of Texas P, 1981.

Bogle, Donald. *Toms, Coons, Mulattoes, Mammies, and Bucks: An Interpretive History of Blacks in American Films.* Expanded ed. New York: Continuum, 1989.

Bordwell, David, Janet Staiger, and Kristin Thompson. *The Classical Hollywood Cinema: Film Style and Mode of Production to 1960.* New York: Columbia UP, 1985.

Buck-Morss, Susan. *The Dialectics of Seeing: Walter Benjamin and the Arcades Project.* Cambridge, Mass.: MIT P, 1989.

Burke, Peter. "The 'Discovery' of Popular Culture." *People's History and Socialist Theory.* Ed. Raphael Samuel. London: Routledge and Kegan Paul, 1983. 215–22.

Calinescu, Matei. *Five Faces of Modernity.* Durham, N.C.: Duke UP, 1987.

Cook, David A. *A History of Narrative Film.* New York: Norton, 1990.

Cripps, Thomas. *Black Film as Genre.* Bloomington: Indiana UP, 1979.

Diawara, Manthia. "Black Spectatorship: Problems of Identification and Resistance." *Screen* 29.4 (Autumn 1988): 66–79.

Durgnat, Raymond, and Scott Simmon. *King Vidor, American.* Berkeley: U of California P, 1989.

Dyer, Richard. "Entertainment and Utopia." *Genre: The Musical.* Ed. Rick Altman. London: Routledge and Kegan Paul, 1981. 175–89.

Eliot, T. S. *Selected Prose.* Harmondsworth, Eng.: Penguin, 1953.

Feuer, Jane. *The Hollywood Musical.* Bloomington: Indiana UP, 1982.

Fordin, Hugh. *The Movies' Greatest Musicals.* New York: Ungar, 1984.

Gates, Henry Louis, Jr. "The Trope of the New Negro and the Reconstruction of the Image of the Black." *Representations* 24 (Fall 1988): 129–55.

Harvey, Stephen. *Directed by Vincente Minnelli.* New York: Harper, 1989.

Horkheimer, Max, and Theodor W. Adorno. *Dialectic of Enlightenment.* 1944. New York: Seabury, 1972.

Hughes, Langston. *Five Plays by Langston Hughes.* Ed. Webster Smalley. Bloomington: Indiana UP, 1968.

Jameson, Fredric. *Postmodernism, or, the Cultural Logic of Late Capitalism.* Durham, N.C.: Duke UP, 1991.

Lardner, David. "The Current Cinema." *New Yorker* 29 May 1943: 79.

Lewis, Ramona. "'Cabin' Picture Called Insult." *Amsterdam News* (New York) 12 June 1943: 17.

Locke, Alain. "The New Negro." *Black Voices.* Ed. Abraham Chapman. New York: Mentor Books, 1968. 512–23.

Marchetti, Gina. "Ethnicity, the Cinema and Cultural Studies." *Unspeakable Images: Ethnicity and the American Cinema.* Ed. Lester D. Friedman. Urbana: U of Illinois P, 1991. 277–307.

Minnelli, Vincente, with Hector Acre. *I Remember It Well.* Garden City, N.Y.: Doubleday, 1974.

Mordden, Ethan. *The Hollywood Studios.* New York: Simon, 1989.

Nowell-Smith, Geoffrey. "On Kiri Te Kanawa, Judy Garland, and the Culture Industry." *Modernity and Mass Culture.* Ed. James Naremore and Patrick Brantlinger. Bloomington: Indiana UP, 1991. 70–79.

Papers of the NAACP. Dec. 1940 and Apr. 1942.

PM Magazine 1 June 1943: 10.

Ray, Robert. *A Certain Tendency of the Hollywood Cinema, 1930–1980.* Princeton, N.J.: Princeton UP, 1985.

Schrank, Joseph, and Marc Connelly. "Cabin in the Sky." Mimeographed film script. 21 Sept. 1942. Revisions dated 20 Oct. 1942.

Shohat, Ella. "Ethnicities-in-Relation." *Unspeakable Images: Ethnicity and the American Cinema.* Ed. Lester D. Friedman. Urbana: U of Illinois P, 1991. 215–47.

Stallabras, Julian. "The Idea of the Primitive: British Art and Anthropology, 1918–1930." *New Left Review* 183 (1990): 95–115.

Stam, Robert. "Bakhtin, Polyphony, and Ethnic/Racial Representation." *Unspeakable Images: Ethnicity and the American Cinema.* Ed. Lester D. Friedman. Urbana: U of Illinois P, 1991. 251–76.

Torgovnick, Marianna. *Gone Primitive: Savage Intellects, Modern Lives.* Chicago: U of Chicago P, 1990.

Williams, Raymond. *The Country and the City.* New York: Oxford UP, 1973.

Wood, Robin. "Ideology, Genre, Auteur." *Film Genre Reader.* Ed. Barry Keith Grant. Austin: U of Texas P, 1986. 59–73.

Doubling, Music, and Race
in Cabin in the Sky

ADAM KNEE

To explore the racial politics of Vincente Minnelli's all-black musical *Cabin in the Sky* (1943), I will analyze structures of doubling throughout the text. I will delineate a number of mirrored or doubled relationships that are foregrounded at several levels, and I will argue that this formal tendency is a key textual means of negotiating issues of race: throughout *Cabin in the Sky*, dichotomous relationships operate as a substitute for, while also pointing toward and elaborating, the displaced and far more crucial racial relationship of black and white. Although the film represses racial differences by largely absenting it from any overt narrative discourse,[1] the text simultaneously sets up a conceptual framework grounded in numerous Manichaean oppositions—a framework in which the black realm inevitably comes up the negative term, an inadequate mirror of a white sphere all too present by its absence. It will be seen, moreover, that one particularly significant opposition is in the realm of the film's music: *Cabin in the Sky* links its moral conflicts with musical contrasts, endowing different African American musical idioms and performance styles with different moral values.

James Naremore's recent work on *Cabin in the Sky* has been rightly praised for its thorough and impressively researched examination of the film within its cultural context (see, for example, Diawara 6); his close reading of the text carefully and convincingly situates it in relation to a range of popular discourses and historical forces. While the argument offered here concurs with many of the specific points in Naremore's reading, it differs in what I think is a significant way. Naremore indicates the presence of several substantial ideological contradictions within

Cabin in the Sky, suggesting that opposing cultural influences are a central part of what shapes the film, and he further acknowledges that the work is "saturated with inferential forms of racism" (107), despite its progressive aspects. But he also implies at points that the film's contradictions are ultimately a positive force, endowing the text with what he somewhat vaguely terms a "complex ideological potential" (119). I will be arguing that this posited potential might in fact be more accurately termed a *symptom* of the contradictory positioning of blacks within American culture, that the "cultural schizophrenia" Naremore delineates within the film is very deeply rooted in problems of race, and that many of the oppositions which he suggests are delimited and resolved within the text are in fact pervasive and persistent.

The return of the film's dichotomous repressed makes itself evident first in a seemingly offhand exchange in the initial establishing shot, as Reverend Green greets a woman who has chosen to bring her twins to church that day. Before long we meet the film's main protagonist, the naive and wayward "Little Joe" (Eddie "Rochester" Anderson), as he looks at his reflection in a mirror (the first of many throughout the film) and readies himself for his first visit to church in some time. His loving and God-fearing wife, Petunia (Ethel Waters), has been trying to get him to give up gambling and repent, but shortly after arriving at church, Joe is coerced into sneaking out and gambling for the money he owes some creditors. He is soon shot for using the dice the creditors have given him, apparently innocent of the fact that they were loaded. Joe falls unconscious, and when his departed spirit sees his body, it declares, "I ain't never been twins before!"

Perhaps Joe has not been twins before, but his dual nature now seems his chief defining characteristic, and the film's resolution becomes predicated upon his reconciling his divergent selves. Owing to Petunia's powerful prayers on his behalf, Joe is given the chance to avoid perdition if he manages to live the next six months without giving in to temptation. The difference between the living Joe and the dead one, and ultimately between the heaven-bound and hellbound Joes, now turns on the man's repressing his weaker self in favor of his moral self. The narrative framework of the scene later retroactively redoubles the split: the entire moral dilemma is revealed to have been dreamed up in the wounded Joe's delirium, so we have superimposed the dualities of health and illness, waking and dreaming, reality and fantasy.

The notion of a split subject is further suggested in the specific form the "death" scene's dramatization takes. The forces of evil line up on one side of Joe's bed, low-lit and dressed in black Hotel Hades bellhop uniforms, while the soldiers of heaven commandeer the other side, dressed in light-colored military uniforms and emanating a bright glow. Representatives of each side let Joe know that both heavenly and hell-sent suggestions will be made to his unconscious mind during his trial period, that it will be up to Joe to determine the moral path. The dual casting of a number of the otherworldly messengers also draws attention back to the doubled nature of the dramatic situation. Lucifer Jr., introduced through the double constituted by his shadow, is played by Rex Ingram, who also plays the most coercive of Joe's earthbound creditors; while the heaven-sent General and Sgt. Fleetfoot are played by Kenneth Spencer and Oscar Polk, who appropriately also have the terrestrial roles of Reverend Green and the Deacon.

The moral drama of the two warring sides of Little Joe is projected into and played out largely through his relationships with the two loves of his life, who are also two of the most important sources of musical entertainment and of spectacle in this film: devout Petunia and the temptress Georgia Brown, played by Lena Horne. The otherworldly agents let us know right away that Petunia has a special closeness with the Lord, while Georgia is the Devil's favorite. Petunia embodies the moral polarity of goodness through her emphatic domesticity and her asexuality, spending many scenes involved with laundry or cooking, wearing drab, purely functional clothes, and rarely leaving her home. In direct opposition to Petunia is the scantily clad free agent Georgia Brown, clearly the object of Joe's sexual desire. Georgia owes allegiance to no one in particular and is part of what attracts Joe to the establishment where he gambles, known as Jim Henry's Paradise—the ironic name of which again suggests a thematic of spiritual doubling and duality. Waters and Horne, the two most important vocalists in *Cabin in the Sky*, are aligned with a musical polarity as well as a moral one. Waters works with church spirituals, such as the first song of the film, and ballads of domestic bliss, such as "Happiness Is a Thing Called Joe" and "Cabin in the Sky," both performed and filmed in a highly restrained style that emphasizes the smile on Waters's face rather than any physical movement. (In one instance, Waters performs the former song with Joe's laundry rather than Joe himself, a gesture that at once fetishizes the domestic realm and drains it of any earthly corporeality.) Horne, on the other hand, is linked with black music as a popular and hardly sacred entertainment, as when she performs the suggestive "Honey in the Honeycomb" at Jim Henry's.[2]

Indeed, Jim Henry's, although clearly posited as the locus of moral transgression, is also the site of much of the film's more exciting musical entertainment, including performances by Duke Ellington and the film's most elaborate dance sequences. This is in fact where one of the film's most important contradictions lies. It is at the nocturnal world of Jim Henry's that most of the film's illegal and/or immoral (from the church's perspective) activities take place along with most of the film's most overtly sexual dialogue and interactions. For this reason, none other than God himself (as explained later on) destroys the club near the film's conclusion. Yet it is simultaneously the space of some of the film's freest African American self-expression, a realm that allows sexually allusive dialogue, open physical movement and dancing combined with sweeping camera dollies, and spontaneous performance in the relatively free, unrestrained idioms of jazz. While inviting us to enjoy this performance (as much of Little Joe's African American community clearly does), to vicariously partake of the thrill of this space of transgression, *Cabin in the Sky* ultimately condemns and destroys it. Thus, while black music and self-expression is the lifeblood of the film, the text is forced to render such self-expression (and, by implication, black leisure activity generally) safe through moral judgment and containment by situating it in a distinct and subsequently obliterated space.

One could also note that the specific forms this self-expression takes in the performance scenes at Jim Henry's provide an additional kind of safe containment. The performance may be highly energetic, but it and the camerawork are precisely measured and choreographed; the music may be jazz, but it is, to use Naremore's phrase, "an uptown face of jazz" (109), performed by Duke Ellington's orchestra throughout the final scenes at the club, with the camera repeatedly moving back to Ellington himself. Ellington, who is billed as himself within the diegesis, was a key figure in imbuing jazz with a more sophisticated cachet; he was featured in a major Carnegie Hall concert the winter before *Cabin* was released, an event that marked a new mainstream acceptance of his work (see Collier 209–23). Indeed, by 1943, jazz itself was receiving an unprecedented level of mainstream acceptance (Leonard 133–53), although *Cabin*, in the polarities it constructs, paradoxically harkens back to the morally based denigration of the form more prevalent twenty years earlier.

In relation to such polarities, Naremore does argue that "*Cabin* is based on a paradigmatic tension between city and country"—the worlds of the nightclub and the cabin, respectively—and he further indicates that the film's "racist implications become especially apparent when we realize how often the two opposed realms are depicted respectively in shades of blackness and whiteness" (112). At the same time, however, Naremore suggests that the film achieves a level of synthesis between the two realms, bringing together performance, sexuality, and sacred marital bliss. The examples he gives as evidence of such a synthesis are strained and hardly convincing. He briefly cites Petunia's appearance at Jim Henry's as one example, but as argued below, this sequence contains a good deal of crucial conflict. He cites as well Petunia's cabin performance of "Taking a Chance on Love," yet as I will indicate, this very performance is most emphatically restrained when it starts to threaten too much sexual self-expression; the little cabin simply cannot accommodate it. While it may be accurate to claim that in comparison to jazz clubs represented in other movies, Jim Henry's is "no smoky den of iniquity" (113), it is difficult to argue that the film "contains no Manichaean musical oppositions" (113) or that the club is "treated as relatively innocent fun" (114). There is indeed levity present in the Jim Henry's sequences as in much of the film, but the establishment's evident "innocence" is undoubtedly a function of mainstream Hollywood conditions of representation in 1943; within the film's own dichotomous moral structure, the nightclub's position remains clear.

Little Joe's choice between performance idioms, between women, between social spaces and life-styles, between moral paths, and, ultimately, between two sides of his own self proves to be a difficult if not impossible one in the world of *Cabin in the Sky*—a world in which genuine personal fulfillment appears out of the question for the protagonist. The morally righteous path, a return to home and Petunia and religion, is always clear, but it is posited as requiring a relinquishing of sexual gratification in favor of other domestic comforts. These comforts, moreover, are themselves difficult to maintain: we are constantly reminded that Joe and Petunia have an economically marginal existence, their dilapidated home full of leaks and drafts and lacking in any vaguely modern conveniences. A context of financial hardship even asserts itself in the monetary terms in which Joe's moral struggle is often cast: he is seen to have a deficit in the Lord's ledger. Such economic exigencies are presumably part of what cultivates Joe's other weakness besides Georgia Brown—his gambling, which in fact tends to leave Joe even worse off both economically and physically. He is thus trapped between perdition and hardship, and this partially accounts for the schism in his psyche.

The film does allow Little Joe and Petunia one route of escape, in the form of a shared dream of ascendance to the heavenly cabin of the film's title, a site, presumably, of happiness and intimacy. In other words, the film can only allow closure for these characters if they move utterly beyond their present inadequate realm, a transition predicated on their demise. This space of potential personal fulfillment is so outside the usual boundaries of the diegesis as to render it largely unrepresentable; it is conjured up only in such special registers of the filmic discourse as an emblematic drawing behind the credits and a sung reference in the titular musical number. That Petunia is linked with a moral choice that is ultimately a deathly one makes the opposition between her and Georgia not only one of morality versus sexuality, or of reality principle versus pleasure principle, but of Thanatos versus Eros.

To return to my opening contentions, I would argue that the absolute nature of this schism is a function of the social structure and racial politics of the film: the defining dichotomy of the film is racial, and the impossibility of Little Joe's dilemma is rooted in the bifurcated space of black male subjectivity. The Manichaean nature of many of the film's oppositions has already been worked out by Naremore (112): the light and dark costuming and the lighting of God's and the Devil's servants clearly designate opposing moralities. This chromatic scale of moral values is immediately reinforced with such lines of dialogue as a command to Little Joe to "white-wash" his soul and a description of Georgia as "a long black mark" against Joe. One invidious irony of the "black mark" comment is that in the American cinematic discourse, Georgia Brown can only be a "black mark"—that is, an object of sexual desire—because she is played by a light-skinned African American.[3]

This chromatic value scale translates directly into a racial value scale in a text that strongly stresses race through its emphatic process of repressing it, not to mention a viewing context immersed in racism. The novelty of the all-black casting refers the viewer back to an opposed, primarily white musical genre that this lower-budgeted film can only emulate; the film is positioned as an inadequate mirror of a white form. Indeed, I do not think it would be too farfetched to propose that *Cabin in the Sky* has a specific double in the world of the white musical—*The Wizard of Oz* (1939). Both musicals, produced by Arthur Freed for MGM, concern a protagonist propelled by a physical trauma into a fantasy world peopled by members of disenfranchised groups, some of whom bear uncanny resemblances to characters in the initial reality frame. Both narratives revolve around the protagonist's efforts to return to this reality and are resolved when the protagonist comes to in a sickbed with a loving mother figure waiting nearby. Both films also pivot around unexpected tornados, the later film borrowing tornado footage from its predecessor, and both films were released in sepia-toned prints.

While *Cabin in the Sky* is set up in opposition to the white Hollywood musical, it is clearly positioned in opposition to the race film as well.[4] Where the independent race film is aimed primarily at a black audience, this MGM musical opens with a direct address to what is clearly a white audience, in an effort to disavow any nonhegemonous cinematic discourse, to deny the validity of the black subject. The address, in the form of a scrolled text of truisms of dubious grammar and coherence, is worth quoting in its entirety here:

"Throughout the ages, powerful and inspiring thoughts have been preserved and handed down by the medium of the legend, the fable, and the fantasy.

"The folklore of America has origins in all lands, all races, all colors.

"This story of faith and devotion springs from that source and seeks to capture those values."

This barely connected series of statements reassures the white audience of its centrality by reference to sources and values that are Other, at the same time using internal incoherence as a means of denying the very black culture the film is premised on: the phrases "that source" and "those values" in the last sentence have no specific discernible antecedent.[5] This strategy is typical of the genre of Hollywood-produced all-black features, of which *Cabin in the Sky* is the fourth in the sound era. The folk-religious spectacle *Green Pastures* (1936), for example, opens with a similar text condescendingly referring to the way "the Negroes in the Deep South" conceptualize God and heaven, while the musical *Hearts in Dixie* (1929) is introduced by a direct address from a wizened white patriarch who tries to set the film comfortably into context.

Although not as pointedly condescending toward blacks as were many Hollywood films, *Cabin in the Sky* makes substantial use of the stereotypes that pervade these films and numerous race films as well. Such stereotyping is made all the easier in the narrative's doubly fantastic frame, that of a dream within a musical, where toms and bandana'd mammies gather and sing on cue, untroubled by poverty and oppression. Petunia and Georgia fit the stereotypes described by Donald Bogle as the aunt jemima and the tragic mulatto (*Toms, Coons* 9), while other characters follow previous screen African Americans in weaknesses for gambling, sex, alcohol, and cigars, as well as in illiteracy, sloth, and poor analytical skills. Important popular black performance forms are themselves placed into moral doubt here (although these forms are also the key source of spectacle and entertainment within the film); that far more scenes take place at the overflowing Jim Henry's than at the church in turn implies a moral corruption of the entire community.

The context of racial polarity also surfaces indirectly, but significantly, in a number of references to the film's actual wartime context—a context, just as in the previous world war, of segregated troops and tensions arising from racism within the military. Indeed, 1943 also saw the production of *The Negro Soldier*, an Army training film aimed at assuaging racial tensions and promoting black involvement in the war effort.[6] Given the feelings of resentment among some African Americans over fighting a "white man's war," over having to risk one's life in Europe and the Pacific to return to a second-class citizenship at home, it is interesting that the war references—specifically, Lucifer Jr.'s claim that Little Joe has been "1-A on our list for a long time" and his complaint that "I'm stuck with a bunch of B-idea men; all the A-boys is over there in Europe"—both pertain to conscription.

Cabin in the Sky attempts to resolve some of its many dualities in a climactic sequence at Jim Henry's Paradise, the name of which itself brings the heavenly into confrontation with the earthbound while also suggesting a mirroring relationship between the two. Early in the sequence, Domino Johnson, the man who has previously shot little Joe, performs a song containing what may be the film's only explicit verbal references to race; among its lyrics are, "Just because my hair is curly, just because my teeth are pearly, . . . just because my color shade's a wee bit different maybe, that's why they call me shine."[7] Again, however, what gets dramatized here is not racial tension, thrust outside the plot by way of casting, but a tension between two versions of the feminine, embodied in Petunia and Georgia. Petunia has previously kicked Joe out of their house, wrongly believing that Joe was forsaking her for Georgia, while in fact he was only thanking Georgia for the information that he had won a sweepstakes prize. Now, months later, Joe is spending his money on Georgia at Jim Henry's, and his wife shows up to claim her share. The two women exchange insults and attempt various forms of one-upmanship—most significantly, a musical showdown of sorts.

Consistent with this conflict, another more basic duality begins to come to the fore—sexual difference. Part of what has been disavowed through a focus on Little Joe's trouble in choosing between Petunia and Georgia is his trouble in dealing with the feminine at all, in "being a man" in the face of these two powerful women. Little Joe's diminutive name and stature, along with his being wounded at the film's start and having to use a cane to move about when no longer bedridden, are all common symbols of impotence and castration. He is, moreover, physically confronted, if not threatened, by both women during the course of the film. Georgia is aggressive in her attempts to seduce him, forcing him into a face-off with her bare legs and uplifted skirt, while Petunia gets him to leave their home by threatening him with raised fists. In another telling moment, Petunia unexpectedly shifts from her usually devout and reserved stance while singing "Taking a Chance on Love," letting loose a couple of guttural notes and moving sensuously; Little Joe and a delivery man are instantly terror-stricken by this unleashed feminine power and rush to quiet her.

I would suggest that part of why moments emphasizing a male/female binarism are so rare up to the final sequence at Jim Henry's is that the binarism is, for this text, perilously similar to the more deeply repressed black/white binarism. Joe's experience of sexual difference largely parallels his experience of racial difference—an experience of fear, confusion, frustration, and belittlement stemming from a relationship to members of a group with an inherent physical dissimilarity. It is when the dream/drama reaches a crisis point in the final sequence that this less concealable substitution of sex for race is engaged. Georgia Brown starts broadcasting her sex as soon as she arrives at Jim Henry's, lifting her dress up to reveal what she terms her "accessories," while also wearing the racial repressed on her sleeve in the form of a striking white outfit with a large white feather boa. Little Joe, highly agitated by this undue emphasis on the feminine, reminds Georgia that she is now "a lady," to which she responds that she merely wants to remind fellow club patrons of this fact. From here she starts her "Honey in the Honeycomb" number.[8]

When Petunia arrives, she herself announces a previously repressed big-boned femininity, having cast aside her former simple garb for a form-fitting sequined gown as loud as Georgia's. Little Joe is clearly startled by this side of his wife, which he had previously caught only a brief glimpse of, now stuttering that she is beautiful. Georgia claims that Petunia is "just jealous cause she ain't got what I got," to which Petunia proudly responds, "I got what you got and a whole lot more." Petunia then fulfills what she calls a "musical urge" by performing her own version of "Honey in the Honeycomb." ("Ask the boys to put me in the mood," she suggestively demands, "so I can give out.") Clearly, the earlier formal and moral opposition between the two women no longer obtains here in the same way: Petunia is now actually trying to beat Georgia at her own game, both women unsettling Joe with the spectacle of difference. Heavyset Waters's version of the song does not become the grotesque satire one might expect, but rather it is used to show off her skill in moving her weight nimbly around the dance floor; this is not femininity lampooned so much as it is femininity writ large, echoing the earlier moment when Petunia lets loose during her performance of "Taking a Chance on Love."

Petunia's shift here can be read not only as a reemergence of difference, but also as an instance of the return of self-expression with which the nightclub is associated, both diegetically and on the level of star discourse. Just as Petunia can now reveal another side of her persona, so can Ethel Waters now demonstrate other aspects of her talent, previously held in check by her role. Accounts of Waters's feistiness during the production, her insistence on a say in the creation of her character, would appear to support such a reading (Waters 258; Bogle, *Brown Sugar* 114–16); it is in all likelihood largely Waters's own input that allows the scene to be expressive rather than purely mocking. The shift also seems to allude to tensions within Waters's own star persona—the once lanky singer billed as "Sweet Mama Stringbean" now playing matronly roles on stage and screen.

Significant in terms of the film's discourse of difference is that it is dark-skinned Domino, the film's most overt signifier of blackness, with whom Petunia now proceeds to dance in her more sexually oriented identity. Joe continues to be agitated and confused by the sudden transformation of his formerly desexed wife, directly confronted with her corporeality as she dances with the other man. When Petunia finds Domino's advances too aggressive and calls to Joe for help, he quickly leaves Georgia's side to take advantage of the opportunity to reestablish his manhood. At this, however, Joe will ultimately prove unsuccessful. During his ensuing fistfight with Domino, Petunia, evidently still pious after all, prays to God to destroy the "wicked place" that is Jim Henry's. Although the tornado that immediately appears has been sent by a male God, the phenomenon is clearly linked to the feminine forces that have recently been let loose: Petunia is causally linked to it by way of her prayer, while Georgia is given a visual connection in a medium shot framing her and the tornado together as she stands at a window. Indeed, in its aforementioned intertextuality, this swirling vortex metonymically refers us back to the female object of director Minnelli's own as-yet unrequited desire, the star of *The Wizard of Oz.*

Tornado or no, Little Joe finds himself shot once again by Domino, this time fatally, and Petunia meets the same end. Judgment time arrives, and Petunia manages to convince the Lord to let Joe ascend to the heavens with her. They start to climb stairs to their cabin in the sky, but Joe begins to feel oddly tired. Just as the text's inability to resolve its major oppositions in the Jim Henry's scene results in the appearance of a particularly surprising deus ex machina, so does the unrepresentability of any resolution for Joe now force the text to reveal the dream status of most of the foregoing narrative; Joe's ascent to the promised cabin suddenly ceases as he wakes up in his bed, substantially recuperated. The film then rather abruptly ends with Joe having his dice burned and Petunia singing in her earlier "safe" performance style a quick final refrain of "Taking a Chance on Love," as though we need to be whisked away from the scene, as though the text wants to keep us from remembering that numerous conflicts and numerous schisms are as yet unresolved. We hardly get the sense of full closure that accompanies fellow dreamer Dorothy's parallel return to reality in *The Wizard of Oz*. It seems that for Little Joe, as for the black soldier in World War II and the black subject in white Hollywood, there truly is no place like home. None at all.

Notes

1 In expounding the notion of "structuring absence," Stam and Spence point out how, "The all-black Hollywood musicals of the twenties and thirties . . . tend to exclude whites because their mere presence would destroy the elaborate fabric of fantasy constructed by such films" (638).

2 Ed Guerrero has recently argued that such a musical polarity, evident in *Cabin in the Sky* and a number of other "black-focused mainstream cinema spectacles," is directly counter to the reality of black music, which "works to represent life in all its paradoxical, contradictory (w)holeness and complexity. Conversely, in these films, Gospel or church music occupies the realm of absolute good, while the pervasive black popular idioms of jazz and blues are depicted as a seductive evil" (51).

3 See Roberts (esp. 114–29) for an in-depth and compelling discussion of Lena Horne's paradoxical positioning in racial terms—both in *Cabin in the Sky* and in her star discourse generally.

4 One could argue that *Cabin in the Sky* has a race film "double" as well, in Spencer Williams's *The Blood of Jesus* (1941), a work Naremore cites for comparison a number of times. Produced during the years between the Broadway and Hollywood versions of *Cabin*, *The Blood of Jesus* mirrors that mainstream text's plot in several ways. The race film, like the musical, deals with a poor and devout woman's efforts to positively influence her husband; however, it is interestingly *she,* and not her husband, who is felled by a bullet early in the film and who must undergo a moral trial of sorts—choosing between the road to eternal life and the road to hell and destruction—before being returned to her formal mortal existence.

5 Naremore sees the ambiguity of this particular text somewhat more positively as "opening the possibility for a more playful reading" (111) that takes into account both the film's "refined" Broadway origins and its other sources of inspiration.

6 See Cripps, chap. 4, for a historical account of the production and distribution of *The Negro Soldier.*

7 Domino's name itself has a racial/racist aura, with its invocation of a black/white contrast and its stereotypical reference to gambling. See also Naremore's comments on the racist implications of the figure, 121–22 n.

8   Roberts argues that the racialized erotic threat Lena Horne poses in this particular
     scene—and elsewhere in her star discourse—is negotiated in part through "the
     displacement of her eroticism onto food discourse" (145); Horne's thematic was
     consistently one of honey. See esp. 141–46.

Works Cited

Bogle, Donald. *Brown Sugar: Eighty Years of America's Black Female Superstars.* New
     York: Da Capo, 1980.
——. *Toms, Coons, Mulattoes, Mammies, and Bucks: An Interpretive History of
     Blacks in American Films.* Expanded ed. New York: Continuum, 1989.
Collier, James Lincoln. *Duke Ellington.* New York: Oxford UP, 1987.
Cripps, Thomas. *Making Movies Black.* New York: Oxford UP, 1993.
Diawara, Manthia. "Cinema Studies, the Strong Thought, and Black Film." *Wide
     Angle* 8.3–4 (July–Oct. 1991): 4–11.
Guerrero, Ed. *Framing Blackness: The African American Image in Film.* Philadelphia:
     Temple UP, 1993.
Leonard, Neil. *Jazz and the White Americans.* Chicago: U of Chicago P, 1962.
Naremore, James. "Uptown Folk: Blackness and Entertainment in *Cabin in the Sky.*"
     Arizona Quarterly 48.4 (Winter 1992): 99–124. Reprinted in this collection. 169–
     92.
Roberts, Shari. " 'Stormy Weather': Lena Horne and the Erotics of Miscegenation."
     Chap. 3 of "Seeing Stars: Feminine Spectacle, Female Spectators, and World War II
     Hollywood." Diss. U of Chicago, 1993.
Stam, Robert, and Louise Spence. "Colonialism, Racism, and Representation: An
     Introduction." *Screen* 24.2 (1983). Reprinted in Bill Nichols, ed. *Movies and
     Methods.* Vol. 2. Berkeley: U of California P, 1985. 632–49.
Waters, Ethel, with Charles Samuels. *His Eye Is on the Sparrow.* Garden City, N.Y.:
     Doubleday, 1951.

JAZZ

AND

DANCE

Divine Frivolity: Hollywood Representations
of the Lindy Hop, 1937–1942

ROBERT P. CREASE

I n the beginning, jazz was dancing music. From Congo Square and the second line to parties, parades, burlesque houses, street corners, speakeasies, honky-tonks, and nightclubs, dance flourished on an amateur or vernacular level as a natural and organic concomitant to jazz music.[1] Dance remained integral to the jazz scene until the end of the swing era in the late 1940s. The big bands of the 1930s and 1940s supported themselves by playing not concerts but large ballrooms, amusement parks, hotels, and other venues for dancing. Meanwhile, professional dancers were a staple of revues and musicals of the swing era; a typical show at the Cotton Club in the late 1930s, for instance, would include several different varieties of dance performances, among them tap, flash, and exotic, as well as a team of Lindy Hoppers.

Jazz dance ought, therefore, to be a legitimate and productive branch of jazz studies, but so far the literature, except with respect to tap dancing, is pitifully small.[2] Accounting for the neglect would be worthy of an article itself. Documentation is a major problem. Another is the difficulty inherent in discoursing about dance—the embodied art, the art that concerns itself with the sensuous presence of the body and that does not fit easily into the traditional philosophical classification schemes of the arts in the West (Levin; Sparshott). A final difficulty arises from the fact that vernacular dance is still often dismissed as a form of popular culture (as jazz music once was). For all these reasons, jazz dance tends to be treated as marginal in jazz studies. Sam Donahue's remark (cited by Knight in this volume's opening chapter) that he wanted to see a film about jazz that did not cover it up "with a lot of jitterbug dancing and stuff" typifies the reaction even of established jazz scholars and historians.

The potential scope of jazz dance studies is vast. It would encompass several different dance traditions, each with different histories and posing different kinds of issues and problems. It would concern itself with the origins, dissemination, and evolution of the various jazz dances, as well as with race and class relations, cultural transformations under slavery, the economics of nightclubs and dance halls and their changing social roles, the interplay of vernacular practice and stage representations, the relation of the dance to the music, improvisation, exoticism, and so forth.

In this article I shall restrict myself to a small part of that prospective field of studies—a discussion of the representations in Hollywood films of the Lindy Hop (the basic jazz vernacular dance) from 1937 to 1942. The year 1937 was the date of the Lindy's first appearance in Hollywood films, by a group called Whitey's Lindy Hoppers who operated out of Harlem's Savoy Ballroom, while 1942 was the year Whitey's Lindy Hoppers disbanded. Even this narrow focus will broach a number of issues that cannot be treated in depth here. One is the continuance in the movies of the vaudeville tradition of compiling on the same bill numerous unrelated variety acts—from songs and dances to acrobatic feats and humorous sketches—as discrete bits of entertainment unrelated to the narrative thread. This practice intersects with a second issue, involving Hollywood practices in depicting African Americans. As Ernie Smith mentions in his article on "Films" in *The New Grove Dictionary of Jazz*, the Hollywood response to segregationist box-office reality was either to produce all-black cast movies (such as *Cabin in the Sky*, discussed in the essays by Naremore and Knee), or to restrict scenes involving African Americans to discrete and self-contained segments that could be excised for screenings in the South.[3] A third issue relates to the observation, by Henry Louis Gates and others, of the role of the vernacular in African American literature and art—for example, the use of vernacular traditions by writers and poets to subvert dominant conventions and ideologies, disguising within an apparently stereotypical and nonthreatening discourse a powerful and potentially subversive message.[4] It has been claimed that African American dance was used to this end as well (Hazzard-Gordon 46). If this is true, however, it is much less a factor in the persistence of the form than is the case with literature and poetry, given that the range of what vernacular dance (movement styles) can subvert is of necessity much more restricted than what is available to a vernacular form with a linguistic dimension.

What interests me, however, is certain cinematic problems involved in representing this dance. The Lindy does not lend itself readily to representation through traditional cinematic methods, though this may not be apparent at first to those who have benefited from the cumulative effect of having seen it in situ and who have watched a number of films in which it was featured. As a jazz dance, it (like jazz music) is both an improvisational and individualistic practice and a collaborative one. To capture that antinomic character involves somehow representing the performer both as individually creative *and* as involved in a give-and-take with a community of other performers. In addition, vernacular dances like the Lindy are unlike stage dances in that they are not composed to be performed on stage before an audience from a privileged perspective. Rather, the performer of a vernacular dance is always alongside others in an organic and multiperspectival event admitting of no privileged perspective; the performer of a vernacular dance is always interstitial.[5] Neither the proscenium approach, in which the camera is located in the best possible position in the audience, nor a sequence of cuts between close-ups and overviews, effectively captures the spirit of this kind of dance.

Moreover, the Lindy was able to lend itself to several vastly different significations. In the Hollywood film clips that are the subject of this article, the dance was made to signify an apparently paradoxical posture—on the one hand, of irreverence and indulgence in this-worldly enjoyment; on the other, of transcendent and redemptive freedom from earthly cares and constraints. With selective emphases to suit Hollywood conventions, the Lindy Hop was made to exhibit an attitude akin to what Nietzsche called the "divine frivolity of the dancer" (427).

The Lindy developed in Harlem nightclubs and ballrooms of the late 1920s and is based on African bodily movements with European-style recurring footwork.[6] The African bodily movements are hip-centered, low to the ground, syncopated, and improvisational; the recurring-style footwork involved an eight-count (two-bar) basic step. What distinguished the Lindy from other dance practices from which it evolved (in particular the Collegiate) was the "breakaway," where the partners separated at arm's length for part of a step or even for several steps; occasionally, the partners would separate from each other entirely. In most couple dances (the waltz or fox-trot, for instance), the partners hold each other closely enough so that they generally need to do identical footwork with reverse parity lest they tread on each other's feet. The development of the breakaway, however, made possible a flexible couple dance with room for improvisation. Partners could do markedly different steps—even ones unknown to and unanticipated by one's partner—as long as the basic rhythm was preserved. The basic eight-count step, in which the partners separate at arm's length and in the course of which they circle 360 degrees, is called a "swing-out." But a wide variety of other steps was possible, including numerous kinds of spins, twirls, throws, and dips; moreover, the flexibility of the dance made it possible for the Lindy to incorporate footwork from other dances, including the Charleston. The name was inspired by aviator Charles Lindbergh, who flew across the Atlantic alone in May 1927 to become an overnight folk hero. The sharpies of Harlem nightclubs and ballrooms—in particular, a flashy dancer named George "Shorty" Snowden and another called "Twist Mouth George"— soon dubbed their dance with its characteristic breakaways, or solo hops, the "Lindy Hop," with the name reaching the attention of the public during the Negro Dance Marathon at the Manhattan Casino, from 17 June to 4 July 1928 (Stearns, chap. 39). Later, when the dance became popular among young white dancers, their version of it generally would be called "jitterbug"; still later, professional dance teachers would refer to their cleaned-up version of each as "swing" dancing, borrowing the term from the music.

By 1929, songs were being written specifically for the Lindy, and references to the dance begin to figure in literature, including the poems of Langston Hughes. Carl Van Vechten calls the dance "Dionysian" in *Parties* (1930). "To observe the Lindy Hop being performed," he writes, "at first induces gooseflesh, and second, intense excitement, akin to religious mania." Then Van Vechten makes an observation that is an important clue to the Lindy's later representation in Hollywood films; he tells the reader that it is "not erotic" and that "the dance is not of sexual derivation, nor does it incline its hierophants towards pleasures of the flesh" (Van Vechten 184–85). Physical stimulation without carnality, Dionysus without Eros—the claim at first astounds. But it was often repeated; when in 1945 Sweden's leading newscaster, Gunnar Skoglund, visited Nalen, Stockholm's citadel of the Lindy, he reassured concerned parents that so much energy is required to do the dance that "it's constitutionally impossible to think about sex." The contention is not as counterfeit as it might seem. The movements of the dance are at times so acrobatic, the individual steps so precipitate, the partners often so far apart, that no trace seems to emerge of a caress-like lingering over the flesh of the other. For this reason, even the fall-down jig walk step, where chest is firmly planted against chest, pelvis thrust into pelvis, the bodies of the two partners rhythmically twisting back and forth and up and down together, can be executed without appearing sexual, at least to some eyes.

But the Lindy is not always so furious, nor sex so languid; moreover, other factors enter into the constitution of the erotic. To appreciate that "Dionysian but asexual" was but one possible signification of the dance, consider that others held the Lindy to be disruptive, barbaric, and obscene. In the United States the dance was denounced from time to time as a throwback to primitivism, a form of mass hysteria, and as leading to sexual deviation. As one reader, "H. N., California," wrote to *Hygeia*, a magazine of the American Medical Association, "Isn't it possible that 'jitterbug' dancing incorporates sufficient sex expression to create a minor perversion among adolescents who consciously or subconsciously form the habit of partial expression of sex to the accompaniment of 'hot' music?" Professional dance teachers, among them Irene Castle, declared it unseemly, ungraceful, and unsuited to the ballroom, and professional dance organizations regularly passed resolutions opposing it or asserting that it was dying out (see articles in the *New York Times* and *Newsweek*, "'Jitterbug' Dying Out"; "Farewell to the Jitterbug?"; among others). Others found the Lindy disturbing because it was generally the dance of choice in nightspots and ballrooms where blacks and whites freely mingled. Overseas, too, the dance was condemned and occasionally banned. Nazi commentators on American culture, whose opposition to jazz has been amply documented, disliked jazz dance equally strongly, viewing it as revealing the insanity of American ambitions to achieve racial equality.[7] In 1937, the *Black Corps*, the newspaper of Hitler's Elite Guard, published photographs of black Lindy Hop dancers and remarked, "On the one hand, equality of all men; on the other, the Lindy Hop—a mixture of cannibalistic abdominal contortions and obscenity. Such a reckoning simply does not balance" (see *New York Times*, "Equality of Negroes" and "Swing Dancing Is Banned"). Leftist opponents of the Nazis, too, criticized the dance, with sociologist Theodor Adorno warning of its latent "authoritarian impulses" (Adorno, "On Jazz," etc.). In Sweden, where the dance was adopted by some as a symbol of rebellion against the hegemony of Germanic culture, it was viewed by others as a sign of barbarism and sin. Religious authorities condemned it as "Satanic fool's play," "a refined form of masturbation," and "negroid mating rites" (Frykman).

Thus the Lindy had a wide variety of potentially available significations, some contradictory. Most of its early appearances on films are in newsreel- or documentary-like footage of individual couples or couples performing unrelated routines, or with the dancers as accessories to music. The earliest known Lindy on film, *After Seben*, filmed in 1928 and released in 1929, includes a brief scene with Shorty Snowden. In

1931, Pathé News released footage of the dance.[8] For several years, too, stage versions were restricted to talent contests and virtuoso exhibitions in Harlem nightclubs. Even when Snowden became the first to land a job outside Harlem around 1934, dancing with Paul Whiteman at the Paramount, his act consisted of an exhibition by individual couples who came out on stage one by one in three different routines in three different Lindy styles, "comedy," "smooth," and "flash." In 1935 the *New York Daily News* began sponsoring harvest moon balls. While most of the contest was given over to (all-white) ballroom dancers, by far the most exciting single moment was the (all-black) Lindy Hop contest. This event, the biggest exhibition yet of Lindy Hoppers on stage, brought the dance to the attention of the New York public, although still as a dance for amateurs.

That changed the following year, thanks to a team of dancers from the Savoy Ballroom known as "Whitey's Lindy Hoppers," though for individual jobs the group was sometimes called by other names. "Whitey" was Herbert White, a former prizefighter who had worked at Baron Wilkins's club as a dancing waiter and then as a bouncer at the Savoy when it opened in 1926. During his scouting of the ballroom floor, White came to realize the Lindy's potential as a show in itself, and he picked out and began to train the more active and nimble of the young dancers. White was tough in promoting his own dancers over others, yet he was equally fierce in demanding that those who hired his Harlem kids treat them with respect—which sometimes cost him jobs. In the next half-dozen years, nearly all show-business jobs for Lindy Hoppers were filled by members of Whitey's Lindy Hoppers because of the dominance of New York Lindy Hopping over Lindy Hopping elsewhere, of Savoy Lindy Hopping over that of the rest of New York, and of White over the Savoy.

White's team of dancers included Frankie Manning, who in 1936 was twenty-two years old and the most innovative of the Lindy Hoppers. In 1935 and 1936, Manning introduced into the Lindy three features—one stylistic and two choreographic—that expanded its possibilities as a stage dance. The stylistic innovation was to crouch down low instead of dancing erect; this evened the momentum flow in swing-outs and gave the dance a smoother and faster look. The two choreographic innovations were ensemble dancing and air steps. In ensemble dancing, individual couples are still featured, but at the beginning and/or end of the number the couples line up and perform the identical high-speed routine at the same time. In an air step, one partner lifted, flipped, tossed, or threw the other. Both developments made the dance more exciting and more appropriate as an act in revues and musicals, and the opportunities for White's dancers expanded. In the fall of 1936, White was contracting three separate teams of dancers. A troupe consisting of Manning and Naomi Waller, Mildred Cruz and Billy Williams, and Lucille Middleton and Jerome Williams was one of the acts performing with Cab Calloway at the Cotton Club, opening downtown on 24 September 1936. Another, including "Tiny" Bunch (who was 6'2" and weighed almost four hundred pounds, but was light on his feet) and Dorothy Moses, Thomas Lee and Wilda Crawford, and Billy Ricker and Helen Bundy, was at the Harlem Uproar. A third team, consisting of Norma Miller and Leon James, George Greenidge and Ella Gibson, and Snookie Beasley and Willamae Ricker, went on tour with Ethel Waters. This last team brought the Lindy Hoppers their first movie. While performing in Los Angeles at the Paramount theater, someone involved with the making of the Marx Brothers' *A Day at the Races* (which was initially a stage show) spotted them and called White, who convinced the producers to hire a fourth dance couple, Dorothy Miller and Johnny Smalls, and himself as an extra.

MGM's *A Day at the Races* (1937) was the first Hollywood film in which Whitey's Lindy Hoppers appeared. The preceding sequence is this: the Marx Brothers and the two protagonists (Allan Jones and Maureen O'Sullivan) are being pursued by the sheriff and two other foes, with O'Sullivan particularly melancholy because she is on the verge of losing the sanitarium she runs. She begins to cry in front of a window, which happens to look out over the black section of town, and a few black children can be seen among the farm animals happily engaged in innocent play, scampering and skipping rope and playing catch. Jones tells O'Sullivan that she, too, is "just a kid" and should laugh and be happy. Though gloomy himself, he nevertheless sings to her that "tomorrow is another day."

Harpo then picks up a tin pipe to serenade the sorry couple, a drum begins to pound in the background, and the black children, calling him Gabriel, tag along behind and dance as he walks through the black quarter, piping away gaily. They come across a circle of older kids throwing dice; they, too, quit their game and follow Gabriel. Next, Harpo encounters a shack of adults in which everybody is singing their troubles—but when Harpo/Gabriel pokes his head in the window and blows on the pipe, they abruptly stop singing and come out to join him. Finally, they come to a house literally swaying with the rhythm of blacks dancing and making music, and even the musicians welcome Harpo, call him Gabriel, and let him be their conductor. From the crowd Harp coaxes singer Ivie Anderson, who begins her song with a lamentation; "I got a frown / you got a frown / all God's chillun' got a frown on their face." Cut to the lovers: O'Sullivan is frowning and Jones trying to jolly her out of it. Cut back to Anderson: "Take no task / with that frown / a song and a dance / turn it upside down!"—the tempo heats up and Anderson sings "All God's Chillun' Got Rhythm," which had already been used as the opening instrumental theme of the movie. The tempo becomes still faster, and the Lindy Hoppers take over.

The dance sequence begins with Harpo standing in the middle of the barn, still piping. The four couples shoot into the clearing, seizing the space; feigning fright at the sudden maelstrom of activity, Harpo backs away. The four couples do three swing-outs together, then one couple (Dorothy Miller and Smalls) moves center stage and twirls around several times while the others step to the edge of the crowd to clap and applaud. (White himself is in the scene; he is the one in suspenders and a black shirt with a white streak in his hair, rocking from side to side, clapping and shouting to the dancers.) They are followed by Norma Miller and James; James spins wildly, does some "legomania" (the term was generic for fancy leg movements, but James had some signature legomania), then falls to his knees while Miller somersaults over his back. Ricker and Beasley come center stage, and Beasley then does *his* signature move, the "lockstep," twisting his legs around each other and freezing momentarily in that position while clinging to his partner's waist. Beasley picks Ricker up, tosses her through his legs, and throws her in the air so that her feet reach for the ceiling. Greenidge and Gibson do a series of furious Charlestons before he flips her over his shoulder. Meanwhile, the three other couples have lined up and begun to swing out, and Greenidge and Gibson fall in line for some ensemble dancing. The dancers then pile on top of each other, one person holding up two others—a finale known as "doing the horses"—and disappear into the crowd.

As the music suddenly switches to the blander and clunkier "Three Cheers for the Red, White, and Blue," Harpo reappears with brothers Chico and Groucho—but meanwhile so have the sheriff and the two other cronies. The Marx Brothers, thinking to escape by blending in, smear axle grease over their faces and prance about in this goofy blackface. The locals, however, know that the presence of authorities spells trouble; "Da sheriff!" one shouts, and the whole crowd scrams in fright, bumping into each other helter-skelter. Still, when the movie recovers what narrative thread there is, the euphoria is still present, and the film is en route to a conclusion; the protagonists discover their horse's skill at jumping and the existence of a steeplechase to enter him in, whose stakes will rescue the sanitarium, etc.

The sequence is unusual in terms of its representation of African Americans. First, short and discrete as the sojourn in the black quarter is, at nearly eight minutes it was unusually long for a Hollywood movie of the day. Second, the sequence is not easily excisable. The arrival of the white authorities does effectively banish the black characters so that the antics in the barn can continue without them. Still, enough plot development has occurred during the sequence that the narrative thread would be disrupted if it were cut. Third, "All God's Chillun' Got Rhythm" is the movie's theme song that plays not only during the opening credits but returns (along with some of the black characters in the barn scene, except for the Lindy Hoppers) at the movie's finale. As Thomas Cripps observes, these facts did not go unnoticed and unappreciated by the black press when the movie appeared, and the reviewer for the *Amsterdam News* referred to it as "A Day at the (Negro) Races" (Cripps 115).

The filming of the sequence is fairly traditional and is shot mostly from one camera position (low, looking up), with one cut to a trumpet player (which does not interrupt the flow of the dance) and two close-ups, one of Norma Miller, the other of Leon James. These do interrupt the flow of the dance, and the one of James is especially troubling. Miller is shown shaking her head and wagging her finger, doing the "truckin'," a popular step that year. James, on the other hand, is shown grinning antically and rolling his eyes skyward, Sambo-style. This disturbs because it recalls a stereotype that the Lindy Hoppers precisely were in the process of surpassing. Their dance involved the genuine recovery and celebration of African rhythms and body movements—it was through the Lindy Hop, declares Malcolm X in his autobiography, that he rediscovered his "long-suppressed African instincts." The view of most of the Lindy-Hopping couples is blocked during the ensemble; one feels a little too close to the action. A few cheap sound effects are added—a slide tin-whistle noise dropped in above the orchestra mainly on the air steps. Just as the close-ups disrupt the flow of the dance, inviting us to contemplate not the bodily movements of the dancers but their facial expressions, so do the sound effects; this makes it seem as though the air steps are not thrilling enough by themselves but need to be accompanied by fanfare and to invite the viewer to isolate these steps from those that precede and follow them.

Moreover, the musical editing of the sequence loses its coordination with the dancers (which, as was customary, was recorded to a guide track).[9] Smalls and Dorothy Miller enter during the bridge of the song, and dance for a mere eight bars; Norma Miller and James replace them at the top of the next sixteen-bar chorus (with the clarinet lead) and dance until its conclusion. Beasley and Ricker enter with the trumpet lead-in on the next chorus, but a series of edits begins to interrupt the song form, and what we hear from then on is a pastiche of solos, new material, and previous instrumental passages. Beasley and Ricker wind up dancing about twenty-four bars uncoordinated with any chorus structure, as do Greenidge and Gibson. These musical edits disrupting the song structure of the instrumental arrangement betray a general lack of attention to the connection between the music and the dance.

But so strong is the dancing that the musical disruptions are barely noticeable—and one's memory of Ivie Anderson's powerful vocals also helps suppress recognition of them. The sequence captures the spontaneous, physical, improvisational, and anarchic character of the Lindy in several different ways. In the initial throw-out, Gibson slips slightly, then immediately recovers; in the first solo Smalls twice leaps in the air with both feet off the ground; in their solos both Beasley and James do what are obviously signature steps—moves which, like the characteristic sounds of jazz musicians, are individually creative, must be worked at to perfect, and are difficult to imitate (and even successful imitations are patent imitations). In all but one of the solos the partners separate momentarily at least once to whirl around independently of the other, and all but one couple do at least one air step. By the end they are sweating, with perspiration under their arms testifying to how physically taxing that ninety seconds of performance had been.[10]

It is a small but significant scene—as much of a denouement as *A Day at the Races* has, and not only because "All God's Chillun' Got Rhythm" is the theme song. For while Anderson has counseled everyone that the way out of their troubles is to sing and dance, and provided the song herself, the Lindy Hoppers complete the equation. They embody the movie's "message," such as there is: the pleasures, on the one hand, of joyful enthusiasm in physically active behavior with others (one hardly needs to add how important slapstick is to the Marx Brothers' humor), and, on the other, of anarchy and irreverence. For in their sudden terrified exit the crowd acknowledges guilt that, instead of dancing, they should have been at work. The scene thus shares the same spirit as that of the Marx Brothers themselves: it culminates the scene that began with Harpo's upbeat piping. The scene also retains, however, a margin of independence and integrity. With the entry of the Lindy Hoppers and the departure of Harpo, it is finally black performers calling their own tune.

The MGM musical *Everybody Sing!* (1938), was to have been the Lindy Hoppers' second movie. It was a Judy Garland vehicle, the first in which she received star billing. The plot called for Garland (a budding young per-

former inspired by MGM's version of swing) at one point to go through
Harlem on a bus; next to the Savoy, at the corner of 140th Street and
Lenox Avenue, she was to pass the clubhouse of the famous Lindy Hoppers, arriving just in time to catch them do the Big Apple and then the
Lindy. The scene was never included. Frankie Manning, who was to have
been in the scene, recalls that at one point Garland complained of fatigue
and wanted to rest her legs, and when White made a point of demanding
equal time off for his dancers to rest, a quarrel ensued and the scene was
dropped (Manning). The fact that the movie was over budget and behind
schedule and that its producers were already cutting major scenes also
may have contributed. (The stars go on an uneventful bus trip to China-
town instead.) The context was thus essentially similar to that of *A Day
at the Races:* white stars happen across blacks entertaining themselves in
their own neighborhood in a hot and exciting but nonthreatening manner; they are duly impressed and appreciative of the performance (being
performers themselves), but they are able to leave it behind simply by
driving off.

Fortunately for the Lindy Hoppers, another film soon came their way,
Radio City Revels (1938), RKO's vehicle for the comedy pairing of Bob
Burns and Jack Oakie. Burns is Lester Robins, a budding songwriter from
the Mississippi banks of Arkansas, who takes mail-order songwriting
lessons from a New York instructor but is frustrated because the beautiful tunes that come to him in his sleep are promptly forgotten on waking.
After making the decision to go to New York to learn from his mail-order
mentor in person, Robins happily joins an outdoor community barbecue,
where the entertainment is music ("Swinging in the Corn") and dancing.
Two white novelty dancers perform, one after the other (Melissa Mason
and Buster West); the second (West) performs a move startling to contemporary audiences when, dressed in a suit, he throws himself down and
spins, breakdance-style, on his shoulders. At this point Burns walks
away and lies down to nap (hence, he is about to receive inspiration).
While he is sleeping, the musical pulse changes from a hoedown rhythm
to a swing-like rhythm with a big-band orchestration, and the Lindy
Hoppers appear.

Once again, a total of four couples perform, and White is in the scene as
an extra. The sequence begins with Mildred Pollard (who later changed
her name to Sandra Gibson after quitting the group to become a showgirl
and marrying tap dancer Albert "Gip" Gibson) "truckin' " in the background with her sassy and inimitable signature boogie-woogie wiggle.
White walks over to the food table in the foreground with a tray, bounc-
ing his knees to the rhythm while serving himself. Behind him, Frankie

Manning is shown all too briefly swinging out in his characteristic low-down posture with Lucille Middleton. Pollard and Eddie Davis are followed by Greenidge and Eleanore (known as "Stumpy"—her last name is unknown) and then Tiny Bunch and Dorothy Moses, before all of them line up ensemble to do a series of long-legged Charlestons followed by an air step in which the men lock arms with the women and flip them over their backs; the men then leapfrog over the women. The group lines up together, and all of them fall back on one another like so many dominoes. Cut back to Burns, who is dreaming, a song on his lips. The Lindy Hoppers are on film all of a minute.

Here the music and its edits *are* obtrusive. First of all, the song the Lindy Hoppers dance to is only loosely speaking jazz. The instrumentation is for a fairly standard big band of the era (it is performed by the RKO studio orchestra), but there is an oom-pah to the rhythm that makes the music feel more like a strange hybrid of square dance and swing—the swing is more "in the corn" than doubtless was intended. And the music has been chopped up and poorly edited, with noticeable cuts disrupting the cohesion of the song, which rambles in the first place.

Moreover, the way the scene was filmed hinders the dancers' attempts to rescue it. The camera is farther from the action than in *A Day at the Races,* and the dancers perform against a wall of dozens of people in the background; the scene feels cramped even though it is in the open air. By far the best part of the sequence is seeing Tiny Bunch and Dorothy Moses perform—a huge giant of a dancer and a waif. In the fifteen seconds they are on screen, he swings her out; they do two fall-down jig walks; he swings her around and around, her legs flailing through the air like a rag doll's; he throws her down so that her feet scrape the ground; and finally he sends her upward with her legs pointed skyward as if she were as light as cotton. She floats and soars, he is agile and sometimes appears about to take off with her like some huge balloon, and the two seem freed from the ordinary earthly bonds of gravity—the liberation of the repressed. In fact, the dance happens during Burns's reveries; the performance of the Lindy Hoppers, as it were, assumes the place of his divinely inspired dream.

That year a film clip of the Lindy Hoppers doing the Big Apple, a popular circle dance of the day, was made and appeared the next year in a black-cast film shot in New York (*Keep Punchin'*, 1939, Film Arts Studio). Several news footage-type film clips were also taken around this time. Russian ex-dancer Mura Dehn sometimes put a camera on the Savoy Ballroom floor and brought over Lindy Hoppers to record them (see Backstein's essay in this collection). The Lindy Hoppers also performed in several Broadway shows, including *Knickerbocker Holiday* (1938), where they played Indians on the warpath against Walter Huston, and *Hellzapoppin* (1938), a vehicle for the comedy team of Ole Olsen and Chic Johnson, which redefined "zany" and, though panned by critics, ran for three years to become the longest-running Broadway musical up to that date. In *The Hot Mikado* (1939) the Lindy Hoppers danced during the Three Little Maids number, and in *Swinging the Dream* (1939) twenty-six Lindy Hoppers played the forest spirits.

The Lindy Hoppers did not return to Hollywood until 1941, when Olsen and Johnson made *Hellzapoppin*, the movie, which was only loosely based on the stage play. For the first time, the Lindy Hoppers get a credit (in the beginning as the "Harlem Congaroo Dancers," at the end simply as the "Congaroo Dancers"). Their performance, choreographed by Manning specifically for the movie, involved four couples, William Downes and Francis "Mickey" Jones, Billy Ricker and Norma Miller, Al Minns and Willamae Ricker, and Manning and Ann Johnson. This is probably the finest performance of the Lindy Hoppers—and one of the hottest dance sequences—on film. The movie involves Olsen and Johnson as two prop men who are helping their housemate Jeff (Robert Paige) produce a show, part of a benefit staged at a fabulously wealthy Long Island estate, "in the big outdoor theater back of the greenhouse." At one point, two porters (Slim Gaillard and Slam Stewart) carry some equipment backstage for the orchestra. When no one else is looking, they divert themselves on the instruments; Slim, for example, bangs prankishly on the piano with the backs of his hands. The playful melody and engaging syncopated rhythm attracts the attention of the other help; we briefly see a mechanic and then two maids drop what they are doing to listen. More help join the impromptu band, which swells to a sextet. "This might turn into something," Slim says, at the end of a little ditty. "If I ain't mistaken, here comes something now!" The rhythm heats up, the music changes to a fuller orchestra, and the camera sweeps just in time to discover a mechanic and a maid (Downes and Jones) jumping into the air in an empty clearing amid the props. Their solo is followed by solos by Billy Ricker and Miller, Minns and Willamae Ricker, and Manning and Ann Johnson. All four couples line up to do an ensemble, and then each does a different air step in turn, with the camera sweeping down the line barely in time to catch each (a "waterfall"). The men next throw the women over their heads and then leapfrog over the heads of the women into splits; at the concluding strains of the song, the women leapfrog over the heads of the men into splits, and they all fall over, face-down. They hear a noise and look up to see—white folks! Olsen, Johnson, and Paige are watching and applauding, and the dancers, terrified, scramble to get back to work.

Comparing this scene with the one in *A Day at the Races* four years earlier (two of the dancers are in both scenes) reveals not only how much the dancers developed as artists but how much the choreography and filming improved in that time. The sequence lasts for only two minutes, but the music is fast—faster than the typical swing tune and considerably faster than the dance music in *A Day at the Races*, so that much more dancing ensues. Despite the increased speed, the steps are smoother and executed with more finesse. While in *A Day at the Races* many of the air steps consisted of lifting or flipping or vaulting, here the dancers are *thrown*, and without missing a beat—and not only do men throw women, but women throw men. The improvisational character of the dance is suggested by some peculiar positions in which the dancers find themselves: Downes exits his solo snaking off the floor on his back; Jones goes off his solo in a crab walk; and Minns at one point is held above the ground, upside down, by his partner. In *A Day at the Races* one can often detect the dancers readying for each air step with hesitations or preparatory steps, and close-ups and sound effects are used to focus attention on individual moves. None of that occurs in *Hellzapoppin*, not even for the most vigorous of the air steps. The dance is filmed as a seamless whole, one continuous discharge of energy.

Contributing to that feeling of smoothness is the coordination between dancing and music. A guide track ("Jumpin' at the Woodside") was used, but in a reversal of traditional practice the music was apparently arranged and played *for* the dance *after* the scene was shot (Manning). The song form is integral—thirty-two-bar choruses, with each couple entering at the top of the chorus, and the ensemble entering on an interlude with new material at the end. Moreover, when Manning, who is physically the largest dancer as well as the most exciting, enters with Ann Johnson, the music modulates upward, building in intensity. The musical intensity culminates during the dance ensemble, with a trumpet entering as the music goes back to the bridge and continuing over the top until the end.

Other elements adding to the general feeling of frenzy are the hats—Downes's, Mickey's, and Miller's—that are thrown or fly off. And a significant improvement on the earlier film sequences is in the interaction between the soloing couple and the others. Nobody stands by quietly; there is a constant chatter as the dancers egg each other on, and nearly as much motion takes place in the background as in the foreground. At one point Manning follows Billy Ricker and Miller while bobbing his head like a chicken (a move called "peckin'"), and when Minns flips Willamae Ricker, Downes falls to the ground in mock astonishment. When Ann Johnson slides through Manning's legs and across the room on her rear, Jones has to jump up to get out of the way, and Johnson sails by underneath. When Johnson returns to grab Manning again, she is accompanied part of the way by an applauding Minns. And in the final chorus, when the camera travels down the line in time to catch each couple in an air step, the viewer gets a feeling of coordinated yet individual motion.

With its careful filmwork, the sequence owes as much to Hollywood as it does to the Savoy Ballroom floor. It would be difficult to represent the entire sequence, solo and support couples, in front of a live audience to the right effect. It has been tried, and I am told that the effect was wooden and stagy. It is not difficult to imagine why. On film, the camera can catch the solo couple from different angles, while still picking up interaction with support couples; by manipulating the play of what is visible and what is invisible, what is present and what is absent, the sequence manages to preserve the feeling of simultaneous improvisation and collaboration (figures 1 and 2). The waterfall, for example, is a carefully staged motion among all four couples, but with the camera drifting down the line, just in time to catch an air step from each one, the moves seem almost spontaneous and unconnected, arising out of chaos. Even in a highly choreographed event, the camera creates the illusion of interstitial viewing.

As to signification, the Lindy once again appears as a pleasure verging on the demonic, yet without a trace of anything sexual or lurid. Bodies fly through the air with the fierceness and power of a horse race, but also with the coordination of an orchestral performance. The Lindy is also portrayed as an interruption of normal human activity: the dancers are neglecting their duties. Yet that spirit, while not encouraged, is at least tolerated. Olsen, Chic Johnson, and Paige applaud and smile knowingly as they witness the help dash back to work ("Too bad they're not in the show," one of them says); the help, evidently not realizing that the film's stars bear about the same relation to their wealthy employers as the Marx Brothers did to the sheriff in *A Day at the Races*, no doubt are ready to protest that they had been working all along.

The Lindy Hoppers' contract at Universal called for them to do a second movie after *Hellzapoppin*. But, as war loomed, no picture materialized. White had been asked to send a team of dancers to Rio de Janeiro to perform in a casino there, and he talked his way out of the contractual

Figure 1. Whitey's Lindy Hoppers in *Hellzapoppin*. Couples from left to right: William Downes and Francis "Mickey" Jones, Albert Minns and Willamae Ricker, and Frankie Manning and Ann Johnson; Billy Ricker and Norma Miller are out of the frame to the left. Courtesy of the Academy of Motion Picture Arts and Sciences.

obligation. Before the dancers left, in November 1941, they made *Hot Chocolate* ("*Cottontail*"), a soundie released the next year.[11] Soundies were the music videos of the day, played on machines called Panorams that might be found in bars, hotels, and restaurants from 1940 until 1947.[12] They were shot in a hurry, and often low production values showed in the form of simple backgrounds, basic costumes, and sound-tracks poorly synchronized with the visuals. Fortunately, the Lindy Hoppers were paired with the Duke Ellington orchestra; Ellington would have insisted on carefully supervising anything with his name on it. The simple set (a near-empty railway station) worked to advantage; the only indication of below-average production values is an occasional conti-nuity error (Downes wears a hat in one cut and is without it in the next) and the fact that most of the dancers are wearing coats in the scene because they were filming on a chilly fall day on an open-air stage.

It is refreshing to see the Lindy Hoppers without a flimsy excuse for their appearance, and their dancing simply unfolds. *Hot Chocolate* even has an arty look. When Ellington appears at the piano, a sculpture of a

Figure 2. Trio of couples from Whitey's Lindy Hoppers in *Hellzapoppin* (Universal Pictures, 1941). Courtesy of Fotofest.

staff of notes casts shadows against the wall in the background; and there is a mysterious cut wherein a microphone changes into a radio speaker—the band is now playing live over the radio. A few seconds later, just before the dancing begins, there is an extremely effective and mood-setting shot in which the camera pans down the line of Lindy Hoppers who are gently nodding their heads and shoulders to the music. (Miller, either distracted or copping an attitude, is perversely looking away at the end.) "Cottontail" is a conventionally structured, thirty-two-bar swing tune played at a medium tempo, and while the dancers are not always coordinated precisely with the succession of choruses, they all enter and exit at key musical moments. Manning and Johnson are once again the final dancers, and they enter at the top of a chorus—a shout chorus, the only one in the arrangement and the point at which its musical intensity culminates. The dancers begin their ensemble when the orchestra is also playing a tutti section; the music then switches back to the main melody and diminishes in intensity as the dancers exit on "horses" as they had in *A Day at the Races.* Nobody has to run away or apologize for their actions.

After three of the four couples spent eight months in Brazil (Downes and Jones remained in the States), the team rejoined in the United States.

Most of the male members were subsequently drafted, and the team broke up for good. A few more soundies were made in 1942 with other members of the group (*Sugar Hill Masquerade, Outline of Jitterbug History, Tuxedo Junction*). In 1944, Columbia put out a ten-minute short featuring Cootie Williams and his orchestra with two pairs of Lindy Hoppers (*Film Vodvil*, ser. 2, no. 2). Later, some of the Lindy Hoppers' earlier footage was rereleased in repackaged form. RKO, for instance, issued a series of variety-type movies in the late 1940s and early 1950s incorporating material from previous movies: the picnic scene from *Radio City Revels* appears in *Footlight Varieties* (1951). A ten-minute excerpt from *Keep Punchin'* including the Big Apple scene, entitled *Jittering Jitterbugs*, was later issued by Sack Enterprises; an excerpt from the Sack reissue appears in a documentary that has appeared on PBS entitled *Rock and Roll: The Early Years*, misidentified as being from the mid-1950s.

The year 1943 was the high-water mark of the Lindy's respectability. *Life* magazine devoted a cover story to it (photographed by Gjon Mili), and an organization of professional dance teachers began to teach the "Lindy/Jitterbug." White jitterbuggers had turned up briefly in a few movies before this time, including *Bachelor Mother* (1939) and *City for Conquest* (1940). These scenes typically involved teenage couples enjoying themselves at parties, dance marathons, or other occasions in which no apology is needed for their activity.[13] After 1943, white jitterbuggers appeared more and more frequently (*Stage Door Canteen* [1943] and the short *Groovie Moovie* [1944]). A number of black-cast movies also had Lindy Hoppers, of which the best-known is *Cabin in the Sky* (1943). Dozens of soundies were issued with some dancing couples, though none compare with the performances of the Lindy Hoppers. A troupe of white youngsters, the "Jivin' Jacks and Jills," appeared in fourteen low-budget movies from 1942 until 1944, among them a number of good dancers including Grace McDonald, Donald O'Connor, and Peggy Ryan (Frank, chap. 21). GIs took the dance all over the world, and Betty Grable danced it at the close of each show of her USO tour with a handful of servicemen from the audience. Manning, as it happened, was one of her chosen partners in the Philippines. A white movie star Lindy Hopping on a public stage with a black serviceman without, apparently, any innuendo—the dance was now much more than a hot and exciting black vernacular dance; it had become a symbol of America, the great melting pot.

The Lindy would have a profound influence on later African American and jazz dancing, both vernacular and theatrical, and two of the Lindy Hoppers (Manning and Miller) would later choreograph for the stage and in movies.[14] But the way the Lindy was represented on film changed. It had previously been presented as an activity which, on the one hand, was frivolous and distracting, something indulged in while AWOL from work; on the other hand, the Lindy was an innocent celebration of something good in and of itself, something valuable for its sheer existence alone and thus could be characterized as sacred and divine. This curious, apparently ambivalent signification—which, as Suzanne Langer has remarked, has characterized dance from its beginning (184)—is approximated by the Nietzschean phrase, "divine frivolity" (427). Nietzsche's ideas about the signification of dance ran further and deeper, of course. For him, dance encapsulated the spirit of the Overman, who rejects the spirit of gravity, who artfully experiments and improvises in every situation, and who knows there is nothing "other-worldly" and that this is the only world. Likewise, there is nothing Nietzschean in the sexually sanitized. With these qualifications, however, the borrowed phrase still serves to characterize the Lindy's signification in these Hollywood films.

Henceforth, the representations would be appropriated in a number of different ways and on a number of different levels for some other end. They would be used, for instance, as evocative of the jazz scene (*Jammin' the Blues*, 1944); of an era (*1941*, 1979; *A League of Their Own*, 1992); of black heritage (*Malcolm X*, 1992; the TV movie *Stompin' at the Savoy*, 1992); of energy and vitality (soft drink commercials); or of nature, peace, and togetherness (Timmy Thomas's 1992 pop video, *Why Can't We Live Together*, featuring a collage of shots of wild animals in their native habitats, starving children, African American leaders such as Martin Luther King, and an interracial group of Lindy Hoppers at Covent Garden).

Each of these occasions faced and resolved in a different way the same kinds of problems faced by prewar films in representing this dance on film. These problems involved, first, representing a practice that for the individual performer is at once improvisational and collaborative, and second, representing an event involving numerous performers that is organic and multiperspectival in which each performer, even when "soloing," is always alongside others. Finally, whereas jazz music has a temporal integrity that demands to be maintained, jazz dance requires the additional maintenance of a spatial integrity that is easily disrupted by film editing. Though the assigned significations of the Lindy have changed, the basic problems and difficulties associated with representing it remain.

Notes

In jazz studies one often finds oneself having to seek out the help of scholars and enthusiasts who have made it their business to know particular corners of the jazz world in exhaustive detail. In preparing this article I have profited from the help of several such individuals, whose knowledge was as extensive as their generosity: Mark Cantor (who is working on a book about Panoram soundies based on the original production files), Frankie Manning (who was *in* most of the movies made by Whitey's Lindy Hoppers), Ernie Smith (the original collector of jazz films), and Stephanie Stein (possessor of an uncannily perceptive musical ear). The "Jazz Oral History Interview" with Frankie Manning is used with permission of the Jazz Oral History Project, Smithsonian Institution, National Museum of American History, Washington, D.C. I am grateful to Al Vollmer for translating the Frykman essay from the Swedish for me.

1   Although it sounds overly academic, I use Stearns's "vernacular" for want of a better term. "Social dance" implies dressiness and elevated environments; "popular dance" bespeaks short-lived fads and widespread acceptance (the Lindy has been around for more than six decades and is not exactly widespread); and "folk" sounds nostalgic, ethnic, or political. I like Marcellus Blount's definition of vernacular as involving "an interaction between performer and audience that relies on linguistic, paralinguistic, kinesic, and thoroughly contextual codes and conventions" (583).

2   The most important work in this field is still Stearns (reprinted in 1994), but also see Emery; Frank; Haskins; and Hazzard-Gordon.

3   The same clips that were excised in the South might also be advertised as attractions in the North; see Cripps.

4   On the vernacular as the key to understanding African American literature, see Gates; Marcellus Blount makes a similar point regarding poetry in "The Preacherly Text."

5   This is wonderfully captured, for instance, in the swimming pool scene of Les Blank's 1983 documentary on Polish polka dancing, *In Heaven There Is No Beer!*

6   These body rhythms are discussed in chapter 2 of Stearns. For other sources on the Lindy, see the three essays by Crease and part ten of Stearns, although this account is distorted and occasionally erroneous because of the author's excessive reliance on Al Minns and Leon James as sources; moreover, James is misidentified in the picture of "Whitey's Hopper Maniacs."

7   For the Nazis on jazz, see Kater; see also the impressionistic and at times distorted account in Zwerin as well as the film *Swing Kids* (1993). For a novelistic account of the Lindy in France during World War II, see Loiseau.

8   For information on this and similar footage, see Ernie Smith's bibliography of jazz dance on film in the back of Stearns, as well as Frank's supplement in the back of Frank.

9   On the music of this scene, see Stratemann. In keeping with the prevailing opinion of jazz scholars, Stratemann argues against the previous assumption that members of Ellington's band are in the recording orchestra of this scene.

10 Consider, too, the great contrast between the Lindy Hop sequence and the other dance number earlier in the film—the lavish, well-choreographed, and interminable Water Carnival scene. The one takes place in a barn, with straw on the floor

and a wagon in the corner, while the other takes place on a lavish set equipped with fountains and bridges transversing bodies of water; the one involves mainly a series of wild solos, while the other involves careful choreography sometimes involving dozens of dancers executing the same motions simultaneously; the dancers in the one are wearing farm clothes, while those in the other are in elaborate costumes; and the one zips along for a mere ninety seconds, while the other seems endless at slightly more than four minutes.

11 The contract for this soundie is dated 8 November; the recordings were done the week of 24 November; and the filming of the Lindy Hoppers was probably done that week as well.

12 On soundies, see Terenzio, MacGillivray, and Okudo.

13 One might also mention a dance sequence excised from *The Wizard of Oz*, which though named "jitterbug" barely resembles it.

14 Manning won a 1988 Tony Award for his role in the choreography of *Black and Blue*.

Works Cited

Adorno, Theodor. "On Jazz." Trans. Jamie Owen Daniel. *Discourse* 12.1 (Fall–Winter 1989–90): 45–69.

——. "On the Fetish-Character in Music and the Regression of Listening." *Zeitschrift für Sozialforschung* 7 (1938).

——. "Popular Music." *Introduction to the Sociology of Music*. Trans. E. B. Ashton. New York: Seabury, 1976.

Blount, Marcellus. "The Preacherly Text: African American Poetry and Vernacular Performance." *PMLA* 107 (May 1992): 582–93.

Crease, Robert P. "The Lindy Hop." *Proceedings of the International Early Dance Institute* 1:1 (1988): 1–11.

——. "Swing Story." *Atlantic* Feb. 1986: 77–82.

——. "Last of the Lindy Hoppers." *Village Voice* 25 Aug. 1987: 27–32.

Cripps, Thomas. *Slow Fade to Black: The Negro in American Film, 1900–1942*. New York: Oxford UP, 1977.

"Equality of Negroes in U.S. Angers Nazis: Paper of Elite Guard Asserts Pictures of Lindy Hop Show Race Can't Be Civilized." *New York Times* 28 Feb. 1937: 30.

Emery, Lynne Fauley. *Black Dance from 1619 to Today*. Princeton, N.J.: Princeton Book Company, 1988.

"Farewell to the Jitterbug? Teachers Enlist Irene Castle in War on Swing Dance Style." *Newsweek* 14 Aug. 1939: 30–31.

Frank, Rusty E. *Tap!* New York: Morrow, 1990.

Frykman, Jonas. "Dansebane elandet." *Den dolda historien*. Ed. Ronny Ambjörnsson and David Gaunt. Stockholm: Författarförlaget, 1984. 297–318.

Gates, Henry Louis, Jr. *The Signifying Monkey: A Theory of Afro-American Literary Criticism*. New York: Oxford UP, 1988.

Haskins, James. *Black Dance in America*. New York: Harper Collins, 1990.

Hazzard-Gordon, Katrina. *Jookin': The Rise of Social Dance Formations in African-American Culture*. Philadelphia: Temple UP, 1990.

"H. N., California." "Questions and Answers, Dancing." *Hygeia* Dec. 1939: 1131.

" 'Jitterbug' Dying Out, Dance Masters Agree." *New York Times* 1 Aug. 1939: 16.

Kater, Michael H. *Different Drummers: Jazz in the Culture of Nazi Germany.* New York: Oxford UP, 1992.

Langer, Suzanne K. *Feeling and Form.* New York: Scribner's, 1953.

Levin, David Michael. "Philosophers and the Dance." *What Is Dance? Readings in Theory and Criticism.* Ed. R. Copeland and M. Cohen. New York: Oxford UP, 1983. 85–94.

Loiseau, Jean Claude. *Les Zazous.* Paris: Sagittaire, 1977.

Manning, Frankie B. "Jazz Oral History Interview." Interviewer Robert P. Crease. 22–23 July 1992.

Nietzsche, Friedrich. *The Will to Power.* Trans. Walter Kaufmann and R. J. Hollingdale. New York: Random, 1968.

Sparshott, Francis. *Off the Ground: First Steps in the Philosophical Consideration of the Dance.* Princeton, N.J.: Princeton UP, 1988.

Stearns, Marshall, and Jean Stearns. *Jazz Dance: The Story of American Vernacular Dance.* 1968. New York: Da Capo, 1994.

Stratemann, Klaus. *Duke Ellington Day by Day and Film By Film.* Copenhagen: JazzMedia, 1992.

"Swing Dancing Is Banned in Reich Town as Menace." *New York Times* 6 May 1938: 8.

Terenzio, Maurice, Scott MacGillivray, and Ted Okudo. *The Soundies Distributing Corporation of America: A History and Filmography of their "Jukebox" Musical Films of the 1940s.* Jefferson, N.C.: McFarland, 1991.

Untitled article. *New York Times* 2 Apr. 1939: X, 8.

Van Vechten, Carl. *Parties: Scenes from Contemporary New York Life.* New York: Knopf, 1930.

Zwerin, Mike. *La Tristesse de Saint Louis: Swing under the Nazis.* London: Quartet Books, 1985.

Keeping the Spirit Alive: The Jazz Dance Testament of Mura Dehn

KAREN BACKSTEIN

Jazz is a one-legged proposition without dancing—and Negro art without danc-ing is unthinkable.—Mura Dehn

Somewhere around 1940, dancer/filmmaker Mura Dehn poi-gnantly lamented to jazz critic Marshall Stearns: "The true mas-ters of jazz dancing are drowning in silence. They can't even scream. So much of Negro dancing has died unrecorded. We can only guess what minstrelsy was really like . . . one would have to fish it out, in traditional vaudeville mannerisms. That is a difficult job that could probably still be done now, but ten years from now it will probably be too late" (Mura Dehn files, New York Public Library Dance Collection at Lincoln Center; hereafter cited as Dehn files). In this perception of the gradual death of an art form lay the impetus for *The Spirit Moves: A History of Black Social Dance on Film, 1900–1986*, Dehn's decades-long project to record the evolution of African American vernacular dance. Her undertaking remains unequaled in scope, covering reconstructed plantation dances, low-down burlesque, hot nights at the Savoy, freestyle rock and roll, and the street cool of break dance.

Dehn's film is unique in that it sets out to be a historical document, designed to preserve and contextualize jazz and its progeny, rather than to provide entertainment per se. She began filming in the 1950s, and, until her death, she continued recording the newest manifestations of African American dance. *The Spirit Moves* consists of four "volumes," each dedicated to different dance styles and eras. Volume 1 is divided into two parts, both shot around 1950. The first section presents traditional jazz dances—the strut, cakewalk, boogie woogie, snake hips, black bottom,

Big Apple, and calypso—restaged in a studio. The featured performers include Pepsi Bethel, James Berry, Teddy Brown, Sandra Gibson, Leon James, Esther Washington, Frankie Manning, Thomas King, and Albert Minns—among the finest dancers of their generation. Their torsos ripple, their bodies swing freely into sudden tumbles and shimmies, and their feet move in intricate crisscrossing patterns. Then, languid, fluid blues inspires the first real couple dance, with the woman leaning against the man, doing low, tango-like kicks and half-shifts of weight. Her arms caress her body in an image of elegant sensuality, and, in a movement that recalls earlier plantation dances, she slowly swivels her hips. The volume's second part, by contrast, consists of live footage taken at the Savoy Ballroom in Harlem, where talented amateurs and professionals mingled as they danced the bebop Lindy and mambo, the applejack and the Charleston, the Lindy Hop and the aerial Lindy, all in preparation for the Harvest Moon Ball; bodies fly through the air (with the women taking on some of the athletic partnering) and feet slide along the floor, executing deceptively simple shuffles that alternate with tapping steps in complex rhythms. No other filmmaker ever received permission to shoot at that legendary club.

Volume 2, "The Postwar Era," covers a wide span, from 1950 until 1975, and it also consists of two parts. The first focuses on bebop and on mambo dancers at New York's Palladium. In "bebop time" the dancers play with the music's extreme syncopation, teasingly keeping their bodies constantly on the edge of balance, half-teetering. A dancer leans forward, falls back and air-boxes, stumbles, trips, and walks stiffly; the camera turns on its side in a freedom that mirrors the performer's alternation between sudden action and unexpected pauses. Then three couples perform the mambo, some of them incorporating bebop's tricky timing and dance vocabulary; a Latino couple dances a more typical mambo, with its mixture of jazz and rhumba. The volume's second part plunges into the thoroughly modern age, capturing Mama Lu Parks's company performing the rock and roll repertoire (the pony, waddle, twist, funky chicken, and mod squad) with all its African retentions.

Volume 3, "Artists of the Theater" (shot in the 1980s), goes back in time again, offering minstrel jazz, the Charleston, and nondance burlesque skits. Finally, volume 4, in two parts, is devoted to "Artists of the Street," in particular break dancing. The performers include The Magnificent Force and the VTB dancers. Several shots focus on the physical isolations in which break-dancers specialize; the movement travels from one extremity to the other as the dancers shiver and twitch in loose, rubbery movements before finally executing a panoply of acrobatics. Dehn filmed this last volume from 1984 until 1986.

The work in its entirety reveals the constant shifts of direction taken by black vernacular dance, and it makes explicit the transition between jazz dance proper, with its richly dialogic give-and-take between musician and dancer, and later dance forms, where the dancer either faced a fixed musical text (as in resolutely unimprovised rock and roll) or musicians who at best ignored or at worst deliberately obstructed the dancer's progress.

The Spirit Moves offers the opportunity to examine the cinematic translation of vernacular and theatrical jazz dance in a work that explicitly employed cinema for its recording properties. At the same time, this was not an "ethnographic" or library study but one designed (as its title suggests) to capture the dance's *spirit*. The film raises a host of issues surrounding jazz dance and film stylistics, all the more important when one considers that the cinema was, for jazz dance, the equivalent of recordings for jazz music, in terms of capturing actual, contemporary performances; one might even argue that, given the difficulty of transcribing movement into written form (especially for techniques without standardized steps), and the ephemeral quality of dance, cinema played an even more pivotal role for choreography than records did for the music.

To what extent were Dehn's fears and assumptions about the fading away of jazz dance justified? And how can the work of this self-appointed keeper of the flame be seen in relation to both film and dance history? Before looking at *The Spirit Moves* as a text, that text needs a context— one that takes into account race, gender, artistic appropriation, and the theatrical enterprise.

Race and Artistic Appropriation

The importance of Jazz Dance for the modern world is not in the fact that black Americans originated it, nor that it has its roots in Africa.

Jazz is important because it became the national dance of the U.S.A. . . . [because] white people absorbed this black contribution as the main element of their own dancing.—Mura Dehn, "The Spirit Moves: Preliminary Version of an Unpublished Manuscript" (undated)

On the surface, Dehn, a Russian immigrant with little exposure to jazz, seems an unlikely historian of black culture. She had trained in the movement style of Isadora Duncan, which scorned African "wildness" in favor of Greek "serenity." But Dehn saw Josephine Baker dance in Paris, which piqued her already nascent interest in jazz, and she came to the United States in 1930 to search out the finest dancers and learn from them. Even though she had not shared the roots that nourished black jazz musicians and dancers, Dehn quickly established herself, and she soon formed, directed, and danced in her own troupe. By 1945 she and her company toured Africa on U.S. State Department funds. Dehn also wrote articles on the history and theory of jazz dance for important trade periodicals such as *Dance Magazine,* and she prepared a written script to accompany *The Spirit Moves,* which contains comments on each dance and its social context.

Dehn became one of many white artists and impresarios who took it on themselves to present, imitate, or dance alongside black jazz performers. She, however, allied herself more closely with the intellectual "artistic" community than with the entertainment industry that had heretofore controlled stage exhibitions of African American culture—such as the Theater Owners' Booking Association of the early 1900s, colloquially known as "Tough on Black Artists" (Stearns and Stearns 78). Among these artists concerned with black cultural practices, many shared Dehn's Eastern European background. They included George Balanchine, who, in 1940 purchased the rights and then directed *Cabin in the Sky* on Broadway; he also choreographed the show *House of Flowers* with dancers Alvin Ailey and Carmen de Lavallade. Igor Stravinsky's music also played with complex syncopations, and Maya Deren devoted herself to documenting Haitian vodoun.

Dehn fit snugly within the intelligentsia, who, from the turn of the century and continuing even today (especially among New Agers who use Native American and African religious rituals and drumming to get in touch with their "primitive selves"), tended to valorize "folk" forms with links to tradition, spirituality, and community. And she shared the desire of many practicing artists to transform popular vernacular forms into concert pieces, even as Béla Bartók and Zoltán Kodály in Hungary transcribed folk songs for concert halls, Agnes de Mille brought square dancing to ballet and Broadway, and Ted Shawn rechoreographed Native American dances for his all-male group. "Dying arts" were of particular concern; Jill Drayson Sweet describes how intellectuals and artists "encouraged the stereotype of the Pueblo Indians as artists . . . [and] felt it was important to encourage [them] to revive forgotten dances and arts." This sympathy had its limits, however, and an examination of Dehn's work can shed some light on the problems inherent in the almost "paternalistic" undertaking of these "cultural saviours" and the gap between them and the communities whose output they either documented, scooped up for inspiration, or, at worst, simply plundered.

Intellectuals desirous of speaking for the unheard and aggrandizing the fringe in order to distance themselves from the middlebrow perpetuated errors about and unnoticingly asserted their supremacy over the cultures they heralded. Dehn, for example, even after devoting decades of her life to the perpetuation of jazz, could still insist in her film's narration that the motion of blues dance "was decidedly of an African heritage . . . but the dancers were not aware of it," suggesting an unpleasantly superior attitude toward those who actually created the dance. The statement reeks of unintended irony: Dehn, who understands the constant change and loss that mark the history of jazz dance, questions neither why the form constantly redefines itself, nor why its history might have been suppressed. Certainly, whites had no desire to valorize Africanness at the time, and until the 1960s blacks could gain no honor from claiming ties to a civilization so denigrated by hegemonic culture.

Robert Farris Thompson's thorough study of African retentions in the United States provides an interesting comparison to Dehn and her refusal to consider that blacks actually knew the African origins of their art. In *Flash of the Spirit,* Thompson describes the attempts of Harlem artists during the 1960s to research and reconfigure Yoruban art to reflect their own time and their own struggles; he also notes the persistence of African-derived rituals throughout black communities in the South. For Thompson, "the grand message of Yoruba Atlantic art, wherever it is found . . . is this: sheer artlessness may bring a culture down but a civilization like that of the Yoruba, and the Yoruba-Americans . . . will safeguard the passage of its people through the storms of time" (97).

Dehn does not implicate the hegemonic culture's role in the effort to foster forgetfulness, at least partially by a constant failure to credit and recognize Africanisms within society. Thompson wryly states, "Many a Ki-Kongo-derived word has been described by etymologists as 'origin unknown'" (104).

Because jazz (and the musical/dance forms that followed in its footsteps) remains the most important and widespread form of indigenous American culture, arguments have always raged over its origins. From as far back as the 1700s, white dancers in blackface appeared onstage mimicking, satirizing, and otherwise appropriating African American dance traditions. These performers seized choreographic credit for borrowed work, while at the same time denigrating the folks they robbed from. Although no one now refutes jazz's African American antecedents, in the past many white Americans' views of this style fluctuated according to whether the form was classified as black or white. When the dance remained wholly within the African American world, whites refused to admit its artistic value. Then, as jazz's artistic currency increased, they hotly denied the role of blacks in its creation. According to this view, tap became merely a variation of Irish clog dancing rather than a rhythmic and choreographic reconceptualization in terms of African principles. When whites did acknowledge African American creativity, they often did so in a negative, backhanded manner, marveling at blacks' "natural" sense of rhythm and dance prowess—which, like Dehn's casual assumption of historical ignorance on the part of the dancers, removed the *intellectual* component from African American artistic creation. Ultimately, this imputation of "naturalism," of bodily energy and power outside the realm of intellect, proved to exercise an irresistible attraction for Caucasian artists.

The fascination felt by white intellectuals for African American culture (if not always for the African Americans themselves) has a long and complex history, both inside and outside the United States. Andrew Ross in *No Respect: Intellectuals and Popular Culture* examines the reactions of white artists to black culture, particularly during the late 1940s and early 1950s. From Jack Kerouac's "desire to become negro" to Norman Podhoretz's admiration of "negroes' physical grace," Ross traces the history of an almost jealous admiration felt by these intellectuals for African American art and their nostalgia for the "folksy" world from which this art had emerged and from which they were forever excluded.

Ross also details the angry response of African American intellectuals to this innocent idealization, as well as to white co-optation of black stylistics: they disavowed or altered their art to challenge and alienate Caucasian spectators. Influential writers such as Amiri Baraka touted musicians who scuttled the more accessible aspects of black music and developed a barrage of artistic strategies to make their work immune to appropriation by those outside their own community. In the process they partially severed the sacrosanct link between jazz music and dance. This in part explains why Dehn saw jazz dance as a dying art: other than jazz in its later stages, African American culture regarded music and movement as a whole; the music was the lifeblood on which the dance fed, and in turn (especially in jazz), the musicians answered and adapted to the rhythms developed by the dancers. Theorists of African and African American culture such as Portia K. Maultsby, Joyce Ashabranner, Pearl Primus, and Marshall Stearns firmly emphasize the intertwined nature of the two forms (See Stearns and Stearns; Emery; Maultsby). But the struggle between whites and African Americans for control of black culture changed this. As Dehn herself realized, "the separation has begun—the music for some reason is the luckier of the two . . . I guess our civilization is basically anti-dance" (Dehn files). While Dehn correctly locates white civilization's bias, the aggrandizement of jazz and jazz dance by whites had as strong an impact on the development of the dance as the Bible-thumping Puritan sermons denouncing it. To some extent, what Phyllis Rose refers to as exoticism and primitivism were operating in the popularity of jazz dance with whites. Rose's analysis of the dynamics of Josephine Baker's extraordinary Paris success provides an interesting contrast to Ross's examination of American white reactions to black culture.

Rose characterizes Parisian thinking as "racialist" as opposed to "racist," which views differences of race as something fearful, calling for separation and violent oppression. She considers the two connected, however, pointing out that both believe "differences between races are meaningful and enduring." She further distinguishes between "primitivism" and "exoticism." "The primitivist tends to believe in a mixture of various racial qualities as an ideal, whereas the racist is disgusted by the idea. But they are in the same ballpark. The very term primitivism suggests a hierarchy of racial values whose usual order the primitivist chooses to invert" (Rose 36). In exoticism, Rose sees "an enthusiasm for black flesh . . . compared with racism, exoticism is merely decorative and superficial. Exoticism cares mostly about its own amusement and tends to find differences of color amusing. . . . Exoticism is frivolous, hangs out at nightclubs, will pay anything to have the black singer or pianist sit at its table" (Rose 44). In either exoticism or primitivism, as Rose stresses, color remains a forceful issue, as potent as it is in racism. One can see their operation in the popularity of African American dance in the twenties, which became for young women a sign of freedom, youth, and rebellion *because* of the meanings that had clustered around that dance. But cultural victory did not equal political victory, and embracing the movement did not mean embracing those who developed it; these jazz babies did black dance without partaking of black society. Joyce Ashabranner and Katherine Dunham, along with many theorists and historians of African American dance and theater, bluntly consider the acceptance to have taken place only in terms of entertainment.

Gender remains an unexplored issue for Rose and for most who have looked at issues of the attraction for and co-optation of African American art by whites. Given the coding of dance as "feminine" that has pervaded the American conscious, and the often explored linkage of women with oppressed racial groups, this issue deserves greater elaboration. Andrew Ross saw the temptation that the "myth of superior black masculinity" had for the white male writers he spoke of; but this myth acted like a fence that closed the men off from an innocent Eden they longed to enter. Rose's view would appear, unlike that of Ross, to offer a potential for a woman's perspective as well as a man's. But ultimately she returns to focusing on the male, metaphorizing white Frenchmen's admiration and desire for African women as akin to their hunger for colonial exploration—one possesses the colonies, and the people in them.

Women remained exempt from this metaphor, neither explorers nor, in the Western world, persons who would, apparently, find the "sexuality of the savage" appealing. What remains unstated is what women found compelling in the choreographic forms from the African diaspora: an almost utopian image of physical liberation, of movement forms free of traditional European constraints. This image could have particularly captured Dehn, given her background in Isadora Duncan's teachings, which however little respect they had for African-based dance, espoused freedom of the body and a return to nature. Of course, the way this fascination is acted out is culturally determined; not surprisingly, Dehn did not come from American society, with its overwhelmingly negative views of African American culture, but from a country where African-based art was practically nonexistent. While Americans could not look at their own black culture as exotic, a non-American could see it with eyes similar to those with which Americans might see African-based art from other countries. Dehn, unlike Kerouac and his compatriots, did not see herself as exiled from the African American cultural scene, a lonely child peering into a happy folk community she could not join.

Dehn still sees with the prurient vision of the racist and the missionary, but, as with Rose's primitivist, she overturns the hierarchy, privileging what had been damned. Her unpublished writings on the mambo shed interesting light on her attitude on and fascination for African American dance. Using rich, overheated language, Dehn described mambo night at the Palladium in 1951: "The outspoken sensuality and primitiveness of posture was [sic] never seen before. Along with formal society tables one could see people squatting on the floor admiring a dancer who was crawling on his arms . . . he would hug the floor with a cheek and then propel himself with undulating shocks . . . [a] girl on all fours let a constant bump pass through her rear end and torso. . . ." Significantly, Dehn's critiques often metaphorize cultural mixing as miscegenation, in a confusion of art and marriage: "The way black and white dancers make up mambo is ferocious. They give themselves to it like a cult. The whites in their way, the negroes in theirs. Ballet and Africa, Spain and New York mixed in a extatic [sic] marriage. It is an orgy of creativity" (Dehn files).

The insistent focus on sexuality and animal frenzy in her writings reveals the extent to which Dehn views such behavior as outside Western proprietal norms; African Americans still projected images of "darkest Africa." Her excitement solidly typifies the attitudes and writing on non-Western culture by Western artists, especially regarding the body and dance. Marianna Torgovnik in *Gone Primitive* examines writer after writer and artist after artist, who all, in their fashion, find themselves alternately attracted and repelled by "the primitive." Her analysis of D. H. Lawrence, with its dual focus on pleasurable and violent ritual, captures his sense of longing and fear: "It is significant that [he] chose the dance as an important synecdoche for primitive life, he later chose a ritual of human sacrifice; both imputed aspects of primitive societies embody the values of collectivity and proximity to the cosmic . . ." (Torgovnick 164).

If Dehn—along with other female dance filmmakers such as Maya Deren—felt she could participate in the culture (Dehn originally believed that she "danced just like the black dancers" until the Savoy regulars set her straight), Dehn's role as historian has its problematic aspects, problems shared by many outsiders reporting on a culture they do not fully comprehend. One of Dehn's most troublesome assumptions concerns what the communities producing vernacular dance know about their cultural history. Just as she doubted African Americans' knowledge of the roots of the blues, she doubted Latinos' knowledge of mambo's roots. She noted that a young Puerto Rican dancer's beautiful arm movement precisely matched a gesture common to one of the Nigerian gods, but she felt "it [had] no significance for that dancer" (Dehn files). Given the widespread practice of Santeria, the African-based religion practiced by many Cubans and Puerto Ricans, the dancer may well have known the exact meaning of his motion; even more important was the ability of these subaltern groups to retain their culture—even *spread* the culture— in the face of societal forces that attempted to impose forgetfulness.

Jazz and Cinematic Representation

Dehn's insistence on the need to record jazz dance belies the fact that this art has a long history on film: from the moment cameras started cranking, they captured African Americans tapping, strutting, and high-kicking. Many of the older dances that Dehn restaged for the camera—

such as the cakewalk—already existed on film, caught near the height of their popularity, performed by dancers who specialized in those styles. Although the filmmakers of the late 1890s and early 1900s may not have proceeded with Dehn's sense of posterity and historic mission, their work nonetheless provides a fascinating document of contemporary dance and racial attitudes.

In cinema the dance experienced its first radical change in presentation: it severed the link between dancer and spectator, an essential bonding for African-based dance, and drained it of its carnivalesque impetus and spontaneity. Most important, the films themselves do not capture the acrobatics that defined the dance's technique; often the nervous, unsmiling performers looked uncomfortable with the situation. And racist narratives focusing on watermelon thieves or "lazy slaves" anchored the dance in denigrating humor, with qualities of movement and choreography becoming of secondary importance.

But the Hollywood musical's dependence on jazz had perhaps the strongest effect of all. Through this genre, white dancers and choreographers helped change jazz from a specifically black form into a general notion of "popular dance" that was color-blind on the surface but ignored those who had developed the technique and stylistics. Ella Shohat refers to "inferential ethnic presences, that is, the various ways in which ethnic cultures penetrate the screen without always literally being represented by ethnic or racial themes or even characters" (223). Once jazz mingled with ballet and ballroom, the obvious racial antecedents of Fred Astaire's and Gene Kelly's dance had been effaced. Black performers like Bill Robinson often were called on to tap beside blond mop-top Shirley Temple or, like the Nicholas Brothers, in the background behind Gene Kelly in *The Pirate* (1948).

Of course, no dance form remains stagnant without dying; and in a multiracial society influence clearly flows back and forth between communities—even if only one group has the power to try to claim the cultural products of the others. How does the development and history of jazz dance compare with other dance forms—ballet, for example? Marshall and Jean Stearns, in their seminal book *Jazz Dance: The Story of American Vernacular Dance*, note that ballet, like jazz, had its origins in folk dances, which then underwent theatricalization (xiv). Classical ballet reached its first creative peak in the 1800s in its birthplaces in France and Italy; then dance theater in those countries weakened, and technical developments came to a halt. Only an infusion of energy from imported Russian ballet brought classical dance back to life in Europe and, eventually, in the United States.

Interestingly, Dehn compares her work to that of Diaghilev, stating that he rescued ballet from its death throes: "Thanks to Diaghileff's [*sic*] deliberate efforts, there is now a true renaissance of ballet all over the world. I just want to stress that it would not have happened inevitably" (Dehn files). Without arguing for the moment the correctness of her statement in terms of ballet history (ballet was in fact fairly lively both in Denmark and Russia in Diaghilev's time, which accounts for his ability to bring together a company that could galvanize Europe), it sheds light on how she saw both her work and the state of jazz at that period, while leaving aside some significant differences between the two forms of movement. Ballet had become highly codified technically and fully theatricalized; whatever folk roots had gone into its creation had withered, and while new folk forms may have refreshed individual pieces of choreography, they did not affect the basic technique. Jazz, on the other hand, had not traditionally possessed a codified technique; its creators valued playful invention and competition more than standardization.

Under such conditions Dehn's project could not have been analogous to Diaghilev's. While Diaghilev renewed ballet by extending its technical boundaries and taking a fresh approach to music, costume, and scenery, *The Spirit Moves* captures existing jazz but does not innovate. Nor could her dance troupe serve that role, for jazz dance has never been renewed by theatrical means alone. In examining the history of jazz dance in the United States, we see a constant push-and-pull between the vernacular and the theatrical, "high art" and "low art," and invention and appropriation.

A subtle issue must be raised in relation to jazz dance and its disappearance. Unlike other countries in the African diaspora, where African retentions retain much of their original appearance, the African roots of black art in the United States are often deeply buried, although still yielding potent fruit. As Maultsby notes, "Over the centuries specific African elements either have been altered or have disappeared from the cultures of New World blacks altogether. Yet the concepts that embody and identify the cultural heritage of black Americans have never been lost" (187). The malleability of African-based dance, its ability to consume and transform dance material, leads to a constant shifting of styles. A specific dance may die away, but the *principles* of African American movement forms remained.

The work of Mura Dehn focused on secular dance. *The Spirit Moves* aimed to reconstruct for posterity the dances of the plantation, the minstrel show, and the first black musicals, and to capture contemporary black dances as they developed and became widespread. The historical situation that had given birth to the earliest of the dances that interested Dehn had passed, as had many of the dances' movements, which lived more in the memories of older dancers and in re-created versions than in active performance. Dehn was fortunate, for, as she noted, "Dancers in the jazz idiom hate to change a single step or sequence once they have worked them out; they hand them down like 'folk say,' a tradition to be observed by succeeding dancers" ("Is Jazz" 24).

Dance scholar Joanne Kealiinohomoku, in a carefully considered discussion of the imprecise category known as folk dance, employs Felix Hoerberger's distinction between a "first and second existence" of folk art: "in the first existence, 'folk dance is an integral part of a community,' whereas in the second existence it is no longer a functionally integral part of the community but has become the property 'only of a few interested people'" (385, 386). Dehn's recordings capture black jazz dance in both its "first and second existence," and, in one interesting case, that of break dance, dance that falls in what could be called "the first and a half existence." Her cinematic strategies for each differ markedly. What are the political and cultural ramifications of these cinematic choices? And what are the effects of reconstructing culture?

Dehn rejected a self-effacing camera style purporting merely to capture the dance in favor of more reflexive filmmaking. The reconstructions appear in a cinematic no-man's-land, all the more starkly empty and ghostlike for their contrast with the lively, energetic space where the majority of the contemporary dances occur.

Gilles Deleuze in *Cinema: Movement-Image* contrasts saturated and rareified framings: "The frame is therefore inseparable from two tendencies: towards saturation or towards rarefaction. The big screen and depth of field in particular have allowed the multiplication of independent data . . . [while] Rareified images are produced, either when the whole accent is placed on a single object . . . or when the set is emptied of certain sub-sets" (12). Dehn's choice of extreme rareification for the reconstructions posits, to a certain degree, both a lack of information—could one honestly reconstruct the world in which these dances developed?—as well as an indication of the professional, choreographed nature of these dances in our day, rather than their formerly participative, improvisational nature.

For Dehn, the theatricalization of jazz requires a balance between choreography (the organization of space and patterns) and improvisation. "The architecture of jazz choreography can be pursued only in general terms, in grouping, in the relation of planes, in floor patterns worked out like a mathematical problem. . . . Jazz is such an elastic form that to confine the dancer to a set pattern would be to destroy his creativeness at its very roots" ("Is Jazz" 24, 25). In *The Spirit Moves* the camera becomes a choreographic principle that affects the presentation of the dance—but not the dancer's creation of the dance. The bare studio, in combination with Dehn's artsy cinematic arabesques—turning the bodies into abstract shadows against a blank wall, focusing in on a swirling skirt—and erratic cutting, in which the dances seem at times to be put together like little puzzle pieces that do not quite fit, firmly sever the dance from the cultural context in which it flourished. Additionally, Dehn makes almost no adjustment for skin color, leaving her (African American) dancers to fade into the darkness of the space.

Dehn particularly plays with the Charleston: contrasting fast and slow motion highlights the dance's freneticism and grace. First, legs and arms fly wildly at an impossible pace, fully stretched in oppositional motion to ensure balance; then, in half-time, legs lift and flow langorously and weightlessly. To illustrate the fragmentation of the body in the Charleston, in contrast to classical Western dance where every part of the body moves in relation to the other to produce a single, "graceful" line, Dehn places lights on the dancers' arms and legs. The lights shine and bob like fireflies in the darkness as the dancers' bodies whirl and shift weight, their legs constantly turning in and out from the hips, every limb moving independently of the others. The body, like the music, works polyrhythmically.

The contemporary sequences, which range from live filming of the aerial Lindy, Big Apple, and mambo at the Savoy to the deliciously joyous steps of the mod squad, twist, and bump in the rock and roll section, have a fullness denied to the Charleston, cakewalk, and strut. At the Savoy, dancers crowd the floor and create that most traditional of formations—the circle—around the central performers. The rock dancers, professionals all, take turns doing their solos, and in an inspired cinematic move that more effectively illustrates the relationship of black American dance to its roots than all of Dehn's dry narration, she overlays the contemporary dance with traditional African music. In that moment it seems as if the dancers, with their bodies bent forward toward the earth, their torsos flexible and their feet pounding the ground, might be dancing the dances of their ancestors.

The sheer scope of *The Spirit Moves* permits the spectator to see nearly a century's worth of dance in quick succession; from the bent-over body of the cakewalk, which Africanized the quadrille, to the sliding and shimmying of the jerk and waddle, to the looseness and fragmentation of the limbs in break dance, the film demonstrates continuity as much as change. What perspective does Dehn impose on this work with her narration?

Verbal contextualization remains at a minimum throughout the film. But those words set the dance firmly in relation to Caucasian culture. Dehn describes the cakewalk, for example, as the "first dance created by blacks accepted by whites"; similarly, with the Charleston came the "shock of a complete revolution against caucasian grace and bodily unity." The film includes the mambo and calypso, but no commentary speaks of Latino culture, African retentions outside the United States, or the desire of African Americans to show solidarity with blacks elsewhere by incorporating a different version of African-based culture; these dances stand in marked contrast to Dehn's dismissal of historical knowledge on the part of the dancers, proving their recognition of a shared heritage.

An alternate history could be constructed from these dances. Instead of pointing out that the Charleston reconceptualized the quadrille, one could mention that this reconception also mocked the prancing of the white masters who danced those quadrilles. Similarities between the steps in African American dances and dances from other countries in the African diaspora could be made: the cakewalk includes a cross-step similar to Brazilian *frevo,* and the way a woman doing a slow and sultry blues dance runs her arms over the outline of her body resembles the movements of several goddesses in Yoruban religion. And, when Dehn examines the break-dance phenomenon, she points out that it began as a fighting dance; overlooked entirely is the history of dance fights, such as Brazilian *capoeira,* in slave cultures of the African diaspora.

The most telling references to oppression occur not in the overarching narrative but by the performers themselves in the few verbal routines taken from vaudeville and burlesque. In one skit a man holding a bag filled with money (some of which his friend would like to get ahold of) bluntly asks his friend:

"Are you in there? [pointing to the bag]
"No."
"Then you ain't my friend."

In another routine a cop accosts two drunk men singing "Sweet Adeline"; the scene culminates with the policeman kicking and beating them.

Dehn does, however, see societal forces as shaping the dance. She saw the Lindy as a "dance of hope, expressive of a time when black people thought they would gain equality," while break dancing "shows young people displeased because they really have no place in the world." *The*

Spirit Moves captures the efforts of a people to *make* a place for themselves in the world in cultural terms, to keep history alive, to remind each other of their past in terms of the language that comes from the past—even when others would have them speak a new tongue.

Notes

I would like to thank Roberta Pearson and Robert Stam, who read earlier drafts of this article.

Works Cited

Cohn, Emma. "Mura Dehn: The Preservation of Black Jazz Dance on Film." *Sightlines* (Spring 1987): 8–11.

Dehn, Mura. Unpublished writings, including letters to Marshall Stearns, the preliminary manuscript for *The Spirit Moves*, and notes on mambo. Files at the New York Public Library Dance Collection at Lincoln Center. Cited in the text as Dehn files.

———. "Is Jazz Choreography?" *Dance Magazine* Feb. 1948: 24–25.

Deleuze, Gilles. *Cinema 1: The Movement-Image.* Trans. Hugh Tomlinson and Barbara Habberjam. Minneapolis: U of Minnesota P, 1986.

Emery, Lynn Fauley. *Black Dance from 1619 to Today.* Princeton, N.J.: Dance Horizons, 1988.

Kealiinohomoku, Joanne Wheeler. "Folk Dance." *Folklore and Folklife.* Ed. Richard M. Dorson. Chicago: U of Chicago P, 1972. 381–404.

Maultsby, Portia K. "Africanisms in African-American Music." *Africanisms in American Culture.* Ed. Joseph E. Holloway. Bloomington: Indiana UP, 1990. 185–210.

Rose, Phyllis. *Jazz Cleopatra: Josephine Baker in Her Time.* New York: Doubleday, 1989.

Ross, Andrew. *No Respect: Intellectuals and Popular Culture.* New York: Routledge, 1989.

Shohat, Ella. "Ethnicities-in-Relation." *Unspeakable Images: Ethnicity and the American Cinema.* Ed. Lester D. Friedman. Urbana: U of Illinois P, 1991. 215–47.

Stearns, Marshall, and Jean Stearns. *Jazz Dance: The Story of American Vernacular Dance.* New York: Schirmer, 1968.

Sweet, Jill Drayson. "Entrepreneurs, Artists, Intellectuals, and Missionaries: Some Non-Indian Reactions to Indian Dance in the 1920s." *The Myriad Faces of Dance.* Proceedings of the Eighth Annual Conference of the Society of Dance History Scholars. 1985.

Thompson, Robert Farris. *Flash of the Spirit: African and Afro-American Art and Philosophy.* New York: Vintage, 1984.

Torgovnick, Marianna. *Gone Primitive: Savage Intellects, Modern Lives.* Chicago: U of Chicago P, 1990.

PICTURING

JAZZ

Jazz and the New York School

MONA HADLER

Before Willem de Kooning left Holland for New York in 1930, he conjured up an America of "broad clean streets in a glare of white light and everywhere the sound of Louis Armstrong's trumpet" (Blesh 257). Jimmy Ernst, the only child of the Surrealist Max Ernst, also thought of America as a country of African American music and Native American art as he fled Europe for the States (interview). The accounts of these two artists suggest how Abstract Expressionism can be opened up to noncanonical figures and "low art" influences such as jazz.[1] And the artists' fascination with jazz provides yet another context for understanding Abstract Expressionism in a richer, post-Greenbergian framework.[2]

In the light of its impact on Abstract Expressionism, jazz itself might also be conceptualized in a broader framework, especially since the painters who claimed jazz as an influence did not always listen to precisely the same artists subsequently canonized by many jazz writers.[3] For example, the unlikely group of musicians who performed at the opening of Stuart Davis's 1943 exhibition included W. C. Handy, Mildred Bailey, Red Norvo, George Wettling, Duke Ellington, and Pete Johnson, among others (Davis 186). Or, consider the sculptor Seymour Lipton's inclusion of the Johnson Singers with Louis Armstrong and Scott Joplin in his list of favorites (interview). Finally, we must come to terms with the inspiration that the Surrealist poet Philippe Soupault derived from the music of Paul Whiteman.[4]

The era of the 1940s and 1950s when artists in New York ardently listened to jazz was bracketed on one end by Piet Mondrian, the prime advocate of jazz in New York, and on the other by Larry Rivers, the musician-artist. Satirical murals, including one by Ad Reinhardt, decorated the walls of Barney Josephsen's jazz club, Café Society (interview), and Roy de Carava's camera expressed the intensity of the moment. Romare Bearden has testified to the enthusiasm that greeted Samuel Kootz's suggestion of organizing the show "Homage to Jazz" in 1946 (interview). In addition to Bearden, the participants included William Baziotes, Byron Browne, Adolph Gottlieb, Carl Holty, and Robert Motherwell. In describing her husband Jackson Pollock's love of the music, the artist Lee Krasner has said that Pollock "would get into grooves of listening to his jazz records—not just for days—day and night, day and night for three days running until you thought you would climb the roof! . . . Jazz? He thought it was the only other really creative thing happening in this country" (Du Plessix and Gray 51).

Among the other New York School artists, Franz Kline's paintings on the theme ranged from a more realistic canvas of 1940 entitled *Hot Jazz* to the 1958 abstraction *King Oliver*, named after the musician. According to Peyton Boswell, Philip Guston possessed an immense collection of swing records (Boswell 3). Likewise, members of the Beat Generation of poets, who stressed the spontaneous in their writings, were jazz devotees. Jack Kerouac began his 1959 volume of poems *Mexico City Blues*, "I want to be considered as a jazz poet, blowing a long blues in the afternoon jam session on Sunday." Some artists such as Larry Rivers did just that, beginning his career as a jazz musician, with Charlie Parker and Lester Young as his heroes (O'Hara 109).

The most apparent connection between jazz musicians and the artists of the Abstract Expressionist generation is their shared commitment to an improvisational process. There was in fact a reciprocity between the artists and musicians in this regard. Ornette Coleman, an originator of free-form jazz or free improvisation, has compared himself to Pollock, stating that Pollock was "in the same state I was in and doing what I was doing" (Mandeles 140).[5] When Coleman's Atlantic LP *Free Jazz* was released in 1961, it bore a reproduction of a Pollock—by then famous—inside its gatefold cover.

Critics of the period often responded to the appearance of spontaneity in Abstract Expressionism with an existential tone, one that reflected Jean-Paul Sartre's own reception of jazz. Sartre expressed his appreciation for the feeling of active participation in a live performance in his 1947 essay, "Nick's Bar": "There's a big man blowing his lungs out trying to follow the gyrations of his trombone. . . . They speak to the best part of you, the most unfeeling and the most free. . . . They make demands on

you. . . . The rhythm grabs you and rocks you. You jump to the beat . . ."
(193).[6]

Jimmy Ernst, who first heard American jazz at the age of ten while
visiting his father in Paris (Harrison 39), was similarly drawn to the
music for its improvisatory quality. Undoubtedly aware of the battles
raging in the press between supporters of swing and New Orleans re-
vivalists,[7] Ernst remembered being familiar with the more orchestrated
sounds of big bands in Europe, but here he came to favor New Orleans
and Kansas City jazz because of what he perceived as its greater sense of
freedom (interview). Judging from the titles of his jazz paintings, Ernst's
taste was more eclectic. Works of 1946 bear titles such as *See See Rider*
and *Mahogany Hall Stomp,* inspired by pianist Montana Taylor's boogie-
woogie recordings of the tune.

In addition to serving as an important witness to the moment, Ernst
formed a major link between the Surrealists and Americans in New York
in the forties. One would expect the Surrealists with their emphasis on
instinct and automatism to be drawn to the music, but the situation was
more complex. On one level, the response to jazz was generational, with
younger figures such as Ernst and the Chilean Surrealist Matta appreciating the music, and older figures such as Max Ernst and André Breton
rejecting it. But even in the original Surrealist group, responses varied.
Although Breton was reported to have been hostile to the music, some
Surrealists were more positive. Not only were poets Robert Desnos, Paul
Éluard, and Philippe Soupault admirers of jazz; Soupault apparently composed his 1926 poem "Georgia" while listening to a recording of Paul
Whiteman (Goffin 62).

Breton recanted somewhat in the forties (Breton 265), even attending
jazz concerts while he was in New York. However, an incident remembered by Jimmy Ernst is provocative. At dinner with Breton in an Italian
restaurant in New York, Ernst played a Glenn Miller recording on the
jukebox. Breton became furious and "screamed" that "the music was the
Germans" (interview). Breton's reaction raises several questions. Was he
returning to his earlier rejection of jazz? Did he understand and oppose
the lack of spontaneity in Miller's orchestrated sound? Did he know of
Miller's military orchestra at that time?[8] The answers cannot be known,
but the many implications of the story are tantalizing. Yet it is only when
one fleshes out the canon to include both Ernst and Miller that a wider
play of cultural forces can emerge. Indeed, by examining Breton's antip-
athy to Miller, Ernst's choice of the music, and Soupault's receptivity to
Whiteman, we can avoid what Bernard Gendron has called the "exclu-

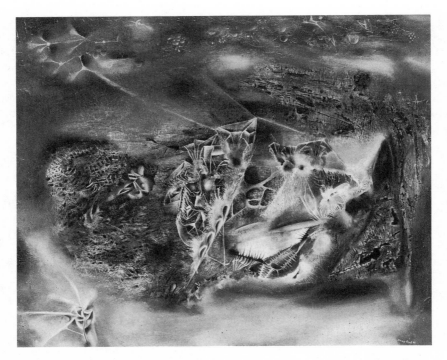

Figure 1. Jimmy Ernst, *Echo-Plasm* (1944), oil on canvas, 27" × 32", whereabouts unknown.

sionary rereading" of jazz history that bypasses "those early types of jazz which do not fit into the trajectory leading to modern jazz or give sense to its aesthetics. . . ." ("Jamming at Le Boeuf" 14).

Not surprisingly, it was in the circle around Bataille and in the magazine *Documents* that jazz had the greatest significance. In the twenties André Masson together with Georges Limbour and Michel Leiris spent many late evenings in bars, drinking and listening to jazz. According to Leiris, jazz was for them "an orgiastic banner to the colors of the moment" (189).[9] Leiris compared the effect of jazz to a form of possession, to a religious experience, involving music, dance, and eroticism, which evoked the "derangement of the senses" coveted by the Surrealists. One cay say that for this group, jazz had an essential link with coded perceptions of "black bodies—their vitalism, rhythm, magic erotic power, etc.— as seen by whites" (Clifford 197). Leiris and Masson later collaborated with Bataille on *Documents*, which was published in 1929 and 1930. The magazine covered jazz and included, for example, an article on Ellington with a double-spread photograph of his band.

The improvisational component of jazz appealed to Jimmy Ernst because of the primary role that automatism played in his art in the early forties. He clearly expressed the conjunction of jazz and automatism in paintings of 1944 such as *Blues From Chicago* and *Echo-Plasm* (figure 1). Ernst began *Echo-Plasm* and many other paintings of the period by using an automatic technique he called "sifflage," which involved blowing on thin oil paint until it spread in weblike patterns on the canvas. In essence, we can call it "blowing the blues."

Ernst wrote in 1944, "Sounds and voices, bearing witness to multimillion epochs are encased within the crevices of *Echo-Plasm*. A given pitch will release all sounds, re-echoing history from the thunder of the falling walls of Jericho to the wail of Benny Goodman's swing" (Janis 103). Like Matta's paintings, which influenced Ernst at this time, the shapes in *Echo-Plasm* suggest the germinations of organic forms. Ernst, like other artists in the forties, evokes a metaphor of growth from the beginnings of the painting—automatism—to the beginning of life—plasm. In his statement he suggests that sounds, too—for him the sounds of jazz—can trigger associations and "re-echo history" to the primordial beginnings of time.

Similarly, Seymour Lipton, a sculptor from the period whose works include *Blues Player* of 1942 (figure 2), inspired by Louis Armstrong, has

Figure 2. Seymour Lipton, *Blues Player* (1942), walnut, 24", estate of the artist.

called jazz "ancestral voices" and says he has been drawn to it on a "subliminal level," as he is drawn to primitive art for its "ancestral rhythms," its relationship to "voodoo drums, magic and the unconscious"—for its roots in African music and ritual (interview). Lipton here is placing jazz in an anthropological and Jungian context typical of the forties—a discourse on the "primitive" as representing the ancestral nature of humanity accessible to the artist through an instinctual process (Polcari 37). In Jung's words, "To our subconscious mind contact with primitives recalls not only our childhood, but also our prehistory. . . ." (196).[10] Jazz, in essence, stirs up ancestral memories. As Torgovnick, among many others, has pointed out (99), the danger in this discourse is its construction of an evolutionary model that positions the "primitive" as earlier or lower than Western man. Nevertheless, this view was extremely attractive to a group of artists who relished jazz as something quite unlike the art music that much of it has since become.

Lipton's attitude must also be seen in the context of the modern artist's wide-ranging fascination with the so-called primitive. Jazz of course retains its West African elements even today, and there are atavistic qualities in jazz pieces such as Ellington's "jungle" dances, even though Ellington was surely using the term with a degree of irony. Yet the music can hardly be called "primitive." In fact, with its combination of African and European elements, jazz, in this sense, is comparable to the work of contemporary painters such as Picasso (Hadler, "Jazz and the Visual Arts" 91–92). On the other hand, jazz flourished in urban centers and came to be associated with advanced technology and the dynamism of the modern city. Hence it attracted artists such as Mondrian and Léger, just as "noise music" appealed to the Futurists. With its complex dissonant sounds and dynamic energy, jazz impressed some painters as a fitting analogue for modern life. Count Harry Kessler, whose diaries form a major document of Germany in the twenties, expressed these ideas clearly when he recorded his impressions of the "negro revue" performing in Berlin: "All of these shows are a mixture of jungle and skyscraper elements. The same holds good for the tone and rhythm of their music, jazz. Ultramodern and ultraprimitive" (282).

The oscillating perception of jazz as an image of twentieth-century modernity on the one hand, or as a facet of an outmoded pastoral myth on the other, was a subject of particular importance to intellectuals in the forties. With the growing number of African Americans fighting in the war, a new discourse on race was emerging that critiqued the vestigial folkloric tradition of the 1930s in part for its simplified rural typecasting.

In 1942 the NAACP attacked Hollywood, calling for an end to the plantation stereotypes with which American films consistently portrayed black people.[11] A tension existed in configuring blackness as urban or primitive. In essence, de Kooning's image of an America of broad, clean streets with the sound of Armstrong's trumpet countered Lipton's ancestral voices. Lipton, in fact, had come from the folkloric tradition of the thirties that often identified the image of African Americans with progressive social causes. Indeed, three of his 1942 sculptures, *Blues Player*, *Spiritual*, and *Swing Low*, grow out of the culture of the thirties and, in his own words, out of "a humanism related to the times" (unpublished statement).

Jazz, in Kessler's words, bridged extremes. Not the least of these extremes, for the Abstract Expressionists, was the urban and the primitive. In this context, jazz played a major role in the reconfiguring of Abstract Expressionism as a more complex and less "pure" movement. Abstract Expressionism should also be rethought to include more urban references along with the well-known de Kooning "glimpses" and his T-zone mouths cut from advertisements. We should also consider Abstract Expressionism in relation to film noir (Leja 109–18) and to the love of an artist such as Baziotes for Raymond Chandler and boxing—"life in a squared ring" (Baziotes, Hunter College Teaching Notes). In this reappraisal, jazz becomes more than an anomaly or another source but a key element. In spite of its naïveté, Surrealist Philippe Soupault's 1930 assessment of American influence in France is provocative:

> European music for several centuries has been divided into two branches, popular music (songs, marches, operettas), and highbrow music, that is to say, concert music. American music, on the other hand, is of a single sort. Neither popular nor purely artistic (hermetic, one might say), it belongs utterly to life. And one need not fear to emphasize always this characteristic in whatever comes from the United States. One of the most definite qualities of the American influence resides in the close relationship between art and life. (Soupault 20)

The reception of jazz in the United States is a complex story in its own right. Jimmy Ernst, recently arrived from Europe as a refugee from Hitler (his mother was Jewish), had a particular empathy for the uneasy place that jazz and its musicians inhabited at that time. In recalling the historic 1938 "Spirituals to Swing" concert at Carnegie Hall organized by John Hammond, Ernst wrote,

Until this particular evening the histories of lynchings and segregation that I had been all too familiar with before coming here had existed only as exaggerated European notions of some dim postcolonial past. There was something in that music that was trying to reach my sensibilities. There was the fleeting thought, at some point in the night, that, hidden in the intricate structures of boogie-woogie, Kansas City, New Orleans and, yes, the blues, was the image of an architecture. I recall fantasizing the picture of a man, both hands tied, trying to build a house with his voice while sitting on a cot in his jail cell. I felt deep empathy with the only white face onstage, that of the organizer of the concert, John Hammond, who seemed awed by the artists around him, obviously honored to call them his friends.

I had come so far from the green soccer fields of my recent youth because there were genes in me that made me an outcast. And suddenly, on this new island of refuge, I had come face to face with the pain of the rejected expressed through a new music that I had heretofore associated with dancing.[12] (Ernst 145–46)

The notion of jazz as architecture rather than automatic process grew on Ernst and informed the bulk of his paintings on jazz from the mid-forties such as *Riff* of 1946 (figure 3). His ideas countered the "primitivist myth" of jazz as pure inspiration, produced in a trance, and devoid of intellectual content—a widespread attitude in Surrealist circles (Gioia 30–31). To be sure, improvisation was an important aspect of jazz, but the history of the music also includes the carefully arranged music of the big bands not to mention small groups such as the Modern Jazz Quartet, the John Kirby Sextet, and the septets and octets organized by Duke Ellington. Moreover, in listening to the twelve-bar blues and thirty-two-bar song forms that prevailed in jazz during that period, artists of the New York School possibly were awakened to the idea that jazz was a combination of improvisation and structure. This in itself was important for many artists and made jazz analogous to their own work. Ernst was not alone in appreciating the architecture of jazz, but in this regard he can be classed with artists such as Stuart Davis, Bearden, and Mondrian.

All three of these artists were inspired by structural aspects of the music. For Mondrian, the rhythms of the boogie-woogie pianists were analogous to the formal innovations of his late paintings such as *Broadway Boogie Woogie* (1942–43). Bearden, too, whose involvement with the music predated his artistic career (Fats Waller and other celebrated musicians were friends of his family), was encouraged by the then senior

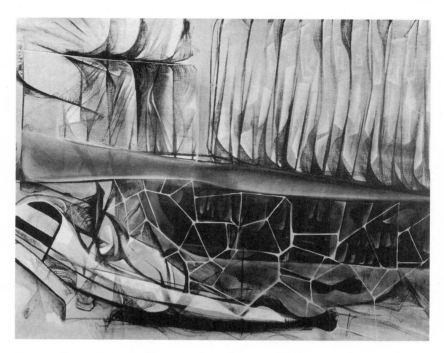

Figure 3. Jimmy Ernst, *Riff* (1946), oil on canvas, 22″ × 26¾″, collection of Dr. and Mrs. Sidney I. Kreps, New York.

artist, Stuart Davis, to study the formal elements of the music to further his understanding of avant-garde painting. Davis entreated him to seek out visual analogies for Earl Hines's piano improvisations. Bearden ultimately "developed his style of working with the separations between colors and the different values of a given color by studying the expressive use of intervals in the piano style of Earl Hines" (Murray 18). Bearden has recalled that Davis criticized one of his watercolors for having equal spacing on both sides and told him to listen again to the variety in Hines (interview).

Ernst's own movement from process to structure, or a greater combination of the two elements, is evidenced in his shift from *Echo-Plasm* (figure 1) to *Riff* of 1946 (figure 3) and *Dallas Blues* (figure 4) of 1947. He ultimately aimed "to capture the structure of riffs" in his works (interview). *Echo-Plasm* maintains a crusty surface and amorphous space resulting from the automatic process "sifflage" reminiscent of his father's "frottages," or rubbings. The fluid background and organic shapes suggest the interconnectedness of life forms. The artist, as conduit of the

Figure 4. Jimmy Ernst, *Dallas Blues* (1947), oil on canvas, 36″ × 28″, estate of the artist.

flow of imagery, "re-echoes history." In *Dallas Blues* the free application of paint, visible is quick touches of red paint at the top right, is countered by the more prismatic geometric structure of the whole. *Riff*, above all, conjures up architectonic elements of jazz in the vertical lines that repeat and vary throughout the top section of the painting. Indeed, the entire abstract language of the painting is one of repetition and variety within a theme, what Ernst called "a progression of riffs" (interview).

For all of Ernst's structural vocabulary, we must remember that when he saw the blues as an image of an architecture, he fantasized an African American man sitting on a cot in his jail cell trying to build his house with his hands tied. And Ernst identified with this man as he himself was as an outsider in America and had suffered racial persecution in his native Germany. It is in these complex relationships that we can see the multiplicity of jazz's meaning, which, like so much else, shifts, mutates, and avoids fixity. As many of the essays in this collection and its companion volume demonstrate, jazz is crucial to the various discourses on multiculturalism, primitivism, mass culture, race, gender, and the body. For the same reasons, it is one key to a new understanding of Abstract Expressionism as well. How the painters actually experienced the music may even help forge a better understanding of jazz at a time when it had not yet been defined as an art music with a canon.

Notes

I would like to thank Krin Gabbard for many stimulating discussions during the writing of this essay.

1   This essay expands on work begun in my earlier article, "Jazz and the Visual Arts." The term Abstract Expressionism will be used interchangeably here with New York School to include artists working in New York in the 1940s and 1950s.

2   Also see Peter Wollen's discussion of Jackson Pollock in *Raiding the Icebox*.

3   Perhaps the most prominent examples of canonizing tendencies in jazz writing can be found in the work of Martin Williams. In addition to selecting the recordings for the *Smithsonian Collection of Classic Jazz*, Williams lavishly praised the artistry of a select group of jazz musicians in his *The Jazz Tradition*. Krin Gabbard has discussed the formation of a jazz canon in his introduction to *Jazz Among the Discourses*.

4   See Goffin 62. Soupault's interest in Whiteman is provocative, notwithstanding his limited access to a greater variety of jazz musicians.

5   Also see Jones 234.

6   For more on Sartre and the artists of this era, see Hadler 199–200.

7   For a thorough account of the schism among jazz writers in the 1940s, see Gendron.

8   Erenberg (235–37) discusses Glenn Miller's role in American culture in "Things to Come."

9 Also see Beatty; Torgovnick 111.
10 Also see Leja.
11 In his contribution to this volume, James Naremore proposes four conflicting discourses about blackness and entertainment in the United States during World War II, two of which are the folkloric tradition from the 1930s and the emerging issues of race, foreshadowing the civil rights movement to follow.
12 Arthur Knight's essay on *Jammin' the Blues* in this anthology discusses John Hammond and racial-political issues.

Works Cited

Baziotes, William. Hunter College Teaching Notes, 1952–62. Archives of American Art, Smithsonian Institution, Washington D.C.

Beatty, Frances Fielding Lewis. "André Masson and the Imagery of Surrealism." Diss. Columbia U, 1981.

Blesh, Rudi. *Modern Art USA*. New York: Knopf, 1956.

Boswell, Peyton. "Hipped to the Tip." *Art Digest* 1 Apr. 1934: 3–27.

Breton, André. *What Is Surrealism? Selected Writings*. Ed. Franklin Rosemont. New York: Pathfinder, 1978.

Clifford, James. *The Predicament of Culture: Twentieth-Century Ethnography, Literature, and Art*. Cambridge, Mass.: Harvard UP, 1988.

Davis, Stuart. "Memo on Mondrian." 1961. *Stuart Davis*. Ed. Diane Kelder. New York: Praeger, 1971. 183–86.

Du Plessix, Francine, and Cleve Gray. "Who Was Jackson Pollock?" *Art in America* May–June 1967: 48–59.

Erenberg, Lewis A. "Things to Come: Swing Bands, Bebop, and the Rise of a Postwar Jazz Scene." *Recasting America: Culture and Politics in the Age of the Cold War*. Ed. Lary May. Chicago: U of Chicago P, 1989. 221–45.

Ernst, Jimmy. *A Not-So-Still Life*. New York: St. Martin's, 1984.

Gabbard, Krin. "The Jazz Canon and Its Consequences." *Jazz Among the Discourses*. Ed. Krin Gabbard. Durham, N.C.: Duke UP, 1995. 1–27.

Gendron, Bernard. "Jamming at Le Boeuf: Jazz and the Paris Avant-Garde." *Discourse* 12.1 (Fall–Winter 1989–90): 3–27.

———. "Moldy Figs and Modernists: Jazz at War (1942–1946)." *Discourse* 15.2 (Fall–Winter 1992–93): 130–57.

Gioia, Ted. "Jazz and the Primitive Myth." *The Imperfect Art: Reflections on Jazz and Modern Culture*. New York: Oxford UP, 1988. 19–49.

Goffin, Robert. "Jazz and Surrealism." *America (Cahiers France-Amerique-Latinité)* 5. Special Issue "Jazz 47." June 1947: 61–65.

Hadler, Mona. "David Hare: A Magician's Game in Context." *Art Journal* 47.3 (Fall 1988): 196–201.

———. "Jazz and the Visual Arts." *Arts Magazine* June 1983: 91–101.

———. Interview with Barney Josephson. 12 Oct. 1982.

———. Interview with Jimmy Ernst. 1 Dec. 1982.

———. Interview with Romare Bearden. 23 Nov. 1982.

———. Interviews with Seymour Lipton. 2 and 16 Nov. 1982.

Harrison, Helen A. *Jimmy Ernst, A Survey, 1942–1983.* Exhibition Catalog. East Hampton, N.Y.: Guild Hall, 1985.

Janis, Sidney. *Abstract and Surrealist Art in America.* New York: Reynal and Hitchcock, 1944.

Jones, LeRoi (Amiri Baraka). *Blues People: Negro Music in White America.* New York: Morrow, 1963.

Jung, Carl J. "Your Negroid and Indian Behavior: The Primitive Elements in the American Mind." *Forum* Apr. 1930: 193–99.

Kessler, Harry. *In the Twenties: The Diaries of Harry Kessler.* New York: Holt, Rinehart and Winston, 1971.

Leiris, Michel. *L'Age d'Homme.* Paris: Gallimard, 1971.

Leja, Michael. *Reframing Abstract Expressionism: Subjectivity and Painting in the 1940s.* New Haven, Conn.: Yale UP, 1993.

Lipton, Seymour. Unpublished statement. Nov. 1982.

Mandeles, Chad. "Jackson Pollock and Jazz: Structural Parallels." *Arts Magazine* Oct. 1981: 139–41.

Murray, Albert. "The Visual Equivalent of the Blues." *Romare Bearden: 1970–1980.* Exhibition Catalog. Charlotte, N.C.: Mint Museum, 1980.

Naremore, James. "Uptown Folk: Blackness and Entertainment in *Cabin in the Sky.*" *Arizona Quarterly* 48.4 (1992): 100–124. Reprinted in this collection. 169–92.

O'Hara, Frank. Interview with Larry Rivers. *Art Chronicles 1954–1966.* New York: George Brazilier, 1975.

Polcari, Stephen. *Abstract Expressionism and the Modern Experience.* Cambridge: Cambridge UP, 1991.

Sartre, Jean-Paul. "Nick's Bar, New York City." *The Writings of Jean-Paul Sartre.* Ed. Michel Contat and Michel Rybalka. Vol. 2. Evanston, Ill.: Northwestern UP, 1974.

Soupault, Philippe. *The American Influence in France.* Seattle: U of Washington Book Store, 1930.

Torgovnick, Marianna. *Gone Primitive: Savage Intellects, Modern Lives.* Chicago: U of Chicago P, 1990.

Williams, Martin. *The Jazz Tradition.* Rev. ed. New York: Oxford UP, 1983.

Wollen, Peter. *Raiding the Icebox: Reflections on Twentieth-Century Culture.* Bloomington: Indiana UP, 1993.

The Tenor's Vehicle: Reading
Way Out West

MICHAEL JARRETT

Cadenza

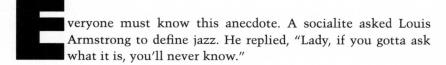

veryone must know this anecdote. A socialite asked Louis Armstrong to define jazz. He replied, "Lady, if you gotta ask what it is, you'll never know."

Confessions of a Record Reviewer

For some time, I've reviewed jazz recordings for Tower Records' magazine *Pulse!* In March 1990, my column began: "Sonny Rollins's tone is something like the sonic equivalent of my wife's Newfoundland dog. It's burly, warm and smart. Nobody, but nobody, sounds like the Saxophone Colossus. He remains one of jazz's great originals, a prodigiously gifted improviser . . ." (74). I continued in this vein, singling out Rollins's then-current album, *Falling in Love with Jazz*, for special praise, rehearsing its particular virtues.

Like all descriptions of music or, for that matter, like all descriptions of art, mine relies on tautology and simile. I call *Falling in Love with Jazz* "a paradigm of what great jazz can be" (a tautology), but qualify my approval by admitting that it "lacks the intensity of, say, *G-Man* [an earlier recording], or the sheer visceral punch of Rollins live" (a simile). I, thereby, fall back on what Roland Barthes calls "a vast commonplace of literature" and, in effect, declare that this record is a repetition of the "previously played," the "already written." He states: "Beauty cannot assert itself save in the form of a citation"; deprived of "anterior codes," it "would be mute" (*S/Z* 33–34). The critic's task, then, is to store up signs—reference codes—for the sake of predicating beauty, bringing it into language.

As a record reviewer, I've done that. I've cultivated a set of ideological biases (or, more generously, I've accepted an aesthetic shared by fellow reviewers) and acquired an institutionally sanctioned discourse; I've processed so much music that I can tell whether a disc is "good" or not after listening for only a few minutes. More honestly, I can normally determine whether I'll like a recording by merely glancing at its cover. I am prejudiced by names, typography, and graphics. I listen, the first time through, in order to confirm or contradict what the album's jacket has already told me. After that, I listen either for pleasure or out of a sense of professional obligation. Finally, I translate the musical work "into the poorest of linguistic categories: the adjective" (Barthes, *IMT* 179).

The goal of my journalistic work is also the goal of all "normal" criticism or scholarship: "both a *mathesis* ['the closure of a homogeneous body of knowledge'] and a *mimesis*" (Barthes, *Grain* 238, 237). In exegesis the critic seeks to fashion, out of institutionally dictated predicates, an utterance that readers will decode as *literal*, as discourse transparently representing an object of study. He avoids sets of predicates that might be perceived as entirely predictable (redundant or conventional) or completely ineffable (entropic or unmotivated) and, thereby, constructs a work that will pass as at once original (a genesis) and definitive (an apocalypse).

Image-Music-Text

There is, however, another way to write. "The scholar's choice," Barthes declares, "is finally between two *styles:* the plain (*écrivance*—'clarity, suppression of images, respect for the laws of reasoning') or the rhetorical (*écriture*—writing or 'the play of the signifier')" (quoted in Ulmer, "Discourse" 65). The *plain style,* "the regular discourse of research" or language used literally, produces a "Work." If its claims are evident, this Work is received as "science"; if its claims are considered "secret, ultimate, something to be sought out," then it "falls under the scope of a hermeneutics, of an interpretation (Marxist, psychoanalytic, thematic, etc.)" (*IMT* 158). The *rhetorical style,* "writing" or language used figuratively, produces "Text" ("a *mise en scène* . . . not of content but of the detours, twists, in short the bliss of the symbolic") (*Grain* 238).

How is this done? What could it mean to write rhetorically? Barthes answers this question when he likens writing and the "scarcely differentiated activity" of reading-as-production to *playing*—the generation of perpetual signifiers. He elaborates:

> "Playing" must be understood here in all its polysemy: the text itself *plays* (like a door, like a machine with "play") and the reader plays twice over, playing the Text as one plays a game, looking for a practice which re-produces it, but, in order that that practice not be reduced to a passive, inner *mimesis* (the Text is precisely that which resists such a reduction), also playing the Text in the musical sense of the term. The history of music (as a practice, not as an "art") does indeed parallel that of the Text fairly closely: there was a period when practicing amateurs were numerous (at least within the confines of a certain class) and "playing" and "listening" formed a scarcely differentiated activity. (*IMT* 162)

Writing as "*playing* with the text" or reading as coauthorship does not struggle against adjectival tyranny ("diverting the adjective you find on the tip of the tongue towards some substantive or verbal periphrasis"— 180). Neither does it seek to merely retrieve a hidden Work, give it "expression." Rather, in rupturing what Marjorie Perloff calls "the mimetic pact between artist and audience," it changes the object of study itself, altering our "perception or intellection" of the way it presents itself to discourse (Perloff 117). Text allows and, therefore, demands that readers map and remap: brand and rebrand. Works give rise to commentary (plod the dusty trails of criticism); Texts prompt affabulation (wander an open range of associations). They proceed parasitically, "alongside of" or "aside from."

In the following paragraphs I want to collapse "reading" (writing as interpretation) and "writing" (writing as invention), treat them as "scarcely differentiated" activities; I want to model a "*third form*" of writing that cuts across or combines the stylistic categories described by Barthes: "neither a text of vanity, nor a text of lucidity, but a text with uncertain quotation marks, with floating parentheses (never to close the parenthesis is very specifically: *to drift*)" (*Barthes* 106). Because it projects the rhetorical style onto the plain style, the metaphorical axis of language onto its metonymic dimension, my hybrid Work/Text might be regarded as a reinvestigation of allegory (Owens 72).[1] Autobiographical, journalistic, and anecdotal materials—the novelistic—are "played out" in order to evoke (and, then, resist reduction to) the critical and theoretical—the essayistic. Its reliance on what Craig Saper dubs "rigorous unsystematized thinking" should also prompt readers to identify this type of writing with the more recent experiments of Florida School theorists such as Gregory Ulmer, Robert Ray, and Saper himself (Saper 393).[2] Simply put, it is applied grammatology: oriented toward the pleasures of theory, the development and popularization of a poststructuralist writing practice. Without abandoning the philosophical critique of literature (identified with the Yale School and deconstruction) or the critique of culture and institutions (identified with the University of Birmingham Centre for Contemporary Cultural Studies and the Center for Twentieth Century Studies at the University of Wisconsin), it aims to employ popular culture (the entertainment industry) as a source of and means to theoretical invention and innovation.

Amateur de musique

For a long time, between eighth and eleventh grades, I was an amateur musician. I played B-flat clarinet in school bands. Nowadays, my instrument sits unused in a bedroom closet, and I listen to recordings made by professionals (among clarinetists, I dote on Barney Bigard, Artie Shaw, Jimmy Giuffre, and Don Byron). Playing music has become, for me, a matter of consumption, not production (my condition parallels that of readers who have delegated literary work to specialists: critics, theorists, and authors—*S/Z* 4). And what to play has become a problem. Because record companies send me many new releases, I own hundreds of discs; I readily admit, however, that my collection reflects not so much what I like (though I like what I collect), but what I hope to find the time one day to "really" enjoy.[3] Nevertheless, to a certain degree my situation—a *simulation* of unlimited resources—is not unique. It is replicated whenever anyone has unrestricted access to libraries, archives, galleries, the inventory of a store, and data bases.

Record reviews channel my listening. Writing them provides a means of managing overchoice: an effect of mechanical reproduction and the commodification of music (the reduction of "playing" to "listening"). But writing also, contradictorily, exacerbates, or at least makes more than theoretical, information overload. With the writing of reviews come more recordings, more choices. Thus we should observe that the top-ten or desert-island list, a staple of journalistic criticism, signifies an eschatological dream: the end of choice, the end of commodity fetishism. It is predicated on an apocalyptic fantasy that allows writers to imagine themselves surviving some beneficent catastrophe that has winnowed the positively essential from the merely engaging, thus granting a release from the burden of actually attending to what they have hoarded (while at the same time holding forth the promise of a new beginning).

That off my chest, here is a list: My Top-Ten Record Covers. These images—closely entwined with sounds I love—enthrall me without my knowing exactly why ("such ignorance is the very nature of fascination"—*Grain* 3).

> (1) *Way Out West* Sonny Rollins (Contemporary, 1957); designer, Guidi/Tri Arts; photographer, William Claxton (figure 1).
>
> (2) *Murmur* R.E.M. (I.R.S., 1983); designer, Ann Kinney, Carl Grasso, and Sandra Lee Phipps; photographer, Sandra Lee Phipps.
>
> (3) *Sweetheart of the Rodeo* The Byrds (Columbia, 1968); designer, Geller and Butler Advertising; illustration, Jo Mora, 1933.
>
> (4) *Porgy and Bess* Miles Davis (Columbia, 1958); photographer, Roy de Carava.
>
> (5) *Elvis Presley* (RCA, 1956); designer, Colonel Tom Parker; photographer, Popsie [William S. Randolph].
>
> (6) *London Calling* The Clash (Epic, 1979); designer, Ray Lowry; photographer, Pennie Smith.
>
> (7) *The Basement Tapes* Bob Dylan and The Band (Columbia, 1975); designer, Bob Cato; photographer, Reid Miles.
>
> (8) *This Is Mecolodics* The Universal Congress of (SST, 1988); designer, Jason Kahn; photographer, Martin Lyon.
>
> (9) *Dancing in Your Head* Ornette Coleman (A&M, 1977); designer, Dorothy Baer.
>
> (10) *Underground* Thelonious Monk (Columbia, 1969); designer, John Berg and Dick Mantel; photographer, Horn/Griner.

Just as writing is traditionally conceived as supplementary to speech (and allegory is conceived as subordinate to symbol),[4] so too a sartorially motivated nomenclature determines that jackets, covers, and sleeves supplement records.[5] They *add* to that which is present (are, therefore, accessories appended to music), and they *replace* that which is not present (i.e., the musician's image) (Johnson xiii). They can be read, writes John Corbett, as an "attempt to reconstitute the image of the disembodied voice," "to stitch the cut that separates seeing from hearing in the contemporary listening scenario" (85–86). "Yet it can be shown that this project of reappropriation is inherently self-subverting" (Johnson xi). Insofar as they imply absence ("the lack of the visual, endemic to recorded sound"), album jackets, covers, and sleeves point toward a *desire* for presence, not toward some lost but recuperable plenitude. They mark a fundamental and originary lack: one that initiates the desire from

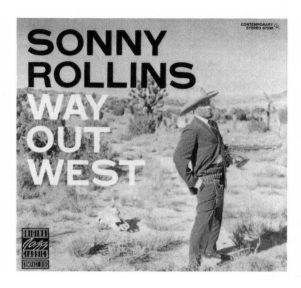

Figure 1. Album cover
of *Way Out West*,
Contemporary Records,
1957.

which all recording technologies spring, "the erotic spark that drives the
music industry motor" (Corbett 84, 88).

The Rustle of Language

After deciding to write about two photographs that became front covers
to Sonny Rollins's *Way Out West* (1957), I submitted to that urge which
drives the endeavors of all specialists. Like Flaubert's characters Bouvard
and Pécuchet, I sought to arm myself with knowledge; I borrowed lots of
books from the library (stacked on the floor of my bedroom, they reminded me of Monument Valley). For example, on the subject of cowboys, I thumbed through the following:

> Edward Douglas Branch, *The Cowboy and His Interpreters*
> Mark H. Brown and W. R. Felton, *Before Barbed Wire*
> Jenni Calder, *There Must Be a Lone Ranger*
> Edward Everett Dale, *Cow Country*
> David Dary, *Cowboy Culture: A Saga of Five Centuries*
> Philip Durham and Everett L. Jones, *The Negro Cowboys*
> Emerson Hough, *The Story of the Cowboy*
> William MacLeod Raine, *Cattle, Cowboys and Rangers*
> William W. Savage, *The Cowboy Hero: His Image in American
>   History and Culture*

Richard W. Slatta, *Cowboys of the Americas*
Lonn Taylor and Ingrid Maar, *The American Cowboy*
Jane Tompkins, *West of Everything: The Inner Life of Westerns*
Will Wright, *Sixguns and Society: A Structural Story of the Western*

Thumbed though them, mind you. I did not peruse. As Marianna Torgov-nick notes: "No one who gets around to writing a book, or even an essay, ever reads everything that has been written about its subject" (27). Besides, I am not only bored by but suspicious of works that lay bare myths constructing the West. Demythologizing is most often an excuse for aggression. The traditional critical essay, observes Jane Tompkins, re-produces the western's confrontational structure. As an imagined arena in which truth is not yet established (an intellectual frontier), it legiti-mates conflict as an epistemology, much as its analogue romanticizes violence as a solution to moral and social dilemmas. In traditional schol-arship the hero-scholar, provoked by what he considers an insult, retali-ates, "proving his moral superiority" (585–86).

But what if, as Tompkins recommends, we heed the voice of Amy (Grace Kelly) in *High Noon* (1952)? Just before Will (Gary Cooper) shoots it out with Frank Miller's gang, she exclaims: "I don't care who's right or who's wrong. There has to be some better way to live!" In other words, what could an alternative to the traditional critical essay look like? Or as Gregory Ulmer puts it, how might one drop the struggle for truth (ex-pressed by the scholar's affection for classical reasoning and problem-solving) as the means of organizing knowledge (*Teletheory* 50)?

Sax and Violence

In 1846, Adolphe Sax, son of the largest wind instrument producer in Eu-rope, took out a patent on a family of instruments he called saxophones. Writes music critic Mike Zwerin: the saxophone combined "the speed of woodwinds with the carrying power of brass" and was intended "to replace clarinets, oboes, and bassoons in military bands." In fact, it accomplished this aim after Sax won a "battle of the bands held on Paris's Champs de Mars," thus securing numerous orders for the instrument from the government of King Louis-Philippe. "The Revolution of 1848, however, intervened and official support dried up. Sax went bankrupt."

In the course of his life Sax "declared three bankruptcies, and jealous competitors made three attempts to kill him." "On occasion his prem-ises were trashed, furniture wrecked, and expensive tools stolen. One hapless employee, on an unusually late call to Sax, was stabbed through the heart. As the victim and Sax were of a similar build, an inquest concluded that the inventor had been the intended target." All told, Sax took out forty-six patents; one, significantly, was for the " 'Saxocannon,' a monster mortar that could fire a shot of 550 tons" (102–04).

Cock-and-Bull Story

The following textualist parable from Texas speaks of the most frequently visited commonplace of semiotics: the arbitrariness and the iterability of the sign. The story goes that in 1847, Samuel A. Maverick, a lawyer living on the San Antonio River, acquired four hundred head of cattle as settlement for a debt. Unwilling to forsake his legal practice, he entrusted the beasts to one of his slaves. "The Negro," write Philip Durham and Everett Jones, "neglected to do much branding, and the cattle roamed free, growing and multiplying on the open Texas range." In 1856, Maverick sold his land, cattle, and brand to A. Toutant Beauregard, a rancher with ambition. He, in turn, "sent . . . men riding over several counties, searching for Maverick's cattle." Whenever they found an animal unbranded, they claimed it as Maverick's: that is, as their own (14–15).

(1) Rollins's improvisations on *Way Out West*—aberrant readings of "I'm an Old Cowhand" and "Wagon Wheels"—and his appropriation of the iconography of the American West for the album's cover (figure 2)— his "rewriting" of the image of buffalo soldier—are comparable to the textualist practice Gregory Ulmer identifies as a "new mimesis." This "representation without reference" or mavericking by other means— practiced most notably by Barthes, Jacques Derrida, Michel Foucault, Gilles Deleuze, and Félix Guattari—amounts to a perversion of the Western construct of *properness:* property and propriety ("Object" 91–92). Poststructuralists respond to "State philosophy" (Western metaphysics) as Beauregard's cowboys responded to unbranded cattle and as jazz musicians respond to the products of Tin Pan Alley (i.e., to "standards").

(2) Originally, Marlboro cigarettes were considered "prissy," a brand women smoked, but in 1955, Philip Morris invented the Marlboro man. He captured the young men's market. Today, Marlboro is the biggest-selling cigarette in the United States (Savan 53).

(3) ABC introduced *Maverick,* a television series that parodied every convention of the western, in 1957, the very year that Contemporary Records released *Way Out West.* It was at this "exact moment," writes Robert Ray, that "mythological self-consciousness began to appear prominently in American popular culture" (256–57). In the summer of

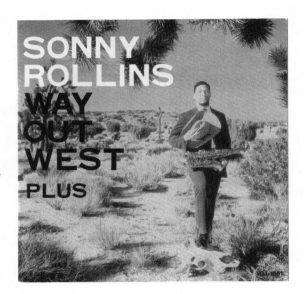

Figure 2. Senator Ted Stevens (R, Alaska): "I've asked my staff to look into things that you've been doing. I think you've got a political agenda" (qtd. in Deitcher, 39). Album cover of *Way Out West Plus*, Contemporary Records, 1957.

1994, *Maverick* was remade as a movie, and the White House was, of course, occupied by a saxophonist.

(4) Malcolm McLaren, the provocateur who packaged the Sex Pistols, describes rap's scratch or "Do-It-Yourself" process on the record cover of "Buffalo Girls" (1982). "Two manual decks and a rhythm box are all you need. Get a bunch of good rhythm records, choose your favorite parts and groove along with the rhythm machine. Use your hands, scratch the record by repeating the grooves you dig so much. Fade one record into another and keep that rhythm box going. Now start talking and singing over the record with the microphone. Now you're making your own music out of other people's records. That's what scratching is" (quoted in Taylor 14). McLaren, of course, did not invent scratching. He merely heard a good idea (the "dubbing" practiced by New York and Jamaican disc jockeys) and appropriated it. "He's very clever," said Boy George, "but he takes the credit for everything, including the things he never touched" (quoted in Taylor 12).[6]

(5) In this age of mechanical reproduction we do well if we learn to maverick. Listening to "The Surrey with the Fringe on Top" (Rollins), *Duck Rock* (McLaren), and "Fight the Power" (Public Enemy), reading "Limited Inc a b c . . ." (Derrida), *S/Z* (Barthes), "Derrida at the Little Bighorn" (Ulmer), and *Flaubert's Parrot* (Julian Barnes), or looking at Marcel Duchamp or Sherrie Levine's ready-mades is to witness an exploitation of *copyright*, a concept that "now means the right to copy

anything" (Ulmer, "Object" 96). These texts celebrate the demise of the print medium, and they anticipate the advent of hypertext. Walter Benjamin writes: "Quotations in my works are like robbers by the roadside who make an armed attack and relieve an idler of his convictions" (quoted in Arendt 38). Robert Coover: "We are always astonished to discover how much of the reading and writing experience occurs in the interstices and trajectories *between* text fragments" (24).

(6) "Allegorical imagery," writes Craig Owens, "is appropriated imagery; the allegorist does not invent images but confiscates them. He lays claim to the culturally significant, poses as its interpreter. And in his hands the image becomes something other (*allos* = other + *agoreuei* = to speak)" (69). In one of his notebooks, Leonardo da Vinci wrote:

> Seeing that I cannot choose any subject of great utility or pleasure, because my predecessors have already taken as their own all useful and necessary themes, I will do like one who, because of his poverty, is the last to arrive at the fair, and not being able otherwise to provide himself, chooses all the things which others have already looked over and not taken, but refused as being of little value. With these despised and rejected wares—the leavings of many buyers—I will load my modest pack, and therewith take my course, distributing, not indeed amid the great cities, but among the mean hamlets, and taking such reward as befits the things I offer. (1)

Conversation With a Colossus

Having lost interest in telephone interviews with good and great musicians, I wanted to commune with the godhead. I contacted Fantasy Records and asked Terri Hinte, director of publicity, if she could hook me up with Rollins, a saxophonist *Rolling Stone* magazine dubbed "one of the most inventive improvisers in the history of music"—"the last remaining titan" (Spencer 148). Months passed, but, as always, Terri came through. Rollins and I talked for nearly an hour. *Cadence* published the interview (after *Interview* rejected it): that is, it published everything except the following exchange (which I held back).[7]

> *Jarrett.* My favorite record cover of all time is the one to *Way Out West.* Was it your idea?
> *Rollins.* The one on *Way Out West*—it happened a long time ago. I'm pretty sure that it was my idea: the hat and the gun belt and all that stuff.
> *Jarrett.* So how was it received? Was that a kick for your friends?

Rollins. It was very striking, very unusual. It was a big kick at the time. In fact recently I ran into a guy—there's a young tenor player in England called Courtney Pine. He came up to me and told me a story. He said that he didn't know what he wanted to do. He was just a kid, and when he saw this album—*Way Out West*—he realized that he wanted to be a musician. So it's kind of nice when something like that happens. It was an unusual thing at the time, but I thought it went well with playing unusual songs for a jazz album. I thought that the whole thing was really right.

Jarrett. It's incredibly funny, ironic, anticipating one of the best jokes in *Blazing Saddles*. I look at it and laugh and then think, "This isn't funny. It's true. There were plenty of black cowboys."

Rollins. Exactly.

Jarrett. And jazz is metaphorically associated with the myths of the American West: the musician as outlaw hero; the music as a movement or push outward. The cover says that. It works on many, many different levels.

Rollins. That's right. I've never thought of it in those words, but that's quite true. When I was a boy, I had seen these all-black films. There was a fellow who used to sing with Duke Ellington's Band, Herb Jeffries. He was in an all-black western. I remember that. I've forgotten whether it was *Rhythm on the Range* or *Bronze Buckaroo*, but that made an impression on me. And of course, as we all know, there were black cowboys. All of these things were in my mind.

Swinging Cowboys

Some estimates state that at least one-fourth of the working cowboys in the late nineteenth century were African Americans; one-fourth of the Hollywood films made between 1910 and the late 1950s were westerns. Still, writes J. Hoberman, "the demographics of the western remained overwhelmingly white up until the eve of the genre's demise," when confidence in its "ethos of limitless growth and personal freedom" ebbed "in response to the struggle for civil rights at home and the question of imperial ambition abroad" (53) (figure 3).

Herb Jeffries played the leading role in *Bronze Buckaroo* (1938, directed by R. C. Kahn). He also starred in *Harlem Rides the Range* (1939, directed by Sam Newfield). Rollins (born 7 September 1930) was eight or nine when he saw one or both of these films. I was born in 1953, the year Paramount released *Shane*; twenty years later Herb Jeffries appeared in Barry Shear's *Jarrett* (1973) (Meeker).

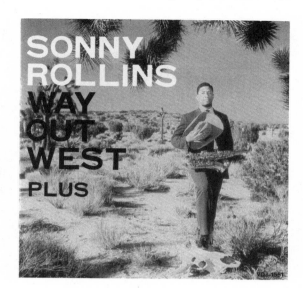

Figure 3. John Wayne (1969): "They tell me everything isn't black and white. Well, I say why the hell not?" (qtd. in Hoberman, 49).

The Voice of the Camera

When I spoke with William Claxton in January 1990, he was working for *Motor Trend* magazine and living in Beverly Hills, California, but back in the mid-1950s, when he shot available-light photographs that made Art Pepper, Gerry Mulligan, Shorty Rogers, and Chet Baker icons of West Coast cool, he worked for Contemporary Records. At that time, stimulated by the rise of the long-playing record, jazz was enjoying a period of renewed prosperity, and Lester Koenig's new company was doing well. Contemporary was "the first jazz label to introduce 45 rpm singles, stereo and attain national distribution" (Carr et al. 113). But prosperity brought its own set of artistic challenges. The speed with which photographers and graphic artists had to generate ideas matched the fast tempos of bebop.

The photo session for *Way Out West* developed out of a conversation between musician and photographer.[8] Rollins, Claxton recalls, "liked western things" and wanted to do something that would complement the material he was recording, plus commemorate his first trip to the West Coast. Claxton agreed but suggested that Rollins maintain the jazzman's air of urbanity. "I told him to keep his Brooks Brothers suit and skinny black tie." Claxton says:

> I knew the desert pretty well, so I knew exactly where to get the right kind of Joshua trees and cactus in the background. I went to a prop

house and rented a steer's head—a skeleton—because I couldn't depend on finding one out there. And we put a holster on him.

I picked him up. He was a terrific guy to be with, very nice, and we just drove out to the high desert, near Mojave. I had shot pictures there before. I put the skull out in the sand, and he put one foot up on it. He had this long, thin body. He looked great. He just posed beautifully. And he had great fun doing it. We laughed a lot.

Before he photographed Mel Brooks and Carl Reiner, at a sitting that yielded the cover to the comedians' first record album, Claxton showed them his recently completed work for *Way Out West*. Brooks liked what he saw and, perhaps, remembered the image of Rollins as cowboy when he directed his own western. "The ultimate desecration," writes Hoberman of *Blazing Saddles* (1974); it was also the highest-grossing western before *Dances with Wolves* (1990), capping "the assorted anti-, post-, spaghetti, revisionist, psychedelic, black, and burlesque westerns of the early '70s" (52). It boasted an African American actor, Cleavon Little, as the sheriff of Rock Ridge, and in one memorable gag, predicated on the audience mistaking diegetic for nondiegetic music, Brooks filmed the Count Basie orchestra playing jazz in the desert.

Joshing in the Mojave

Comedy, Aristotle claims in the *Poetics*, arose in the "outlying districts," as "those who led the phallic songs (that even now are still customary in many of our cities) . . . improvised" (Golden 8).

Theory of Album Covers

Record covers mirror back our perceptions of particular types of music, perceptions that are to a great extent visually and not musically determined (the modern age, notes Heidegger, grasps the *real* as picture), shaped by past experiences with other texts representing aural "texts" (131). They not only represent—encode in visual form—the myths associated with music, they contribute to the construction of those myths. They are part of the process that imbues music with meaning, gives it voice.

Easily dismissable as a period piece, an egregious example of West Coast kitsch, the cover to *Way Out West* is, in fact, a tightly packed bundle of highly charged metaphors: the jazz equivalent of the *Primavera*. Think of it as a dream image, a case of transference or projection

(*metapherein* means "to transfer"). It establishes a correspondence between two remote images. It speaks of modern jazz—conventionally
understood as the ceaseless exploration of uncharted musical territory by
social and artistic outsiders[9]—and of the West. Shane becomes the jazzman; California becomes jazz. Rollins, Claxton, and their audience gain
symbolic knowledge of this music (it enters language) by identifying it
with traditional mythological categories perpetuated by film, literature,
theater, painting, television, and other media.

Claxton and Contemporary Records portrayed Rollins as outlaw hero
(much as Andy Warhol would later portray Elvis Presley), and, in so
doing, they anticipated an image that the counterculture would appropriate and refunction—maverick—in less than ten years. At that time,
through what Robert Christgau calls a "barstool-macho equation of gunslinger and guitarschlonger" (120), the musician as outlaw was apotheo-
sized, and his image, formerly signifying values approved by a few mav-
ericks ("bohemians"), became an icon recognized by all and embraced by
many. He stood for "freedom from restraint, a preference for intuition
as the source of conduct, a distrust of the law, a prolonging of adoles-
cence, and a bias against technology, bureaucracies, and urban life." The
radical left of the 1960s, notes Robert Ray, was obsessed with the iconography of the American West. "Clothes (jeans, boots, buckskins) and
hairstyles (long and unkempt, moustaches) derived from daguerreotypes
of nineteenth-century gunfighters; and pop music returned repeatedly to
frontier images: The Buffalo Springfield's 'Broken Arrow,' The Grateful
Dead's 'Casey Jones,' The Band's 'Across the Great Divide,' James Taylor's 'Sweet Baby James,' Neil Young's 'Cowgirl in the Sand,' Creedence
Clearwater Revival's 'Proud Mary,' The Byrds' *Sweetheart of the Rodeo*,
and the Eagles' *Desperado*" (255–56). Rock, however, had followed a trail
blazed by jazz. The quest for a unique sound, a privileging of invention
over interpretation, an infatuation with drugs, sex, and spirituality. Both
musics glorified an ideology founded on individualism (figure 4).

Fish Out of Water

For a semester I tutored Scott, a freshman at Penn State–York, on his
writing skills, but the work of remediation never kept us from talking
about more engaging matters. One day our conversation turned to fish-
ing. Scott told me that he planned to major in wildlife management; I
told him that I used to live in Atlanta, not far from Lake Lanier, where the
world-record largemouth bass was caught.

"Really?" he said. "I have a calendar in my bedroom that shows pic-

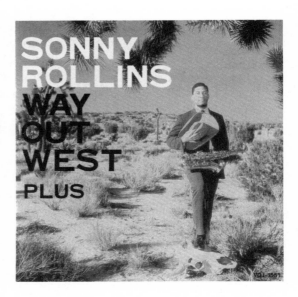

Figure 4. Sonny Rollins
to Gary Giddins: "Don't
ever shrink from the
belief that you have to
prove yourself every
minute, because you
do" (qtd. in Balliett,
1991:58).

tures of fish. It lists the size of a world-record catch, then tells where it
was caught. Did you know that the world's largest pike was caught in
Germany?"

I confessed that I didn't.

"Yeah," he said. "Sometimes I just look at that picture and think,
'Damn, how'd it get all the way over there?'"

Sometimes I look at Rollins—born in Harlem, the child of immigrants
from the Virgin Islands—and wonder, "How'd he end up way out West?"

Go West

The search for work (gold by any other name) motivated my first trip
west. Having completed all required courses at the University of Florida,
I traveled to San Francisco and the Modern Language Association convention, in hopes of landing a teaching position. Although I had managed
to schedule interviews with only a few of the hundreds of schools gathered for this annual convention, I got lucky. The Pennsylvania State
University hired me.

The Joshua Tree

In her analysis of the mythic significance of the West, Joan Didion describes both a physical and a social geography. She writes: "California is a

place where boom mentality and a sense of Chekhovian loss meet in uneasy suspension; in which the mind is troubled by some buried but ineradicable suspicion that things had better work here, because that immense bleached sky is where we run out of continent" (quoted in Schrag 171).

The Joshua tree (*Yucca brevifola*) was named by Mormon pioneers who fancied that it resembled the biblical Joshua "pointing the way with uplifted arms to the Promised Land" (*Encyclopedia Americana*). Their spiritual quest—for transcendent identity and a traceable genealogy—was (and is) directed by the metaphor of the *root-tree:* i.e., by the arborescent model theorized extensively by Deleuze and Guattari. It led them to conceptualize the West as a garden (Eden or Gethsemane) and to erect a bureaucracy: making property the basis of government; negotiating land through litigation and marriages.

Mormons repressed knowledge of "the rhizomatic West, with its Indians without ancestry, its ever-receding limit, its shifting and displaced frontiers" (Deleuze and Guattari 19). They could not shake arborescence, were unwilling to abandon faith in roots and radicles: "classical" trees. To them, the Joshua tree did not look upside down, its limbs—strangely forked and spreading in all directions—signifying nothing so much as indeterminacy.

If Charlie Parker Were a Gunslinger

When I see an African American dressed as a cowboy . . . I supply the signified: outlaw with a bad case of irony (figures 5–7). Does that make me a Mormon?

The Truth in Photography

After sitting down to write on a group of drawings by Valerio Adami, Jacques Derrida observed: "As for painting, any discourse on it, beside it or above, always strikes me as silly, both didactic and incantatory, programed, worked by the compulsion of mastery, be it poetical or philosophical" (65). His statement strikes a resonant chord in me. I am somewhat embarrassed by my "Theory of Album Covers." *It assumes too little.* If *Way Out West* communicates perfectly well—speaks the truth about jazz—then I should shut up and let signification do its work. *And it assumes too much.* If this photograph needs me—let us say that it speaks the truth, albeit in signs so oblique that only well-trained eyes can discern them—then what will keep my version of its truth from renewing, reproducing, and reintroducing the very obliqueness I hope to allay? (2).

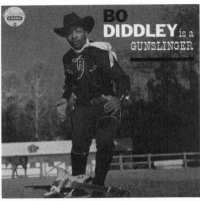

Figure 5. Jimi Hendrix wielding a six-gun. Album cover of *Smash Hits*, Reprise Records, 1972.

Figure 6. Bo Diddley reaching for his guitar. Album cover of *Bo Diddley Is a Gunslinger*, Chess Records, 1960.

What I am looking for is an alternative to silence and formalism, a way to break away from writing that aims to represent an object of study mimetically. I want to respond to John Leavey's question: If no referent, no transcendental signified regulates Text, how is writing to proceed, writing which in the classical sense is anchored by the referent? (74). More importantly, I want to stage my answer, show how one might go about "representing" an object of study without falling back on a system of truth "as adequation or as unveiling" (*Truth* 367). That is why I am interested in the cover to *Way Out West*. It is, to borrow a phrase Barthes uses to describe *A Night at the Opera* (1935), "allegorical of many a textual problem" (*IMT* 194). It suggests another way to write criticism, one which Ulmer describes as "fully referential, but referential in the manner of 'narrative allegory' rather than of 'allegoresis.' 'Allegoresis,' the mode of commentary long practiced by traditional critics, 'suspends' the surface of the text, applying a terminology of 'verticalness, levels, hidden meaning, the hieratic difficulty of interpretation,' whereas 'narrative allegory' (practiced by post-critics) explores the literal—*letteral*—level of the language itself, in a horizontal investigation of the polysemous meanings simultaneously available in the words themselves—in etymologies and puns—and in the things the words name."[10] In short, allegory, unlike allegoresis, is not *hermeneutics* (puzzle-solving); it "does not restore an original meaning that may have been lost or obscured" (Owens 69). Instead, it is *heuretics*—invention. It dramatizes or enacts

Figure 7. George Clinton riding two dolphins bareback. Album cover of *Parliament's Motor-Booty Affair,* Casablanca Records, 1978.

"letteral" truth, enlarging on the possibilities of linguistic transference ("Object" 95).

The allegorist does not analyze so much as he invents. He concerns himself with recomposition—how to compose a "nonidentical, staggered, discrepant 'repetition'" of what is, in fact, already a "repetition" (*Truth* 30). This is what aligns him with the jazz musician (an artist whose every note is a response to earlier texts). His method consists of joining the idiomatic (e.g., autobiographical materials) with the institutional (e.g., the recognized "grammar" of a discipline) in order to interrogate an object of study.[11] Ulmer labels this contribution of one's personal style (or story) to "problem-solving in a field of specialized knowledge" *mystory* ("Textshop" 767–68), and he distinguishes it from what Barthes calls *reading,* a pleasureless "activity" that has become nothing more than a *referendum* (*S/Z* 4). We should note that mystory and other Florida School applications of critical theory (grammatology) are founded on the notion that the signifier *joshes:* points the way with strangely forked arms. It is comic, "laughter being what, by a last reversal, releases demonstration from its demonstrative attribute. What liberates metaphor, symbol, emblem from poetic *mania,* what manifests its power of subversion, is the *preposterous . . .*" (*Barthes* 80–81). Allegoresis—normal criticism—is serious, an extrapolation of the simple form of the riddle; its features are examination and catechism. Allegory or mystory is an extrapolation of the simple form of the joke; by "'loosening intelligibility' through play" it attempts to model a type of writing that evades "the inhibitions and compulsions of reason and criticism" (*Teletheory* 52–53). Normal criticism is to mystory as *Shane* (1953) is to *Blazing Saddles.*

The Tenor's Vehicle

Craig Saper anticipates the question of how theory might assist us in displacing the emotion—melancholia—that necessarily accompanies writing reproducing the confrontational structure of the western. He states that the "swerve of affect from alienated thought to carnivalesque thinking occurs by exploiting the indirections of metaphors, images, and key words employed in theoretical explanations or metalanguages" (375). Craig Owens recommends a similar tactic (though that is too confrontational a word) in his instructions for actualizing the allegorical potential of texts. He points out that allegory proceeds according to a "pictogrammatical" logic. In it "the image is a hieroglyph; an allegory is a rebus—writing composed of concrete images." It confuses "the verbal and the visual" (74–75).[12]

Looking again at the cover of *Way Out West* and capitalizing on this insight, we discover that a confusion of "the vernal and the visual," made manifest by the substitution of tenor saxophone for (the obviously absent) six-gun, yields what Ulmer calls a "research pun" and what Barthes labels an "amphibology."[13] The *tenor* that Rollins holds (*tenere* = to hold) in Claxton's photograph might recall Sax's invention (the saxophone or saxocannon), but it also winks at I. A. Richards's distinction between the "tenor" and "vehicle" of a metaphor (comparable to Saussure's distinction between "signified" and "signifier"). It allows us to seize the cover to *Way Out West* as a pictogrammatical set of instructions, a tutor-text on how to make other texts.[14] (Ulmer writes: "What the baroque or romantic allegorist conceived of as an emblem, the post-critic treats as a model"—"Object" 99.) We may read *Way Out West* as an allegory of allegory—i.e., as an allegory about metaphor—or exploiting Claude Lévi-Strauss's theory of the *charivari* (introduced in *The Raw and the Cooked*), we may observe that it illustrates how to make *noise,* generate what we might call "knowledge effects." The "unnatural union" of jazzman and desert—or of saxophone and cowboy—recommends that invention proceed through mavericking. A conventional syntagm (cowboy and desert; jazzman and New York City) is interrupted and into this same sequence a "foreign" element intrudes: an element that appropriates one term of a sequence brings about a distortion (Lévi-Strauss 289ff).

Way Out West teaches a textualist lesson: Tenors are vehicles. It models Derrida's main point in "White Mythology: Metaphor in the Text of Philosophy." Interpretation (hermeneutics) and Western metaphysics begin with the in(ter)vention of metaphor. Without it "we cannot imagine what it is to be someone else," writes Cynthia Ozick. "Metaphor is the reciprocal agent, the universalizing force: it makes possible the power to envision the stranger's heart" (67). "Metaphors," Hannah Arendt notes, "are the means by which the oneness of the world is poetically brought about" (14). Invention (heuretics), on the other hand, begins when the concept of metaphor dissolves, that is, when tenor and vehicle collapse or when, as in allegory, structure is projected as sequence. *One plays a tenor by causing a read to vibrate* between literal and figurative levels of language; one finds an alternative to a hermeneutics of truth by unsettling "what turns out to be *the* metaphysical distinction, between words [signifiers] and meanings [signifieds]" (Cooper 26).

But we might ask with Jean Baudrillard: "[H]ow far can we go in the extermination of meaning, how far can we go in the non-referential desert form without cracking up and, of course, still keep alive the esoteric charm of disappearance?" (63–64). His answer ("a fundamental rule"): "[A]im for the point of no return. This is the key" (10).

Coda

When I lived in Chattanooga, I occasionally spent Sunday afternoons at a downtown flea market. One day, while browsing around, I happened onto a whole table of combination locks. Interested in purchasing one, I asked a woman sitting behind the table if she had a list of the combinations, since I saw none attached to any of the locks I had examined.

"No," she said.

I asked, "Well, then, how do you get them open?"

She said, "You try it. Some people get it right off."

Notes

1 Owens describes allegory as the projection of structure as sequence, reminding us that, "in rhetoric, allegory is traditionally defined as a single metaphor introduced in continuous series" (72).

2 For a historical placement and discussion of the Florida School, see Saper, esp. 392–94; his edition of *Visible Language* is the best single-volume introduction to its aims and methods, collecting essays by Gregory Ulmer, Robert Ray, Avital Ronell, Ellie Ragland-Sullivan, and Bonnie Sparling.

3 Jacques Attali argues that the time people spend producing the resources to buy recordings ("of other people's time") cancels out time available for using those recordings. Hence accumulation becomes its own reward (101). While this point is compelling, Attali fails to acknowledge that "time spent producing the means to buy recordings" frequently coincides with time spent consuming recordings. Music permeates all phases of our lives, serving to blur conventional distinctions between production and consumption. "When you whistle while you work" (e.g.,

listen to Muzak, a car radio, or a homemade cassette tape), work becomes a form of leisure, or, as in the case of the one who writes about music for money (or tenure), leisure becomes work.

4   Owens argues that the symbol was, to Saussure, "never wholly arbitrary," and was, thus, the antithesis of allegory, "the domain of the arbitrary, the conventional, the unmotivated" (82–84).

5   The landmark critique of supplementary logic appears in Jacques Derrida's discussion of Rousseau's *Confessions* in ". . . That Dangerous Supplement . . . ," *Of Grammatology*, trans. Gayatri Chakravorty Spivak (Baltimore: Johns Hopkins UP, 1976): 141–64. It is, however, in Jonathan Swift's allegory of church history, found in *A Tale of a Tub*, that the coat (an addition to and a substitute for the Father's will) is made the image of supplementarity.

6   McLaren's appropriative practice is underwritten by politics that are decidedly leftist and Gallic—Situationist in their origin. For a discussion of his art school training and his affiliation with the Situationist International, see Taylor; Simon Frith and Howard Horne, *Art Into Pop* (London: Methuen, 1987); and Greil Marcus, *Lipstick Traces: A Secret History of the Twentieth Century* (Cambridge, Mass.: Harvard UP, 1989).

7   My interview with Rollins appeared as "Sonny Rollins," *Cadence*, 16.7 (1990): 5–8, 28. Rollins's comments on *Way Out West* were also later published: "Sonny Rollins—Tenorman Amidst the Joshua Trees," *Jazziz*, Apr.–May (1990): 21. This second piece became the germ of this text.

8   Telephone interview with William Claxton, 21 Jan. 1990.

9   The classic study of the jazz musician as deviant is Howard Becker, *The Outsiders: Studies in the Sociology of Deviance* (New York: Free Press, 1963). See also Hebdige; this study of postwar British youth culture argues that "it is on the plane of aesthetics: in dress, dance, music; in the whole rhetoric of style, that we find the dialogue between black and white most subtly and comprehensively recorded, albeit in code" (44–45).

10   The citation is from Ulmer ("Object" 94), but he is citing and extending an argument begun by Maureen Quilligan, *The Language of Allegory* (Ithaca, N.Y.: Cornell UP, 1979): 30–33.

11   For the jazz musician, this means projecting one's inimitable "sound" onto the "grammar" of jazz (e.g., a blues scale) in order to recompose a Tin Pan Alley song, or "standard."

12   Owens also adds that the confusion of "the verbal and the visual" is but one aspect of allegory's "hopeless confusion of all aesthetic mediums and stylistic categories (hopeless, that is, according to any partitioning of the aesthetic field of essentialist grounds)" (75).

13   An amphibology is Barthes's term for a "precisely ambiguous" word; it has two meanings and is used in such a way that both of these meanings are kept: "*one and the same word, in one and the same sentence, means at one and the same time two different things*" (*Barthes* 72).

14   My maneuverings in this section virtually recapitulate Ulmer's allegorical reading of the Marx Brothers film, *A Night at the Opera* (*Teletheory* 73–81). I am, obviously, deeply indebted to this work. I must add, however, that I had noticed the inventive possibilities of the pun made available by "tenor" before reading Ulmer, a point which, to my mind, substantiates his theories on heuretics.

Works Cited

Attali, Jacques. *Noise: The Political Economy of Music.* Trans. Brian Massumi. Minneapolis: U of Minnesota P, 1988.

Arendt, Hannah. "Introduction." *Illuminations.* New York: Harcourt, Brace and World, 1968.

Balliett, Whitney. "Jazz: Rollins Rampant." *New Yorker* 29 July 1991: 58–59.

Barthes, Roland. *The Grain of the Voice: Interviews 1962–1980.* Trans. Linda Coverdale. New York: Hill and Wang, 1985.

——. *Image, Music, Text.* Trans. Stephen Heath. New York: Hill and Wang, 1977.

——. *Roland Barthes.* Trans. Richard Howard. New York: Hill and Wang, 1977.

——. *S/Z.* Trans. Richard Miller. New York: Hill and Wang, 1974.

Baudrillard, Jean. *America.* Trans. Chris Turner. London: Verso, 1988.

Carr, Roy, Brian Case, and Fred Dellar. *The Hip: Hipsters, Jazz and the Beat Generation.* London: Faber and Faber, 1986.

Christgau, Robert. *Christgau's Record Guide: Rock Albums of the Seventies.* New Haven, Conn.: Ticknor and Fields, 1981.

Cooper, David E. *Metaphor.* Oxford: Basil Blackwell, 1986.

Coover, Robert. "The End of Books." *New York Times Book Review* 21 June 1992: 1, 23–25.

Corbett, John. "Free, Single, and Disengaged: Listening Pleasure and the Popular Music Object." *October* 54 (1991): 79–101.

Deitcher, David. "A Newer Frontier: The Smithsonian Revises the Old West." *Village Voice* 25 June 1991: 39–40.

Deleuze, Gilles, and Félix Guattari. *A Thousand Plateaus: Capitalism and Schizophrenia.* Trans. Brian Massumi. Minneapolis: U of Minnesota P, 1987.

Derrida, Jacques. *The Truth in Painting.* Trans. Geoff Bennington and Ian McLeod. Chicago: U of Chicago P, 1987.

Durham, Philip, and Everett L. Jones. *The Negro Cowboys.* Lincoln: U of Nebraska P, 1965.

Golden, Leon, trans., and O. B. Hardison, Jr., commentary. *Aristotle's Poetics: A Translation and Commentary for Students of Literature.* Englewood Cliffs, N.J.: Prentice-Hall, 1968.

Hebdige, Dick. *Subculture: The Meaning of Style.* London: Methuen, 1979.

Heidegger, Martin. "The Age of the World Picture." *The Question Concerning Technology.* Trans. William Lovitt. New York: Harper, 1977. 115–54.

Hoberman, J. "How the Western Was Lost." *Village Voice* 27 Aug. 1991: 49–53.

Jarrett, Michael. "Jazz Greats Still in Transition: Sonny Rollins and Cecil Taylor." *Tower Records' Pulse!* Mar. 1990: 74.

Johnson, Barbara. "Translator's Introduction." Jacques Derrida. *Dissemination.* Chicago: U of Chicago P, 1981. vii–xxxiii.

Leavey, John, Jr. "Time Signatures: Post*.* Responsibilities." *Strategies* 1 (1988): 64–81.

Leonardo da Vinci. "Observations and Aphorisms." *Notebooks.* Trans. Edward MacCurdy. New York: Modern Library, 1957. 1–33.

Lévi-Strauss, Claude. *The Raw and the Cooked: Introduction to a Science of Mythology: I.* Trans. John and Doreen Weightman. Chicago: U of Chicago P, 1969.

Meeker, David. *Jazz in the Movies.* New and enlarged ed. New York: Da Capo, 1981.

Owens, Craig. "The Allegorical Impulse: Toward a Theory of Postmodernism." *October* 12 (1980): 67–85.

Ozick, Cynthia. "The Moral Necessity of Metaphor." *Harper's.* May 1986: 62–68.

Perloff, Marjorie. *The Futurist Moment: Avant-Garde, Avant Guerre, and the Language of Rupture.* Chicago: U of Chicago P, 1986.

Ray, Robert B. *A Certain Tendency of the Hollywood Cinema, 1930–1980.* Princeton, N.J.: Princeton UP, 1985.

Saper, Craig, ed. "Introduction." *Instant Theory: Making Thinking Popular. Visible Language* 22 (1988): 371–97.

Savan, Leslie. "Let's Face It." *Village Voice* 11 June 1991: 49–53.

Schrag, Peter. *The End of the American Future.* New York: Simon, 1973.

Spencer, Scott. "The Titan of Jazz." *Rolling Stone,* 13–27 Dec. 1990: 148–56, 230.

Taylor, Paul, ed. "The Impresario of Do-It-Yourself." *Impresario: Malcolm McLaren and the British New Wave.* Cambridge, Mass.: MIT P, 1988.

Tompkins, Jane. "Fighting Words: Unlearning to Write the Critical Essay." *Georgia Review* 42 (1988): 585–90.

Torgovnick, Marianna. "Experimental Critical Writing." *Profession* 90 (1990): 25–27.

Ulmer, Gregory L. "The Discourse of the Imaginary." *Diacritics* 10 (1980): 61–75.

——. "The Object of Post-Criticism." *The Anti-Aesthetic: Essays on Postmodern Culture.* Ed. Hal Foster. Port Townsend, Wash: Bay P, 1983. 83–110.

——. *Teletheory: Grammatology in the Age of Video.* New York: Routledge, 1989.

——. "Textshop for Psychoanalysis: On De-Programming Freshmen Platonists." *College English* 49 (1987): 756–69.

Zwerin, Mike. "Sax and the Man." *Elle* Feb. 1990: 102–04.

VOCALESE:

REPRESENTING

JAZZ

WITH JAZZ

Purple Passages or Fiestas in Blue?
Notes Toward an Aesthetic of Vocalese

BARRY KEITH GRANT

Although jazz is commonly conceived of as an instrumental music, the voice has been crucial to jazz history from the beginning. Indeed, as every jazz history tells us, the voice was the first instrument, and jazz playing developed when musicians began to use their instruments to emulate its flexible phrasing. Even in the prehistory of jazz—the work songs, arhoolies, and early blues—the voice was central and often, as in the first two of these forms, unaccompanied. In the golden age of the classic blues singers following the surprising commercial success of Mamie Smith's "Crazy Blues" (1920), Bessie Smith, Ma Rainey, Ida Cox, and others consistently were accompanied by the most important jazz musicians of the day. Whether, as legend would have it, Louis Armstrong was the first to do so when he sang nonsense syllables in a manner resembling the way he played his cornet on the Hot Five's recording of "Heebie Jeebies" (1926), he inaugurated the venerable tradition of scat singing later developed by such practitioners as Ella Fitzgerald, Anita O'Day, Clark "Mumbles" Terry, and others. Since then, many jazz musicians have also sung, approaching singing like they do their instruments. Chet Baker, for instance, is often identified with the "cool school" of the 1950s, quite different in style from Armstrong, but Baker also sang in the same manner as he played his trumpet; Slam Stewart blended voice and instrument, bowing his bass in unison with his vocals.

Additionally, many jazz composers and arrangers have incorporated voices in their arrangements. Duke Ellington employed the voice as one possible color in his orchestral palette (listen, for example, to Adelaide Hall in his 1927 version of "Creole Love Call" or Kay Davis in the ethereal "On a Turquoise Cloud" of 1947). Tadd Dameron, George Russell, Charles Mingus, Horace Silver (a popular composer with vocalese artists)—in fact, almost all of the major figures in modern jazz—have recorded with voices as part of the musical setting rather than as mere background embellishment (although, unfortunately, some have succumbed to embellishment as well). In short, the voice has been so important to jazz that, as Leslie Gourse has noted, "Almost any American can recognize the voices of Louis Armstrong, Bing Crosby, Nat King Cole, Ella Fitzgerald, Billie Holiday, Frank Sinatra, Tony Bennett and others with lightning speed. Few Americans recognize the voices of any world leaders so readily . . ." (Gourse 21).

Yet jazz singing has inspired much contention, unfairly minimized by many jazz historians, and so, I think, needs to be further examined. Not only is it unclear whether specific vocalists are or are not jazz singers—Tony Bennett, Frank Sinatra, Bing Crosby, Rosemary Clooney come readily to mind—it is also unclear what qualifies a vocalist as a jazz singer. This even presents a problem within the work of individual vocalists. For example, early Nat Cole vocals with his trio are commonly considered jazz singing, but his later pop vocals with arrangements by Nelson Riddle or Gordon Jenkins are not. Is it that the voice must sound like an instrument (Berendt 317)? Or is it the jazz sense of rhythm (Friedwald xiv)? Must the singer be able to hit the blue notes? Or improvise on the melody? Will Friedwald begins his 1990 book on the subject by conceding the impossibility of definition but still employs the term for want of a better one (Friedwald xi).

Vocalese, as one particular style of jazz singing, has particularly suffered in the critical discourse on jazz. In Clint Eastwood's *Bird* (1988), the Chan Parker character, on hearing King Pleasure's vocalese version of "Parker's Mood" for the first time, proclaims without hesitation, "I hate the idea. . . . It's horrible." Of course, she is reacting as much to the premature depiction of Parker's death in Pleasure's lyrics as she is to vocalese as a concept, but in a sense the scene is metaphorically resonant of the extent to which the employment of lyrics is said to destroy the art of jazz ("kills" the artist) by diluting its musical "purity." It is not insignificant that commentators usually specify that those early vocalese tunes that achieved commercial success, like Pleasure's 1952 recording, were hits in the *rhythm and blues* market—that is, one that defined itself as a distinctly different, although overlapping, subculture from jazz.

This bias against vocalese among jazz connoisseurs is common, however subtly present it may be. One important jazz encyclopedia, for example, describes vocalese as an "extremely circumscribed exercise" and Eddie Jefferson's pioneering work as "a serious diversion"—a case of damning with faint praise (Carr et al. 518–19). Even Leonard Feather, a critic sympathetic to vocalese—in fact, he is credited with coining the term—refers to Jefferson's early work as "a hobby" (Feather, *Encyclopedia* 268). In his notes for the Blue Stars' American LP, Feather tellingly suggests that because most American listeners do not understand French, they will be forced to pay attention to the group's musical values, as if listening to them as a musical combo somehow makes them more acceptable (Feather, *Blue Stars*). The purpose of the following analysis is to demarginalize vocalese in jazz discourse by analyzing the genre both for its own properties and its aesthetic affinities with other cultural traditions (although the latter is less an attempt to "legitimize" vocalese by association than to elucidate the nature of its discourse)—to locate the voice of vocalese, as it were.

Vocalese involves the setting/singing of lyrics (almost always composed rather than improvised) to jazz instrumentals, both melody and solo parts, arrangement and solos, note for note. Thus vocalese is distinctly different from scat singing both because it is arranged and composed rather than improvised, and because it relies on language rather than simply on sound. Like the bop instrumentalist, the vocalese singer often aspires to speed ("cookin'," as Pleasure called it) and technical facility without slurring the words. (This, of course, is not to be confused with inflection, which is central to any kind of jazz singing.) Hence, the rapidly sung final line in "Moody's Mood"—"Well James Moody, you can come on in and blow now if you want to, we're through"—became "a household word" (Gitler) as a result of Pleasure's recording. Undoubtedly, the supreme vocalese performer in this regard is Jon Hendricks (he is also the one true auteur of vocalese, its "poet laureate" [Feather, *Encyclopedia* 252]), who can sing with astonishing speed while maintaining clear articulation, as in, for example, the tour de force "Cloudburst" (1959)—in clear contrast to, say, Tim Hauser of Manhattan Transfer, who must slur and garble Hendricks's lyrics in order to keep pace. Annie Ross has at least equal technical facility. How many singers have the range she demonstrates when she emulates the final notes of Count Basie's trumpet section in Lambert, Hendricks and Ross's version of "Avenue C" (1957)?

Vocalese can be traced back to the horn-like vocals of Harry "the Hipster" Gibson (among others, "Get Your Juices at the Deuces" [1944]; "Who Put the Benzedrine in Mrs. Murphy's Ovaltine" [1946]), to the private language ("Vout") of Slim Gaillard and the "hi-de-ho" jive of Cab Calloway; and especially to the original vocal approach of Leo Watson (and later bop vocalists like Buddy Stewart, Babs Gonzales, and Joe Carroll, whom Watson influenced), who played with lyrics in a way that can only be called stream of consciousness. Appropriately dubbed the "James Joyce of Jazz" by Leonard Feather (Gourse, 151)—a sobriquet *Time* magazine would later apply to L, H & R—Watson skittered over notes like a trumpet or trombone (listen to what he does with the refrain of "Jeepers Creepers" [1938]), interpolated seemingly inappropriate melodies, and punned with words in a manner that resembled free association or dadaist automatic writing (listen, for example to "Coquette" [1945, with the Spirits of Rhythm featuring, interestingly, none other than Feather on piano], where, more like e. e. cummings than Joyce, he also sings some of the punctuation). Some writers (e.g., Friedwald 233) have cited such recordings as Marion Harris's lyricized version of Beiderbecke and Trumbauer's solos on "Singin' the Blues" (1934), Crosby's lyrics for the end of Beiderbecke's "Way Down Yonder in New Orleans" in his "Someday, Sweetheart" (1934), and the Delta Rhythm Boys' vocalizing of Billy Strayhorn's arrangement of "Take the A Train" as early intimations, if not instances, of vocalese.

But just as the swing era emphatically arrived with Benny Goodman's Palomar Ballroom engagement in August 1935, so vocalese truly begins in February 1952 with the release of King Pleasure's (Clarence Beeks) recording of James Moody's "I'm in the Mood for Love" for Prestige. Released as "Moody's Mood for Love," it became one of the biggest R & B hits of that year. Eddie Jefferson, the composer of the lyrics for "Moody's Mood" and the singer generally credited with inventing vocalese, actually recorded a few sides before Pleasure, but it was Pleasure who made the impact and, ironically, gave a welcomed impetus to Jefferson's own career. Since then, vocalese has been a consistent, although marginal aspect of jazz singing, from L, H & R to Mark Murphy to Joni Mitchell and the Pointer Sisters.

The defining characteristic of vocalese as a particular form of jazz singing is that it employs language, assigning words to already existent (recorded) musical notes. The very premise of vocalese, then, is a challenge to the traditional ideology of Western music, which is constructed as immaterial, the most "pure" of the arts, thus transcendent, capable of speaking directly to the emotions or the soul (Green). Western philosophers (e.g., Nietzsche, Hegel, Schopenhauer, Langer) have commonly described music as an expression of an essence that is itself ideal, spiritual, hence superior to the other arts. But words (with the exception, perhaps, of opera), in providing denotation, "pollute" the "purity" of music, like lead shoes preventing it from rising above the prosaic; words hold onto music by, to paraphrase Roland Barthes, translating it into impoverished linguistic categories (Barthes, "Grain" 179).

Thus words have enhanced vocalese's potential for popularity by providing an easy hook for presumably less "sophisticated" listeners, jazz's equivalent of Adorno's "humming millions" (Adorno 61–62). Thus L, H & R, organized initially as a studio recording group only, for a time was perhaps the most popular vocal group in jazz, rivaled only by the Boswell Sisters in the 1930s. On the pop charts Donna Lynn had a novelty hit with "Java Jones" (1964), a vocal version of Al Hirt's popular recording of "Java" earlier the same year; and the Friends of Distinction were successful with a vocal recording of "Grazing in the Grass" (1969), although they sang only the melody, entirely omitting Hugh Masakela's original trumpet solo. Both Bette Midler (1973) and Joni Mitchell (1974) covered Annie Ross's "Twisted"; and Barry Manilow (yes, that's right! see *Barry Manilow II*, Bell 1314) covered L, H & R's "Avenue C."

Scatting, unlike vocalese, does not taint the music with the impurity of denotation. Certainly fewer scat performances of any sustained length (thus containing short doo-wop riffs) have made the pop charts (one thinks primarily of Billy Stewart), and it is likely for this reason. Hence, scatting is inevitably valorized at the expense of vocalese since, as Friedwald puts it, scatting reaches feelings "so deep, so real" that "they can't be verbalized"; a great scat performer, thus, is able to "bypass our ears and our brains and go directly for our hearts and souls" (37). Just as one musician explained the title of Charlie Parker's "Klacktoveedsedsteen" by declaring "It's a sound, man. A sound" (Williams, *Smithsonian* 33), so scat singing, in avoiding the use of words, is seen to strive for the abstraction, the purity, of the music itself. Dizzy Gillespie, for example, praises Babs Gonzales's vocals because his singing captures the nature of bop: "like 'babadelidee.' Scat words. That's what the music sounds like" (Gourse 151). The land of oo-bla-dee is, by consensus, a very hip place indeed.

(Essentially the same argument is advanced to support the claim that the best rock songs are tunes like "Do Wah Diddy Diddy," "Be-Bop-A-Lula," "Rama Lama Ding Dong," and so on—that is, songs with lyrics that bypass denotation and attempt to capture directly the "primal warblings" [Emerson 224] or "barbaric yawps" [Whitman 55] of American life, of which the raw energy of the music itself is an expression. Thus the premise of the old routine by Steve Allen—himself an occasional jazz pianist—wherein he would solemnly stand at a podium and intone the lyrics of rhythm 'n' blues or rock songs as if reading poetry, comically emphasizing the disparity between denotation and meaning.)

However, despite (or perhaps more accurately, in part because of) its demonstrated commercial appeal, vocalese has been largely denigrated in jazz culture, a particular target of "a highly vocal anti-vocalist lobby among enthusiasts of the music" (Crowther and Pinfold 7). Popular acceptance is for jazz culture more of a taint than an achievement, the result of a strong ideological bias generated by the "hipper than thou" element within jazz culture. When jazz artists move successfully into the pop mainstream, they are invariably perceived as having lost their artistry or "soul," or as no longer "paying their dues" (for example, Armstrong by the 1940s and Nat Cole in the 1950s). However, such judgments are essentially "delineated" as opposed to "inherent" meanings, social relations attached to specific pieces of music or musical styles at particular historical moments (Green)—in this case, the ideological belief that "jazzness" is necessarily rooted in oppression and romantic angst. In any event, this is certainly not true of vocalese artists, who necessarily tend to be more interested in spreading the joyful gospel of jazz—to envision a world in which, as Jon Hendricks puts it, "everybody's boppin'"—than in attaining "commercial" success, as both their choice of material (tunes from boppers like Gillespie, Parker, Silver, and Wardell Gray) and the style's rejection of popular music's usually sacrosanct thirty-two-bar popular song format suggest. If before the bop vocalists the conception of the singer in jazz was that of the "canary" warbling pleasantly and looking pretty in the spotlight (Crowther and Pinfold), the vocalese performer sympathizes more with the introspective artistry of the beboppers. As Jefferson sings about Miles Davis and John Coltrane in his lyrics to one of Coltrane's classic tunes, after their solos, "Well, they walked off the stage, clean out of sight—So what?"

The other reason for the denigration of vocalese has to do with its lack of improvisational quality, which begins immediately with the constraints of its composition. The liner notes for Honi Gordon's solo debut album, in seeking to valorize this singer's method (original material rather than relying on previous recordings) over vocalese, expresses the view of many in asserting that the vocalese performer "labor[s] under crippling constraints—slavishly following rhythmic and melodic patterns originally set down by improvising horns, and adhering to titles that were often carelessly tacked on to originals with little or no thought." That is to say, the lyrics for vocalese are not only scripted, but to some extent they are predetermined, and, furthermore, this situation is a priori a fatal aesthetic straitjacket. The assumption is that lyrics are reductive of music in that they function like denotative anchors, analogous to Roland Barthes's idea of the relation of captions to photographs as "anchorage," a text that "remote-controls" the reader/listener toward a specific meaning or interpretation ("Rhetoric" 38–41).

It is true that we tend to "anchor" music with images (often in the form of memory of specific events or places when we had heard the music in the past), which is why music yoked with film images are so capable of overpowering us emotionally. Hence the nostalgic attraction of *American Graffiti*-type movies, the kind that appeal to the "historical" fantasy of "the good old days" in which the songs are visually contextualized within their specific historical moment. Sometimes the pairing is so effective that it becomes difficult to think of them separately, as, now, say, with Wagner's "Ride of the Valkyries" and the helicopters flying in formation over the Vietnamese jungle in Francis Coppola's *Apocalypse Now* (1979). Similarly, the dramatic opening of Richard Strauss's *Also Sprach Zarathustra* can no longer be conjured in an auditor's mind independent of the apes and monoliths in Stanley Kubrick's *2001: A Space Odyssey* (1968). The scene in Kubrick's *A Clockwork Orange* (1971) where Alex beats and rapes Mrs. Alexander while playfully singing "Singin' in the Rain" is so powerful precisely for this reason, as it conflicts with the viewer's memory of the romantic optimism of Gene Kelly's performance of the same song, an aesthetic assault that parallels the physical one depicted in the sequence.

Perhaps this strong pull of music toward anchorage in the historical world accounts for the predominance of vocalese tunes that rely on prosaic invocations of nostalgia in their lyrics, as in Jefferson's invitation in "Now's the Time" [1968] to "Come reminisce with me / and think about the Bird / Remember every thing he did and all the things you heard." Since, the thinking goes, a vocalese tune is derived from a recording, its shape and content is pre-determined; it therefore lacks the originality (usually manifested in improvisation) of great jazz and works as mere imitation or homage. Generally, to be sure, such uninspired vocalese lyrics as these nostalgia pieces do little more than sing the praises, as it were, of the artist who played the music from which the lyrics derive. Too many vocalese songs invoke the self-congratulatory hipness, the insider's knowledge of jazz in a rather uninspired fashion—what Friedwald calls the "preaching" typified by Bob Dorough's "Yardbird Suite" (1956) (Friedwald 237). Among the numerous examples that spring readily to mind are L, H & R's version of Coltrane's "Mr. P.C." (1961) and Hendricks's lyrics for Benny Golson's "I Remember Clifford." Jefferson's "Dexter Digs In" (1969) offers the listener a litany of musicians, the mere invocation of their names intended as evidence of jazz's greatness.

Such lyrics work more by association than by any inherent aesthetic use of language, and thus they constitute perhaps the least imaginative motif in vocalese. But the best vocalese tunes do not succumb to the backward glance of nostalgia, but rather they look forward to offering aesthetic satisfaction to the listener. In fact, the aesthetic task of the vocalese lyricist need be no more restrictive than that of any other artistic form involving language. According to Samuel Charters, it is the very presence of its rigorous structural constraint (three lines and twelve bars) that, paradoxically, give the blues its poetic potential (Charters 25ff.). Similarly, the vocalese artist may be somewhat restricted by the suggestiveness of a song's title, but it ain't necessarily so—listen, for example, to the way Hendricks ironically embraces for the purpose of flaunting the "constraint" of a title like Basie's "Every Tub" (1958). Moreover, any such constraint is more than compensated for by the freedom the vocalese artist attains in being freed from the structural conventions of the popular song.

As well, consider the distinctly different moods generated by the same lyrics: for example, the versions of "Moody's Mood" by Pleasure, Jefferson (two different recordings), Mark Murphy, Aretha Franklin (1973), and Van Morrison (1993); then there is Jefferson's reprise of "Moody's Mood" as "There I Go There I Go Again" (1968), still another variation of that anthem. Or compare versions of different lyrics to the same original tune: Hendricks's for L, H & R's "A Night in Tunisia" (1962), the same writer's for Manhattan Transfer's "Another Night in Tunisia" (1985), and Jefferson's version of the Gillespie tune (1961); or Pleasure's version (1954) of "Parker's Mood" and Jefferson's (1962), the former a lyrical pastiche of evocative conventional blues images and the latter a narrative scenario about the loss of love. An ear open to textual nuances will easily discern the differences between any of these examples.

Further, lyrics need not be restricted to the literal, denotative level to be expressive. The title of Gillespie's bop standard "Salt Peanuts"— the two words comprising the song's entire lyrical content—ultimately "means" very little, really no more than his "Oop-Bop-Sh-Bam" or "Ool-Ya-Koo," since there is no "exposition" contextualizing them and since the repetition of the words drains them of denotation. L H & R's version of Ellington's "Main Stem" (1960) uses words repetitively to depict the nightlife on the main drag in an abstract way (not unlike the montage of tenement life in Hendricks's lyrics for "Harlem Air Shaft" that is consistent with Ellington's own description of his composition [Williams, *Smithsonian* 31]), a rhythmic expressionism analogous to Mondrian's famous *Broadway Boogie Woogie* canvas. Jefferson's lyrics to "A Night

in Tunisia" make perfectly clear that words in a song need make no denotative sense: "I saw an eskimo climbing up a moonbeam," "a chicken
with lips / a snake with hips," and perhaps the most surreal image of all—
"Dizzy started playing Sammy Kaye"! The verbal images are literally
"impossible" and suggest, perhaps, a drug-induced hallucination or the
"far-out" state of mind induced by "exotic" jazz, not unlike the surreal
visual images of a jazz cartoon like *Tin Pan Alley Cats* (Bob Clampett,
1943).

Perhaps, then, it would be more accurate to describe the relation of the
best vocalese lyrics to the music in terms of what Barthes calls "relay"
rather than anchorage, where both elements exist in a "complementary"
relationship ("Rhetoric" 41). After hearing Hendricks's lyrics to his playing of Basie's "Goin' to Chicago," Buck Clayton said, "The lyric makes
the tune more than it was—and changes it" (Gourse 175). Like Eisen-
steinian montage, the music, lyrics, and performance of vocalese are
parts that exist independently, but together they are capable of expressing something more than the parts individually—"jazz operettas" (Gleason) or better, Dave Lambert's "bopera" (Gourse 168). Indeed, the great
vocalese lyrics not only adorn their musical sources but simultaneously
work as an integral aesthetic element. So, for instance, in "This Is Always" (1962), based on a Moody version of "Roost," when Pleasure protests that his ardor is not merely "midsummer's ma-a-a-adness," his
stretching out of that last word over several notes not only captures the
mellow quality of the Moody source, but also effectively conveys the
simmering desire of a long, hot Tennessee Williams-like summer more
fully than the denotative meaning of the words alone and, as a result,
ultimately belies the narrator's claim.

If, to return to Green's distinction about musical meanings, we concentrate on vocalese's "inherent" qualities, we may discover a rich yet
largely unappreciated tradition of true jazz poetry. Mark Murphy begins
his album *Beauty and the Beat* (1987) by reciting the lyrics of the title
track before singing them, in effect a bold proclamation of vocalese's
poetic potential. Here is merely one concise example, from the lyrics for
L H & R's recording of Ellington's "Rocks in My Bed" (1960)—which, for
one critic at least, are "amateurish" (Tucker). The line "that man is lower
than a snake in a wagon track" conjures a series of visual images that,
aside from paralleling the descending notes of the music, employ a
metric construction in service of its downward "movement" (its thrust
initiated by an opening spondee, insistently carried forward by a series of
iambs, and brought to a halt at the lower depths by an anapest followed
by a final emphatic and symmetrical spondee) and that is in harmony

with the overall bluesy, self-pitying interpretation Hendricks brings to the piece.

Virtually all vocalese writer/performers have remarked on their perception of the music that inspired them as narratives. Pleasure said he perceived instrumental solos as stories (Gitler), Jefferson told Feather that "I always thought that the great jazz solos told a story" (Steingroot), and James Moody said the same thing about Jefferson (Gourse 155). In "Body and Soul" (1962) Jefferson sings about "the story Moody was tellin' " when he played his saxophone. Annie Ross's "Farmer's Market" (1952), based on Wardell Gray's version of an Art Farmer composition, is an instance of concise narrative that arguably fulfills the unity of effect espoused by Poe's philosophy of composition. Nevertheless, the lyrics of vocalese often achieve an aesthetic resonance more characteristic of poetry than prose.

And the poetic tradition embraced most fully by vocalese is, specifically, the Beat aesthetic. The movement's very name, of course, is suggestive of the importance of musical values characteristic of the style, and according to one account of its coinage, John Clellon Holmes claims to have adopted it from jazz argot, where the term was popular in the 1940s (Cook 6). On Mark Murphy's *Bop for Kerouac* album (1981), two of the seven tracks include readings from novels by that patron saint of the Beats who, possibly more than any other American writer, with the exception of Walt Whitman and Gertrude Stein, demonstrated the rhythmic potential of the American language. Jazz and Beat poetry have had a particularly intimate connection. Jazz ("holy the jazzbands marijuana hipsters . . .") is referred to at least five times in Allen Ginsberg's Beat anthem, "Howl" (1956). Lawrence Ferlinghetti's description of "the poet [who] like an acrobat / climbs on rime / to a high wire of his own making" (30) applies equally to the jazz artist. Indeed, the experimental combination of Beat poetry readings accompanied by improvisational jazz (on record, listen, for example, to Ken Nordine's "word jazz" albums) perhaps finds its fullest expression in vocalese.

Of course, while the attempt to define poetry is at least as great a folly as defining jazz or jazz singing (although Gary Snyder's "the skilled and inspired use of the voice and language to embody rare and powerful states of mind" is quite apposite here), it can be said that vocalese is particularly akin to the kind of poetry that Charles Olson, a major influence on the Beat aesthetic, called "projective verse." Olson's understanding of speech as the "solid" of verse (Olson 20), his emphasis for poetry on the physiological capabilities of breathing—on, in short, the voice—invites a musical comparison (in fact, he makes an explicit analogy between the poet and the musician [22]) especially to vocalese. The extended and rhythmic lines of Whitman, Ginsberg, and others seek a bardic quality not unlike that of the vocalese singer. Olson's claim that syllabication is the core of prosody becomes in jazz singing the sense of rhythm, perhaps its most crucial quality (Friedwald xiv); and his sense of "field" may be understood as the song's performance (whether live or recorded).

Vocalese is a form of verbal expression that, like Beat poetry, breathes aesthetic quality into daily *parole*. As Samuel Charters observes, the blues creates poetry out of daily events and objects surrounding the singers, attempting to achieve in the frequent homeliness and concreteness of its language an articulation of lived experience (15–21). The same, of course, could be said about vocalese. This is precisely the raison d'être of Pleasure's "Exclamation Blues" (1952): although not a vocalese tune, it is animated by the same spirit, the lyrics consisting entirely of mundane exclamations—"Great day in the morning," "landsakes alive," and so on, just as in "Old Shoes" Jefferson sings the exclamation "Hey, good Lordy in the morning." Inescapably, we take delight in suddenly discovering inherent musical potential in such mundane phrases when they are sung rather than spoken. (How is it we never noticed the rhythms these phrases fall into so easily?)

So, too, vocalese's frequent reliance on enjambed rhymes—"this beat your feet will understand / I'm a fan, do the sand man," sings Hendricks in "It's Sand, Man" (1957)—and the occasional accent on the wrong beat, as Jefferson does with the Homeric tag phrase "Have *mercy on* me" in "Bless My Soul" (1962), are devices that serve to emphasize discourse's rhythmic qualities. Vocalese's use of other poetic techniques works similarly. Annie Ross's use of surprising rhymes like "Coca-cola" and "gorgonzola" in her "Jackie" (1953), and the frequently forced rhymes of Jefferson's lyrics for Horace Silver's funky "Filthy McNasty" (1968), such as "corn" / "Don Juan," generate a sense of defamiliarization (as well as bespeak the obnoxiously aggressive personality of the eponymous character), making us hear these words in new ways.

In "It Might As Well Be Spring" (1962) Pleasure chants "look at the spider" three times before finishing the line, the quick repetition nicely expressing the simultaneously peripatetic and repetitive work of said arachnid, its mesmerizing injunction carrying over into the line's completion, "keeps spinning daydreams . . ." (compare Ginsberg's "boxcars boxcars boxcars" in "Howl" 11). In "This Is Always" Pleasure exclaims "I want to scream that this is all / I want to scream that this is all / I want to scream that this is always." Cannily halting on the first syllable of the last word the first two times, Pleasure suggests the consuming nature of his passion as well as its temporal infinitude. Additionally, Pleasure's delivery, as in Jefferson's line in "I Got the Blues" (1955) that "the telephone rang rang rang rang rang," not only captures the rhythm of the thing expressed, but is made richer by its performative aspect: in both cases the singer's voice cracks—particularly vivid instances of what Barthes calls the "grain" of the voice (Barthes, "Grain")—the strain in the former further suggesting the intensity of desire (as well as literalizing the "scream") and in the latter conveying the grating annoyance of a persistent telephone. Vocalese singing abounds with many such examples.

Olson goes so far as to claim the typewriter as a significant tool for the projective poet—an awareness of the inevitable relation between technology and aesthetics in art that addresses that inseparable relation between vocalese as music and as apparatus. It is of course true that vocalese would be impossible without recording technology, for the form depends on the ability to listen innumerable times to the same exact performance. Thus the very history of vocalese is intimately connected with the technology of recording. Jefferson invented the form in the late 1930s while on tour as a dancer, amusing his friends by singing along with his partner Irv Taylor to the records played on the portable turntable in their hotel rooms. The first vocalese album, L H & R's *Sing a Song of Basie* (1958), was originally conceived by Hendricks and Dave Lambert as a duo with backing chorus; but when the chorus was not able to achieve the vocal effects the two men wanted, they picked Annie Ross out of the group and spent more than sixty hours in the studio at night overdubbing (secretly, because they had already spent the budget for the recording allotted by producer Creed Taylor). The record may have developed as a historical "accident," but it is nevertheless entirely appropriate that it employed multitracking—that, in other words, the performance on record is an "impossible" one—in order to replicate vocally all the parts of the Basie orchestra. (Lambert and Hendricks sang the reed and trombone parts, Ross the trumpets and piano. The original album's liner notes contain all the lyrics as well as identifying which singer is singing which part.) Indeed, it was only after the success of the record, and of its follow-up, *Sing Along with Basie* (1959), that the trio ventured out of the studio to be enthusiastically received at the 1959 Newport Jazz Festival and to become "the most sought-after singing group in jazz" at live venues (Gourse 169). Significantly, the Double Six of Paris, who began recording shortly after, take their very name from their reliance on overdubbing when recording.

Now a recording is to a musical performance what film acting is to that in the theater: it gives us a *particular* performance—this one and no other (the release of alternate takes is a practice that increased with the ascendance of the compact disc and is usually restricted to rerelease packages)—in this case forever etched, like sculpture, into a material object—vinyl, tape, or compact disc. A record player, in turn, is considerably more than, as Marshall McLuhan called the phonograph, a "music hall without walls" (McLuhan 248). On record (note the derivation of the noun, originally referring to *evidence* in a legal sense), a musical performance thus automatically attains a "definitive" status in that it becomes irrevocable. It might be said that recorded music is to music as literature (however it is defined) is to writing: it is published, enshrined on the public "record." Because it was considered worth preserving, recorded music attains "classic" status (surely it is not coincidental that radios at one time were designed like cathedrals). Other versions of released tunes, although they may be issued subsequently, are designated by the subordinate term "alternate take," forever defined in relation to the original release.

But if this technological music hall reifies the music imprinted in its grooves, it also in another way demystifies it. In our mind's ear we tend to "freeze" our experience of recorded music, so that we know exactly how it should sound. In jazz, this is of particular import, for the experience of being present at an exciting live performance where the musicians are truly taking improvisatory risks in their playing, exploring new territory ("the poet like an acrobat"), inevitably dissipates with each listening on record (although, of course, other aesthetic pleasures may deepen). The original improvisation can be played back innumerable times, in whole or in selected part, until such new terrain becomes familiar, charted, to the listener. This has been, in fact, the most common kind of reception by jazz listeners since jazz is usually performed for relatively small audiences, unlike stadium rock concerts.

Jed Rasula has reiterated the importance of Brian Priestley's observation that the writing of jazz history has been largely based on records, "implying that this was the only jazz worth writing about." Indeed, this history would be entirely different without the mediation of recordings. For instance, it is well-known that both Armstrong and King Oliver had to be spatially distanced from the recording horn and the rest of the Creole Jazz Band during their Gennett recordings; that pads were put under the insistently tapping feet of many peripatetic musicians; that drummers were often restricted to snare drums and woodblocks (Crow 108); and so on. Such examples abound, and they are clear indications that recorded sound, as Alan Williams has convincingly argued, is, because of the mediating apparatus involved, distinctly different from the sonic event it records, that it is, in fact, another "signifying practice." But it is also noteworthy that the very music that was chosen for recording was sometimes determined by the limits of technology. Hence narrative blues, early in the form's evolution, were important, but they were recorded with much less frequency than lyrical blues because of the time constraints of 78-rpm recordings, thus altering their relative importance in the evolving canon (Charters 32). Just six months after Armstrong recorded "West End Blues" (1928), Louis Metcalf was directed by Oliver to duplicate his solo note-for-note; and Red Allen learned to play along with Armstrong's recordings in different keys by adjusting the speed screw on his Victrola (Williams, *Heritage* 224). Because of jazz's ephemeral nature—because it is music but also because of its emphasis on performance over notation—is it not possible to suggest that jazz might be without a history at all if it were not for records?

So it may be true that since vocalese depends on a prior performance, and attempts to duplicate it note for note, it denies the possibility of improvisation—indeed, the "better" a vocalese version is, the more faithful it has been to the original—but this is only to say that vocalese not only returns jazz to its source in the voice, but to its technological base as well. Indeed, vocalese is a particularly interesting kind of jazz practice, for it may be the only form of the music that *inevitably* works at the level of what philosopher Evan Eisenberg calls "phonography."

Eisenberg picks up Williams's idea of recorded music as a "signifying practice" and follows it through to some of its logical aesthetic consequences. With recording, music (despite the tradition, discussed earlier, of its philosophical valorization) becomes a "thing," and *recorded* music becomes a new art—phonography. The masters of phonography, for Eisenberg, include the usual suspects: Glenn Gould, Stockhausen, Phil Spector, Miles Davis, Frank Zappa, and the Beatles—musicians who employed the resources of the studio not just to enhance their sound, but to enrich the expressive vocabulary of their work. He might have added to the list Eddie Jefferson, King Pleasure, and Lambert, Hendricks and Ross, for their music depends on the apparatus of production as much as any of those others. Vocalese, that is to say, is always a metadiscourse, at once a jazz singing and a speaking about jazz.

Rasula concludes that the writing of jazz history produces an inevitable struggle "between grapho-centrism and its phono-eccentric phantoms." This may be true everywhere else in jazz history except in the case of vocalese. For vocalese erases the difference between the two, since the writing of vocalese lyrics based on specific recorded jazz solos simultaneously celebrates what records listeners other than historians actually listened to, and, since they are built on the principle of intertextuality, in the very act of listening to them we are necessarily reminded of their history, their tradition.

L, H & R's *Sing a Song of Basie,* for which Hendricks wrote all the lyrics, is true phonographic art, and not only because of its construction through overdubbing of a studio sound with no referent in the real world. It is also a "concept album"—before the idea was explored by such phonographers as Frank Zappa and the Beatles in the mid-1960s. It is true that the songs on the L, H & R album share the fact that they were composed and recorded by the Basie orchestra, but more importantly, they share a similar vision, exploring what it in fact *means* to "sing a song of Basie." In these songs, characters are consistently depressed and blue—even suicidal, as in "Down for the Count"—yet through singing the songs, by embracing the blues (like Conrad, Hendricks believes that one must "in the destructive element immerse"), one is able to transcend them. (Similarly, Hendricks's lyrics for Rahsaan Roland Kirk's "Bright Moments," recorded with Jon Hendricks & Company in 1982, treats the phrase as mantralike incantation so that the singing of the words themselves become one such epiphanic moment. (Cf. Ginsberg's claim to "make mantra of American language now" in "Wichita Vortex Sutra" ["Sutra" 76].) Thus, the trio is "delighted" when invited to a "Fiesta in Blue," the song's seemingly oxymoronic title summing up the philosophy of the whole album. So if they begin by having the blues "Everyday," then, by the end, they can happily strut down "Avenue C." (Even more than Joe Carroll, Hendricks is "the man with the happy sound"—even to the point that, as he proudly boasts in an original composition, after a fully lived life, "I'll Die Happy.")

As well, *Sing a Song of Basie* is, on another level, a kind of vocalese manifesto, for time and again vocalese performers have insisted that jazz, as Parker said, is "a happiness blues" (Gourse 25). From Leo Watson, who in "Scatting the Blues" (1945) oscillates between being happy and being blue, to King Pleasure, who admits in "Sometimes I'm Happy" (1953) that "Sometimes I feel so blue I don't know what to do," to Eddie Jefferson, who explicitly tells us in "Yardbird Suite" (1969) that he sings what he does because "Bebop's a whole lot of fun," the idea of jazz lifting one's spirit has been the grand theme of vocalese. And it, in turn, gives voice to the animating spirit of all blues and jazz, which developed out of the black experience of oppression in America and which itself was an attempt to combat that condition. Perhaps, then, it is not because of a lack of imagination that so many vocalese songs are about the appeal of jazz and the greatness of particular jazz artists, but because, as so many of these songs insist, the music, whether played on an instrument or with the voice, is itself the message.

Ultimately, then, the great vocalese artists join the elite ranks of jazz royalty—the Count, the Duke (and it is no accident that L, H & R "did" them both), and Ambassador Satch—as jazz artists who have "interpreted" jazz for those humming millions, essentially by embracing rather than refuting the denotative "anchor" of language. By adding lyrics to both melody and improvised parts, vocalese demonstrates that the great jazz improvisers were, in a sense, also great *composers*—a fundamental truth about vocalese that only a few jazz writers have acknowledged (Steingroot; Giddins). Perhaps this is an unavoidable consequence of their phonographic endeavor; nevertheless, for this reason, Ralph J. Gleason is correct to claim that the work of L, H & R "is of more help to the understanding of what jazz is and how it works than all the radio and TV shows put together." Vocalese performers are among the few true oral poets in the age of digital reproduction. Just as Whitman urged the reader to "loose the stop from your throat" (15), so Eddie Jefferson unabashedly proclaims in "I Got the Blues" that "I wrote the words so everybody can sing it."

Note

I am indebted to my colleague Terrence Cox for pointing out to me certain aspects of the reception of vocalese in critical discourse.

Works Cited

Adorno, T. W. *Introduction to the Sociology of Music.* Trans. E. B. Ashton. New York: Seabury, 1976.

Barthes, Roland. "The Grain of the Voice" and "Rhetoric of the Image." *Image, Music, Text.* Trans. Stephen Heath. New York: Hill and Wang, 1977. 179–89, 32–51.

Berendt, Joachim. *The Jazz Book: From New Orleans to Rock and Free Jazz.* Trans. Dan Morgenstern and Helmut and Barbara Bredigkeit. New York: Lawrence Hill, 1975.

Carr, Ian, Digby Fairweather, and Brian Priestley. *Jazz: The Essential Companion.* London: Grafton, 1987.

Charters, Samuel. *The Poetry of the Blues.* New York: Avon, 1970.

Cook, Bruce. *The Beat Generation.* New York: Scribner's, 1971.

Crow, Bill. *Jazz Anecdotes.* New York: Oxford UP, 1990.

Crowther, Bruce, and Mike Pinfold. *The Jazz Singers: From Ragtime to the New Wave.* Poole, Eng.: Blandford P, 1986.

Eisenberg, Evan. *The Recording Angel: The Experience of Music From Aristotle to Zappa.* New York: Penguin, 1987.

Emerson, Ralph Waldo. "The Poet." *Selections from Ralph Waldo Emerson.* Ed. Stephen Whicher. Boston: Houghton Mifflin, 1960. 222–41.

"Falco, Sidney." Album notes for Honi Gordon, *Honi Gordon Sings*. Prestige 7230, 1962.

Feather, Leonard. Album notes for the Blue Stars, *The Blue Stars*. Emarcy 36067, 1956.

———. *The Encyclopedia of Jazz*. 2nd ed. New York: Bonanza Books, 1960.

Ferlinghetti, Lawrence. *A Coney Island of the Mind*. New York: New Directions, 1958.

Friedwald, Will. *Jazz Singing: America's Great Voices from Bessie Smith to Bebop and Beyond*. New York: Scribner's, 1990.

Gabbard, Krin. "The Jazz Canon and Its Consequences." *Jazz Among the Discourses*. Durham, N.C.: Duke UP, 1995. 1–27.

Giddins, Gary. *Ridings on a Blue Note: Jazz and American Pop*. New York: Oxford UP, 1981.

Ginsberg, Allen. *Howl and Other Poems*. San Francisco: City Lights, 1967.

———. "Wichita Vortex Sutra." *The Poem in Its Skin*, by Paul Carroll. Chicago and New York: Follett, 1968. 65–80.

Gitler, Ira. Album notes for King Pleasure, *Original Moody's Mood*. Prestige 7586, 1968.

Gleason, Ralph. Album notes for Lambert, Hendricks & Ross, *The Swingers*. World Pacific 1264, 1959.

Gourse, Leslie. *Louis' Children: American Jazz Singers*. New York: Morrow, 1984.

Green, Lucy. *Music on Deaf Ears: Musical Meaning, Ideology, Education*. Manchester and New York: Manchester UP/St. Martin's, 1988.

McLuhan, Marshall. *Understanding Media: The Extensions of Man*. New York: Signet, 1964.

Olson, Charles. *Selected Writings of Charles Olson*. Ed. Robert Creeley. New York: New Directions, 1966.

Rasula, Jed. "The Media of Memory: The Seductive Menace of Records in Jazz History." *Jazz Among the Discourses*. Ed. Krin Gabbard. Durham, N.C.: Duke UP, 1995. 134–62.

Snyder, Gary. "Poetry and the Primitive." *The Poetics of the New American Poetry*. Ed. Donald A. Allen and Warren Tallman. New York: Grove P, 1973. 395–406.

Steingroot, Ira. Album notes for Eddie Jefferson, *There I Go Again*. Prestige P-24095, 1980.

Tucker, Mark. Album notes for Duke Ellington, *The Blanton-Webster Band*, RCA Bluebird 5659, 3-CD set, 1986.

Whitman, Walt. *Leaves of Grass*. Facsimile ed. San Francisco: Chandler, 1968.

Williams, Alan. "Is Sound Recording Like a Language?" *Yale French Studies* 60 (1980): 51–66.

Williams, Martin. "Jazz, the Phonograph, and Scholarship." *Jazz Heritage*. New York: Oxford UP, 1985. 223–28.

———. Accompanying booklet to *The Smithsonian Collection of Classic Jazz* (LP set P6 11891). Washington, D.C.: Smithsonian Institution, 1973.

Discography

Eddie Jefferson

Letter from Home (Riverside 411/9411, 1962). Reissue: Prestige OJC 307 (CD).

Body and Soul (Prestige 7619, 1968). Reissue: Prestige OJC 396 (CD).

Come Along With Me (Prestige 7698, 1969) (CD).
Things Are Getting Better (Muse 5043, 1974).
The Jazz Singer (Inner City 1016, 1976). Reissue: Evidence ECD 22062 (CD).
Still on the Planet (Muse 5063, 1976).
The Main Man (Inner City 1033, 1977).
The Live-liest (Muse 5127, 1979).
There I Go Again (Prestige P-24095, 1980).
(Jefferson also appears on several of James Moody's LPs from the 1950s.)

King Pleasure
King Pleasure Sings (Prestige 208, 1955).
King Pleasure Sings/Annie Ross Sings (Prestige 7128, 1957). Reissue: Prestige OJC 217
    (CD).
Golden Days (HiFi Jazz 425, 1960). Reissue: Prestige OJC 1772 (CD).
Mr. Jazz (United Artists 14031/15031, 1962). Reissue on Solid State.
Original Moody's Mood (Prestige 7586, 1952).
The Source (Prestige 24017, 1973).
Moody's Mood For Love (Blue Note CDP 7 84463, 1992) (CD).

Jon Hendricks
A Good Git-Together (World Pacific 1283, 1959).
Evolution of the Blues Song (Columbia 1583/8383, 1961).
Fast Livin' Blues (Columbia 1805/8605, 1961).
Salud (Reprise 20167/6089, 1963).
Recorded in Person at the Trident (Smash 27069/67069, 1965).
Cloudburst (Enja 4032, 1972).
Jon Hendricks and Company (Muse 5258, 1982).

Lambert, Hendricks and Ross
Sing a Song of Basie (Impulse A-83, 1957). Reissue: Impulse GRP-112 (CD).
Sing Along With Basie (Roulette 52018, 1958). Reissue: Emus 12004 and LRC CDC
    9008 (CD).
The Swingers (World Pacific 1264, 1959). Reissue: Affinity 131.
The Hottest New Group in Jazz (Columbia 1403/8198, 1959). Reissue: Columbia KC
    32911.
Sing Ellington (Columbia 1510/8310, 1960).
High Flying With (Columbia 1675/8475, 1961). Reissue: The Way-Out Voices of
    Lambert, Hendricks and Ross (Columbia Odyssey 32 16 0292).
Twisted (Rhino R2 70328, 1992 [CD]) (selections from the three Columbia albums
    above. The three Columbia LPs have been reissued separately and in their entirety
    on CD by Japanese Sony.)

Lambert, Hendricks, and Bavan
Live at Basin Street East (RCA 2635, 1963). Reissue: Swingin' Till the Girls Come
    Home (RCA Bluebird 6282-2-RB) (CD).
At Newport (RCA 2747, 1963).
Havin' a Ball at the Village Gate (RCA LPM 2861, 1963).

Mark Murphy

Meet Mark Murphy (Decca 8390, 1956).

Rah (Riverside 395/9395, 1961). Reissue: Prestige OJC 141.

That's How I Love the Blues (Riverside 441/9441, 1962). Reissue: Prestige OJC 367 (CD).

Bridging a Gap (Muse 5009, 1972).

Mark Murphy Sings (Muse 7078, 1975).

Stolen Moments (Muse 5102, 1978) (CD).

Bop For Kerouac (Muse 5253, 1981) (CD).

The Artistry of (Muse 5286, 1982).

Beauty and the Beat (Muse 5355, 1987) (CD).

Kerouac, Then and Now (Muse 5359, 1990) (CD).

Manhattan Transfer

Vocalese (Atlantic 7-81266, 1985). Reissue: Atl 81266 (CD).

Note: Both Eddie Jefferson and Annie Ross are well represented in *The Bebop Singers* (Prestige 7828) and are included, along with most of the others, in *The Jazz Singers* (Prestige P-24113).

Contributors

KAREN BACKSTEIN has written on dance and film for *Cinéaste* and teaches at The College of Staten Island. She is finishing her dissertation at New York University's Department of Cinema Studies.

LELAND H. CHAMBERS, Professor Emeritus of English and Comparative Literature at the University of Denver, concentrates now on literary translation from Spanish. His latest book is *Contemporary Short Stories From Central America* (1994).

ROBERT P. CREASE is Associate Professor of Philosophy at the State University of New York at Stony Brook and Historian at Brookhaven National Laboratory. He is the author of *Play of Nature: Experimentation as Performance* (1993).

KRIN GABBARD is Associate Professor of Comparative Literature at the State University of New York at Stony Brook. His forthcoming book is *Jammin' at the Margins: Jazz and the American Cinema* (1996).

FREDERICK GARBER is Professor of Comparative Literature at the State University of New York at Binghamton. The author of numerous books including *The Autonomy of the Self from Richardson to Huysmans* (1982) and *Self, Text, and Romantic Irony: The Example of Byron* (1988), his most recent work is *Repositionings: Readings of Contemporary Poetry, Photography, and Performance Art* (1995).

BARRY KEITH GRANT is Professor of Film Studies and Popular Culture at Brock University in St. Catherines, Ontario. He is the author of *Voyages of Discovery: The Cinema of Frederick Wiseman* (1992), and of numerous other works on film and popular music. A second edition of his anthology *Film Genre Reader* is forthcoming.

MONA HADLER is Associate Professor of Art History at Brooklyn College and the Graduate Center of the City University of New York. She has published on Abstract Expressionism and guest edited an issue of *Art Journal* on sculpture in Europe and America from 1945 to 1959.

CHRISTOPHER HARLOS teaches in the Department of Communication at North Carolina State University. In addition to his research on jazz nonfiction, he has written on jazz and the fiction film soundtrack. Currently he is editing *The Mary Lou Williams Reader*.

MICHAEL JARRETT is Associate Professor of English at Penn State University, York Campus. He is the author of *Drifting on a Read: Jazzography and Heuretics*, an investigation of jazz as a model for invention ("heuretics"). He regularly writes about jazz and popular music for *Pulse!*, Tower Records' magazine.

ADAM KNEE is a doctoral candidate in Cinema Studies at New York University and former program coordinator in the Communication Department of the New School for Social Research. He has taught film studies at NYU and Pennsylvania State University, and he has contributed articles to anthologies and to such publications as *Film Quarterly*, *Minnesota Review* and *Wide Angle*.

ARTHUR KNIGHT teaches American Studies and English at the College of William and Mary. He is the author of the forthcoming *Dis-Integrating the Musical: African American Musical Performance and American Musical Film, 1927–1959*.

JAMES NAREMORE is Professor of English, Comparative Literature, and Film Studies at Indiana University. His many books include *The Films of Vincente Minnelli* (1993), *The Magic World of Orson Welles* (1988), and *Acting in the Cinema* (1988). He is currently writing a book on *film noir*.

Index

Library of Congress Cataloging-in-Publication Data

Representing jazz / edited by Krin Gabbard.

Includes index.

ISBN 0-8223-1579-3. — ISBN 0-8223-1594-7 (pbk.)

1. Jazz—History and criticism. I. Gabbard, Krin.

ML3507.R47 1995

781.65—dc20   94-37347 CIP

Permission has been granted to use the following previously published articles in this volume: *Krin Gabbard*, "Signifyin(g) the Phallus: Mo' Better Blues and Representations of the Jazz Trumpet," *Cinema Journal* 32, no. 1 (Fall 1992), pp. 43–62; by permission of the University of Texas Press. *Barry Keith Grant*, "Purple Passages or Fiestas in Blue? Notes Toward an Aesthetic of Vocalese," *Popular Music and Society* 18, no. 1 (Spring 1994), pp. 125–43; by permission of Popular Press, Bowling Green State University. *James Naremore*, "Uptown Folk: Blackness and Entertainment in *Cabin in the Sky*," *Arizona Quarterly* 48, no. 4 (Winter 1992), pp. 99–124; © 1992 by the Arizona Board of Regents, reprinted by permission.